State Expansion and Conflict

Lebanon and Israel/Palestine are two political entities that expanded in 1920 and 1967 respectively, and became divided societies characterized by periods of stability and conflict. This book provides the first detailed comparison between the two states and also explores the effects of their expansion on their changing relations. It looks first at how both expanded states attempted to cope with their predicaments, focusing on the relationship between state, community and security, before moving on to analyze the de-stabilizing effects of expansion on Israeli-Lebanese relations. The book draws on previously unpublished official documents, memoirs, media resources and films produced in Lebanon and Israel/Palestine, in addition to existing works on the two states and the Middle East. Bridging the gap between comparative politics and international relations, it will interest students of Lebanon and Israel/Palestine, the Middle East, and conflict and peace.

Oren Barak is the Maurice B. Hexter Chair in International Relations – Middle East Studies and Associate Professor of Political Science and International Relations at The Hebrew University of Jerusalem, Israel. He is the author of *The Lebanese Army: A National Institution in a Divided Society* (2009) and co-author of *Israel's Security Networks: A Theoretical and Comparative Perspective* (Cambridge, 2013, with Gabriel Sheffer).

State Expansion and Conflict
In and Between Israel/Palestine and Lebanon

Oren Barak
The Hebrew University of Jerusalem

CAMBRIDGE
UNIVERSITY PRESS

University Printing House, Cambridge CB2 8BS, United Kingdom

One Liberty Plaza, 20th Floor, New York, NY 10006, USA

477 Williamstown Road, Port Melbourne, VIC 3207, Australia

4843/24, 2nd Floor, Ansari Road, Daryaganj, Delhi – 110002, India

79 Anson Road, #06–04/06, Singapore 079906

Cambridge University Press is part of the University of Cambridge.

It furthers the University's mission by disseminating knowledge in the pursuit of education, learning, and research at the highest international levels of excellence.

www.cambridge.org
Information on this title: www.cambridge.org/9781108415798
DOI: 10.1017/9781108235198

© Oren Barak 2017

This publication is in copyright. Subject to statutory exception
and to the provisions of relevant collective licensing agreements,
no reproduction of any part may take place without the written
permission of Cambridge University Press.

First published 2017

Printed in the United Kingdom by Clays, St Ives plc

A catalogue record for this publication is available from the British Library.

Library of Congress Cataloging-in-Publication Data
Names: Barak, Oren.
Title: State expansion and conflict : in and between Israel/Palestine and Lebanon / Oren Barak, The Hebrew University of Jerusalem.
Description: New York : Cambridge University Press, [2017] | Includes bibliographical references and index.
Identifiers: LCCN 2017034795 | ISBN 9781108415798 (hardback)
Subjects: LCSH: Israel – Politics and government. | Lebanon – Politics and government. | Israel – Relations – Lebanon. | Lebanon – Relations – Israel. | Al-Aqsa Intifada, 2000 – Influence. | State, The – Case studies. | BISAC: POLITICAL SCIENCE / General.
Classification: LCC DS126.5 .B2627 2017 | DDC 956.9405–dc23
LC record available at https://lccn.loc.gov/2017034795

ISBN 978-1-108-41579-8 Hardback

Cambridge University Press has no responsibility for the persistence or accuracy of URLs for external or third-party internet websites referred to in this publication and does not guarantee that any content on such websites is, or will remain, accurate or appropriate.

All happy families are alike; each unhappy family is unhappy in its own way.
— *Leo Tolstoy*, Anna Karenina

Contents

	List of Figures	*page* viii
	List of Tables	ix
	Preface	xi
	Acknowledgments	xvii
	Chronology	xix
	Introduction	1
1	State Expansion and Its Effects	17
2	From Nation-States to Divided Societies: Lebanon and Israel/Palestine	45
3	Lebanon: Weak and Legitimate	60
4	Israel/Palestine: Strong and Illegitimate	95
5	Lebanon and Israel/Palestine Compared	138
6	The Deterioration of Israeli–Lebanese Relations	155
7	Two Conflicts Intertwined	188
	Conclusion	219
	Bibliography	225
	Index	261

Figures

5.1 State, community, and security in Lebanon *page* 152
5.2 State, community, and security in Israel/Palestine 153

Tables

1.1	The process of state formation	*page* 25
1.2	Strong and weak states	28
1.3	Major patterns of inter-communal relations in divided societies	35
1.4	Policy options of expanded states	39
1.5	The security sector in expanded states that are divided societies	40
2.1	Demography in the *Mutasarrifiyya* and in Greater Lebanon	49
2.2	Demography in Israel and in Israel/Palestine	53
3.1	Communal allocation of seats in the Lebanese Parliament before/after Ta'if (1989)	69
3.2	Regional allocation of seats in the Lebanese Parliament before/after Ta'if (1989)	70
3.3	Social background of LAF officers by religion and community	70
3.4	Social background of LAF officers by region	88
5.1	Strong and weak states: Lebanon and Israel/Palestine	142
5.2	Inter-communal relations in Lebanon and Israel/Palestine	147
5.3	The security sector in Lebanon and Israel/Palestine	151

Preface

That Lebanon and Israel/Palestine[1] are comparable, and that one can reach more general conclusions from juxtaposing these two ostensibly disparate cases, did not occur to me before the outbreak of the Second Palestinian Intifada (or al-Aqsa Intifada), following the failure of the Camp David summit between Israeli Prime Minister Ehud Barak, PLO Chairman Yasser Arafat, and US President Bill Clinton in July 2000, and the visit of Israeli Knesset Member and future Prime Minister Ariel Sharon to Temple Mount/Al-Haram al-Sharif in Jerusalem in September 2000, which provoked massive Palestinian demonstrations.

At that time, I was doing research on conflict and peace at Harvard University, having completed an extensive study of the Lebanese Armed Forces (LAF), which revealed the critical role of this institution in regulating conflict in Lebanon since its independence. In particular, I was able to show that, contrary to the prevailing image of the LAF as a weak military that fragmented along the lines of community, clan, and region during Lebanon's long and devastating civil war (1975–1990), this institution had, in fact, made continuous efforts to reconstruct itself not only in the material sense, first with US assistance and later with help from Syria, but also by trying to win the hearts and minds of all Lebanese by presenting itself as an institution that is "from all of Lebanon."[2]

The significance of this finding was emphasized by a research project on "failed states" at Harvard University, in which I participated, which brought together theorists and practitioners dealing with different aspects of "state failure" and experts on African and other non-Western states. In

---

[1] Israel/Palestine (or Palestine/Israel) is the area west of the Jordan River. In Arabic, the term employed to refer to this unit is *Filastin* (Palestine), and in Hebrew the term used is *Eretz Israel* (Land of Israel) or *Eretz Israel ha-Shlema* (the full or complete Land of Israel). The book refers to this area in the period before 1948 as "Palestine" and since 1967 as "Israel/Palestine."

[2] See, especially, Barak (2009a). This finding was based, among other things, on my detailed analysis of the officer corps of the Lebanese Armed Forces (LAF) before and after Lebanon's independence (see Barak [2006]) and on research that I did on the role of the LAF in national integration in Lebanon (Barak [2001]).

addition to demonstrating the usefulness of theoretically driven and comparative research on this topic, this project suggested that Lebanon, when considered from such a broad perspective, was by no means the worst case of state failure, and that its ability to reconstruct itself after the long and devastating conflict was actually quite impressive,[3] albeit not without problems: Syria's efforts to maintain its "special relations" (that is, a form of hegemony) with Lebanon since 1990, the attempt of Hizbullah to legitimize its own special status as a party-militia even after the dismantling of all other local parties-militias, and the thorny question of how to deal with the memory of the civil war.[4] This observation was further reinforced in the wake of the US invasion of Iraq and its aftermath,[5] and following the events of the "Arab Spring," and particularly the conflict in Syria, which suggested that Lebanon was not the worst case of a divided society in the Middle East and that others could actually learn from its experience.[6]

In the meantime, and as part of my research on conflict and peace, I came across many studies on what I refer to elsewhere as "conflict management" and "conflict resolution," including quite a number of works that applied these approaches to the Israeli–Palestinian conflict. At the same time, I found only a few studies that dealt with "conflict regulation" in the context of Israel/Palestine.[7] I found this gap quite puzzling, especially since studies on conflict regulation, which focuses on divided societies, seemed to be as relevant to Israel/Palestine as were works on conflict management and conflict resolution. This was mainly because since the Israeli–Arab War of 1967, and notwithstanding the Israeli–Palestinian peace process in the 1990s, Israel/Palestine seemed to be moving away from, rather than toward, a two-state solution based on the establishment of an independent Palestinian state alongside the State of Israel.

To be sure, there were scholars and practitioners who had doubts regarding the feasibility of partition in Israel/Palestine even before the collapse of the Oslo Process in 2000,[8] and some of these observers were

---

[3] On the project and its findings, see Rotberg (2003, 2004). On Lebanon, see Barak (2003).
[4] Barak (2007a).　　[5] Barak (2007b).　　[6] Barak (2012). See also Abou Lteif (2015).
[7] For more on these approaches, including from a comparative perspective, see Barak (2005a). Broadly speaking, proponents of conflict management and conflict resolution consider conflicts to be terminable through negotiations or informal interactive workshops, respectively, whereas students of conflict regulation see conflicts as stemming from deep and overlapping societal cleavages and posit that so long as these cleavages remain politically significant conflicts shall persist, but also that such conflicts can be regulated. Chapter 1 presents different patterns of conflict regulation in divided societies.
[8] One skeptic was Major General (ret.) Yehoshafat Harkabi, who served as head of the IDF's Intelligence Branch and later taught International Relations at The Hebrew

critical not only of this particular scenario but also of the more general approaches of conflict management and conflict resolution, which underpinned much of the peacemaking efforts between Israelis and Palestinians in the 1990s.[9] But these were a minority among students of Israel/Palestine, and it seems that most observers believed that a peaceful settlement to the Israeli–Palestinian conflict based on a two-state solution would, eventually, be attained.[10] In any case, I decided to integrate some of my conclusions from studying Lebanon – which is all about conflict regulation in a divided society composed of various communities, large families (or clans) and geographical regions[11] – into a paper on the Israeli–Palestinian peace process in 1993–2000 and see whether it could help account for its failure.[12]

Political developments in Israel/Palestine in the decade that followed further reinforced my assumption that Israel/Palestine was indeed comparable to Lebanon since both were, essentially, divided societies. These included, on the one hand, the failed attempts to reinvigorate the Israeli–Palestinian peace process, and, on the other hand, Israel's continued efforts to create more "facts on the ground" in the Territories – that is, to build and expand Jewish settlements, military installations, bypass roads, and the "separation barrier" – so as to preclude a meaningful separation between Israelis and Palestinians.[13] Consequently, what had previously been implicit in my research on Israel/Palestine became more pronounced.

I began to share these new ideas with my colleagues, and wrote another paper that offered a general comparison between Israel/Palestine and Lebanon as two nation-states that turned out to be divided

---

University of Jerusalem. In an interview in early 1994, Harkabi predicted that, in view of the opposition to removing Jewish settlements in the Territories, there will be assassinations of Israeli leaders, even stating that Prime Minister Yitzhak Rabin will not die a natural death. The interview was published in full only after Rabin's assassination in 1995. See Harkabi (1995, 15).

[9] See, especially, M. Benvenisti (1995, 2007). On the application of conflict management and conflict resolution theories and practices in the Israeli–Palestinian conflict, see Barak (2005a).

[10] Barnett (1999). In fact, it was only shortly before his assassination that Rabin acknowledged, in a clear break from the traditional Zionist narrative, that "we did not come to an empty land": namely, that there was another community in Israel/Palestine before the Zionists settled there. Avnery (1997) later observed that "It was for this realization that he was assassinated."

[11] See, especially, Hudson (1968); Hanf (1993). Some scholars who belong to the conflict resolution approach did address the Lebanese conflict of 1975–1990, but their goal, too, was to reach political accommodation between Lebanon's various communities – that is, to regulate the conflict, not to resolve it. See Azar and Haddad (1986).

[12] Barak (2005a).

[13] In December 2015, US Secretary of State John Kerry warned that "current trends are leading for a one-state reality" in Israel/Palestine. Quoted in Ravid (2015). See also Ravid (2016).

societies.[14] But many of the responses that I received from my peers were skeptical, and some wondered aloud about the causes for my "pessimism." Still, the facts on the ground in Israel/Palestine continued to accumulate, the peace process did not resume, and an increasing number of studies (discussed in Chapter 4), suggested that, in fact, Israel/Palestine – and not the State of Israel in its pre-1967 borders – was the relevant unit of analysis.

A few years later I decided to combine my interest in Lebanon and Israel/Palestine in a course entitled "Understanding Israeli–Lebanese Relations." The first part of the course dealt with Israel and Lebanon individually and then compared them; the second part discussed the changing relations between the two states. For me, one of the course's goals was to explore possible comparisons between Israel – and, ultimately, Israel/Palestine – and Lebanon; the other was to look more closely at the two states' relations, a topic that, after a relative lull in the wake of Israel's withdrawal from Lebanon in 2000, became relevant after the War between Israel and Hizbullah (2006) (or the Second Lebanon War).[15] But, as it turned out, the two parts of the course were closely connected, and Israeli–Lebanese relations began to look very different after exploring and comparing the two political entities.

I enjoyed teaching the course and continued to do so for five years, first at the University of Texas at Austin (2010–2011), then at The Hebrew University of Jerusalem (2011–2016), and in between also at Cornell University (2014–2015). Although the title and structure of the course remained basically unchanged, its content was different every year, depending on my changing perception of the two cases and their relations, but also on the reactions of my students (to whom I am greatly indebted). In particular, I became intrigued by the mix of formal and informal (including cultural) aspects manifested in both cases and, ultimately, by the usefulness of considering Israel/Palestine – and not the State of Israel in its pre-1967 borders – as the relevant unit for comparison with Lebanon and other divided societies.

As to my students (and especially the Israelis and Palestinians among them), they were initially puzzled by the comparison between Israel and Lebanon, a neighboring state they felt they knew much about but were by and large unfamiliar with. This became clear to them during the first meeting of the course, when I divided them into groups and distributed three envelopes containing timelines of Lebanon, Israel, and their relations to each group. However, in order make matters more complex, these three timelines were actually "puzzles," since the events and the dates

---

[14] Barak (2005b, 2009b).   [15] Barak (2010).

were disjointed and the students had to use their collective knowledge to match each event with the year in which it occurred and then place the events in the correct order (this timeline served as the basis for the timeline provided below, and readers can test their own knowledge about Israel, Lebanon, and their relations as they go over it). By studying these two cases together under one umbrella, my students and I got to know more not only about these cases but also about ourselves. It was particularly rewarding when students came up with new and interesting areas and topics for comparison between Israel and Lebanon, such as sports, high-tech, films, and food, in addition to the two states' political systems, militaries, societies, economies, refugees, and, of course, their mutual relations.[16]

This book presents the main conclusions that I have drawn from studying and teaching Lebanon, Israel/Palestine, and their relations, and at the same time situates these two cases in a broad theoretical and comparative perspective by employing relevant theories from the fields of political science, sociology, and International Relations (IR). In particular, it seeks to better elucidate these two cases of expanded states that are also divided societies – two terms that will be discussed in more detail below – by juxtaposing them and attempting to "see" each of them through the other's "lens," but also by asking how they actually related to one another – that is, by exploring their changing relations.

On a more general level, the book wishes to better elucidate the triangular relationship between the state, community, and security in divided societies – an issue that has elicited considerable attention since the events of the "Arab Spring"[17] – and also to add a crucial external dimension to the analysis of this complex and multi-faceted relationship. This discussion is also motivated by the case of Iraq since the US invasion in 2003, which suggests that states can be "collapsed" and "failed" due to the actions of others and not only on account of their own weakness.

---

[16] Quite tellingly, every year a number of students in the course were interested in writing papers on Hizbullah but not on other Lebanese factions (or even on the Lebanese state, for that matter). In this sense, the course seemed to reflect broader views in Israeli that Lebanon equals Hizbullah. See, e.g., a telling interview by Major General (ret.) Amos Gilad, head of the political-security bureau of Israel's Ministry of Defense, who argued in 2011 that "Lebanon is a state without a constitution, and a constitution without a state. The president and the speaker [of parliament] are not aware of anything that is happening in the other half of their country ... This vacuum leads to the establishment of what we call Hizbullastan" (Gilad 2011). I present my (different) conclusions regarding Hizbullah's role in Lebanon in Chapter 3 and elaborate on Israel's changing perceptions of Lebanon in Chapters 6 and 7.

[17] Elsewhere, I discuss, with other colleagues, some of the more tranquil states in the "Arab Spring," including divided societies such as Jordan and Lebanon, and try to account for this phenomenon. See Barak and Rahat (2012).

By employing the aforementioned theoretical tools, as well as by adopting a comparative approach to Lebanon and Israel/Palestine, the book attempts to treat these two cases in a non-essentialist manner, thus responding to the valid criticisms raised by Edward Said in his seminal book *Orientalism*.[18] In addition, the book intentionally avoids using politically charged terms such as "terror" and "terrorism,"[19] which are frequently employed when referring to the *other* and its actions but only rarely to *one's own* behavior in Israel/Palestine and Lebanon (and also elsewhere). Finally, when relating to historic events that different actors refer to by using different names (e.g., the War of Independence and the *Nakba* by Israelis and Palestinians, respectively), the book mentions these different names without attempting to decide between them. It is hoped that the aggregate result of these choices is a fair and balanced analysis of the two cases at hand.

---

[18] Said (1979).
[19] On the problems in using these terms, see, e.g., Richard Jackson (2005).

Acknowledgments

This book could not have been written without the generous help of many individuals and institutions. In recent years, I presented parts of this project in seminars and courses at several universities, including Cornell University, the University of Texas at Austin, the University of Toronto, Brandeis University, Tel Aviv University, and The Hebrew University of Jerusalem, as well as in several meetings of the International Studies Association. I thank the participants in these conferences, seminars, and courses for their helpful comments.

A number of colleagues and friends have given me valuable feedback at various stages of the project, and I am indebted to all of them for their time and effort. In particular, I thank Emanuel Adler, Shulamit Almog, Jacques Bertrand, Uri Bialer, Assaf David, Laurie Zittrain Eisenberg, Matthew Evangelista, Orit Gazit, Ran Greenstein, Caroline Hartzell, Piki Ish-Shalom, Peter Katzenstein, Asher Kaufman, Menachem Klein, Ephraim Kleiman, Jeff Kopstein, Liat Kozma, Anna Leander, Lior Lehres, Yagil Levy, Amir Lupovici, Ian Lustick, Joel Migdal, Benjamin Miller, Dan Miodownik, Shaul Mishal, Raya Morag, Galia Press-Barnathan, Avraham Sela, Gabriel Sheffer, Yehouda Shenhav, Daniel Sobelman, Daniella Talmon-Heller, Ilan Troen, Nicholas van de Walle, Yair Wallach, Steven Ward, and Ariel Zellman. However, none of these individuals is responsible for any errors that remain in the text.

At Cambridge University Press, I thank my two editors, John Haslam and Lewis Bateman, Puviarassy Kalieperumal, Bronte Rawlings, and Stephanie Taylor for their valuable help during the production stage, and the anonymous referees for their useful feedback. I also thank Lior Spindel for research assistance, and Colette Stoeber and Helen Cooper for editing the manuscript.

Research for this book was supported by grants from the Israel Science Foundation (grant no. 1561/14) and from the Bernard Cherrick Center for the History of Zionism, the Yishuv, and the State of Israel at The Hebrew University of Jerusalem.

I would also like to express my deep gratitude and love to my family, Orna, Paz, Guy, and Roy, and to my parents, Nurit and Amnon Barak.

This book is dedicated to the loving memory of my grandmother, Miriam Margalit, and my grandfather, Meir Bracha, who would have been happy to see it in print.

Chronology

1861: In the wake of inter-communal violence in Mount Lebanon, an autonomous district, the *Mutasarrifiyya*, is established there, under the auspices of the European powers but within the framework of the Ottoman Empire.

1914–1918: During the First World War, Ottoman forces enter Mount Lebanon and the local population suffers from their conduct. Later, British and French forces occupy the areas that today are part of Lebanon, Syria, and Israel/Palestine and divide this territory among themselves.

September 1, 1920: The French colonial power establishes a new political unit called "Greater Lebanon" (*grand liban*) by formally annexing the areas of North Lebanon, South Lebanon, the Biqa', and the city of Beirut to Mount Lebanon.

July 1922: The League of Nations approves the British Mandate in Palestine and the French Mandate in Lebanon.

1923: The border between Mandatory Palestine and Greater Lebanon (*grand liban*) is delineated by French and British officials.

1932: The last comprehensive population census is held in Lebanon.

1936–1939: The Palestinian revolt against the British Mandate and the Jewish community in Palestine (the *Yishuv*). British forces crush the revolt.

November 1943: The Lebanese emerge victorious from a confrontation with France, the colonial power. Leaders representing Lebanon's major communities reach the National Pact, an informal settlement that has domestic and external aspects.

1945: Lebanon becomes a fully independent state and joins the Arab League (League of Arab States) as a founding member.

November, 1947 – July, 1949: The First Arab–Israeli War – also known as the 1948 War, Israel's War of Independence, the Palestine War, and the *Nakba* – takes place. Tens of thousands of Palestinian refugees arrive in Lebanon and settle in refugee camps.

May 14, 1948: Termination of the British Mandate in Palestine; the State of Israel declares its independence.

May 15, 1948: Several Arab states intervene in the conflict in Palestine. The Lebanese Armed Forces (LAF) maintain defensive positions along the Israeli–Lebanese border.

October 21, 1948: Israel imposes the Military Government (martial law) over most of its Palestinian citizens. It is abolished in 1966.

February–March 1949: Israel and each of Egypt, Lebanon, Jordan, and Syria sign Armistice agreements that put an end to the First Arab–Israeli War. The Palestinians, who have ceased to be an autonomous actor on account of the conflict, do not sign such an agreement. The Israel–Lebanon Mixed Armistice Commission (ILMAC) is formed under the auspices of the United Nations to supervise the agreement.

May 3, 1956: The first Druze and Circassian soldiers from among Israel's Palestinian community are recruited to the Israel Defense Forces (IDF). Later, Bedouins are also recruited to the IDF, but most Muslim and Christian citizens are exempted.

1958: The first civil war in Lebanon leads to US intervention in Lebanon and ends with the election of General Fouad Chehab, the commander of the LAF, as Lebanon's president.

June 5–10, 1967: During the Israeli–Arab War Israel defeats the armies of Egypt, Jordan, and Syria and occupies the Sinai Peninsula and the Gaza Strip from Egypt, the West Bank (including East Jerusalem) from Jordan, and the Golan from Syria.

1968–1969: An Israeli raid on Beirut International Airport leads to the first major crisis between Lebanon and the Palestinian armed factions, which ends with the signing of the Cairo Agreement between the two parties under Egypt's auspices.

1970–1971: The Jordanian Army defeats the Palestinian armed factions in Jordan and many Palestinian activists flee to Lebanon.

1973: The second major crisis between Lebanon and the Palestinian armed factions. An annex to the Cairo Agreement is signed but does not resolve the problems between the parties.

April 13, 1975: The Lebanese civil war begins. The state's institutions, including the LAF, become paralyzed.

1976: Israel steps up its involvement in South Lebanon and extends humanitarian and military support to the local Christian militia as part of its "Good Fence" policy.

March 30, 1976: The Palestinian citizens of Israel organize the Land Day in response to the confiscation of their lands by the government. Six demonstrators are killed by Israel's security sector.

June 1976: Syria intervenes in Lebanon after securing Israel's consent. Arab summits legitimize Syria's peacekeeping role in Lebanon.

November 1977: Egyptian President Anwar al-Sadat visits Israel, paving the way to the Camp David Accords (1978) and the Egyptian–Israeli Peace Treaty (1979).

March 1978: Israel launches the Litani Operation (1978) in South Lebanon in response to a deadly Palestinian attack against its territory. Israel hands over the occupied area to its local ally, the Christian militia headed by a Lebanese officer, Major Saad Haddad, and a UN force (UNIFIL) is deployed in South Lebanon.

April 1982: Israel evacuates all of its settlements in the Sinai Peninsula according to the terms of the Egyptian–Israeli Peace Treaty.

June 1982: Israel launches the Lebanon War of 1982 ("Operation Peace for Galilee") designed to crush the PLO forces in Lebanon, expel the Syrian army, and facilitate the election of Israel's major Lebanese ally, Bashir Gemayel, leader of the Lebanese Forces militia, as Lebanon's president.

September 1982: President-elect Bashir Gemayel is assassinated, and, following the Sabra and Shatila Massacre perpetrated by the Lebanese Forces militia, the Kahan Commission of Inquiry is formed. Its report leads to the removal of Defense Minister Ariel Sharon from office.

May 17, 1983: An Israeli–Lebanese agreement is signed but not implemented due to its rejection by several Lebanese actors (especially Shi'i and Druze militias) and Syria.

June 1985: The IDF withdraws from most parts of Lebanon but leaves a self-declared "security zone" under the control of its local ally, the South Lebanese Army (SLA).

December 1987: After two decades of Israeli occupation, the first Palestinian Intifada erupts in the West Bank and the Gaza Strip. Israel attempts to crush it by force.

October–November 1989: The remaining members of the Lebanese parliament, who had been elected in 1972, convene in the city of Ta'if, Saudi Arabia, and approve the Ta'if Agreement, which is designed to end the civil war and facilitate Lebanon's reconstruction.

October 13, 1990: A joint Syrian–Lebanese military operation terminates Lebanon's civil war.

January–February 1991: During the Gulf War, Iraq fires 39 Scud missiles at Israel. Israel does not respond to the attack.

October–November 1991: The Madrid Conference, co-sponsored by the United States and the Soviet Union, brings together delegations from Israel, Syria, and Lebanon, as well as a joint Jordanian–Palestinian delegation. However, the bilateral talks between the parties make little progress.

June 1992: The Left-Center bloc wins the Israeli general elections and Lieutenant General (ret.) Yitzhak Rabin, leader of the Labor Party, forms a new government.

July 1993: Israel launches a military operation against Hizbullah in South Lebanon ("Operation Accountability").

September 13, 1993: Israel and the PLO sign the Declaration of Principles on Interim Self-Government Arrangements, known as the Oslo Agreement, under US auspices.

May 1994: Israel and the PLO sign the Cairo Accord, also known as the Gaza–Jericho Agreement. A Palestinian National Authority is formed in the West Bank and the Gaza Strip. Hamas and the Islamic Jihad, two radical Palestinian Islamist factions, are opposed to the Israeli–Palestinian peace process and attempt to obstruct it by launching armed attacks against Israel. Some ultra-right Israeli Jews (most notably Baruch Goldstein), launch armed attacks against Palestinians.

October 26, 1994: Israel and Jordan sign a formal peace treaty.

September 24, 1995: Israel and the PLO sign the Interim Agreement on the West Bank and Gaza Strip.

November 4, 1995: Israeli Prime Minister Yitzhak Rabin is assassinated by Yigal Amir, an ultra-right national religious Jew, in Tel Aviv, and is succeeded by Shimon Peres.

April 1996: Israel launches a military operation against Hizbullah in South Lebanon ("Operation Grapes of Wrath"). Israeli fire kills more than one hundred Lebanese civilians in Qana.

May 2000: Israel withdraws from its "security zone" in South Lebanon, and its client, the SLA, collapses.

July 2000: Israel's withdrawal from Lebanon is confirmed by the UN, and the "Blue Line," which approximates the international boundary between Israel and Lebanon, is verified.

July 2000: The Camp David summit held between Israeli Prime Minister Ehud Barak, PLO leader Yasser Arafat, and US President Bill Clinton ends in failure.

September 2000: The Second Palestinian Intifada (or al-Aqsa Intifada) begins in the West Bank and the Gaza Strip.

October 1, 2000: Thirteen Israeli–Palestinian citizens are killed by Israel's security sector during a wave of demonstrations and riots.

October 7, 2000: Hizbullah abducts three Israeli soldiers in the contested Shebaa Farms area.

February–April 2005: Former Lebanese Prime Minister Rafiq al-Hariri is assassinated in Beirut, resulting in mass demonstrations, both for and against a Syrian withdrawal from Lebanon. Syrian troops pull out following domestic and external pressures.

September 2005: Israel completes its Disengagement Plan, a unilateral withdrawal from the Gaza Strip and a small area in the West Bank, including the dismantling of all military bases and settlements in these areas.

July–August 2006: The War between Israel and Hizbullah (or the Second Lebanon War).

December 2008–January 2009: Military confrontation between Israel and Hamas in the Gaza Strip (the "Gaza War," "Operation Cast Lead").

November 2012: Military confrontation between Israel and Hamas in the Gaza Strip ("Operation Pillar of Defense").

June–August 2014: Military confrontation between Israel and Hamas in the Gaza Strip ("Operation Protective Edge"). The confrontation begins with the abduction and killing of three Israeli teenagers by Hamas armed operatives in the West Bank. Later, ultra-right Israeli Jews abduct and kill a Palestinian teenager in East Jerusalem.

October 2016: General (ret.) Michel Aoun, former commander of the LAF, is elected as Lebanon's new president by 83 out of 128 members of the parliament after a 29-month void in the state's highest post. Aoun is the third consecutive LAF commander to become Lebanon's president.

Introduction

In August 1978 Menachem Begin had a secret meeting, in his home Jerusalem, with Camille Chamoun, a Maronite Christian who had served as president of Lebanon. Begin promised his guest that his government will expand the assistance to the Christian community. He likened the Christians in Lebanon to the Jews who were persecuted in the Diaspora because they were Jews. The meeting ended in brave hugs. When exiting the house Chamoun's face suddenly clouded and he stopped. "Your Excellency," he said to Begin, "Do not make the same mistakes we did in Lebanon. The French forced a Greater Lebanon upon us. When we became an independent state, they forced us to annex territories whose population was Muslim. This was the source of our troubles. Don't annex territories with Muslims to your country." Begin listened but did not say a word.

– Daniel Ben-Simon, "Delusions of Lebanon" (1998)[1]

In 1993, *The Formation of Modern Lebanon*,[2] a book by Ben-Gurion University Professor Meir Zamir whose English version had appeared eight years earlier,[3] was made available to Hebrew readers for the first time through a joint effort by the publishing houses of the Israel Defense Forces (IDF) and Israel's Ministry of Defense. In its punctilious academic style, the book discussed the causes for the creation of the political unit of "Greater Lebanon" (*grand liban*) on September 1, 1920, and the long-term implications of this watershed event for Lebanon both before and after it won its independence from France in the mid-1940s.[4]

Contrary to much of the literature on the contemporary Middle East, which emphasizes the role of the European colonial powers in creating the region's states, delineating their borders, and shaping their political,

---

[1] Ben-Simon actually paraphrases David Kimche's version of the meeting. See Kimche (1991, 125). Interestingly – but not untypically for Israeli officials – Kimche adds that "Chamoun had good reason for counselling Israel to take care" but then focuses only on the Lebanese side of the equation.
[2] Zamir (1993). [3] Zamir (1985).
[4] Lebanon's official date of independence is November 22, 1943, although it took several more years before French troops evacuated its territory.

bureaucratic, and military institutions,[5] *The Formation of Modern Lebanon* highlighted the role of an indigenous actor, the Maronite Christian community (hereafter, the Maronites) in Mount Lebanon, in initiating the establishment of Lebanon in its present-day borders. It also demonstrated how, instead of creating the nation-state that some Maronite leaders had envisioned and coveted, the new political unit turned out to be a divided society fraught with perpetual instability and conflict.

Israeli scholars and practitioners, especially from the center and left of the political spectrum, welcomed the book's publication. Yehoshua Porath, an acclaimed historian of the modern Middle East who in the 1992 parliamentary elections was on the list of the left-wing political party *Meretz* but later opposed the Oslo Agreement between Israel and the PLO and in 1996 supported the election of Benjamin Netanyahu as Israel's prime minister, wrote on the back cover: "This book should be of interest to the Israeli public, and ought to be read by those shaping its future."[6] Abba Eban, a former diplomat and government minister from the Labor Party, was even more explicit in his words: "Whoever wishes to grasp the full meaning of Israeli control over the Territories of Judea, Samaria and the Gaza Strip, should refer to this book, which makes no mention of the State of Israel."[7]

Indeed, as these and other positive appraisals of the book suggest,[8] the more informed audience in Israel came to view *The Formation of Modern Lebanon* not only as an objective account of events that had taken place in some distant time and place, but also – and perhaps even more so – as a powerful allegory for Israel's present political conundrum. Indeed, almost six years after the outbreak of the first Palestinian Intifada in the West Bank (including East Jerusalem and the Gaza Strip; hereafter, the Territories), and months before the signing of the Oslo Agreement between Israel and the PLO, the events leading to, and the long-term consequences of, the creation of multi-communal Greater Lebanon were looked upon as a particularly insightful precedent.

Yet, despite these welcoming remarks, no attempt has been made to follow through with a more detailed – and explicit – comparison between the formation of Greater Lebanon in 1920 and the creation of Greater Israel in 1967, and the long-term political ramifications of these two ground-

---

[5] See, especially, Anderson (1987); Thompson (1999); Owen (2000); Massad (2001); Neep (2012). This view is also reflected in former Lebanese President Camille Chamoun's words presented at the beginning of this chapter. Cf. I. Harik (1990).
[6] Zamir (1993).
[7] Zamir (1985). Quite typically for Israeli officials after 1967, Eban used the Israeli names of the Territories.
[8] See, e.g., a review of Zamir's book by Reuven Merhav, a former Mossad official who during the Lebanon War of 1982 served as head of the Beirut mission of Israel's Ministry of Foreign Affairs and was later appointed as its director-general (Merhav 1993).

Introduction 3

breaking events for Lebanon and Israel/Palestine, respectively.[9] This is despite the interesting parallels that can be drawn between the dynamics and trajectories of these two political units since the state's expansion, and the insights that such an inquiry can offer not only with regard to these cases themselves but also more broadly. After all, both cases highlight a more general dilemma facing members of communities or ethnic (or ethnonational) groups:[10] in their quest to establish their own "place under the sun" – that is, a nation-state to satisfy their collective needs, especially identity and security – these communities instead find themselves in divided societies of their own making, in which they have lost, or are on their way to losing, their numerical majority. All of this challenges not only the community's physical but also its ontological security.[11] Furthermore, the two cases of Lebanon and Israel/Palestine provide telling examples of different ways members of these communities have coped with their conundrum, allowing us to assess their success and failure.

This book takes up the challenge and presents a broad comparison between Lebanon and Israel/Palestine since their creation as divided societies in 1920 and 1967, respectively, focusing on the triangular relationship between the state, community, and security. Following the same (implicit) logic of *The Formation of Modern Lebanon*, a logic that has become more pronounced in subsequent decades, the book's basic premise is that Israel/Palestine – namely, the area that until May 14, 1948, was called Palestine and was under British Mandate, which was brought under Israel's control in the Israeli–Arab War of 1967, and which is referred to as the Land of Israel (*Eretz Israel*) by its Jewish inhabitants and as Palestine (*Filastin*) by its Palestinian inhabitants – constitutes a single political unit, though one that, unlike Lebanon, is informal since it is not recognized by any state. This includes Israel, which has refrained from annexing the Territories, on the one hand, or relinquishing them, on the other hand. This basic assumption, which political developments in Israel/Palestine since 1993, and perhaps even more so since 2000, have reinforced rather than diminished, makes Israel/Palestine comparable to

---

[9] Exceptions are Barak (2005b, 2009b). Elsewhere I discuss the dearth of comparisons between Israel and its neighbors; see Barak (2014).
[10] Gurr and Harff (1994, 190) define ethnic groups as "composed of people who share a distinctive and enduring collective identity based on shared experiences and cultural traits. They may define themselves, and be defined by others, in terms of any or all of the following traits: lifeways, religious beliefs, language, physical appearance, region of residence, traditional occupations, and a history of conquest and repression by culturally different peoples." They add that ethnic groups are also called communal groups. See also the useful discussion in Chandra (2009).
[11] According to Mitzen (2006, 344), "Ontological security is security not of the body but of the self, the subjective sense of who one is, which enables and motivates action and choice." See also Giddens (1991); Steele (2005).

other expanded states, including Lebanon (other relevant examples are mentioned in the concluding chapter). Based on this assumption, which challenges studies that limit themselves to Israel within its 1949 borders and overlook or downplay its expansion in 1967 and its long-term implications,[12] this book sets out to explore the effects of the state's expansion on the triangular relationship between the state, community, and security in Lebanon and in Israel/Palestine.

As this discussion suggests, whereas in Israel/Palestine the process of state formation engendered a strong state in the material-coercive sense, but one that, given the decline of its Jewish majority, fewer and fewer of its inhabitants consider to be legitimate, in Lebanon the process of state formation has engendered a weak state that found it difficult to claim a monopoly over the legitimate means of violence, but which gradually became acceptable to most of its citizens, including those in the regions that had been annexed to Mount Lebanon in 1920.

A second conclusion is that in both expanded states, the political and security institutions became increasingly representative, especially as far as members of the periphery were concerned, and that the latter eventually acquired veto power over political decisions that they regarded as detrimental to their interests. But whereas in Israel/Palestine those represented in the state's institutions were mostly members of the dominant Jewish community and those excluded were the subordinate (or subaltern) Palestinians, in Lebanon members of all communities received an equitable share in the state's institutions.

The third conclusion is that whereas Israel/Palestine witnessed militarization and a foreign policy that emphasized the use of military power to achieve the political goals of the dominant Jewish community, Lebanon attempted to de-militarize and tried to become neutral, but instead became the subject of constant foreign meddling, which, at least in part, was invited by its own leaders.

These three "domestically centered" conclusions are further highlighted by discussing the deterioration in the relations between Lebanon and Israel/Palestine in the period since 1967, which suggests that this outcome stemmed from Israel's expansion and its ramifications, and not only from the weakness, or even "failure," of the Lebanese state in this period.

Although numerous works deal with each of Lebanon and Israel/Palestine, only a few studies discuss both cases, including from a broader theoretical and comparative perspective.[13] By contrast, this book suggests

---

[12] These studies are dealt with in Chapter 4.
[13] An exception is Dekmejian (1975) which deals with the political elites in Egypt, Israel, and Lebanon, focusing on cabinet ministers. An early study that compared Mandatory

Introduction 5

that juxtaposing these two cases and identifying both their similarities and differences can shed new light on these and possibly also other divided societies that have faced, or still face, similar conundrums.[14] More broadly, it offers a critical perspective toward the applicability of the model of the nation-state in divided societies in the Middle East but also more generally.[15] As it suggests, in both Lebanon and Israel/Palestine the vision of the nation-state, which was promoted by the dominant group – the Maronites and the Jews, respectively – soon confronted a multi-communal reality, but whereas in Lebanon this vision was ultimately – and painfully – adjusted to fit the reality, in Israel/Palestine persistent efforts were made to change the reality to fit the vision, with devastating consequences for all.

As far as Israeli–Lebanese relations are concerned, they are usually dealt with by emphasizing "realist" factors, such as Israel's broader "security dilemma" in the Middle East, or, if domestic factors are considered, by focusing on Lebanon's "failure" in the mid-1970s and its consequences for the two states' relations.[16] However, the impact of developments that took place in both Lebanon and Israel/Palestine since 1967 – and especially Israel's expansion and its ramifications – on these actors' relations has not been sufficiently addressed. By exploring this factor, the book suggests that expanded states that are divided societies face a specific set of considerations in their foreign policy, and that this particular type of "domestic-external entanglement"[17] can become even more complex when the interaction is between two expanded states that are divided societies. More broadly, the book suggests that it is useful to ask how two political entities *stand in relation* to one another, based on a thorough comparison between them, in order to answer the question of how these political entities *actually relate* to one another, and to identify elements of change and continuity in these two inter-

Palestine and Lebanon is Dan Horowitz (1982). In addition to Zamir's implicit comparison between Israel/Palestine and Lebanon (Zamir 1985; 1993), exceptions from the period before the Oslo Process that deal with Israel (and Israel/Palestine) and Lebanon in the same context are Smooha and Hanf (1992) and Yiftachel (1992). Recent works that compare the Israeli and Lebanese personal status legal systems and their militaries, respectively, are Mikdashi (2011) and Childs (2012), but both focus only on the Lebanese and Israeli states. Slyomovics (2013) discusses memory studies in Lebanon and Israel/Palestine, but does not compare the two cases or ask why the question of memory is relevant to both of them. A recent work that compares several successful and unsuccessful peace processes, including those in Israel/Palestine and Lebanon, is Tonge (2014). A popular but problematic depiction of Lebanon and Israel/Palestine in the 1980s, which includes some comparative insights, is T. Friedman (1989). For criticism, see Said (1989).
[14] Some of these cases are mentioned in the concluding chapter.
[15] Ra'anan (1990); Connor (1994); Barrington (1997); I. Young (2005); Miller (2007).
[16] These studies are dealt with in Chapter 6.   [17] Putnam (1988).

connected aspects. In this sense, the book highlights yet another important link between the fields of comparative politics and International Relations.[18]

The remainder of this introductory chapter presents an overview of Lebanon, Israel/Palestine, and their changing relations. It then presents the rationale and structure of the book.

Lebanon

The Republic of Lebanon became independent in November 1943, following a major crisis between the Lebanese and France, the colonial power that controlled the Levant – the area comprising the present-day states of Syria and Lebanon – since its occupation from the Ottoman Empire during the First World War.

However, when dealing with the creation of the Lebanese state within its present borders, one needs to go back to September 1, 1920, when, in response to the demands of their local allies, the leaders of the Maronite Christian community in Mount Lebanon, French officials proclaimed the establishment of a new political unit called "Greater Lebanon" (*grand liban*). To this end, they annexed the territories of North Lebanon, South Lebanon, the Biqa', and the city of Beirut to Mount Lebanon, which, until 1914, had been an autonomous district (*Mutasarrifiyya*) within the Ottoman Empire.[19]

However, instead of becoming a Maronite (or, for that matter, a Christian) nation-state, as envisaged by Maronite leaders, Greater Lebanon turned out to be a divided society. By 1932, Christians amounted to slightly more than half of the population in Lebanon.[20] After a short period of ruling Lebanon on their own, albeit with French tutelage, and following regional and international mediation, Maronite leaders reached, in 1943, a political settlement known as the National Pact with leaders of Lebanon's Muslim communities – especially Sunnis but also others, including Shi'is and Druze – who, for their part, had gradually come to terms with the "separate" existence of Greater Lebanon. This informal inter-communal

---

[18] Ibid., 459.
[19] Maps of the *Mutasarrifiyya* are inconsistent. Among the available maps, see (and compare) an Ottoman map from 1893, at: https://commons.wikimedia.org/wiki/File:Osmanli_Orta dogu.jpg (accessed November 10, 2016); "Rare Map of Ottoman Lebanon during World War I," at: www.midafternoonmap.com/2014/01/rare-map-of-ottoman-lebanon-during .html (accessed November 10, 2016); and Akarli (1993, 8) at: http://publishing.cdlib .org/ucpressebooks/data/13030/6t/ft6199p06t/figures/ft6199p06t_00000.gif (accessed November 9, 2016). I thank Asher Kaufman for bringing these maps to my attention.
[20] Zamir (1985, 98). See also Figure 2.1.

settlement included two elements: first, power sharing among members of all of Lebanon's major communities; second, a compromise regarding Lebanon's identity and external orientation that was acceptable both domestically and in the eyes of Lebanon's Arab neighbors.

The political settlement reached in Lebanon enabled its communities to govern the state together for more than three decades, and to evade most (but not all) regional turbulences and crises from the late 1940s until the Israeli–Arab War of 1967. However, from then onwards, this settlement faced mounting domestic and external challenges. Lebanon's growing Shi'i community, but also members of other communities (Sunnis, Druze, and some non-Maronite Christians), harbored social, economic, and political grievances toward Lebanon's political and socioeconomic elite. These they regarded as dominated by conservative Maronite leaders and their Sunni allies, the political bosses (*zu'ama'*). Major political and military backing for the opposition's political claims came from the Palestinian armed factions, whose members had stepped up their activities in Lebanon after the 1967 War and especially after their forced expulsion from the Territories and Jordan. The Palestinians launched armed operations against Israel from Lebanon's territory, Israel responded with retaliatory raids against the Palestinians but also against Lebanon, and the Lebanese state began to lose its monopoly over the legitimate use of violence in the Israeli–Lebanese border area. In the meantime, Syria, Lebanon's Arab neighbor, which stabilized in the early 1970s, exploited Lebanon's weakness and attempted to bring it under its influence.

In April 1975, Lebanon's civil war began and the government in Beirut quickly lost control over most of its territory. The Palestinian armed factions soon joined the fighting, and Israel, too, became involved, first in the Israeli–Lebanese border area and then in other parts of Lebanon. Fearing Lebanon's disintegration and its partition according to communal lines, Syrian leaders decided to send their troops into Lebanon in June 1976, a move that was later sanctioned by the Arab League. But Lebanese leaders failed to reach a settlement in place of the 1943 Pact and the conflict in Lebanon lingered. Mounting Israeli–Palestinian tensions in South Lebanon led to two Israeli invasions into Lebanon: the Litani Operation (1978) and, on a much larger scale, the Lebanon War of 1982. However, Israel and other states that became involved in Lebanon, most notably the United States and France in the period 1982–1984, failed to bring stability, and the Lebanese conflict continued, and even escalated, in the late 1980s, leading some groups to establish their own autonomous regions ("cantons") there.

The Lebanese conflict finally came to end on October 13, 1990, after the Ta'if Agreement, an inter-communal settlement that had been reached by the remaining members of the Lebanese parliament a year earlier following intensive inter-Arab mediation. The agreement introduced major reforms in Lebanon's power-sharing settlement, which made it more acceptable to Lebanon's Sunnis, Shi'is, and Druze, and at the same time formalized Syria's "special relations"– that is, a form of hegemony – with Lebanon. Syria, for its part, was instrumental in Lebanon's disbanding of most local and foreign violent non-state actors in its territory, with some notable exceptions: Hizbullah, the Shi'i party-militia, which retained its military capacities, which it referred to as the "resistance"; and Israel's proxy, the South Lebanese Army (SLA) in the "security zone" that Israel had established in 1985 following the First Lebanon War. In any case, the Ta'if Agreement and the end of the conflict in Lebanon facilitated the state's reconstruction under the leadership of Rafiq al-Hariri (Sunni), a wealthy and charismatic leader who enjoyed Saudi and Syrian support. However, inter-communal relations in Lebanon remained tense, and the continued existence of Hizbullah and its "resistance," and also Israel's occupation in Lebanon, were a perpetual source of instability. Still, at no point did Lebanon slide back into conflict.

In May 2000, Israel withdrew its forces from Lebanon, and almost five years later, in April 2005, following the assassination of former Lebanese Prime Minister Hariri (possibly by Syria, Hizbullah, or both), Syria's forces in Lebanon were compelled to leave due to massive demonstrations in Beirut and external pressures by the United States, France, the UN, and several Arab states. But the relationship between Hizbullah and Israel continued to be tense, and another major confrontation, the War between Israel and Hizbullah (2006), broke out, leading to many casualties and great devastation. Despite the deployment of the LAF in South Lebanon in the wake of the conflict, Lebanon found it difficult to maintain domestic stability and also, from 2011, to keep a safe distance from the Syrian civil war, which sometimes spilled over into Lebanon in the form of almost 1.5 million Syrian refugees who arrived in its territory[21] and occasional violence, particularly along the Lebanese–Syrian border but also between Alawites and Sunnis in the mixed city of Tripoli. Thus, for example, Lebanon remained without a president for a period of 29 months, until the election of Michel Aoun, former commander of the LAF, to this post in October 2016. Still, Lebanon's state of "stable instability," whereby its leaders are "not able to find a final resolution to a range of issues" but are still "able to manage disagreements and reach temporary compromises,"[22] was preserved.

[21] Assi and Worrall (2015, 16).   [22] Ibid., 16–17. See also Barak (2012).

Introduction 9

Although demographic data on Lebanon remains partial – a comprehensive population census has not been carried out in the state since 1932 – estimates are that Lebanon's Christians are no longer the majority in the state, and that the Maronites, who had initiated the creation of Greater Lebanon, are no longer the country's largest community.[23]

Israel/Palestine

On May 14, 1948, after the termination of the British Mandate in Palestine, Jewish leaders officially proclaimed the independence of the State of Israel. But many of the political, bureaucratic, and security institutions of the new state, as well as informal aspects of its political system – to say nothing of the relations between the two communities in the area west of the Jordan River, the Jews and the Palestinians – can be traced to the period of the British Mandate in Palestine, which began after the Allied forces had occupied the area from the Ottomans during the First World War.

During the war, Zionist leaders managed to persuade the British government to make a formal commitment to establishing a Jewish "national home" in Palestine, which the latter did – albeit by adding the need to preserve the rights of the indigenous community, the Palestinians. In the period of the British Mandate, colonial officials were generally supportive of the Jewish community in Palestine (the *Yishuv*) but the latter's rapid growth and territorial expansion was resisted by the Palestinian community, resulting in open confrontations in 1929 and especially in the period 1936–1939, during the Palestinian revolt, which also targeted the British.

On November 29, 1947, the UN approved the Partition Plan for Palestine and the conflict between the Jewish and Palestinian communities escalated. In addition, a host of foreign volunteers (including some from Lebanon), came to fight alongside the two belligerents. Then, after the British left Palestine, the armies of several neighboring Arab states, including Egypt, Transjordan, Syria, and Iraq, as well as troops from other countries, intervened in the conflict. Although Lebanon, too, was involved in the First Arab–Israeli War, its military, the LAF, adhered to a defensive role and fought only one battle against the IDF in Malikiyya, a village located on the border between Israel and Lebanon, on June 5–6, 1948.

In 1949, the First Arab–Israeli War came to an end not by Arab–Israeli peace treaties, but by a series of Armistice agreements that were signed

[23] M. Young (2010, 10).

under the auspices of the UN between Israel and each of Egypt, Lebanon, Transjordan, and Syria, though not with the Palestinians. By then, hundreds of thousands of Palestinians had left their homes – many were expelled by the Israeli forces and others fled in fear of Jewish violence – and settled in the remaining areas under Arab control in Palestine or in the neighboring Arab states.[24]

After the end of the war, Israel had a clear Jewish majority of about 85 percent and a relatively small Palestinian minority of close to 15 percent.[25] Members of the Palestinian community in Israel were granted Israeli citizenship and participated in the general elections, and Palestinian candidates were elected to the Knesset. At the same time, Jewish leaders generally perceived members of Israel's Palestinian community as a threat to their national security and imposed the Military Government – that is, martial law – on them. In addition, the state's institutions confiscated large portions of the Palestinians' land, allegedly because of security considerations. In 1966, Israel's leaders officially abolished the Military Government, and Israel appeared to be on its way to becoming a Jewish nation-state, albeit with a sizable Palestinian minority of about 11 percent.[26]

But in June 1967 all of this changed profoundly. Rising tensions between Israel and Syria led Egypt's president, Gamal Abdul Nasser, to threaten Israel by sending his troops to the Sinai Peninsula, closing the Straits of Tiran, and entering into an alliance with Syria and Jordan, two of Israel's other Arab neighbors. For Israel's political leaders, this was a *casus belli*, and after some deliberations – including intense pressures from members of the general staff of the IDF – Israel decided to launch a pre-emptive war against its Arab foes. Within six days, the IDF defeated the armies of Egypt, Jordan, and Syria and occupied the West Bank (including East Jerusalem) from Jordan, the Sinai Peninsula and the Gaza Strip from Egypt, and the Golan from Syria. As a result, a new political unit, a "Greater Israel," which included all areas that had been part of Mandatory Palestine until 1948 – referred to hereafter as Israel/Palestine – came into being.[27]

---

[24] See Chapter 4.   [25] Haidar (2005, 14).
[26] According to Haidar (ibid., 11), Israel's official statistics, which include the Palestinians in East Jerusalem and the Golan, two areas that Israel occupied in 1967 (it later imposed its jurisdiction there as well), put this community at 18 percent of Israel's population.
[27] For official Israeli maps of the State of Israel since 1967, which omit the "Green Line" and present "Greater Israel" or Israel/Palestine as one unit, see, e.g., www.govmap.gov.il/ (accessed November 10, 2016); Israel Ministry of Foreign Affairs (hereafter, MFA), "Israel in Maps," at: http://mfa.gov.il/MFA/AboutIsrael/Maps/Pages/Israel%20in%20Maps.aspx (accessed November 10, 2016) (see also Chapter 1 and Chapter 4). For a map of Jewish settlements in the West Bank, see www.btselem.org/download/201411_btselem_map_of_wb_eng.pdf (accessed November 17, 2016).

In the decades after the 1967 War, consecutive Israeli governments did their utmost to settle the West Bank and the Gaza Strip (hereafter, the Territories) and, to a lesser extent, also the Sinai Peninsula (which was returned to Egypt following the Egyptian–Israeli peace treaty of 1979) and the Golan so as to make them inseparable from Israel. Still, despite all efforts made by Israel's leaders to maintain a Jewish majority in Israel/Palestine – the new political unit that they had created in 1967, albeit informally – the turn of the twenty-first century saw the Jewish majority there declining considerably, and according to some experts Jews have already lost, or will soon lose, their majority vis-à-vis the Palestinians (see Chapter 2).[28]

In December 1987, after two decades of Israeli occupation of the Territories, the Palestinians in these areas launched the first Intifada, a popular uprising against Israel's military rule over them. However, Israeli leaders, who were taken by surprise, did not relinquish the Territories, and it was only in 1993, after the Gulf War and following the intensification of inter-communal violence in Israel/Palestine, which sometimes spilled over into Israel's territory, that an Israeli–Palestinian peace process was initiated. However, the Oslo Process, which aroused great expectations in Israel/Palestine and beyond, did not lead to the partition of the shared land, and the number of Jewish settlers in the Territories doubled in the period 1993–2000 (see Chapter 4). A second, more violent Palestinian Intifada (or al-Aqsa Intifada) broke out in September 2000, but it, too, failed to lead to the contraction of Israel/Palestine and to the creation of an independent Palestinian state alongside Israel.

In August 2005, and following mounting domestic and external pressures, Israeli Prime Minister Ariel Sharon – a hawkish leader who had played a major role in Israel's efforts to settle the Territories, initiating the Lebanon War of 1982, and igniting the Second Palestinian Intifada – decided, despite considerable opposition within the Jewish community in Israel/Palestine, on a unilateral Israeli withdrawal from the Gaza Strip and several small settlements in the West Bank. Consequently, Israeli troops and several thousand Jewish settlers were evicted from the Gaza Strip, together with several hundred settlers from four small settlements in the West Bank. However, there was no delineation of an international border between Israel and the Gaza Strip, and Israel imposed a land and sea blockade on the latter area. Consequently, some actors continued to

---

[28] On the struggle over demographics in Israel/Palestine, see Lustick (2013). This struggle is reminiscent of the struggle over demographics that took place in Lebanon before 1943, and especially concerning the population census of 1932. See Maktani (1999).

regard the Gaza Strip as subject to Israeli occupation, and several violent confrontations occurred between Israel and Hamas – the Palestinian armed faction which in June 2007 took over the Gaza Strip – in 2008–2009, 2012, and 2014 – as well as clashes between the IDF and international activists who tried to break Israel's sea blockade. More than a decade after the Israeli pullout from the Gaza Strip, Israeli–Palestinian relations remain volatile there and in other parts of Israel/Palestine, including between the Jewish and Palestinian citizens of Israel.[29]

In sum, Israel/Palestine, the political unit created on account of Israel's expansion in 1967, has remained intact, although it lacks formal recognition. As mentioned earlier, this makes Israel/Palestine comparable to other divided societies – formal and informal – including Lebanon, which, at the time of its creation in 1920, but also in later periods, including during some phases of the conflict of 1975–1990, was regarded as an "artificial" entity.

Israeli–Lebanese Relations

The relationship between Israel and Lebanon is unique among Israel's relations with its Arab neighbors in that it witnessed a shift from relative stability before the Israeli–Arab War of 1967 to perpetual instability and, occasionally, open confrontation in the aftermath of the conflict. Chapters 6 and 7, which focus on Israeli–Lebanese relations before 1967 and on the relations between Israel/Palestine and Lebanon since 1967, address the question of how domestic processes in both states, and especially Israel's expansion, have affected this relationship.

Before Israel's independence and the First Arab–Israeli War, Maronite leaders in French-controlled and, later, independent Lebanon had connections with Jewish leaders in Mandatory Palestine, and some members of the two communities envisioned the establishment of peaceful relations between them. However, in 1943 most Maronite leaders chose to accommodate their Muslim compatriots and the Arab states, and Maronite–Jewish relations became largely irrelevant. As mentioned earlier, the First Arab–Israeli War saw little fighting between the Israeli and Lebanese armies, and in 1949 Lebanon was the second Arab state to sign an Armistice Agreement with Israel.

In the two decades after the war, Israel's relations with Lebanon were the most stable among all of Israel's interactions with its neighbors (which also include Egypt, Syria, Jordan, and the Palestinians). This led some Israeli leaders to suggest that, given the right circumstances, peace

---

[29] See, e.g., the views expressed in Eglash (2015).

between the two states was possible. More grounds for optimism, at least on the Israeli side, were seen in the facts that the two states had no major territorial disputes, that their political systems were relatively free, and that they were both pro-Western in external orientation, although Lebanese leaders expressed commitment to the all-Arab cause.

However, following the Israeli–Arab War of 1967, in which Lebanon did not participate, the relations between Israel/Palestine and Lebanon began to deteriorate, resulting in tensions, escalation, and large-scale violence across their shared border. This change was partly due to factors exogenous to Israeli–Lebanese relations: the consolidation of the Baath regime in Damascus in the early 1970s, under President Hafez al-Assad, and its more assertive policy toward Lebanon (and toward Syria's other weaker neighbors, Jordan and the Palestinians); and the increased role of other Arab states such as Iraq and Libya (and, to a lesser extent, Iran) in Lebanon's affairs. The major cause of this change was, however, the growing role of the Palestinian armed factions in Lebanon, especially after their suppression by Jordan in the events known as "Black September" in 1970–1971 and Israel's military reprisals. Both of these developments are closely tied to the transformation of Israel/Palestine since 1967.

The conflictual relations between Lebanon and Israel/Palestine were demonstrated in several Israeli military operations against Lebanon's territory in the late 1960s and early and late 1970s, which often followed Palestinian attacks from Lebanon's territory or attacks that had originated from it (e.g., in 1968). After the civil war in Lebanon began, Israel increased its involvement in the Israeli–Lebanese border area, and its control over the area was consolidated after the Litani Operation in 1978. In June 1982, and following contacts between Israeli and Maronite leaders, Israel launched a major military operation designed to crush the Palestinian armed factions in Lebanon, expel the Syrian forces, and install a pro-Israeli government in Beirut headed by Israel's major Maronite ally, Bashir Gemayel, leader of the Lebanese Forces, the militia of the Phalanges Party. But the plan succeeded only in part. The Palestinian armed factions were expelled from Lebanon under Israel's pressures, but President-elect Bashir Gemayel was assassinated and his militia perpetrated the Sabra and Shatila Massacre against the Palestinians. Following a partial Israeli withdrawal from Lebanon in 1985, the IDF controlled a "security zone" in South Lebanon but faced a mounting challenge from the Lebanese Shi'i party-militia Hizbullah and other local factions.

Although the Lebanese civil war came to an end in 1990 and the Lebanese state and its institutions began to reassert themselves, Israel refused to withdraw from its "security zone" in Lebanon. It decided to so only in May 2000, after the IDF had waged an unsuccessful struggle against Hizbullah, including several major operations in 1993 and 1996. In 2006, following a cross-border attack by Hizbullah against Israel, the IDF launched yet another massive military operation against Hizbullah but did not manage to defeat it. Although in accordance with UN Security Council Resolution 1701, units of the LAF and an upgraded UNIFIL were deployed throughout South Lebanon in the aftermath of that confrontation, the relations between Israel/Palestine and Lebanon have remained volatile.

Rationale and Structure of the Book

This book explores the significant changes that have taken place in the triangular relationship between the state, the community, and security in Lebanon and in Israel/Palestine in the wake of the state's expansion in 1920 and 1967, respectively. As it suggests, in both cases a political unit that was on its way to becoming a nation-state, as envisioned by the community that had initiated the state's expansion – the Maronite Christians and the Israeli Jews, respectively – instead resulted in a divided society, in which this community had to deal with the reality that its numerical majority had declined. In both cases, the clash between the national vision and the multi-communal reality eventually led to conflict – at times regulated and at other times violent, but in the end unresolved. Thus, and like most other states in the Middle East, Lebanon and Israel/Palestine remain divided societies to this day.[30]

Both of the cases dealt with in this book are, in other words, not "ideal" since, as noted by many of their students, each presents its own particular mix of peace and conflict, stability and instability. At the same time, ideal types – which, according to Max Weber, do not exist in reality, but are constructs that facilitate scientific research[31] – can be used to better elucidate these two cases and to reach more general conclusions from analyzing them.

In discussing and comparing Lebanon and Israel/Palestine, the book draws on, and seeks to add to, more general debates concerning the relationship between the state, community, and security on both the domestic and external levels, but also to examine the effects of state expansion on this relationship. It does this while noting the significance

---

[30] On the region's divided societies, see Esman and Rabinovich (1988); Ibrahim (1998). For a broader perspective, see Miller (2007).

[31] Weber (1949, 92).

of informal (including cultural) political settlements and practices, in addition to the state's formal institutions, in various facets of this relationship. In addition, and as mentioned earlier, the book challenges the divide between the domestic and external spheres by asking how particular characteristics of states, which are identified by comparing them to other states, affect their relations with these other states.

With regard to Lebanon and Israel/Palestine, the book draws on numerous published works, including those few studies that compare the two cases or deal with them in the same context. However, since its emphasis is on the triangular relationship between state, community, and security – issues that are often dealt with separately by scholars – and on identifying elements of continuity and change in both cases, it provides a fresh reading of some of these texts, especially those that treat these cases as "unique" or limit themselves to a particular period in their history. In addition, and in order to fill important gaps, particularly concerning the relations between Israel/Palestine and Lebanon, the book makes use of primary sources, including archival materials, memoirs, media resources and films, produced in the two states, although the considerable length of the period under discussion and the imbalance between the two cases in terms of the availability of primary resources means that not all of the primary resources that can be accessed were consulted.

The remainder of this introductory chapter presents the structure of the book and provides a brief description of each of its chapters.

Chapter 1 provides the theoretical and comparative tools that are used to analyze Lebanon and Israel/Palestine in the wake of the state's expansion. These include theories of state expansion (and state contraction) and theories regarding the process of state formation, patterns of intercommunal relations in divided societies, and domestic and external security. The chapter also highlights important connections among these factors, which are further explored in the remainder of the book.

Chapter 2 discusses the actual circumstances of the state's expansion in Lebanon and in Israel/Palestine, which, as mentioned earlier, resulted in divided societies instead of the nation-states that Maronite and Jewish leaders, respectively, had coveted. At the same time, the chapter notes several important dissimilarities between the two cases, which had a considerable impact on their different trajectories after the state's expansion.

Chapter 3 examines the triangular relationship between state, community, and security in Lebanon both before and after the state's expansion, and Chapter 4 does the same with regard to Israel/Palestine. Each chapter begins by briefly presenting the main approaches or themes in the study of the particular case that it discusses and then moves to address the three above-mentioned issues and their interplay in different periods, but especially after the state's expansion, identifying elements of continuity and change.

Chapter 5 draws on the foregone analysis in order to compare Lebanon and Israel/Palestine, highlighting important similarities and differences, and attempts to situate the two cases in a broad theoretical and comparative perspective.

Chapter 6 draws on the discussion of the two cases, including the comparison of them, to discuss the relations between Israel/Palestine and Lebanon, but emphasizing the period after the Israeli–Arab War of 1967 that saw a change from stability to conflict in these relations. The focus on this chapter, which connects it to the previous discussion, is on the inter-linkages between Israel's expansion and the creation of a divided society in Israel/Palestine, and its changing relations with Lebanon.

Chapter 7 continues this discussion by focusing on the period of the Lebanon War of 1982 and its aftermath. As it suggests, this war represented a conflation between, on the one hand, Israel's state expansion and the attempts to assert Jewish hegemony over all of Israel/Palestine, and, on the other hand, the efforts of some Maronite actors in Lebanon to dominate the state. However, both actors failed in their quest, and the result was an ingrained image in Israel of Lebanon as a "non-state" and even as predatory actor, while overlooking Israel's role in, and responsibility for, this outcome.

The concluding chapter presents and discusses the main findings of the book, and suggests questions for further research, particularly on the nexus between comparative politics and International Relations.

1 State Expansion and Its Effects

In September 2014, a new Israeli coffee chain by the name of *Cofizz* published a map of its branches under the appealing slogan, "We have expanded for your comfort." However, what distinguished this from other maps of Israel that have been published by both government agencies and private firms since 1967 was that it presented Israel in its pre-1967 borders and left out the occupied West Bank and the Golan. This omission resulted in an immediate public outcry, including threats, insults, and obscenities directed at the firm and its managers. One commentator stated: "Politics has entered our coffee!!! A national catastrophe!!! I would rather drink cyanide than your coffee even if it's free!!" So great was the outrage that the coffee chain's owners were compelled to issue a lengthy apology, in which they explained that the error was accidental; that the owners of the studio that had drawn the map had themselves originated from the Territories and thus an anti-Israeli position on their part was absurd; and that the coffee chain had provided free products to Israeli soldiers on the front and to the residents of the south during Israel's confrontation with Hamas in the summer of 2014, thus proving its patriotism. Finally, and to dispel all remaining doubts, the "flawed" map was promptly removed from the firm's Facebook page and was replaced by a new and "correct" map, which included not only the two aforementioned regions but also the Gaza Strip, an area that Israel had withdrawn from in 2005 and that was now under the control of the Palestinian group Hamas.[1]

What is interesting about this anecdote is that Israel's expansion into the occupied territories of the West Bank and the Gaza Strip during the Israeli–Arab War of 1967 was never formally acknowledged by Israel and was, moreover, not recognized by any other state, including Israel's closest allies.[2] Indeed, even with regard to East Jerusalem and the

---

[1] Kristal (2014).
[2] Thus, for example, consecutive US governments have refrained from moving their embassy to Jerusalem, and the Department of State does not recognize "Jerusalem, Israel" as the birthplace of US citizens.

Golan – the two occupied areas that Israel formally incorporated into its territory in 1980 and 1981, respectively (the former area had already been incorporated in 1967) – its government only imposed its jurisdiction and did not use the more explicit term "annexation."[3] Still, any attempt to challenge Israel's expansion, even in a map published by a private firm, elicited immediate resistance that originated, quite interestingly, not from state officials but from the Israeli public, which had come to see the Territories as an integral part of its state.

This chapter explores the long-term effects of state expansion on the triangular relationship between state, community, and security.[4] As it suggests, state expansion is sometimes seen as the outcome of political and social processes, and at other times it is viewed as their cause. This chapter, while attentive to both positions, nonetheless leans toward the second view, which appears to be more relevant when dealing with two expanded states that have been around for nearly a century (Lebanon) and a half-century (Israel/Palestine). Accordingly, the chapter first discusses the more general phenomenon of state expansion (and its opposite: state contraction), including its causes and some of the factors that help sustain its outcomes over time. The bulk of the chapter, however, discusses the impact of the state's expansion on the three above-mentioned spheres and their interplay, especially over a long period.

Causes for State Expansion

When do states expand, and what can account for this process? What factors, moreover, help prevent the state's contraction in the aftermath of expansion? Existing works on the expansion and contraction of states suggest that both rational (or interest-based) and cultural factors are at work when the state expands into, or contracts from, an outlying territory (or territories).[5]

---

[3] Lustick (1997a). See also Yishai (1985); Dumper (2014); Klein (2014).
[4] State expansion differs from military occupation, a topic that has received attention both generally and in the Israeli–Palestinian case. See, especially, Zacher (2001); Edelstein (2004, 2008); Fazal (2007); Stirk (2009). Military occupations are usually undertaken with the purpose of forceful regime change, support for an existing regime (or the establishment of a friendly state in a contested area), or for strategic purposes. In contrast, state expansion includes full or partial imposition of the state's jurisdiction in the outlying areas, the considerable blurring of the boundaries between the state and these areas, and, in some cases, the settlement of citizens of the occupying state in these areas. On this last aspect, see Haklai and Loizides (2015). Importantly, military occupations of outlying territories can result in the state's formal or informal expansion.
[5] On Imperial expansion, see Arendt (1973 [1951]); Snyder (1991). On rational, cultural and structural explanations for political behavior, see Lichbach (1997).

In the introductory chapter to an edited volume entitled *Right-Sizing the State: The Politics of Moving Borders*,[6] Brendan O'Leary explains that the term "right-sizing" the state refers "to the preferences of political agents at the centre of existing regimes to have what they regard as appropriate external and internal territorial borders."[7] But who exactly are these political agents, and how do they manage to get their way? Ian Lustick, in a pioneering study, places the onus on members of the political elite in the expanding state, specifically their perception of the outlying territory, in a state's decision to retain or withdraw. He then focuses on three cases: Britain's withdrawal from most of Ireland in 1922, the French withdrawal from Algeria in 1962, and Israel's policy toward the occupied West Bank and the Gaza Strip since 1967.[8] Lustick contends that expanded states must cross two distinct "thresholds" in order to incorporate an outlying territory: First, the "regime threshold," which is "the point at which a government interested in relinquishing the areas finds itself more worried about civic upheavals, violent disorders, and challenges to the legitimate authority of governmental institutions than with possible defections from the governing coalition or party." The question, in other words, is whether the state's leaders are autonomous in deciding on the fate of the disputed territory, and whether they can implement their decision. The second threshold, however, signals a "deeper kind of institutionalization," which "begins when the absorption of the territory ceases to be problematic for the overwhelming majority" in the expanding state.[9] Here, the question is whether there is a new hegemonic conception of the state's territory.

But are these the only relevant factors in determining state expansion, and do they apply to all types of states? During their contraction from most of Ireland and Algeria, Great Britain and France were already established states (both were also world powers), which meant that leaders in both states were relatively autonomous in defining their national interest in a manner that even their political opponents had to accept.[10] However, in less-established states, including the two cases discussed in this book and possibly others, political leaders are far more dependent on societies' acquiescence[11] – or, put differently, they are more vulnerable to social contention.[12] This means that in these contexts, political leaders

---

[6] O'Leary et al. (2001).   [7] O'Leary (2001a, 2).
[8] Lustick (1993). See also Lustick (2001); Spruyt (2005).
[9] Lustick (2001, 85). Cf. O'Leary (2001b, 65–67).
[10] See the discussion of the trials of the French officers who launched the revolt against President Charles de Gaulle to prevent the French withdrawal from Algeria, in Schmitt (2004 [1963], 59). See also Kimmerling (2001, 81); Thomas (2014, 331–332).
[11] Migdal (2004, 62–71).   [12] Tarrow (2012).

may find it difficult to bring about the expanded state's contraction even when they conclude that it is in the state's best interest.

Another issue is the importance that state leaders and other members of society attach to the outlying territory. According to Baruch Kimmerling, who compared France and Algeria with Israel and the Territories it occupied in 1967,

> The territories in the domain of Israeli control since 1967 do not amount to a conventional colony within Israel ... A pure colony is a form of political and socioterritorial arrangement that, notwithstanding foreign control, is located outside the boundaries of the colonial state itself, and to which that state relates essentially instrumentally. The West Bank and Gaza Strip represent an integral part of the building and expansion efforts of the territorial self-image of at least one of the versions of collective identity of this immigrant settler state [Israel]. In some cases, when a colony begins to represent a heavy burden for the colonial power, the forces controlling the state begin to make cost-benefit calculations, and if these parties reach the conclusion that the game isn't worth the candle, they abandon the colony as fast as possible. But these parties will never concede control over an area perceived as integral to the state itself, even if continuation of the control represents a sacrifice and a cost exceeding any benefit that comes from possession: in this case, the price of maintaining the territory does not matter.[13]

A telling case concerns Israeli Prime Minister Rabin, who, since assuming his post in the wake of the 1992 elections, has been repeatedly called on by many Israelis, Palestinians, and others to follow the example of French President Charles de Gaulle and withdraw from the Territories Israel occupied in 1967. However, Rabin and his colleagues soon discovered that despite their best efforts to decide on the fate of these regions (which Rabin, as the IDF's chief of staff, had helped "liberate" in 1967), they remained constrained by powerful political forces in Israel/Palestine, and sometimes also beyond its borders, that opposed the state's contraction and, moreover, were prepared to use all means at their disposal to preclude such a scenario. The result was that the attempts made by Israel's leaders to cross the political and ideological "thresholds" were, ultimately, unsuccessful. These attempts were, in any case, limited since the Oslo Agreement fell short of dismantling Jewish settlements in the Territories and did not lead to the creation of an independent Palestinian state. Thus, on November 4, 1995, Prime Minister Rabin was assassinated by an Israeli Jewish extremist who later claimed that he acted "for God, for the [Jewish] people and for the country,"[14] which, to him, stood *above* the state.

---

[13] Kimmerling (2001, 81). This raises the question of how a territory becomes one that is perceived as integral to the state. See Goddard (2010). I address this issue later in this chapter.

[14] State of Israel vs. Yigal Amir (1996, 20).

Another relevant question, particularly with regard to less-established states, is whether international actors, and especially the great powers, support the state's expansion openly or in a tacit manner. As we shall see in Chapter 2, France, the colonial power in the Levant, supported the state's expansion in Lebanon in 1920 and, moreover, helped bring it about. In the Israel case, too, the role of the great powers since the state's expansion has been significant. It is interesting, for example, to compare Israel's occupation of the Territories in 1967 to its occupation of the Sinai Peninsula from Egypt during the Suez War of 1956. In the latter case, despite the intentions of some Israeli leaders, especially Prime Minister David Ben-Gurion, to hold on to this territory, the United States and the Soviet Union applied effective pressure on Israel to withdraw. By contrast, in the wake of the Israeli–Arab War of 1967, the US government led by President Lyndon B. Johnson was reluctant to pressure Israel to withdraw from the Arab territories it occupied, not least because of the failure of the international mechanisms that had been installed in the Sinai Peninsula after 1956.[15] This US position has, since then, facilitated Israel's expansion, although it should be noted that in those places where the status quo proved to be untenable and security arrangements accepted by Israel could be installed, such as in the Sinai Peninsula, the United States supported an Israeli withdrawal.

When attempting to assess the external impacts on state expansion and contraction, however, one should consider the significant changes that have taken place in the international community, especially since the end of the Second World War but also after the Cold War, which have imposed strict normative barriers on states' expansion.[16] Thus, for example, in August 1990, when Iraq invaded and formally annexed its weaker neighbor Kuwait, a broad international coalition was assembled under the leadership of the United States and the state's expansion was forcefully reversed. Similarly, in April 2005, Syria's 29-year military presence in Lebanon, which had been sanctioned by the Arab League in 1976, came to an end following domestic and external pressures, especially by the United States, France, and the UN, but also by regional actors that claimed Syria had overplayed its hand in Lebanon.

It would be an error to conclude, however, that the practice of state expansion has ceased in 1945. Often, state expansion is not presented as such (Iraq's formal annexation of Kuwait is an exception);[17] some states

---

[15] Gorenberg (2006).
[16] Zacher (2001). See also Atzili (2006); Fazal (2007). See also the discussion of the "decolonization norm" in Goertz and Diehl (1992).
[17] Examples include Turkey and Northern Cyprus, Morocco and Western Sahara, and China and Tibet. I return to this issue in the Conclusion.

claim their occupation of outlying territories is "temporary," implying that it can be reversed, even when it lingers for years and even decades.[18] In some cases, moreover, this informal state expansion is accompanied by a political discourse specifically designed to preclude and fend off criticism both domestically and externally. It should be noted that this discourse is also convenient for other international actors – states, international organizations, and NGOs – that wish to interact with the expanded state without acknowledging its expansion.[19] For the state's leaders, this discourse is useful when they wish to hold onto the outlying territory without having to grant citizenship to all of its inhabitants, or even acknowledge the latter's collective rights.[20] Israel's informal expansion since 1967, which is discussed in Chapter 4, is quite telling in this regard.

In sum, political elites in well-established states, particularly those that enjoy the status of world powers, are relatively autonomous when trying to expand into, or relinquish, outlying territories when their national interest so demands and when the majority of their citizens supports such a move. However, since 1945, states generally refrain from expanding into outlying territories, although there are exceptions to this "rule."[21] At the same time, leaders of less-established states are more dependent on

---

[18] According to Edelstein (2004, 52), "[o]ccupation is the temporary control of a territory by another state that claims no right to permanent sovereign control over that territory. An occupying power must intend at the onset of the occupation to vacate the occupied territory and return control to an indigenous government. A precise date for evacuation need not be specified, but the occupying power's intention must not be to stay indefinitely. The intended temporary duration of occupation distinguishes it from both annexation and colonialism."

[19] Thus, for example, Freedom House, a US-based NGO that gauges the extent to which the world's states are democratic, categorizes some expanded states as "free" (democratic) notwithstanding their expansion to outlying territories. Examples are Israel, which in 2014 received a rating of 1.5 out of 7 (the West Bank, however, was rated 5.5 and the Gaza Strip was rated 6.5; both were categorized as "not free," i.e., non-democratic), and India, which in the same year received a rating of 2.5 (but Kashmir was rated 4 and was categorized as "partially free" – that is, partially democratic). At the same time, Turkey, which expanded into Northern Cyprus in 1974, was categorized in 2014 as "partially free" with a rating of 3.5, whereas the outlying territory under its control was ranked 2.0 and categorized as "free." Interestingly, these (and other territories with similar characteristics) still appear in separate list of "Disputed Territories." See Freedom House (2014).

[20] Kimmerling (2001, 79–80).

[21] A recent exception is Russia's expansion into the Crimean Peninsula. However, it should be noted that in conquering this area, which is formally part of Ukraine, Moscow was careful to employ unmarked security personnel. Later, a referendum was held in the outlying territory, which was aimed to show that a majority of its inhabitants supported its incorporation into Russia, and this was followed by a formal treaty between Russia and the self-declared Republic of Crimea, which absorbed it into the Russian Federation. BBC News (2014).

their societies' consent and are vulnerable to their dissent, especially when some actors within the state, or even in the outlying territory, perceive the territory as crucial to the well-being of the nation, which they sometimes see as superior to the state.

The above discussion underscores the critical importance of a state's autonomy from its society,[22] and how this factor must not be taken for granted – by the state's leaders or by relevant outside forces – when the state expands or attempts to contract after its expansion, and especially when the state itself is not well established, as is the case in many non-Western settings, or when the state's expansion lasts for long periods of time. However, since the autonomy of the state is not a given but is an outcome of the process of state formation, and since this autonomy itself is affected by the relationship between the state and its society, there is a need to explore these two issues more closely and ask how they are affected by the state's expansion, and to address the effects of the state's expansion on the inter-connected area of domestic and external security.

Effects of State Expansion

While scholars generally focus on the factors that facilitate state expansion and contraction, others consider a state's expansion (including shifts in its boundaries) as a watershed event affecting the state and its society (but, to a lesser extent, its security) in a myriad of ways. A noted example is Joel Migdal, who, in an important contribution from 2001, focuses on the impact of Israel's changing boundaries in the wake of the Israeli–Arab War of 1967 on the state and society, as well as on their relations. Drawing on this second approach, the following subsections examine the effects of the state's expansion – formal and informal – on the triangular relationship between state, community, and security: first by considering each of these spheres separately, and then by discussing their inter-linkages.

State Expansion and the Process of State Formation

For many centuries, political entities such as empires, kingdoms, and states were not considered to be autonomous from their societies, and the rulers of these political entities regarded them as their personal property. The slogan *Ultima Ratio Regum* ("The Final Argument of Kings"), inscribed on French cannons before the Revolution, projected this idea in

---

[22] According to Kimmerling, "the term 'state autonomy' refers to the ability of the state to prevent unsolicited interventions from, and the imposition of particularistic definitions of collective identity by, one or another segment of civil society." See Kimmerling (2001, 58–59).

unmistakable terms. Later, however, things began to change in this respect, and states, especially in Western Europe and North America, gradually acquired material and cultural attributes that rendered them more autonomous from their societies. This, in turn, enabled the leaders of these states to define their national interest (*raison d'état*), which was, at least in theory, distinct from their personal interest. "Governments," in F. Scott Fitzgerald's words, have become "impersonal."[23]

This significant change was facilitated by the process of state formation. Drawing on numerous works on various aspects of this process, it can be argued that it is composed of three main sub-processes (or dimensions), referred to here as state building, state construction, and national integration (see Table 1.1). Together, these have culminated in the modern state as it is known to us, first in Western Europe and North America, and then in other parts of the world, albeit with significant variations from one place to another. Importantly, these three sub-processes were not only internal but also had external – that is, international – dimensions, and these, too, ought to be considered.

The first sub-process – state building – consists of measures that promote "territorial consolidation, centralization, differentiation of the instruments of government, and monopolization of the means of coercion."[24] One outcome of state building has been the increased material and coercive strength of the state, which it acquires by gradually penetrating society and extracting increasing amounts of material and human resources from its citizens, especially for preparation for war. Indeed, students of this sub-process attach great importance to the dialectics of state-making and war-making.[25] On the international level, state building included the delineation of states' borders and the attempts to control violence across them, which helped buttress these states' sovereignty vis-à-vis other states and eliminate some, but not all, violent transnational non-state actors.[26]

The second sub-process – state construction – refers to more subtle but no less significant processes and mechanisms that sought to ingrain the state in its citizens' minds using various state institutions, such as the military, bureaucracy, the school system, and prisons, as well as a host of other formal agencies. The result of these efforts was a gradual shift from coercive power to disciplinary power (or infrastructural power).[27] In order to achieve this end, states have developed modern techniques of supervision and control of their citizens, and precise distribution of time, space,

[23] Fitzgerald (1986 [1925], 149).
[24] Tilly (1975, 42). See also Evans, Rueschemeyer, and Skocpol (1985).
[25] Tilly (1975, 192); Tilly (1992). See also Barnett (1992).
[26] Thomson (1994); Barak and Cohen (2014). [27] Mann (1986).

Table 1.1 *The process of state formation*

Sub-process / Main attributes	State building	State construction	National integration
Emphasis	Institutional	Cognitive	Emotional
Description	Consolidating the state's territory, centralizing authority, differentiating the instruments of government, and monopolizing coercion.	Strengthening the state's power and authority vis-à-vis society by ingraining the idea of the state in its citizens' minds.	Creating maximum overlap between the political community (the nation) and the state's territory by eliciting popular identification with the state.
Means adopted	Building institutions such as a bureaucracy, military, police, and school system.	Acquisition of disciplinary power through the state's institutions.	Disseminating a national ideology by the state's institutions.
Specific techniques	Penetrating society and mobilizing, through taxation and conscription, both material and human resources, particularly for the purpose of war-making.	Distribution of time and space; striving to achieve maximum control over citizens' bodies.	Reinterpreting (or inventing) shared identities, myths, and symbols.
Desired outcomes	Increase in the state's coercive power vis-à-vis society and other states.	Increase in the state's disciplinary power in relation to its citizens, who perceive the state to be outside or above society.	The state and society are seen as identical and the state's and the nation's interests overlap.

and motion.[28] One of the outcomes of these efforts was the creation of physical and perceptional boundaries between the state and society, promoting the view of the state as an entity that stands "outside" or "above" society – that is, the creation of the state's autonomy vis-à-vis its citizens.[29]

Finally, the third sub-process – national integration – consists of centrally based efforts to inculcate the state's citizens with a common identity based on shared myths, narratives, values, and symbols.[30] Whereas state building and state construction are, in a sense, two sides of the same coin, national integration efforts commenced later, when rulers realized that the states they had built were becoming exceedingly distant from their citizens, who, for their part, felt alienated from them.[31] By evoking the concept of the nation, these rulers sought "to eliminate the perception that the state stands above society and to foster an alternative view, that the state and the society are indistinguishable in purpose, if not in form."[32] The voluntary participation of millions in the two world wars and a host of other conflicts attests to their success. However, George Mosse, who discusses this process, notes that there were also those who volunteered to participate in other struggles besides those waged by states, and provides the example of Lord Byron and his comrades during the Greek War of Independence (1821–1833).[33]

When dealing with the sub-process of national integration, however, one needs to differentiate between states that have fostered a national identity that preceded ethnic, religious, tribal, and other sub-state affiliations of their citizens, on the one hand, and states that sought to embrace the latter types of identities, on the other hand. In the first type, the state is autonomous from the various communities that make up its society; in the second, it is not.

Now, if we consider the three sub-processes of the process of state formation as complementary and not as contradictory, then the power and viability of the modern state can be better appreciated, especially when juxtaposed to earlier forms of government.[34] The modern state developed institutions, mechanisms, and tools that enabled it to extract material and human resources from its citizens on an unprecedented scale, and used more violence than at any other period in history.[35] But

---

[28] Foucault (1979); Mitchell (1991); Steinmetz (1999).   [29] Mann (1986).
[30] Gellner (1983); D. Smith (1986); Hobsbawm (1990); Anderson (1991); Geary (2002). This might also include labeling others as the state's enemies and going to war or acting otherwise on the international arena with the aim of strengthening the state from within. See Anderson (1991); Mansfield and Snyder (2005). See also the saying attributed to Renan quoted in Chapter 2.
[31] Fahmy (1997).   [32] Migdal (1997, 227).
[33] Mosse (1990). On this and other examples, see Barak and Cohen (2014).
[34] Spruyt (1996).   [35] Finer (1975); Howard (1979); Tilly (1975, 1990).

at the same time it sought to dominate its citizens' bodies, to take hold in their minds, and all this while fostering a hegemonic belief that it and they shared the same identity and had common interests.[36]

In time, the modern state gradually became a global phenomenon, largely due to colonialism, which carried the idea and practices of the state to the new territories conquered by European (and, occasionally, other) powers. However, the process of state formation itself was not similar everywhere.[37] In many "new states" in the non-Western regions, the political, bureaucratic and security institutions remained weak and did not acquire autonomy in relation to society.[38] Indeed, many studies identify the phenomenon of state weakness, and even "state failure," which they ascribe to partial, incomplete, or even reversed state-building efforts.[39]

It is worth adding, however, that in some cases this weakness stemmed not only from domestic but also from external factors. In the case of Iraq since 2003, for example, the weakening of the state was the result of the US invasion, the subsequent disbanding of the Iraqi army by the US authorities in Iraq, and the failure to create strong and legitimate political and security institutions there later. As we shall see, in Lebanon, too, the state's weakness and its "failure" – but also its stability in earlier periods – was closely inter-linked to its environment.

At any rate, it is important to note that weak and "failed states" exhibit significant variations: in some cases, including several African and Asian states, the state lacked both coercive capacities and a shared identity among its citizens;[40] in other cases, such as Lebanon, while the state was weak in the material-coercive sense, many of its citizens did identify with it, especially when it managed to accommodate the major societal actors – communities, large families (or clans), and geographical regions – and when all other alternatives proved to be untenable.[41]

One of the problems facing the state's efforts in non-Western regions, alluded to earlier, was that the state was often seen as an actor that had no autonomy from the various segments of society, but that was, rather, a tool in the hands of a dominant community for suppressing other communities within the state's purview. It is thus not surprising that state formation efforts, particularly in divided societies, were sometimes

---

[36] Lustick (1999). [37] Chatarjee (1993).
[38] Huntington (1968); Migdal (1988, 2004); Robert Jackson (1990); Herbst (2014).
[39] Rotberg (2002, 2003, 2004). For criticism, see Bilgin and Morton (2004).
[40] Several examples are provided in Rotberg (2002, 2003). See also Hebrst (2014).
[41] Migdal (2004). The opposite is also true. Some states, such as the Soviet Union and Yugoslavia, had considerable coercive capacities but ultimately failed to win their citizens' support. See Kimmerling (2001, 59).

Table 1.2 *Strong and weak states*

Broad identification / Coercive and disciplinary power	Strong identification	Weak identification
Strong coercive and disciplinary power	1) Most Western states; **Israel (1949–1967)**	2) USSR & Yugoslavia before their disintegration; South Africa before 1994; Iraq before/after 2003; Syria before 2011; Libya before 2011; Sudan before 2011; Serbia; **Israel/Palestine (1967–)**
Weak coercive and disciplinary power	3) **Lebanon (1943–1975, 1991–)**	4) Failed States (especially in Africa); **Lebanon (1975–1990)**

resisted by members of these subordinate communities who wished to preserve their particular interests and identities.[42] States that were strong in the material-coercive sense could accommodate members of these different communities by employing their formal agencies. But in order to succeed, especially over the long haul, these states' rulers needed to distance these institutions from the dominant community – that is, to increase the state's autonomy in relation to it, on the one hand, and to try to accommodate other communities, on the other hand.[43]

Based on the foregoing discussion, it is possible to differentiate, very broadly, between four types of states[44] (see Table 1.2). The first category includes states where the sub-processes of state building and state construction engendered a strong state in terms of its coercive capacities and disciplinary power, and where national integration efforts have led to a broad identification with the state. This category includes established states that are, moreover, relatively autonomous from their societies. Most Western states belong to this first category. As far as the state's expansion and contraction are concerned, these states' leaders are

---

[42] Connor (1994). Even in Western states the notion of the "nation-state" has been challenged by the rising political demands of members of indigenous communities (e.g., the Basques in Spain and the Scots in Britain) and by the arrival of new immigrants.

[43] Migdal (2004). Yiftachel (2001, 361–364) mentions the need to "right-shape," and not merely "right-size," the state in multiethnic settings.

[44] Cf. Kimmerling (2001, 59–60). Miller (2007, 56–59) presents a useful distinction between state-building and nation-building (national integration), but his main focus is on the regional level. Interestingly, his typology of states sometimes omits Israel as a "revisionist" state (ibid., 58, 101, 176–177) – though since 1967 it appears to fall within this category – and at other times treats it as such (ibid., 195–196).

generally capable of redefining those issues that they deem critical to the state's security, as occurred in France with regard to Algeria and in Britain with regard to Ireland, and of implementing their decisions even in the face of considerable domestic opposition. However, since 1945 these states must also consider the international barriers to state expansion, although in some cases (e.g., Russia and Ukraine) they do not heed them.

The second category includes states where the sub-processes of state building and state construction have led to the emergence of a strong state in terms of its coercive capacities, but where national integration efforts did not lead to a broad identification with the state, which is seen as belonging to one (or few) communities but not to others.[45] In addition to the Soviet Union and Yugoslavia in the period before their disintegration and South Africa under Apartheid, this type of state can be found in Iraq before and after the US-led invasion in 2003, in Sudan before its partition and the creation of the Republic of South Sudan in 2011, and in Syria and Libya before the events of the "Arab Spring." As subsequent chapters suggest, this type of political unit, albeit informal in nature, has emerged in Israel/Palestine on account of Israel's state expansion in 1967. If leaders of these states wish to relinquish parts of their territory, and particularly those areas where members of both the dominant and subordinate communities reside, they might face opposition from actors within the dominant community who wish to retain these disputed lands for ideological, economic, or strategic considerations. Since national integration efforts in the state are still underway, moreover, these actors can appeal "against the state to the nation, and against legality to a higher kind of legitimacy."[46] This description seems to fit Prime Minister Rabin's assassin and other opponents of Israel's contraction in the 1990s.[47]

In the third type of states, the two sub-processes of state building and state construction have not produced a strong state in terms of its material and coercive capacities, but the state's efforts to accommodate social groups and to foster a common national identity, however limited, did result in a broad identification with the state. These states thus enjoy an autonomous status vis-à-vis their society in certain respects but not in

---

[45] Esman (1988, 278).   [46] Schmitt (2004 [1963], 59).
[47] The following case is telling: During the Israeli–Palestinian peace process, some Israelis proposed holding a referendum in Israel on the Territories. When asked about her opinion on this matter, Daniella Weiss, one of the leaders of the Jewish settlers in the Territories, replied that she is in favor of a referendum but that it will have to include 70 generations of Jews. When her interlocutor replied that this was technically impossible since most of these are dead, Weiss replied that, if this was the case, holding a referendum was impossible. Barak (2005a, 723).

others. Lebanon before and after the civil war of 1975–1990, as well as other weak-but-not-failed states, belong to this category.

Last but not least, there are states where all three sub-processes of the process of state formation – state building, state construction, and national integration – made little headway or were dramatically reversed, especially on account of internal conflict, massive foreign intervention, or both. Most of the states that are sometimes referred to as "quasi states"[48] or "failed states," and which are mostly found in the non-Western regions, fall within this fourth category, as did Lebanon during the civil war (1975–1990), but not before or after it. As suggested by Robert Jackson, the international community has gone to great lengths to preserve these "quasi states" and prevent their disintegration, and this seems to have an effect also on their possible contraction.[49] Indeed, as we shall see in Chapter 3, opposition to Lebanon's partition during the civil war of 1975–1990 was not only domestic but also included external – including regional and international – actors.

In view of the above, it is now possible to comprehend the effects of a state's expansion on its process of state formation, which also has bearing on its capacity to contract in later periods.

As far as the sub-process of state building is concerned, the emergence of independent power centers in the outlying territory is liable to challenge the centralization of power in the state, and if this territory itself is administered by the security sector (the military and other security agencies), this may hinder the differentiation of the instruments of government not only in the outlying territory but also within the state itself.[50] As for the sub-process of state construction, boundary changes, especially when they are informal in nature, can cause uncertainty and promote an elusive and fluid image of the state in the eyes of its inhabitants, resulting in major political and social crises.[51] Finally, when the state's expansion leads to the imposition of its rule over members of other communities, this is liable to interrupt the state's national integration efforts by reshaping its pattern of state–society relations.[52] At the same time, when the outlying territory itself has, or is invested with, symbolic meaning to the

---

[48] Robert Jackson (1990). [49] Ibid. [50] Cf. Mendelsohn (2016).
[51] Migdal (1996, 195). See also Migdal (2001, 150). Barnett (1999, 10) argues that "changes in territorial boundaries" are a factor that can "enliven the debate over the national identity."
[52] Writing on Israel, Migdal (2001, 151) posits that its boundary change in 1967 replaced the "principle of universal citizenship," which had previously been used as a method of exclusion against Jews from Middle Eastern backgrounds, with "a contending ethnonational set of principles" which the latter "found much more exclusive." However, this set of principles was now employed to exclude the community in the outlying territory, i.e., the Palestinians (ibid.).

dominant community, the state's hold over the national repertoire of myths, symbols, and narratives is liable to be affected, thus opening the way for other actors besides the state's leaders to speak in the name of the nation and its interests.

In sum, the state's expansion not only has a considerable impact on its autonomy – which, as mentioned earlier, is a critical factor when its leaders want to contract the state in later periods – but it is also liable to move it away from the first above-mentioned category of states that are strong in terms of both their coercive power and broad identification, to the second category of states that are strong in terms of the former but not of the latter. It is here that political traditions and historical legacies of statehood and government can play a role – as shown, for example, in the case of France and Algeria, when President de Gaulle was able to bring about the state's contraction. On the other hand, the lack of or weakening of such factors, as in the case of Israel since 1967, can frustrate leaders' contraction efforts and have dire consequences for them and for their states, as demonstrated in the case of Prime Minister Rabin.

State Expansion and Inter-Communal Relations

As suggested earlier, the state's expansion is liable to create a divided society, whether formally acknowledged (as in Lebanon) or continuously denied (as in Israel/Palestine), and this obliges the state's leaders to find ways to cope with the relations between its various communities. Thus, in addition to discussing the process of state formation, there is a need to explain what divided societies are, what major patterns of inter-communal relations can be identified in them, and how these patterns relate to the process of state formation in the wake of the state's expansion.

Divided societies are composed of diverse communities, defined along ethnic, national, religious, tribal, family, or regional lines, and in some cases with a certain overlap between these various foci of identity. In divided societies, moreover, communal divisions are politically salient, and communal considerations often dominate all spheres of public life, including politics, society, the economy, culture, and security, and tend to assume precedence over all other considerations.[53]

---

[53] On politics in divided societies, see Nordlinger (1972); Lijphart (1977, 2004); Lustick (1979); Donald Horowitz (1985); McGarry and O'Leary (1993); Sisk (1996). These social divisions can ameliorate over time. Lijphart (1968) argues that divisions in the Netherlands, which necessitated a power-sharing settlement between its social "pillars" in the period 1917–1967, later declined.

Andreas Wimmer, Lars-Erik Cederman, and Brian Min contend that "the modern state is not an ethnically neutral actor or a mere arena for political competition, but a central object of and participant in ethnopolitical power struggles."[54] Indeed, one of the major challenges facing the state's leaders in divided societies is how to build political, bureaucratic, and security institutions that will not only have material (including coercive) capacities, but will also be acceptable to members of different communities. However, until recently, many studies on divided societies have overlooked this dual challenge, putting the emphasis on "nation-building" (in effect, state-building, as defined above), which, they posit, was indifferent to social divisions or sought to expunge them altogether. Studies that acknowledge these divisions, for their part, focus on political mechanisms that regulate inter-communal conflicts but tend to ignore the state. In particular, they accord insufficient attention to its ostensibly non-political institutions such as its bureaucracy and security sector (the military and the other security agencies).

The first approach, which was part of the modernization school that dominated the social sciences in the 1950s and 1960s and was also influential in policy-making circles, considered communal identities in non-Western states to be anachronistic and expected them to make way for modern Western-type national identities. However, in some non-Western states that are divided societies, efforts to integrate members of different communities by eradicating or simply neglecting their particular identities sparked resistance and violence on a massive scale.[55] This important lesson was lost decades later, in 2003, following the US invasion of Iraq, when the United States engaged in state-building efforts but without considering the political needs, grievances, and demands of all of Iraq major communities: Sunnis, Shi'is, and Kurds. Thus, for example, Major General J. D. Thurman, US commander of the Fourth Infantry Division, which was charged with controlling Baghdad, argued, "When you're forming a government, you can't form it with any kind of sectarian element ... That's got to be put aside, particularly with military forces."[56] As is well known, this "nation-building" project led to continuous inter-communal violence, not least because Sunnis, who had dominated the state in Iraq before 2003, were marginalized by Shi'is, which now presided over its institutions, including its security sector, which was looked on by the Sunnis as a tool of inter-communal control.[57]

---

[54] Wimmer, Cederman, and Min (2009, 316). See also Cederman, Wimmer, and Min (2010).
[55] Connor (1994).   [56] Quoted in Wong (2006).   [57] Barak (2007b).

An alternative to the modernization school emerged in the late 1960s and early 1970s, which acknowledged the embedded pluralism of certain non-Western societies and sought to regulate conflicts between their communities. But it erred as well by overlooking the need to build an institutional framework that could support the political mechanisms that its members identified in, and sometimes prescribed for, these divided societies. Thus, for example, earlier works on inter-communal power sharing dealt with Western and non-Western states in the same context[58] but without giving due attention to the considerable differences in the level of institutional development between established states and new states. It was only later that the state itself – including its political, bureaucratic, and security institutions – began to receive more attention.[59]

Broadly speaking, students of conflict regulation identify four major patterns of inter-communal relations in divided societies: power sharing, control, repression, and stalemate. These patterns will now be presented, along with the relation between the pattern of inter-communal relations and the process of state formation after the state's expansion in each pattern.[60]

Some scholars have posited that the best way to regulate inter-communal conflicts in divided societies while maintaining domestic stability and democratic practices is to acknowledge the existence of social divisions in the state and to establish political mechanisms to ensure that members of all communities participate in decision-making processes that affect their lives. Political settlements based on power sharing thus include a government of a grand coalition with representatives of all communities, and three complementary tools: mutual veto, designed to protect the vital interests of minorities; proportionality in representation, appointments, and the distribution of public funds; and autonomy of all communities.[61] As mentioned earlier, this pattern of inter-communal relations was initially presented as separate from the state and its institutions, including in non-Western regions where states were less established. However, later works have accorded more attention to how the state and its bureaucratic and security institutions sustain these settlements, including in post-conflict settings.[62] Based on the above, it can be

---

[58] Lehmbruch (1974); Lijphart (1977).
[59] Hartzell and Hoddie (2003, 2015); Lijphart (2004).
[60] Cf. O'Leary (2001b); Yiftachel (2001, 364–366).
[61] Lijphart (1977, 1998). For criticism, see Barry (1975); Lustick (1979, 1997b); Roeder and Rothchild (2005). A response to these criticisms, see Lijphart (1998). Recent works that deal with power sharing are Guelke (2012); McEvoy and O'Leary (2013); McCulloch (2014).
[62] See, e.g., Hartzell and Hoddie (2003, 2015).

argued that if a divided society emanates from the state's expansion, which disrupts its state formation process, it may take some time before the communities in the outlying territory become part of a power-sharing settlement, if at all. Still, as the case of Lebanon demonstrates, this is not impossible.

Other students of conflict regulation, for their part, have maintained that in some cases, particularly in non-Western settings, the relationship between the various communities in divided societies is characterized not by power sharing but by control. Control exists when one community in the divided society mobilizes its superior coercive power in order to enforce political stability in the state by limiting the political actions and possibilities of another community (or communities). When inter-communal control is effective and does not encounter significant resistance, it can be maintained over time, thereby regulating conflict in the state.[63] It should be noted, however, that whereas students of power sharing describe and prescribe these mechanisms, students of control only suggest that control is sometimes preferable to more violent measures.[64] When the divided society is a product of the state's expansion, the dominant community can attempt to impose control over the subordinate community that resides in the outlying territory. This was the policy adopted by Jordan in the West Bank in the period 1949–1967 and by Israel in the Territories in the period 1967–1987. However, as this case suggests, control is difficult to sustain over time, especially when the subordinate community mobilizes and asserts itself.

Although there are considerable differences between power sharing and control, both are essentially non-violent patterns of inter-communal relations. However, in some divided societies, including Lebanon and Israel/Palestine, inter-communal relations are (or were) violent, and we must also consider such violent patterns.

The first violent pattern of inter-communal relations is repression, and it occurs when the dominant community in the divided society employs the state's coercive apparatus against other communities with the goal of asserting its hegemony throughout its territory. James Ron, who discusses the use of violence in Israel/Palestine and Serbia, differentiates between two types of regions where repression occurs. These are "frontiers," which are "peripheral regions unincorporated into a power state's legal zone of influence, and as such are more prone to acts of lawless nationalist violence," and "ghettos," which are "repositories of unwanted and marginalized populations" who are "nonetheless included within the dominant state's legal sphere of influence, classifying them as quasi-members of the polity" and "are more likely to be policed than forcefully

[63] Lustick (1979, 1980). See also Yiftachel (2006).   [64] Lustick (1979).

deported."[65] When the divided society emanates from the state's expansion, and when the state has sufficient coercive power, it can attempt to delineate a particular territory as either a "frontier" or a "ghetto" – as shown, for example, by Israel's different policies toward, on the one hand, the West Bank, which has mostly been treated as a "ghetto" since 1967, and on the other hand, the Gaza Strip, which was treated as a "ghetto" for many decades, but since 2005 has become a "frontier" due to Israel's withdrawal. It is worth noting, however, that a marked decrease in the level of violence in a "ghetto," especially as the result of effective policing, may transform the pattern of inter-communal relations there to control, which, as suggested earlier, is a non-violent pattern of inter-communal relations.

The second violent pattern of inter-communal relations is a stalemate, which occurs when an open struggle wages between some or all of the communities in the divided society but no single community is able to dominate the state.[66] This pattern of inter-communal relations suggests a serious setback in the process of state formation, and particularly in the sub-process of state building. If a stalemate occurs in the wake of the state's expansion, this might ultimately lead to the state's contraction, that is, to its partition,[67] although the strict barriers imposed by the international community on border change might apply in these cases as well.

These four patterns of inter-communal relations in divided societies are presented in Table 1.3, although it should be noted that these are ideal types and in reality it is sometimes difficult to distinguish between them since some states fall into more than one category or frequently oscillate between categories. A telling example is Syria in the wake of the uprising against President Bashar al-Assad and his Alawite-dominated Baath regime since 2011, a case that has oscillated between repression by the regime and a stalemate, but without moving toward power sharing or control. Indeed, one of the questions that needs to be asked, and which is also pertinent to Lebanon and Israel/Palestine, is not only why some states remain in one category whereas others move between several categories, but also why some

Table 1.3 *Major patterns of inter-communal relations in divided societies*

Domination / Violence	No communal domination	One community is dominant
Not explicitly violent	*Power sharing*	*Control*
Massively violent	*Stalemate*	*Repression*

[65] Ron (2003, xii). [66] Luttwak (2013). [67] Kaufmann (1996).

states move between one category and another but do not move to other categories.

What are the effects of the state's expansion on the pattern of intercommunal relations in the outlying territory and also in the state itself? The dominant community can try to forcefully subdue the subordinate community in the outlying territory, including by turning "ghettos" into "frontiers," or vice versa. But it can also try to impose a pattern of intercommunal control, for example, by integrating it economically but not politically. However, these practices, whether violent or not, may aggravate the community in the outlying territory and elicit even more resistance to the state's expansion, which, in extreme cases, can result in a stalemate. In order to effectively repress or control the subordinate community, moreover, the dominant community must maintain its own cohesion, including by providing its members with material and symbolic benefits. Alternatively, the dominant community can try to accommodate the subordinate community in the outlying territory – for example, by means of a power-sharing settlement – thus enhancing the legitimacy of the expanded state in the eyes of all of its inhabitants.[68] At any rate, the long-term use of violence by the dominant community against the subordinate community is liable to result in militarization of both communities and in the "role expansion" of the state's security sector, which might not be confined to the outlying territory and may permeate the state itself.

State Expansion and Security

Thus far, the discussion has focused on the process of state formation in expanded states and the inter-connected issue of their pattern of intercommunal relations in those cases where the outcome of the state's expansion is a divided society. This discussion will remain incomplete, however, without considering the issue of security, which is crucial in these contexts.

As suggested earlier, war-making, domestic security, and cross-border violence have played a central part in all facets of the process of state formation in many states in Western Europe and North America. In addition, many non-Western states have faced pressing domestic and external challenges to their security since their independence, which their leaders responded to in quite different ways.[69] Divided societies, too, are often characterized by mutual fears and feelings of insecurity

---

[68] Yiftachel (2001, 361–362).
[69] Job (1992); Ayoob (1995). See also Alagappa (2001); Cawthra and Luckham (2003).

and distrust between, and sometimes also within, their various communities.[70] How, then, does the expansion of the state affect its national security?

Before addressing this question it is worth noting that "security" itself is not an objective, or politically neutral, concept, and that various actors – chiefly the state and institutions, but also others – can "securitize" civilian issues – that is, turn them into security-related issues – in order to gain more leeway and legitimacy in dealing with these issues in particular, but also generally.[71] In divided societies, moreover, it is not always clear whether the concept of "security," and the notion of "national security," relate to all communities in the state or only to the dominant community, whose members consider other communities a threat to their privileged position in the state. In other words, in divided societies security in inexorably tied to the state's pattern of inter-communal relations, and securitization can sometimes be a strategy of inter-communal control.

These very basic questions of "what is security?" and "whose security?" have important implications for the security policies that expanded states that are divided societies will adopt, as well as for the type of security sector that they will build in order to carry out these policies. Let us consider both of these issues.

If the primary goal of an expanded state is to preserve its territorial integrity and prevent the loss of an outlying territory it had incorporated, and which its leaders deem crucial to its security, then one can expect the state's security policy to be geared toward achieving this end. Earlier it was suggested that leaders in established states are relatively autonomous in matters related to the state's expansion (and contraction), whereas leaders of less-established states are more dependent on their own societies and on international support. Another problem, especially since 1945, has been that formal annexation of outlying territories has become taboo in the international system.

What, then, can expanded states do to maintain their hold over an outlying territory that their leaders deem crucial for their national security? First, the expanded state can try to win the support of the great powers by reaching tacit understandings with them, for example by refraining from formally annexing the outlying territory. On the domestic level, too, the expanded state's leaders can practice ambiguity, signaling that "political options remain open and everything is fluid," and thus preserve

---

[70] Enloe (1980); Donald Horowitz (1985); Posen (1993); A. Peled (1998); Barak (2009a). See also Barak (2007a) and the sources cited therein.
[71] Buzan, Wæver, and De Wilde (1998). On the role of security networks in securitizing various civilian issues, see Sheffer and Barak (2013).

domestic stability.[72] But the state's leaders can also try to persuade the population of the outlying territory to accept the state's rule by integrating its members into its political, bureaucratic, and security institutions and/ or by offering them material incentives. Finally, the expanded state can attempt to convince its neighbors, which are liable be concerned over its expansion, to accept this as a fait accompli by providing them with assurances for their sovereignty and their security, and this, in turn, can guarantee the expanded state's security.

Another way to preserve the expanded state's territorial integrity, however, is to build a security sector that would be capable of defending the state's extended borders. However, this policy can be problematic in several respects. The state may need to enlarge its security sector, and this may require additional resources and lead to militarization.[73] Furthermore, if the state's expanded borders lack international legitimacy, the state may find it difficult to launch pre-emptive strikes against its enemies even when the latter pose a threat to its security.[74] But expanded states can also forge military alliances with other states, big and small, including those that face similar challenges. In addition, they can try to encourage their allies to help them weaken potential or actual threats to their rule over the outlying territory, including by military means. Thus, for example, France, which was an expanded state in 1956, launched the Suez War in collusion with two other states, Great Britain and Israel, with the purpose of weakening Egyptian President Gamal Abdul Nasser, whom French leaders regarded as a major supporter of the Algerian revolt and thus as a threat to their state's territorial integrity.[75] The alliance between Israel and Maronite actors in Lebanon before and during the Lebanon War of 1982 (discussed in Chapter 7) is another case in point.

---

[72] M. Benvenisti (1986). On the stabilizing role of ambiguity, see, especially, Sharkansky (1999, 9). This external factor, and not only domestic considerations, can prevent states from fully annexing an outlying territory. Cf. Lustick (1993). A similar consideration can prevent states from crossing the nuclear threshold and admitting that they have nuclear capacities. See A. Cohen (1998).

[73] There are, however, ways to acquire such resources, e.g., by garnering external support and by providing various incentives for society. See Barnett (1992); Levy (2007).

[74] Herein lies the logic of the joint Egyptian–Syrian surprise attack against Israel on October 6, 1973. So long as the Egyptian and Syrian armies did not disclose their intentions to go to war with Israel, the latter, which, at that time, was an expanded state and occupied the Sinai Peninsula and the Golan, could not attack them in fear of losing external, especially US, support. This became clear to Israel's leaders on the morning of the Egyptian–Syrian attack, and they refrained from ordering a pre-emptive Israeli strike against Egypt and/or Syria. See Israeli Government (2011).

[75] According to Shlaim (1997, 514), the French military "had three priorities at that time: Algeria, Algeria, and Algeria," and it assumed that if Nasser were toppled this would end the rebellion.

We see, then, that the leaders of expanded states can pursue quite different security policies in order to preserve their extended borders in the wake of their expansion. These policy choices, moreover, have important consequences for the state: fighting to preserve the outlying territory demands considerable human and material resources, which, in turn, requires a certain degree of militarization.[76] If the population in the outlying territory rejects the state's rule, it could become hostile and constitute a domestic security threat to the expanded state, in addition to the external threats that the state might face. This, in turn, may require beefing up the state's security sector, including the military and other security services. At the same time, attempts to legitimize the state's expansion through diplomacy, especially if accompanied by neutralization and de-militarization of the state, may weaken the state in the coercive-military sense, and may even invite foreign interference in its affairs.

Table 1.4 summarizes the security policy options available to leaders of expanded states that wish to retain outlying territories, differentiating between four different "audiences" to these policies: the great powers and other states and organizations in the international system; the state's neighbors; the state's citizens; and the population of the outlying territory. In the following chapters, we will see examples of these policies in Israel/Palestine and Lebanon as well as in the relations between these two political entities before and after Israel's expansion in 1967 and the subsequent creation of a divided society in Israel/Palestine.

Turning now to the expanded state's security sector, we can consider four main aspects thereof: its composition; its command structures and

Table 1.4 *Policy options of expanded states*

Audience	Policy
Great powers and other states and organizations in the international system	Legitimizing the state's expansion by practicing ambiguity regarding the outlying territory; forging alliances; weakening or forcefully removing external opponents to state expansion
State's neighbors	De-militarization of the state; security assurances; neutrality; threats; military operations
Population in outlying territory	Integration into the state's institutions; material incentives; suppression of resistance to the state's expansion
State's citizens	Ambiguity regarding the outlying territory; militarization; suppression of political dissent

[76] Kohn (2009).

Table 1.5 *The security sector in expanded states that are divided societies*

Inter-communal relations / Attributes of security sector	One community is dominant	No communal domination
Composition	Recruitment focuses on members of dominant community; most members of other communities do not serve in the security agencies	Recruitment is open to all communities, including from the outlying territories
Command and Civilian Control	Security agencies commanded and controlled by members of the dominant community	Commanding and controlling bodies of the security agencies include members of all communities in the state
Identity	The security sector promotes a national identity but with an emphasis on the identity of the dominant community	The security sector promotes a national identity that is supra-communal
Actual Operations	The security sector reinforces the position of the dominant community by suppressing members of the subordinate community (or communities)	The security sector attempts to preserve the inter-communal balance, as well as its own cohesion, by accommodation and by refraining from using its coercive capacities

the controlling civilian bodies; its identity and missions; and its actual operation in the wake of the state's expansion. As suggested by studies on security in divided societies, all of these areas are critical in these contexts, and it is important to ask how they are affected by the state's expansion and the attempts made to uphold it. The following paragraphs discuss each of these four areas, or spheres, differentiating between divided societies in which one community is dominant and divided societies that lack such a hierarchy (see Table 1.5). It should be emphasized, however, that important changes might occur in all of these areas over time, and these, too, ought to be considered.

As far the composition of the security sector is concerned, it matters a great deal who serves and who does not serve – that is, who is excluded from (or refuses to join) – in the security agencies, and this is also relevant to expanded states. When examining this question, we need to focus on the security sector's recruitment policy and how it affects the composition of its agencies. Generally speaking, in divided societies with one dominant community, those serving in the security agencies are mostly members of that community, whereas members of other communities are largely excluded.[77] However, where no single community is dominant, recruitment to the security sector is, at least in theory, open to all.[78] As suggested earlier, however, important changes can occur in this realm: inhabitants of the outlying territories can join the state's security agencies, and especially the military, thus indicating the success of the state's national integration efforts.[79] There can, moreover, be discrepancies between the communal makeup of the security sector, on the one hand, and the pattern of inter-communal relations in the state's political institutions, on the other hand, and this, too, is significant.[80]

The second issue to address concerns who commands the security agencies, who the civilian officials exercising control over them are, and whether these security and civilian officials are members of one or all of the major communities in the state. These questions are important in divided societies since in some cases the rank and file of the security sector is heterogeneous – that is, drawn from all or most of the communities in the state but only members of one community "call the shots."[81] In divided societies that have one dominating community, members of that community also occupy the commanding bodies of the security agencies and the controlling civilian bodies. But where there is no such domination, both types of bodies are made up of members of all communities. Another way to create a diverse command of the security sector is to appoint members of different communities as the heads of the various security agencies. This has been done in the security sector in postwar Lebanon (see Chapter 3) and to an extent also in the security apparatuses of the Palestinian National Authority following its establishment in the 1990s (although it is not a state).[82]

The third issue of relevance is the identity of the security sector, a term that refers to the general values that its agencies attempt to project onto their own members and also onto society at large. In expanded states that are divided societies, two patterns emerge in this regard: in expanded states with one community dominating the security sector, the latter might try to foster a national identity, but it will emphasize symbols, myths, and narratives of the dominant community; however, where no community is dominant, efforts will be made, at least ideally, to foster a national identity that supersedes communal divisions and can thus serve as meeting place for members of all communities. In either case, this

---

[77] Enloe (1980); Donald Horowitz (1985).   [78] Barak (2009a).
[79] Cf. A. Peled (1998); Krebs (2006).   [80] A. Peled (1998).   [81] Quinlivan (1999).
[82] Lia (2006, 307–309).

identity itself is not fixed and it is important to identify changes over time.[83]

The fourth, and final, issue to examine is the actual operation of the security sector – namely, how its agencies perform in the area of security. Here it is important to ask not only which security agencies are employed (e.g., the military, the police, and others), but also how these agencies present their practices to their own members and to others. This is because these agencies can, for example, amplify threats, securitize civilian issues, and frame all kinds of political activities as terrorism. It is also worth knowing how members of different communities perceive these actions. In expanded states that are divided societies, we can, again, identify two distinct patterns: where one community is dominant, the main task of the security sector is, necessarily, to reinforce that community's hegemonic position in the state vis-à-vis others; but where no such domination exists, the security sector is expected to abide by, and help preserve, the inter-communal balance.[84] Adrian Guelke differentiates between three major strategies for maintaining order in divided societies, which derive from how the state treats politically motivated violent offenders: first, accommodation, which indicates that these offenders have legitimate political grievances; second, criminalization, which indicates the state's resistance to addressing such grievances; and third, suppression, which seeks to repress these grievances altogether. Guelke argues that states can pursue different strategies in relation to different kinds of threats, and that these strategies can shift over time even with regard to the same territory. He also notes that these strategies match different forms of inter-communal conflict regulation, such as integration (criminalization), power sharing (accommodation), and control and more violent forms of conflict regulation (suppression).[85]

State Expansion and the Relationship Between the State, Community, and Security

Beyond its effects on the process of state formation, the community (or communities) within the state, and security, a state's expansion also has an impact on the triangular relationship between the state, community, and security, particularly when the state's expansion results in the creation of a divided society.

If, in the wake of the state's expansion, the society remains homogenous – that is, if there is an overlap between the boundaries of the community and

---

[83] See, e.g., Barak (2001). [84] McGarry and O'Leary (1999); Barak (2009a).
[85] Guelke (2012, 55–60).

those of the state – then one can expect internal security issues to be less significant.[86] Moreover, if the neighboring states accept the state's expansion, then external security issues should be less critical. The political settlements in Europe in the aftermath of the two world wars, which involved the shifting of borders, are cases in point, although it is worth adding that these political settlements sometimes included population transfers that contributed to these states' social homogeneity (e.g., in Turkey, Czechoslovakia, and Poland).

However, if the outcome of the state's expansion is a divided society, and if tensions between the various communities that compose this divided society arise, then one can expect security issues to become paramount. One way to deal with this conundrum is to develop conflict regulation mechanisms – and especially power sharing – in the state, including in the area of security, and, ultimately, to promote de-securitization in all aspects of public life.[87] But if one community dominates the state and the subordinate communities resist its domination, the state's leaders, who are also the leaders of the dominant community, will face a constant need to mobilize the members of their community to respond to the challenge – that is, to engage not only in "securitization" but also in "sectarianization" of the political struggle. As a result, the emphasis in the triangular relationship between state, community, and security is liable to shift away from the state – which no longer performs the role of conflict regulator and instead becomes an instrument of control or repression by the dominant community – toward the community and toward security, resulting what might be termed "ethno-securitism" or "ethno-militarism."

Conclusion

This chapter presented some of the major causes and effects of the state's expansion, particularly when the outcome of this move is a divided society. It first discussed the major causes for state expansion (and state contraction), arguing that while rational (or interest-based) and ideological factors (especially on the elite level) are important in these contexts, structural and cultural factors also need to be considered. The bulk of the chapter, however, was devoted to discussing the effects of the state's expansion on the process of state formation, the pattern of intercommunal relations in the state, and the area of security on both the domestic and external levels. As this discussion suggests, all of these spheres, which are sometimes dealt with separately, are in fact closely

[86] Miller (2007).   [87] Wæver (2009).

connected. A common thread running through the chapter has been the issue of autonomy: of political and military leaders who decide on the state's expansion and contraction; of the state and its institutions in general, and in divided societies in particular; and of the area of security in these contexts. A second observation is that in order to better comprehend the triangular relationship between state, community, and security we need to examine not only the state's formal institutions but also the more informal (including cultural) practices and mechanisms at work in these contexts. These observations will guide the discussion of Israel/Palestine and Lebanon in the subsequent chapters.

2 From Nation-States to Divided Societies: Lebanon and Israel/Palestine

This chapter presents a broad, albeit not exhaustive, account of the creation of the two political units of Greater Lebanon in 1920 and Israel/Palestine or Greater Israel in 1967. In particular, it discusses the decisions made by leaders in the Maronite and Jewish communities, respectively, which culminated in the creation of two divided societies in place of the nation-states that members of these communities had envisaged. It also asks why this act was seen as imperative by members of both communities and inquires about the objective circumstances that facilitated the state's expansion in both instances. The emphasis in this chapter on the Maronite community in Mount Lebanon and the Jewish community in Israel/Palestine is warranted by the pivotal roles played by members of these two communities in the state's expansion, and also allows us to draw interesting parallels between the two cases. However, the role played by members of other communities in both political entities, such as Sunni Muslims (hereafter, Sunnis), Shi'i Muslims (hereafter, Shi'is), Druze, and other Christians in Greater Lebanon, and Palestinians (including Muslims, Christians, and Druze) in Israel/Palestine, was also significant,[1] and the chapter makes mention of the (largely negative) response of these other communities to the two expansionist moves that significantly affected their lives. This issue is dealt with also in Chapters 3 and 4, which focus on each of the two cases. Another issue, which is also addressed in these two chapters, is how to consider the Maronites in Lebanon and the Jews in Israel/Palestine, but also the other communities in both cases. Drawing on the useful framework offered by Mark Lichbach, the following discussion treats culture as dynamic and subject to change, and also considers the role of self-interested actors and of structural factors in shaping a community's political behavior.[2] This approach can help explain how language, religion, and ethnic (or ethnonational) sentiments – but also inter-communal conflicts – became crucial to the identity of members of the Maronite community in Mount

---

[1] On this issue, see O'Leary (2001b); Yiftachel (2001, 360–361).
[2] Lichbach (1997); Chandra (2009).

45

Lebanon before the state's expansion in 1920, only to decline in the wake of the National Pact of 1943 and to re-emerge, albeit in different form, before and during the civil war of 1975–1990, and how similar elements became crucial to the identity of members of the Jewish community in Israel/Palestine during and in the wake of Israel's expansion in 1967.

From the *Mutasarrifiyya* to Greater Lebanon

The disintegration of the Ottoman Empire during the First World War and the occupation of the Levant by the Allied Powers placed the Maronites, a Christian community based primarily in Mount Lebanon and its immediate surroundings, for the first time in a position where some of its members, including several of its leaders, could hope to acquire their own "place under the sun" – that is, a nation-state according to the Western model.

For some time, certain prominent members of the Maronite community in Mount Lebanon and in the Lebanese diaspora had been promoting a particular proto-national collective identity, which was actively encouraged by the leaders of the Maronite Church. This development was reinforced by the deepening ties between members of the Maronite elite, on the one hand, and their co-religionists in Western Europe, particularly France, on the other hand. It was also strengthened by the deteriorating relations of the Maronites with their close neighbors in Mount Lebanon, and especially members of the Druze community.[3] Indeed, if a nation is "a group of people who share a fallacy about a common past and dislike the same neighbors,"[4] then the Maronites were on their way to becoming a nation.

In 1861, in the wake of a bloody conflict between Maronites and Druze in Mount Lebanon that left thousands dead, most of them Maronites, the yearning of some political entrepreneurs in the Maronite community for self-rule had been fulfilled, at least in part, with the establishment of the *Mutasarrifiyya*, an autonomous district in Mount Lebanon under the auspices of the European powers but within the framework of the Ottoman Empire.

The *Mutasarrifiyya* was headed by a Christian (but not from Mount Lebanon), who was assisted by a multi-communal administrative council that represented all major communities in the autonomous district (see Chapter 3). A half-century later, Maronites constituted some 60 percent of the population of the *Mutasarrifiyya*, with the total number of

[3] Zamir (1985); Kaufman (2004); Hakim (2013).
[4] This saying is attributed to Ernst Renan.

Christians reaching 80 percent.[5] Importantly, the period from the establishment of the *Mutasarrifiyya* until the First World War (1861–1914) was one of political stability and economic prosperity in Mount Lebanon.[6]

It was, however, the First World War that served as the catalyst for the Maronites' quest for statehood. During the war, the Ottoman army overran the *Mutasarrifiyya*, putting an end to its autonomous status and effectively cutting it off from the outside world, and especially from Western Europe, (The fact that the *Mutasarrifiyya* did not have an outlet to the sea made it all the easier.) The population in Mount Lebanon was subsequently subjected to severe hardships, including starvation, disease, and harsh treatment by Ottoman officials, who could now enter the region as they pleased. Historians later maintained that more than one-fifth, and perhaps even one-third, of the region's inhabitants, mostly Christians, perished during this period.[7]

For members of the Maronite community, as well as for others in the Middle East, the collapse of the Ottoman Empire at the end of the First World War led to crystallization of "ambivalent and inchoate reformist and nationalist programs of the elite ... into full-fledged nationalist agendas."[8] For some Maronite political entrepreneurs, including Patriarch Elias Hoyek, who presented the community's case in the Paris Peace Conference in 1919,[9] this national agenda focused on the restoration of what they regarded as historic Lebanon, which, according to them, had been deprived in 1861 of its "natural and historic boundaries" by the Ottoman Empire and the European powers. For these Maronite activists, the state's expansion was, thus, an imperative, because "to live freely and to prosper, the Lebanese needed not only their political independence but also the extension of their territory to include its natural frontiers."[10]

After the Allied forces occupied the Middle East, and according to series of understandings they had reached during the war (the Sykes–Picot Agreement of 1916) and in its aftermath, France was entrusted with ruling the Levant, which today includes the independent states of Lebanon and Syria. The French army deployed there and defeated the armed supporters of Faysal, the would-be Hashemite king of

---

[5] Zamir (1985, 98).
[6] Akarli (1993). On the rise of sectarianism in Mount Lebanon toward 1861, see Makdisi (2000). On Mount Lebanon before the mid-nineteenth Century, see I. Harik (1968).
[7] Cf. Ajay (1974); Zamir (1985, 36); Hakim (2013, 224). See also Fawaz (2014, 105–106). See also the memorandum presented by the Maronite Patriarch, Elias Hoyek, to the Paris Peace Conference in 1919, in Zamir (1985, 275).
[8] Hakim (2013, 7). Cf. Zamir (1985); Kaufman (2004).
[9] For the text, see Zamir (1985, 269–278).
[10] Hakim (2013, 220, 235, 249). See also Fieldhouse (2006).

Syria.[11] It should be noted that, in this period, French policymakers became highly sympathetic to the Maronite community in Mount Lebanon, which they regarded as a valuable ally in an otherwise hostile land. Indeed, the support extended by French leaders to the Maronite national cause in the years immediately after the First World War – as well as other factors, most notably US President Woodrow Wilson's calls to adopt the principle of self-determination – helped tilt the scales within the Maronite community toward the creation of a political unit that would fulfill its members' collective aspirations and ensure their past traumas not be repeated. The deteriorating situation in the Levant and the "nagging uncertainty" about the area's future[12] made these pro-expansionist actors even more determined.

On September 1, 1920, and after persistent lobbying by Maronite leaders, the community's quest for statehood was realized in full when the local French commander, General Henri Gouraud, announced the creation of a new political unit called "Greater Lebanon" (*grand liban*). In addition to the areas that had formerly been part of the *Mutasarrifiyya* – that is, Christian- and Maronite-dominated Mount Lebanon – this political unit was to include the adjacent regions of North Lebanon, South Lebanon, and the Biqa', with the city of Beirut as its capital. As we have seen, Maronite leaders claimed that the adjacent regions, too, formed part of their historic homeland, and were, moreover, crucial for their community's security and well-being. French officials, although harboring certain reservations about this move and its possible outcomes, were nonetheless willing to play along, and Greater Lebanon became a reality.[13]

However, since the regions annexed to Mount Lebanon were overwhelmingly Muslim (including mainly Sunnis and Shi'is) – a fact that was known to the Maronite leaders and was also acknowledged by some French officials – the result of the state's expansion was that the solid Christian majority in "smaller" Mount Lebanon almost immediately plummeted to about 55 percent in Greater Lebanon, with Maronites dropping to 32 percent and losing the absolute majority in "their" nation-state. By 1932, when Lebanon's last official comprehensive population census was taken, the total number of Christians in the expanded state was already down to slightly more than half of the population (50.7 percent), with Maronites constituting a mere 29 percent (Table 2.1).[14]

Opposition to the establishment of Greater Lebanon, especially by the Muslim inhabitants of the territories that had been annexed to Mount

---

[11] Hakim (2013, 226–231); Fieldhouse (2006). [12] Hakim (2013, 255).
[13] Zamir (1985); Fieldhouse (2006).
[14] Zamir (1985, 98). On the 1932 census, see Maktani (1999).

Table 2.1 *Demography in the* Mutasarrifiyya *and in Greater Lebanon*

Community/Political unit	Christians	Maronites	Muslims (including Druze)
Mutasarrifiyya (1911)	79.5%	58.4%	20.5%
Greater Lebanon (1921)	55.1%	32.7%	44.9%
Greater Lebanon (1932)	50.7%	29.1%	49.3%

Source: Zamir (1985, 98)

Lebanon, was almost immediate, although at first it was mostly limited to protests. This negative response increased the sense of regret among those in Mount Lebanon and in France who had been opposed to the establishment of a multi-communal political unit in Lebanon.[15] But, importantly, it did not lead to the state's contraction. Indeed, in the coming years, Lebanon's Muslims – first Sunnis and later Shi'is and Druze (who are not Muslims but are considered as such for political purposes in Lebanon) – as well as non-Maronite Christians, especially Orthodox and Catholics but also Armenians, all of whom initially rejected the state's expansion, gradually came to terms with the new political reality (see Chapter 3). In fact, despite their "artificial" nature, Lebanon's borders, like those of most Middle Eastern states,[16] have remained almost unchanged since they were first delineated by the Western powers in the aftermath of the First World War.

The atrocities committed by the Ottoman forces in Mount Lebanon during the First World War (which traumatized many Maronites, who witnessed the collapse of their safe haven); the demise of the Ottoman Empire and the occupation of the Levant by the Western powers (especially by France, the Maronites' ally and supporter); the emerging discourse of self-determination in the international arena: all these factors motivated Maronite political entrepreneurs both in Mount Lebanon and abroad to try to expand the territory under their control. This move was presented as crucial for the well-being and indeed the continued existence of the Maronite community in view of the past excesses committed against its members, but also in the face of present security challenges and future uncertainties.

But instead of establishing a Maronite, or even a Christian, nation-state in Lebanon, the result of the state's expansion in this case was the creation of a divided society where no single community, including the Maronites

---

[15] Zamir (1985).
[16] The only exceptions, thus far, have been the establishment of the Republic of South Sudan in 2011, following of decades of civil war between the northern and southern parts of Sudan, and the unification of Yemen in 1990.

themselves, could claim an absolute majority. As a consequence, politics in the new political unit – first French-controlled Greater Lebanon and then the independent Republic of Lebanon – have been a continuous quest to address the social, economic, and cultural needs and demands of about 17–20 distinct communities (or sects), in addition to numerous large families (or clans) and geographical regions.[17] In Chapter 3 we will see how Lebanon's leaders have tried to cope with this challenge.

From the State of Israel to "Greater Israel"

Some writers posit that the creation of "Greater Israel" in June 1967, during the Israeli–Arab War, was accidental, and it seems that this outcome indeed stemmed, more than anything else, from the nature of that particular military confrontation.[18] At any rate, the new political unit that emerged in Israel/Palestine in the wake of the 1967 War, informal as it was, proved to be more durable than other expanded states in the contemporary Middle East, including some that were sanctioned by other states[19] and others that were not.[20] While Israel/Palestine is not the only case of long-term state expansion in the region, it has lasted longer than the other cases,[21] and some even argue that it is "probably the longest [military] occupation in modern international relations."[22]

As with the Maronite community in Mount Lebanon, the breakup of the Ottoman Empire was favorable to the Zionist movement, whose

[17] Hudson (1968); Hanf (1993).
[18] Gorenberg (2006). See also Shlaim (2012, 23). On the creation of Greater Israel or Israel/Palestine in 1967, see Pedatzur (1996); Segev (2007).
[19] Jordan's annexation of the West Bank in 1950 was largely rejected by the international community but was recognized by three states: Britain, Iraq, and Pakistan. See E. Benvenisti (2012, 204). This instance of state expansion was effectively reversed by Israel's occupation of the West Bank in 1967, and in 1988 Jordan formally disengaged from this territory. Syria's military "presence" in Lebanon was sanctioned both by the Arab League in 1976 and by the Ta'if Agreement (1989) and subsequent Syrian–Lebanese agreements, but was reversed in 2005.
[20] Two cases of short-lived state expansion in the region are Iraq's annexation of Kuwait in 1990, which was reversed during the Gulf War of 1991, and the United Arab Republic, the short-lived union between Egypt and Syria (1958–1961). See Malcolm Kerr (1978).
[21] Two other cases of state expansion in the region which have not been reversed are Turkey's rule over Northern Cyprus since 1974 and Morocco's rule over Western Sahara since 1975.
[22] Kretzmer (2012, 208). Stirk (2009, 25) writes that Israel's occupations of the West Bank and Gaza "were unusual in the post-war world because of Israel's relatively open admission of the applicability of occupation law, or at least part of it ... because of the length of the occupation, though prolonged occupations had taken place in the nineteenth century ... because of the uncertainty about the precise status of the territories that Israel had occupied, though such uncertainty was far from entirely novel ... [and] because of the express extension of the jurisdiction of the Israeli Supreme Court to cover acts taken by the occupation authorities."

leaders had, for some time, been propagating the idea of a Jewish homeland in Palestine that would address this community's pressing need for security. During the First World War, Zionist leaders also managed to garner the sympathy of one of the Allies, Great Britain, whose government issued the Balfour Declaration in November 1917, which officially supported their national cause, albeit not unreservedly.[23]

However, unlike the Maronites of Mount Lebanon, who were an indigenous community, the Zionists were, by and large, foreigners to the Middle East, with most (but not all) of their adherents coming from Eastern and Central Europe. This carried certain advantages for the Zionist settlers in Palestine in the late nineteenth and early twentieth centuries: because they were acquainted with – or acquired – Western technologies in the fields of agriculture, industry, and warfare, they had an advantaged position vis-à-vis the indigenous community, the Palestinians. But this factor also caused alienation on the part of the latter, particularly when the Zionist project in Palestine expanded. Indeed, while even the most ardent Maronite activists during Lebanon's two civil wars, in 1958 and in 1975–1990, could be called upon to rejoin the Arab fold, many members of the Jewish community in Palestine were looked upon as, and also considered themselves to be, foreigners in the Middle East – though they did see Palestine as their homeland – even as the newly independent State of Israel absorbed hundreds of thousands of Jewish immigrants from the Middle East and North Africa.[24]

This discussion raises the more general question of whether Zionism itself was, from the outset, a colonialist project or has become one only after Israel's expansion in the Israeli–Arab War of 1967.[25] Nadim Rouhana and Areej Sabbagh-Khoury distinguish between two approaches in this regard: The first approach considers only the Jewish settlements in the Territories occupied in 1967 to be a colonial project, whereas the other approach sees the Zionist project, the establishment of the Jewish State in 1948, and Israeli society (i.e., the Jewish community in Israel/Palestine, including the settlers in the Territories) as a colonial project.[26] However, Gershon Shafir, in a recent contribution, offers a third approach when he posits that "when it comes to colonization, there is a remarkable degree of institutional continuity between the post-1967 era and the pre-1948 years," since this suggests that the period

---

[23] Segev (2000); Fieldhouse (2006, 130–150).
[24] Fieldhouse (2006, 312). On the Zionist settlers' self-perception as Europeans, which was reinforced by their early encounter with the Palestinians, see Dowty (2013).
[25] On this debate, see, e.g., Shenhav and Hever (2004); Friling (2016).
[26] Rouhana and Sabbagh-Khoury (2006, 66). See also Rouhana and Sabbagh-Khoury (2015); Sternberg (2016).

1948–1967 was different than both of these "colonial" periods.[27] This book follows a different path: It notes the points of similarity between Israel's post-1967 settlement project and the period before 1948; it identifies those areas where Israel's behavior since 1967 continued practices that had been adopted in the period 1948–1967; and it is attentive to the important changes that have taken place in Israel/Palestine since 1967 in relation to the previous period.[28]

At any rate, it is clear the leaders of the Zionist movement, and, later, of the independent State of Israel, were quite prudent in setting their national preferences before 1967. Although some political factions in Israel, mainly on the right side of the political system, openly called for imposing Jewish control over all of Mandatory Palestine and, perhaps, over the East Bank of the Jordan River as well, the majority of Zionist leaders, most notably David Ben-Gurion, who in 1948 became Israel's first prime minister and defense minister, were well aware of the limits to their power. This prudent behavior was evident already in November 1947, when these leaders accepted the UN Partition Plan for Palestine although it gave the Jewish community only 56 percent its territory. It was also manifested during the First Arab–Israeli war, when the Israel Defense Forces (IDF) refrained from conquering East Jerusalem, the West Bank, and the Gaza Strip (see Chapter 4).

After the Second World War and the Holocaust, leaders of the Zionist movement redoubled their efforts to garner international support for the establishment of an independent Jewish state in Palestine, and many in the international community supported such a move. The British government, for its part, decided to terminate its Mandate in Palestine on May 14, 1948, and immediately afterwards Jewish leaders proclaimed the establishment of the State of Israel. Almost a year later, in 1949, when the First Arab–Israeli War came to an end with the signing of the Armistice agreements between Israel and each of Egypt, Lebanon, Transjordan, and Syria (but not with the Palestinians), the nascent state controlled not only the areas of Mandatory Palestine that were allocated to the Jewish community according to the UN Partition Plan, but also other regions that were supposed to be part of the Arab state. The remaining areas of the would-be Arab state, which included the West Bank and the Gaza Strip, were, respectively, under Jordanian and Egyptian rule. However, since hundreds of thousands of Palestinians had fled and were deported from the areas that were now under Israel's control, the new

---

[27] Shafir (2016, 799).
[28] Some of these changes are discussed in Bar-Tal and Schnell (2013).

Table 2.2 *Demography in Israel and in Israel/Palestine*

Community/Political unit	Jews	Palestinians
Israel (1949)	89%	11%
Israel/Palestine (1967)	63%	37%
Israel/Palestine (2000)	55%	45%

Sources: Haidar (2005); Efrat (2006)

Israeli state had a solid Jewish majority of 89 percent – that is, more than the Christians in the *Mutasarrifiyya* in 1911 (Table 2.2).

Apart from one major military confrontation – the Suez War in 1956, when Israeli forces, in collusion with Great Britain and France, occupied the Sinai Peninsula from Egypt but quickly withdrew under combined US and Soviet pressures[29] – Israel's borders remained unchanged in the period 1949–1967. But in June 1967, during the Israeli–Arab War, this reality was fundamentally altered. Rising tensions between Israel and Syria prompted Egyptian President Gamal Abdul Nasser to threaten Israel, and Egypt's troops entered the Sinai Peninsula, where a UN force had been deployed since 1956. In addition, Egypt blocked the Straits of Tiran, a vital sea route for Israel, and forged an alliance not only with Syria, whose leaders were fearful of an Israeli attack, but also with Jordan, another neighbor of Israel. Although at least part of the blame for this escalation rested on Israel's shoulders – it was the Israel Defense Forces (IDF) that often provoked Syria in the period before 1967, raising Arab, and also Soviet, fears[30] – Nasser's actions constituted a *casus belli* for Israel. Diplomatic maneuvers commenced, but these proved unsuccessful, and Israel's military leaders, which, since 1953, had been preparing their army for a pre-emptive strike against existential threats to the state,[31] pressured the government to act. The government, led by Levi Eshkol, wavered, but this only increased public apprehensions in Israel and fears of an imminent catastrophe. The combined public and military pressures, together with what seemed to be a US "green light" for Israeli military action, prompted Israel to unleash its military power against its Arab rivals.[32]

In six days in June 1967, Israel scored a dramatic military victory over its Arab neighbors, resulting in its conquest of the Golan from Syria, the Sinai

---

[29] Laron (2013, 4). On the Suez War of 1956, see also G. Sheffer (1996); Golani (2001).
[30] Lieutenant General (ret.) Moshe Dayan, chief of staff of the IDF, quoted in Tal (1997); Goldstein (2003, 535); Laron (2010).
[31] Oren, Barak, and Shapira (2013).
[32] M. Oren (2003); Gluska (2007); Segev (2007); Laron (2010).

Peninsula from Egypt (it was returned to Egypt after the peace treaty of 1979), and the rest of the areas that had formed part of Mandatory Palestine until 1948: the West Bank including East Jerusalem, which Israel occupied from Jordan, and the Gaza Strip, which was occupied from Egypt. As a consequence, Israel expanded and a new political unit – a "Greater Israel," which is referred to herein as Israel/Palestine – came into being, albeit informally. Unlike the State of Israel, which, as we have seen, had an overwhelming Jewish majority in the period 1948–1967, the new political unit was for all intents and purposes a divided society, with its Jewish community constituting only 63 percent of the total population.[33]

Although successive Israeli governments after 1967 refrained from formally annexing the Territories (they did, however, impose Israeli jurisdiction over East Jerusalem, but without using the term "annexation"; see Chapter 1), Israeli leaders, including government ministers, members of various political factions, and Israel's "security networks," which are composed of acting and retired security officials and their civilian partners, actively supported the state's expansion. Together, these actors invested considerable time, effort, and resources into making the Territories practically inseparable from Israel.[34]

Domestically as well as externally, these actors justified their actions in the name of security and by making reference to traumatic episodes from Jewish history, especially the Holocaust. Thus, for example, Foreign Minister Abba Eban famously referred to Israel's pre-1967 borders as the "Borders of Aushcwitz,"[35] signaling that a return to them was tantamount to national suicide. In July 1977, not long after he became Israel's prime minister, Menachem Begin, leader of the Likud Party, told US President Jimmy Carter: "Our concept of national security is not based on aggrandizement or expansion. But our fathers and mothers got killed only because they were Jews and we do not want this for our children."[36] Other actors, especially within Israel's national religious community, evoked ethnonational myths, symbols, and narratives, which held that the Territories were not only an integral part of the Land of Israel (*Eretz Israel*) but were crucial for the continued existence of the Jewish people from a religious standpoint.[37] At the same time, and in order to prevent possible domestic

---

[33] Efrat (2006, 70–71, 148, 167) puts the number of Palestinians in the Territories in 1967 at 1,025,300, including 600,000 in the West Bank, 71,300 in East Jerusalem, and 354,000 in the Gaza Strip. At the time, there were 2,383,000 Jews and 392,700 Palestinians living in Israel. The total population in Israel/Palestine in 1967 was thus 3,801,000 and the percentage of Jews and Palestinians was 63 percent and 37 percent, respectively.
[34] Pedatzur (1996); Gorenberg (2006); Sheffer and Barak (2013).   [35] Eban (1969).
[36] Document 52, FRUS (2013, 343).
[37] Weisburd (1989); Sprinzak (1991); R. Friedman (1994); Gorenberg (2006); Pedahzur (2012).

and external pressures, Israel's leaders insisted that their hold over the Territories was temporary, and that they were needed so long as Israel was not at peace with all of its Arab neighbors.

The fact that Israel's expansion in 1967 remained informal helps explain why it has been tolerated by the international community – particularly by the United States, Israel's patron and ally – as well as by most Israelis for a half-century. As we have seen, in 1956, following the Suez War, Israel declared that it intended to stay in the Sinai Peninsula, but massive US and Soviet pressures compelled it to withdraw. However, in the wake of the 1967 War, Israeli leaders were ambiguous about the fate of the Territories, and while some government ministers and other leaders, including security officials, supported the full or partial integration of these areas into Israel, others opposed it, and yet others, including Prime Minister Eshkol, could not make up their minds. As a result, foreign powers, most notably the United States, whose leaders were familiar with the outcome of the 1956 War, on the one hand, and with the crisis that led to the 1967 War, on the other hand, were reluctant to pressure Israel to withdraw from the Territories before its leaders decided on the matter and without guarantees for Israel's security.[38]

However, and as we shall see in Chapter 4, the lack of a clear and formal Israeli policy with regard to the Territories did not mean that the state's political, bureaucratic, security, and judicial institutions, as well as more informal actors such as the aforementioned security networks, did not operate in these regions and, occasionally, join hands with other social and political actors, most notably the settler movement, that emerged in Israel in the wake of the 1967 War in order to make Israel's presence there more entrenched.[39]

At the same time, the state and its agencies, as well as other organizations that historically were part of the Zionist movement, such as the Jewish Agency and the Jewish National Fund, adopted various measures that were designed to preserve the Jewish majority in Israel/Palestine. These included, on the one hand, the absorption of hundreds of thousands of Jewish (and quasi-Jewish) immigrants in Israel, and, on the other hand, a mix of pressures and incentives that sought to persuade the Palestinians in the Territories to emigrate. But despite all these efforts, the turn of the century saw the Jewish community drop to about 55 percent of the total population in Israel/Palestine,[40] a percentage that is similar to that of all of

---

[38] Gorenberg (2006).
[39] Pedatzur (1996); Zertal and Eldar (2007); Gorenberg (2006); Sheffer and Barak (2013); Pedahzur and McCarthy (2015); Ranta (2015); Gazit (2016).
[40] Efrat (2006, 76). An official Palestinian report from 2003 estimated the number of Palestinians living in Israel/Palestine in 2002 at 4.6 million, compared to 5.1 million

the Christians in Greater Lebanon in the early 1920s, and is, moreover, rapidly approaching parity with the Palestinians.[41] In 2010, a leading demographer, Sergio DellaPergola, stated:

> If people ask when Jews will lose their majority [in Israel/Palestine], then it's already happened ... If one combines the Palestinian population of the Gaza Strip and West Bank, includes foreign workers and refugees, whose numbers have grown rapidly in recent years, and omits Israelis who made aliya [immigration to Israel] under the Law of Return but are not recognized as Jews by the Interior Ministry, then Jews are slightly less than 50% of the population.[42]

Palestinian resistance to the Israeli occupation took the form of demonstrations, protests, and both sporadic and organized acts of violence in the Territories but sometimes also within Israel itself. But only in December 1987, with the outbreak of the first Intifada, did the Palestinian resistance to Israel's expansion become coordinated. Still, Palestinian efforts to dismantle Greater Israel were, on the whole, unsuccessful, and in some respects – especially in terms of the number of Jewish settlers in the Territories – this political unit became even more entrenched.

Following the Madrid Conference in 1991, and after more intercommunal violence in Israel/Palestine, secret negotiations began between Israelis and Palestinians, and on September 13, 1993, the Oslo Agreement was signed between Israel and the PLO. Many believed that this agreement would lead to the partition of Israel/Palestine between Israelis and Palestinians. However, despite some progress in the two sides' relations, including the establishment of the Palestinian National Authority in parts of the Territories in the 1990s, the Israeli–Palestinian peace process failed to redraw political realities in Israel/Palestine, even before its collapse in 2000 (see Chapter 4).

The Second Palestinian Intifada, which began after the breakdown of the peace process, also failed to dismantle Greater Israel. Palestinian demonstrations were met by a massive Israeli response, and violence between the two sides escalated to unprecedented levels. In response to Palestinian attacks against Israel's territory, Israel recaptured many of the Palestinian-controlled areas in the West Bank. Later, Israel began to construct the "separation barrier" with the declared goal of preventing Palestinian armed incursions into its territory. However, much of this

---

Jews. It was estimated that both communities would be numerically equal in 2006. See PCBS (2003, 17).

[41] Efrat (2006, 76). According to this source, the percentage of Jews in Israel/Palestine would decline to 46 percent in 2020.

[42] Quoted in Sheffler (2010). See also DellaPergola (2011). Efrat (2006, 76) argues that the percentage of Jews in Israel/Palestine in 2010 was 51.1 percent.

barrier, which in some places was a concrete wall up to 8 meters high, was built on land that belonged to Palestinians and not on the pre-1967 border, with Israeli forces and Jewish settlers positioned on both sides (see Chapter 4).

Israel's unilateral withdrawal from the Gaza Strip in the summer of 2005 (the Disengagement Plan), for its part, has not been followed by additional steps in and vis-à-vis the Territories, and an internationally recognized border between Israel and the Gaza Strip was not delineated. Indeed, using Ron's terminology, it can be argued that by pulling out of this area, Israel effectively turned it from a "ghetto" into a "frontier"[43] where Israel's security sector, and especially the Israel Defense Forces (IDF), could employ even more violence – as demonstrated, for example, in a series of military confrontations that ensued between Israel and the Palestinian group Hamas in 2008–2009, 2011, and 2014.

As in Greater Lebanon, there were some in Israel/Palestine, and also elsewhere, who realized that if the Israeli state were to maintain its hold over the Territories it would cease to be a Jewish nation-state and a democracy.[44] But these actors, who began to advocate a full Israeli withdrawal from the Territories and a "two-state solution" for Israel/Palestine, have, thus far, failed in their quest to bring about the state's contraction. In November 1995, Israeli Prime Minister Yitzhak Rabin was assassinated following a massive anti-withdrawal campaign launched by the Israeli right, and other Israeli prime ministers who supported Israeli withdrawals from the Territories, including Shimon Peres, Ehud Barak, and Ehud Olmert, were all voted out of office in the elections in 1996, 2001, and 2009, respectively (Olmert had actually resigned in 2008 and did not participate in the elections, but his party, Kadima, did not succeed either). Also, the number of Jewish settlements and Jewish settlers in the Territories has risen steadily since 1967 (see Chapter 4), rendering the partition of Israel/Palestine more difficult – though not impossible – to achieve.

Based on the above, it seems logical to consider Israel/Palestine, or Greater Israel, which has been around for a half-century, as the relevant political unit despite the fact that it is not recognized by any state (including Israel), that most Israelis continue to deny its existence, and that many both within Israel/Palestine and outside its borders seek to undo it. It also seems useful to compare Israel/Palestine to other expanded states that are divided societies, including Lebanon, and to other states and political entities that are divided societies such as South Africa, Northern Ireland, Serbia, Turkey, Jordan, Iraq, and Syria. At the same time, comparing

[43] Ron (2003). [44] Leibowitz (1992, 225–226).

Israel/Palestine to established Western democracies that have not expanded and are not divided societies,[45] or to established Western states (including great powers) that waged colonial struggles but managed to contract,[46] seems less useful.

Conclusion

The Maronites in Mount Lebanon and the Jews in Palestine are two communities that were successful in realizing their national goals after the end of the First World War, with the help of two colonial powers: France and Great Britain, respectively. In so doing, leaders in both communities exploited the disintegration of the Ottoman Empire and also drew on the international discourse of national self-determination to make a persuasive case before the great powers, which extended them their support. Members of both communities, who were fearful for their collective security after having suffered traumatic experiences, believed that the establishment of a state would address this basic collective need. That both communities were successful in their quest is quite remarkable, especially when compared to other groups in the Middle East, such as the Armenians, who had to wait until the demise of another empire, the Soviet Union, before achieving their national goals; the Kurds, who remained divided between Iraq, Turkey, Iran, and Syria; and the Palestinians, who almost a century later are still a stateless people and are divided between Israel, the Territories, and the diaspora.[47] In 1967, during the Israeli–Arab War, the Jewish community in Israel imposed its rule over all of Israel/Palestine, with most international actors, including the great powers (especially the United States, Israel's patron), doing little to reverse this step. However, instead of establishing a nation-state according to the European model, the state's expansion, first in Lebanon and later in Israel/Palestine, led to the creation of a divided society. Almost a century after the proclamation of Greater Lebanon, Christians make up only about a third of the population in their state, mainly due to their higher tendency to emigrate, a higher birthrate among Muslims, and the prolonged conflict of 1975–1990. A half-century after Israel's expansion and the creation of Greater Israel, demographers contend that Jews are no longer the majority in Israel/Palestine, and an official Palestinian report from 2013 predicts there will be a Palestinian majority west of the Jordan River by the year 2020.[48] Based on the two cases of Lebanon and Israel/Palestine, it can be argued that political leaders can promote the

---

[45] See, e.g., Nikolenyi (2013). [46] Lustick (1993); Ben-Eliezer (1998a).
[47] See, e.g., Cizre (2001) and Natali (2001). [48] PCBS (2013, 13).

state's expansion when objective circumstances are forthcoming, and especially in the wake of major collective traumas for their communities, and that their national projects can find formal or tacit support among the great powers, which consider these communities to be their clients in what they perceive as hostile environments. However, attempting to achieve total security for the community through the state's expansion is liable to jeopardize the goal of establishing a nation-state according to the Western model, and can, ultimately, make the community less secure, both materially and ontologically. Still, state contraction, even when the expanded state appears to be a contradiction in terms, is difficult (though not impossible) to achieve, especially when the state itself is not fully established and when its expansion opens up basic questions regarding its identity and gives rise to powerful political actors that do their utmost to preserve the status quo.

3 Lebanon: Weak and Legitimate

This chapter discusses the triangular relationship between the state, community, and security in Lebanon. Its emphasis is on the period after the state's expansion – that is, after the relatively homogenous *Mutasarrifiyya*, the autonomous district of Mount Lebanon, was expanded in 1920, and Greater Lebanon, the new political unit that turned out to be a divided society, came into being. However, in order to better elucidate the impact of the state's expansion on the three above-mentioned spheres and their interplay, the period before this watershed event will also be considered. In order to identify markers of continuity and change in the Lebanese case, the discussion will be divided into five sub-periods: first, the period of the *Mutasarrifiyya* (1861–1914); second, the period of French rule in Lebanon (1918–1943); third, the Republic of Lebanon from its independence to the civil war (1943–1975); fourth, the Lebanese civil war (1975–1990); and fifth, the postwar era (1990–present).

When examining each period, it is important to ask what the political unit was and who presided over it. This is because the borders of the political unit shifted over time (until 1920), as did its rulers' identity. There is also a need to identify the major social groups in the political unit in each period. In Greater Lebanon, these included 17–20 officially recognized communities (or sects), though other foci of identity, including large families (or clans), tribes in peripheral areas such as the Biqa', and geographical regions, were also significant, as were socioeconomic categories.[1] Importantly, the size, power, and identity of all these groups were not fixed but changed over time,[2] not least because of intragroup struggles for hegemony on various levels.[3] Finally, in addressing the above-mentioned issues and their interplay, we need to examine not only the state's formal institutions – its political institutions (presidency, cabinet, parliament, etc.), and ostensibly non-political agencies

---

[1] Hudson (1968); Zamir (1997); Barak (2002).
[2] Makdisi (2000); S. Khalaf (2002); Weiss (2010); Cammett (2014).   [3] Barak (2002).

(bureaucracy, security sector, etc.)[4] – but also its informal settlements, practices, and networks.

Before discussing these issues, however, a note on the major scholarly approaches to Lebanon before and after the civil war of 1975–1990 is in order.[5] Of the many works published on Lebanon over the years, some emphasize the periods of instability and conflict whereas others focus on the more stable and tranquil eras. The group of studies that focus on Lebanon's more volatile periods tends to explain the outbreak of these conflicts in one of two ways. Some works underscore the divisions within Lebanese society – primarily among its communities, but also between other groups – and the failed attempts to regulate the conflicts between them since the creation of Greater Lebanon in 1920 and the state's independence in the 1940s.[6] This "internal" approach, however, is challenged by additional studies that point out the destabilizing role of external actors in Lebanon, in particular its close neighbors (the Palestinians, Israel, and Syria) from the late 1960s onwards, but also others (e.g., Iran).[7] Other studies highlight the disruptive role of foreign forces in earlier periods in Lebanon's history, including Egypt under Mehmed Ali, whose army occupied Mount Lebanon in the period 1832–1840; the European powers, which intervened on behalf of their local clients during the Ottoman period;[8] Egypt under President Gamal Abdul Nasser, which was involved in Lebanon in the 1950s and 1960s as part of the struggle for regional hegemony known as the "Arab Cold War";[9] and the United States, which was involved in Lebanon after its independence, culminating in its military intervention there during the civil war of 1958[10] and in its involvement in different stages of the civil war of 1975–1990), and especially in the period 1982–1984.[11] The second body of work on Lebanon focuses on the more tranquil periods in the country's history, before the creation of Greater Lebanon[12] and after the state's independence.[13] To these one can add

---

[4] Lebanon's security sector includes the Lebanese Armed Forces (LAF), the Internal Security Forces (the police and Gendarmerie), the General Directorate of General Security (also known as the *Surete Générale*), and the General Directorate of State Security.

[5] For previous discussions of these approaches, see S. Khalaf (1987, 2002); W. Khalidi (1979); Hourani (1988); Picard (1996).

[6] Junblat (1959); Qubain (1961); Meo (1965); Hudson (1968, 1988); Johnson (1977, 1986, 2001); Azar (1984); Zamir (1985, 1993); H. Barakat (1988); Salibi (1988); Kedourie (1992); Khashan (1992); Abul-Husn (1998).

[7] Chamoun (1963, 1977); Vocke (1978); Shlaim (1988b); Avi-Ran [Erlich] (1991); Deeb and Deeb (1991); Schulze (1998); Seaver (2000); Naor (2014b).

[8] Farah (2000).   [9] Malcolm Kerr (1978). Cf. Kalawoun (2000).

[10] Alin (1994); Gendzier (2006).   [11] Azar (1984).

[12] I. Harik (1968); Akarli (1993); Fawaz (1994).

[13] Salibi (1965); Binder (1966). For criticism, see Hourani (1976, 1988); Hudson (1988).

studies that examine the political settlements that Lebanon's leaders have reached over the years, and especially the National Pact of 1943, discussed below, but also works that deal with the state's formal institutions and informal settlement in other periods. Here, too, some emphasize the role of domestic actors, whereas others maintain that external actors were the most significant.[14] Among the latter, some suggest that outside actors sometimes played a stabilizing role in some of the major crises in Lebanon, including during the civil war of 1975–1990.[15] Finally, a third group of studies on Lebanon posits that periods both of conflict and of peace in Lebanon should be considered when dealing with this state, and that the role of both types of factors, domestic and external, is relevant when trying to fully comprehend it.[16] This book falls within, and seeks to contribute to, this third approach.

The *Mutasarrifiyya*

The period of the *Mutasarrifiyya* is significant when discussing the process of state formation in Lebanon and its inter-connected pattern of inter-communal relations, since it saw the establishment of institutions that ultimately had an impact not only on Mount Lebanon but also on the expanded state – that is, Greater Lebanon and, ultimately, the independent Lebanese state.[17] This period is less important as far as the area of security is concerned, although some see the origins of Lebanon's security sector in it as well.[18]

The first institution introduced in this period was the governor of the autonomous district of Mount Lebanon, who, according to an understanding between the European powers and the Ottoman Empire, was to be a Christian and a Catholic but not a Lebanese and, consequently, also not a Maronite.[19] The appointment of this official laid the ground for Lebanon's presidency, which would become the state's most powerful institution from the creation of this office in 1926 until the Ta'if Agreement of 1989, which transferred some of the president's prerogatives to the prime minister, creating a multi-communal "troika" at the helm. The appointment of a Christian to this post was significant, and would serve as a precedent both before and after Lebanon's informal inter-communal settlement, the National Pact (1943), which held that the president of the republic shall be a Maronite.[20]

---

[14] Salem (1973); Susser (1986); el-Khazen (1991); Zisser (2000).
[15] Sela and Barak (2014).
[16] Shehadi and Mills (1988); Hanf (1993); Picard (1996); Zamir (1997); S. Khalaf (2002).
[17] On the period of the *Mutasarrifiyya*, see Spagnolo (1977); Akarli (1993); Fawaz (1994).
[18] Fawaz (1994, 217); Akarli (1993, 184).   [19] Akarli (1993, 193).
[20] Akarli (1993); Fieldhouse (2006).

The second institution that was established in this period was the administrative council, which assisted the governor of the *Mutasarrifiyya* in running its affairs. Importantly, the council's 12 members represented the 6 major communities in Mount Lebanon: Maronites, Catholics, Orthodox, Sunnis, Shi'is, and Druze. This, too, was an important precedent that would be followed in later periods, when it was decided that both the Lebanese cabinet and the Lebanese parliament should include members of all major communities in the state.[21] As we will see, the same principle was later applied to Lebanon's security sector (the military and other security services).

In sum, the process of state formation in the *Mutasarrifiyya* was closely connected to the relations between the major communities that resided within its purview, which were represented in its political institutions. However, the pattern of inter-communal relations in this period can best be characterized as Christian, especially Maronite, control, reflecting the overwhelming majority of this community in the autonomous district and the backing that it enjoyed from France. Still, other communities besides the Maronites also had a say in the affairs of the new political unit, and this suggests that there were elements of power sharing as well.

What about other dimensions of the process of state formation? In his book on this period, *The Long Peace*, Engin Akarli concludes that on the eve of the First World War, the *Mutasarrifiyya* in Mount Lebanon "appeared to be quite well prepared for independent self-rule." This was because it was equipped with modern state institutions, including "centralized executive, fiscal, and judicial branches, and a centralized security force, as well as municipal administrations serving the towns":

The government operated under constitutional regulations. Court procedure was formalized, and the law was standardized to a considerable extent. The routine of governmental activities was defined by locally enacted regulations on the basis of local experience and conditions. ... The entire system was financed by locally raised revenue and manned by experienced native personnel. Furthermore, competitive electoral politics had acquired a firm place in Lebanese public life, serving as a link between the government and the people. Finally, political consciousness of the distinctness of the Lebanese and Lebanon had become quite widespread among the population, as witnessed by mass demonstrations, popular publications, and the activities of politically oriented cultural societies.[22]

Akrali notes, however, that this political unit was not without its flaws. It was economically vulnerable and was dependent on two outlying regions: the city of Beirut for export and import of goods and transportation, and the Biqa' for food supply. In the eyes of some political leaders in Mount

---

[21] Akarli (1993); Fawaz (1994).   [22] Akarli (1993, 184).

Lebanon, this made the expansion of the *Mutasarrifiyya* to these outlying territories an imperative.[23]

Indeed, as we saw in Chapter 2, it was in this period that a distinct Lebanese identity, especially among the Maronites, began to take shape, although matters of identity within this community were still quite fluid. In retrospect, it took a series of external shocks – the First World War, during which the Ottomans re-occupied Mount Lebanon and severed its ties with Europe; the subsequent defeat and disintegration of the Ottoman Empire; and the occupation of the Levant by the European powers – for this particular identity to coalesce, and for a more concrete national program, whose focus was on the demand for a "place under the sun" in an expanded political unit, to emerge.[24]

French Rule in Lebanon

The second period to be discussed is the period of French rule in Lebanon, and particularly the period of the French Mandate (1922–1943).[25] As we have seen (Chapter 2), the attempt to create a nation-state for the Maronite community in Mount Lebanon by expanding the borders of the former *Mutasarrifiyya* to include the adjacent territories gave rise instead to a divided society where no single community, including the Maronites themselves, could claim an absolute majority. In addition, all attempts to bring about the state's contraction in later years were unsuccessful.[26] These events had major implications for Lebanon's state formation process, for the relations between its communities, and ultimately also for the area of security. Indeed, it can be argued that since 1920, the major challenge facing Lebanon has been to build a state while satisfying the political, social, and economic needs of 17 to 20 communities (or sects), countless large families and tribes, and several geographic regions.

In addition to delineating the borders of the new political unit and providing it with a flag, a currency, a national museum, and other symbols of statehood,[27] the process of state formation in Lebanon during the period of the French Mandate saw important steps that, again, were inexorably tied to the relationship between its various communities. In 1926, the Lebanese Constitution was adopted after a process in which members of the country's political elite and French officials participated.[28] The new

---

[23] Ibid.   [24] Cf. Zamir (1985); Hakim (2013).
[25] On the period of French rule in Lebanon, see Longrigg (1958); Salibi (1965); Zamir (1985, 1997); Maktani (1999); Thompson (1999); Firro (2002); Kaufman (2004); Fieldhouse (2006).
[26] Zamir (1982, 1985).   [27] Kaufman (2004).
[28] Baaklini (1976); Chalouhi (1978); Zamir (1985, 1997).

constitution established Lebanon as a parliamentary republic, albeit still under French rule. Importantly, Article 95 stated, "As a transitory measure and for the sake of even justice and concord, the communities [in Lebanon] shall be equally represented in public posts and in ministerial composition, without damage to State interest resulting therefrom."[29] In this way, the principle of communal representation in the state's institutions, which, as we have seen, had initially been adopted in the period of the *Mutasarrifiyya*, was formalized, and was, moreover, linked to the need for justice and concord among the state's communities. Although this measure was defined as "transitory," no timetable was set for its abrogation. This, too, was an important precedent that would be followed in future settlements, including the National Pact of 1943 and the Ta'if Agreement of 1989, discussed later in this chapter.

Two additional steps that were taken in the political realm in Lebanon in this period also sought to institutionalize the principle of communal representation in the state's institutions. First, Lebanon's electoral laws (beginning in 1922) reaffirmed the need for proportional representation for all of Lebanon's communities and implemented this principle with regard to its parliament.[30] Second, the Franco–Lebanese treaty of 1936 – and particularly annexes 6 and 6 bis, which became a codename for Lebanon's political settlement – guaranteed the fair representation of all communities in the government and in the administration.[31]

We see, then, that although in this period executive power in Lebanon rested in the hands of the French High Commissioner, and although Christians, and especially Maronites, were the dominant community in Lebanon, a fact that indicates a pattern of inter-communal control, the foundations were also laid for power sharing between Lebanon's communities. Another important development that took place in Lebanon in this period was the emergence of an elite composed of bankers, lawyers, landowners, and entrepreneurs, many of whom were also the leaders of large families and geographical regions, as the most important political and socioeconomic actor in the state. These leaders, who at that time were mostly Christians, not only participated in drafting the Lebanese Constitution in 1926, but also filled most positions in the state's political institutions. In addition, some elite members, together with other actors, played an active role in promoting a distinct Lebanese identity.[32]

In Lebanon's Muslim communities during this period, the leaders – in particular Sunnis, who had rejected the creation of Greater Lebanon and

[29] Lebanese Constitution (1960, 33).   [30] Marayati (1968); Hanf (1993); Zamir (1997).
[31] Salibi (1965); Browne (1976/7); Zamir (1997).
[32] Shehadi (1987); Zamir (1997); Kaufman (2004).

boycotted its political institutions – came to realize that it was in their interest to participate in the Lebanese political system and join the aforementioned elite, which, for its part, was ready to accept them. Thus, already in 1926, only six years after the state's expansion, a Sunni politician defied the Muslim boycott on its institutions and agreed to serve as Speaker of Parliament. In 1937, another member of this community, Khayr al-Din al-Ahdab, a journalist from Tripoli who held Arab nationalist views, became Lebanon's first Muslim prime minister. Lebanese historian Kamal Salibi later wrote that when Ahdab's fellow Arab nationalists attacked him for accepting the post, he replied: "Should the Arabs one day decide to unite, it would not be my presence in the Serail [the government building in Beirut] that would stop them from doing so."[33]

In terms of security, the rule of the French colonial power in the Levant, contrary to their expectations, encountered much resistance. To cope with this challenge, the French recruited soldiers from various social groups in the Levant in different periods according to its policy there and the challenges facing it. Thus, for example, Maronites were given preference over members of other Christian communities and villagers were favored over city-dwellers, and when national unrest among members of the Sunni community in the Levant increased, their influence in the local military units, the *Troupes Spéciales*, diminished, and Christian influence there increased.[34] It is thus not surprising that in the period of the French Mandate in Lebanon, Christians, especially Maronites, were dominant in the security agencies.

The higher number of Christians who served in the *Troupes Spéciales*, and the fact that in August 1945, when these forces were handed over to the governments of the independent states of Syria and Lebanon, they were separated into Lebanese units with a Christian majority and Syrian units with a Muslim majority, led to a situation where mainly Christian, and to a lesser extent Druze, officers served in the nascent LAF. Indeed, data on the composition of the Lebanese military units at the time of their transfer to the national government shows that 57.8 percent of their members were Christians, compared to 38.9 percent Muslims.[35] The disparities among the Lebanese officers were even more pronounced: About three-quarters (71.8 percent) of the LAF's officer corps before 1945 were Christians, and close to half (47.6 percent) were Maronites. The Druze element in the officer corps was also significant (14.6 percent), whereas the total share of Shi'is and Sunnis was relatively low (11.7 percent).[36]

---

[33] Salibi (1988, 183). See also Firro (2002).   [34] Bou-Nacklie (1993, 1994).
[35] Rihana (1984–1988, 1: 175). This figure does not include Alawites.
[36] Barak (2006, 2009a).

But this was not the only significant development in the area of security in this period. At the same time that Lebanon's state institutions and pattern of inter-communal relations were beginning to crystallize, especially on the elite level, other political actors were making their debut. These included a number of parties-militias – that is, organized groups that not only engaged in politics, but also presided over paramilitary units that were autonomous from the state and its security sector. The major parties-militias formed in Lebanon in this period included, first and foremost, the Lebanese Phalanges, a Maronite-led organization whose members were determined to defend the Lebanese state and promote its Christian character. Other parties-militias were the Sunni al-Najaddah, which advocated a pan-Arab platform; the Syrian Social Nationalist Party (SSNP), which propagated the creation of its own expanded state, Greater Syria, and objected to the creation of "separate" political units such as Lebanon and Syria in its place (it would later launch two unsuccessful coup attempts in Lebanon, in 1949 and in 1961); and the Lebanese Communist Party. These parties-militias, which were inspired by and sometimes modeled on the Fascist and Communist movements in Europe in the 1930s, also reflected local interests and identities. In periods of crisis, these violent non-state actors mobilized their members, defended their turf, and sometimes clashed with one another. However, when the time came for a political settlement, they drew on their military power to secure their share in the government.[37]

In a book published during the Lebanese civil war of 1975–1990, Karim Pakradouni, a prominent member of the Phalanges Party who would lead it for several years in the early twenty-first century, described the circumstances surrounding its formation as follows:

The genius of Pierre Gemayel [the founder and first leader of the Phalanges Party] was that he realized the need to establish the Phalanges as a military force that would support the state and serve as its reserve. So long as the formal institutions were capable to defend national independence and the Christian existence [in Lebanon], the Phalanges remained a party that supported it. But when the state collapsed, the Phalanges, which were a strategic reserve force, immediately took its place, even if temporarily. The Phalanges have always been more than a party and less than a state.[38]

In the coming decades, these parties-militias would accompany Lebanon's process of state formation, occasionally stepping in when their leaders felt that the state was weak, hesitant, or not moving in the "right" direction, at

---
[37] Yamak (1966); Suleiman (1967); Entelis (1974); Stoakes (1975).
[38] Baqraduni [Pakradouni] (1984, 112).

least as they saw it, and in the process posing a challenge to the state's claim for a monopoly of legitimate physical force.[39]

From Independence to the Civil War

On November 22, 1943, following a crisis with the French colonial power, Lebanon became an independent state, though a couple of more years would pass before the last French soldier would leave its territory.[40] On the eve of independence, several of Lebanon's leaders, including primarily Maronites and Sunnis but also members of other communities, reached, through regional and international mediation, an informal political settlement called the National Pact. In retrospect, this was the single most important inter-communal political settlement in Lebanon's history.

The National Pact comprised two main parts. First, it was an inter-communal compromise regarding the national identity and foreign policy of the nascent state. Lebanon was defined as having an "Arab face" – that is, a form of Arab identity, but not as a full-fledged Arab state. It was agreed, moreover, that the new state's foreign policy would abide by the principle of "Neither East nor West" – i.e., that Lebanon would not enter into an alliance with the Western powers, like the one propagated by France in 1936, and at the same time will not join a union with the Arab hinterland, as some political factions in Lebanon had advocated. This compromise reflected the recognition among members of Lebanon's two prominent communities, the Maronites and the Sunnis, that the once-illegitimate Greater Lebanon was by now irrevocable – namely, that the state's contraction along communal lines or, alternately, its integration into an Arab union, was not only difficult to achieve but also undesirable.[41] Consequently, Lebanon became one of the founding members of the Arab League in 1945, demonstrating its political and cultural alignment with the Arab states. However, this was only after Lebanon's leaders had ensured that the new all-Arab organization would reinforce the sovereignty of its member states and would not become a vehicle for Arab unity.[42] Importantly, Lebanon's independence was acknowledged by Syria, Lebanon's close neighbor, although some Syrian leaders, as well as certain Lebanese factions (most notably the SSNP), continued to argue that "historically, Syria and Lebanon have

---

[39] Weber (2003, 131).
[40] On the period 1943–1975 in Lebanon, see Salibi (1965); Meo (1965); Hudson (1968); Binder (1966); Baaklini (1976); Goria (1985); S. Khalaf (1987); Hanf (1993); Attié (2003).
[41] See Al-Sulh (1943); Khuri (1960).   [42] Porath (1986); Sela (1998); Barnett (1998).

been one country and one people."[43] Indeed, it would take more than six decades before Syria would establish diplomatic ties with Lebanon.[44]

The second part of the National Pact was a power-sharing settlement between Lebanon's major communities, which provided each of them with proportional representation in all of the state's institutions. Accordingly, the three highest offices of the state – the President, the Prime Minister, and the Speaker of Parliament – were to be held by a Maronite, a Sunni, and a Shi'i, respectively. Furthermore, a 6:5 ratio between Christians and Muslims, as well as proportional representation of all major communities, was to be observed in all branches of the government, including the political institutions, the public administration, and the security sector (see Tables 3.1, 3.2, and 3.3). Despite the fact that this second part of the National Pact was not publicly announced, time has shown that it was no less binding than its first part.[45]

In sum, the National Pact managed to garner domestic and external support for Lebanon's independence, and, ultimately, for the state's expansion, albeit not unconditionally. At the same time, the political settlement reached between Lebanon's leaders created a strong link

Table 3.1 *Communal allocation of seats in the Lebanese Parliament before/after Ta'if (1989)*

Religion and community	Before Ta'if	After Ta'if
Maronites	30	34
Greek Orthodox	11	14
Greek Catholics	6	8
Armenian Orthodox	4	5
Armenian Catholics	1	1
Protestants	1	1
Other Christians	1	1
Total Christians	54	64
Sunnis	20	27
Shi'is	19	27
Alawites	0	2
Druze	6	8
Total Muslims	45	64
Total	99	128

Source: el-Khazen (1994, 17)

[43] Syrian President Hafez al-Assad quoted in Avi-Ran [Erlich] (1991, 6).
[44] This was done in 2008. See *New York Times* (2008).
[45] Salibi (1965); Gaunsen (1987).

Table 3.2 *Regional allocation of seats in the Lebanese Parliament before/after Ta'if (1989)*

Region	Before Ta'if	After Ta'if
Beirut	16 (16.2%)	19 (14.8%)
Biqa'	15 (15.2%)	23 (17.97%)
Mount Lebanon	30 (30.3%)	35 (27.3%)
North Lebanon	20 (20.2%)	28 (21.9%)
South Lebanon	18 (18.2%)	23 (17.97%)
Total	99	128

Source: el-Khazen (1994, 17)

Table 3.3 *Social background of LAF officers by religion and community*

Period/Religion and community	1945–1958	1958–1975	1975–1990	1990–2004
Total Christians	65.5	54.9	51	48
Maronite	43.8	34.8	32.2	30.3
Catholic	11.9	9.9	9.4	7.5
Orthodox	8.1	8.7	7.7	8.7
Armenian	1.7	1.5	1.7	1.5
Jewish	0.6	0	0	0
Total Muslims	34	45.1	49	51.9
Sunni	14.8	15.3	16.9	16.1
Shi'i	9.3	15.3	20.9	26.8
Druze	9.9	14.5	11.2	9

Source: Barak (2006)

among the process of state formation in Lebanon, its pattern of intercommunal relations, and the area of security, a connection that would be maintained for decades to come. Indeed, rather than attempting to build and construct a state that would be autonomous from its various communities, Lebanon's political, bureaucratic, and security institutions were to be shared by members of these groups, and the over-arching national identity propagated by the state was to coexist with, rather than supplant, their particular identities.

In the next three decades, and apart from several political crises – especially the Constitutional Crisis that led to the resignation of President Bechara al-Khoury in 1952, the first civil war of 1958, and the crises between Lebanon and the Palestinian armed factions in 1968–1969 and in 1973 (see Chapter 6) – Lebanon enjoyed relative political stability and economic prosperity. This seemed especially true when compared to its Arab neighbors, specifically Syria, which, until the early 1970s, when President Hafez al-Assad came to power, witnessed long periods of domestic upheaval and foreign involvement.[46] However, by the mid-1970s, intercommunal relations in Lebanon, the process of state formation, and the area of security faced a potent mix of domestic and external strains, which ultimately led to the outbreak of the civil war of 1975–1990 and to the state's "failure."[47] Let us consider some of these factors and their cumulative impact.

First, notwithstanding the stipulations of the National Pact from 1943, political power in Lebanon was not shared equally by members of all of its communities. The Christians, and especially the Maronites, dominated the state's political, bureaucratic, and security institutions before 1975. This state of affairs persisted despite changing political and socio-political realities in Lebanon, especially the steady rise in the number of Muslims relative to the number of Christians. Toward the mid-1970s, the "immobilism" of Lebanon's political system caused resentment among many Muslims (including some Sunnis and Shi'is), Druze, and some Christians (especially non-Maronites), who began to see the pattern of inter-communal relations in Lebanon not as power sharing but as control. Since, as mentioned earlier, inter-communal relations in Lebanon were closely tied to the process of state formation, this political resentment was eventually manifested in these actors' criticism of the state.

A second problem, which was related to the first, is that Lebanon's political and socioeconomic elite refused to open its ranks to new actors, from all communities, who demanded an equitable share in political power.[48] Indeed, instead of accommodating these "newcomers" in the same manner that Lebanon's Muslims, especially Sunnis, had been integrated into the political institutions after the state's expansion, the country's leaders – including Maronites but also their allies, the Sunni political bosses (*zu'ama'*) – resorted to unlawful practices, and even violence, in order to retain power exclusively.[49] Thus, in the civil wars of 1958 and of 1975–1990, some of these leaders – such as Camille Chamoun (Maronite), who in the first conflict was Lebanon's president and in the second conflict was also a prominent political leader – tried to neutralize their political opponents, and even called on outside forces to intervene

---

[46] Seale (1965); Rabinovich (1972); Kerr (1978); Van Dam (1979). [47] Barak (2003).
[48] S. Khalaf (1977); Chalouhi (1978); Ajami (1986); Norton (1987).
[49] S. Khalaf (1977); Johnson (1977, 1986, 2001).

on their behalf. The result was, however, that by the mid-1970s, the strategies that these elite members had employed against these newcomers began to be emulated by the latter, who, in their turn, became convinced that violence was the only way to receive their due share in the state.

But the intertwined process of state formation in Lebanon also encountered difficulties. Members of Lebanon's political and socioeconomic elite, from all communities, were apprehensive of the state, and they put their best effort into curtailing its coercive and disciplinary powers. A noted example of this attitude can be found in the writings of Michel Chiha, a wealthy banker and man of letters who is considered the mastermind of Lebanon's political system. Chiha's writings reveal a strong antagonism and distaste for the state, which he regarded as tyrannical:

> It is well known that foreigners visiting us think that we are a land blessed by the gods. *They see peace and plenty here, whereas we import almost everything and we export practically nothing, which seems a sort of miracle.* Work is more easily done ... here than elsewhere, because the state has not yet got to the stage at which, in the name of would-be economic principles and rigid, harassing social theories, *the public authorities make it impossible to breathe.* Excess in this matter must be abolished forever.[50]

Other aspects of the process of state formation in Lebanon, including national integration, also faced obstacles. The autonomy enjoyed by each community in Lebanon allowed its members to operate their own private schools alongside the government-run educational institutions. The outcome of this state of affairs, as described by one study, is that "[i]n one school, children learn that Lebanese are Phoenicians, in another that they are Arabs. In one school, the ties with the West are stressed, in another ties with the Arab east are emphasized."[51]

In sum, Lebanon's leaders embraced the principle of inter-communal power sharing, but they did not subordinate their particular interests to those of the state, and, to make things worse, they had little respect for democratic norms and practices.[52] In addition, the authority of the state was conditional on these leaders' acceptance, and its political institutions could hardly serve as neutral arbitrators aloof from inter-communal rivalries. This lack of autonomy of the state in Lebanon was particularly acute because the political settlement reached between its leaders in 1943, rather than putting an end to all tensions in its society, sometimes replaced inter-communal rivalries with intra-communal struggles for power, including at the regional level. Since the state was not considered

---

[50] Chiha (1966, 116–117). Emphasis is in the original. [51] Jabra and Jabra (1984).
[52] See, especially, Hudson (1968, 1988); Randal (1983); Johnson (1977, 1986).

a legitimate arbiter, the only solution to such tensions, particularly during elections, was to let these actors manage on their own.[53]

But on the external level, too, Lebanon's process of state formation failed to make significant headway. The state's leaders believed that "Lebanon's strength lies in its weakness"[54] – namely, that it should avoid militarization at all costs and thus keep away from external conflicts. In the wake of the First Arab–Israeli War – in which Lebanon participated, albeit in a limited way, along with the Arab states (see Introduction) – the country's leaders decided that they would remain aloof from regional conflicts, especially the Arab–Israeli conflict but also inter-Arab disputes.[55] Consequently, Lebanon was not obliged, as its neighbors were, to invest significant resources in its security sector. However, this policy had several drawbacks. First, although Lebanon did not get embroiled in external conflicts after 1949, this did not mean that other states and violent non-state actors from the Middle East and beyond did not interfere in its affairs, such as during the civil war of 1958, which became a focal point for regional and international actors.[56] Second, the Lebanese state, which sought to avoid conflict externally, found it difficult to assert its authority within its own territory, where, as mentioned earlier, a host of parties-militias could operate quite freely even before the state's "failure" in the period 1975–1976.[57]

The process of state formation in Lebanon, in other words, engendered a weak state, particularly as far as its coercive and disciplinary capacities were concerned. At the same time, the state did enjoy legitimacy in the eyes of many of its citizens, particularly members of its political and socioeconomic elite, but also those who aspired to join its ranks. This was mainly on account of the power-sharing settlement, which provided representation not only for Lebanon's communities, but also for other social actors such as large families (or clans) and geographical regions. What the state in Lebanon found it difficult to do, and more often than not avoided, was to construct itself as an autonomous actor vis-à-vis society, and to promote a common national identity among its citizens, although it seems that many in Lebanon did identify with the state.

These basic characteristics of Lebanon's process of state formation and pattern of inter-communal relations in this period were reflected in – and were also reinforced by – the area of security. Lebanon's leaders, who, as we have seen, were highly suspicious of the state, sought to ensure that its coercive agencies would remain small and weak and that they would not

---

[53] For details, see Barak (2002, 2003).   [54] Gemayel (1985).   [55] Malcolm Kerr (1978).
[56] On the Lebanese civil war of 1958, see Junblat (1959); Qubain (1961); Chamoun (1963); Meo (1965); Hudson (1968); Alin (1994); Little (1996); S. Khalaf (2002).
[57] Suleiman (1967); Stoakes (1975).

become a tool that could be used against them. Accordingly, these leaders consistently refrained from providing the Lebanese Armed Forces (LAF) and the other security agencies with the means to suppress them.[58] This basic distrust, and even fear, of the state and its coercive power also prevailed in other parts of Lebanese society: for example, some groups were opposed to building military bases near their villages out of fear of the soldiers' behavior.[59] Although the strict limits imposed on Lebanon's security sector were beneficial from an economic perspective, since they did not require levying more taxes that could jeopardize Lebanon's free market economy,[60] they also had significant drawbacks, not least of which was the weakness of the state's coercive institutions in relation to violent non-state actors, local and foreign, before 1975.

Lebanon's main security agency, the LAF, illustrates this conundrum. Since its establishment in 1945, this institution was kept weak and small so that it could not pose a threat to Lebanon's political institutions or to its various communities.[61] At the same time, the fact that the LAF Commander and Lebanon's president were both Maronites ensured that members of this community would dominate this institution, and in the first decades after Lebanon's independence they also presided over its other security agencies. Although other security officials were sometimes members of other communities – the defense minister, for example, was in many cases a Druze – their say in security matters was minimal.

Despite their weakness, however, the state's security agencies, and especially the LAF, did make considerable efforts to foster a national – that is, a supra-communal – identity among their own personnel, making use of their official bulletins as well as a host of other means such as ceremonies, parades, speeches, radio programs, and historical narratives produced and disseminated to their own members and to society at large. However, the fact that Lebanon did not introduce compulsory military service throughout this period and imposed strict limitations on the size of its security agencies meant that the national integration efforts of these institutions were, necessarily, limited.[62]

With regard to the composition of these agencies in this period, the LAF's officer corps was highly imbalanced, and the ratio of Christians to Muslims was 65.5 percent to 34 percent, with 43.8 percent of the officers being Maronites (Table 3.3). Moreover, the identity and actual operations of the LAF still reflected its transformation from an auxiliary force of

[58] Hudson (1968, 3–13, 1988); Hurewitz (1969, 392); Nordlinger (1972, 26–27); Johnson (1986, 100); Hourani (1988).
[59] Rihana (1996, 48). [60] Hurewitz (1969, 392); Shehadi (1987, 29).
[61] Lahoud (1976); Frieha (1980); McLaurin (1984); Aoun (1988); Barak (2009a).
[62] These efforts are discussed in Barak (2001, 2009a). See also Podeh (2011, 207–254).

the French colonial power to a national army. However, the weakness of Lebanon's political system, on the one hand, and the relative cohesion of the LAF, on the other hand, did allow this institution to serve as a mediator between disgruntled sectors in the periphery – that is, in the areas that had been annexed to Mount Lebanon, particularly in the Biqa', – and the government in Beirut, and, occasionally, to use limited force against the former and exert pressure on the latter. In addition, the LAF served as an arbiter between rival political factions, especially during the political crisis of 1952 and, to an extent, in the civil war of 1958.[63] And finally, the LAF controlled the Israeli–Lebanese border area and administrated it quite effectively, at least until 1967 (see Chapter 6).

In the wake of the conflict in 1958, which brought to the fore the grievances of Lebanon's non-Christians, and especially Sunnis and Druze), limited reforms were introduced in the LAF as part of the general reforms in the state. These included the appointment of a Druze officer as chief of staff (previously this position was held by a Catholic), but not as the LAF Commander, a post reserved for Maronites. In addition, the LAF's officer corps became more communally (and, to an extent, also regionally) balanced: The ratio of Christian and Muslim officers was now 54.9 percent to 45.1 percent, with Maronites dropping to 34.8 percent (Table 3.3). However, these reforms still lagged behind political developments in Lebanon because the National Pact had already applied a 6:5 ratio of Christians to Muslims to the political system and the bureaucracy (Tables 3.1 and 3.2).[64]

Until the mid-1960s, when Lebanon's foreign policy conformed to that of other Arab states, the LAF enjoyed a broad consensus domestically and externally. But following the Israeli–Arab War in 1967, the LAF's identity and operations became controversial. Part of the reason for this was the attempt made by a security network composed of officers in the LAF's intelligence branch, the *Deuxième Bureau*, and their civilian partners to dominate politics under President (and former LAF Commander) Fouad Chehab (1958–1964) and his successor, Charles Helou (1964–1970). In this way, these officials sought to bypass Lebanon's traditional leaders and to modernize the state. Another factor that undermined the LAF's legitimacy, especially after the 1967 War, was its inability to, on the one hand, restrain the Palestinian armed factions in Lebanon and, on the other hand, repel Israel's military raids against Lebanon's territory, which became more and more destructive (see Chapter 6). The result was that LAF was criticized not only for its political involvement and for its military weakness, but also for the predominance of the Christians,

[63] Barak (2006, 2009a). See, e.g., Chamoun (1955).   [64] Barak (2006, 2009a).

especially the Maronites, within its ranks.[65] The demands for more equitable power sharing in Lebanon's security sector were rejected by the state's leaders, in particular by the Christians, who dominated the security agencies. This added to the opposition's determination to bring about a profound change in Lebanon, including in the area of security.

In sum, during this period Lebanon's leaders coped with the triangular relationship between the state, community, and security in Lebanon by building a weak state in terms of its coercive capacities; installing inter-communal power sharing primarily with the Maronites (and the Christian communities in general) as primus inter pares; and de-militarization in the area of security, including in the security sector. But by the end of this period these various elements worked to Lebanon's detriment. The inter-communal settlement could not be reformed, and mounting social and political grievances, which could not be alleviated by the state's weak institutions, led to the emergence of new political actors, especially in the periphery, that challenged the status quo. The attempt to shun these newcomers, including by the use of violence, led to militarization and to the sectarianization of the political struggle on both sides in order to rally public support. Lebanon's small and weak security sector, and especially the LAF, which had defused several political crises in the early decades of statehood, could not serve as an effective and legitimate conflict-regulation mechanism because it was now part of the problem. Thus, it could not intervene without leading to its own paralysis. To make things worse, external actors, who in 1943 supported the political settlement in Lebanon, now lent their political and military support to the more intransigent domestic actors, and this, too, had a destabilizing effect on the state, on the pattern of inter-communal relations, and on the area of security.

The Civil War

The basic problems of Lebanon's triangular relationship between the state, community, and security reached their apex with the outbreak of the civil war in April 1975 and the state's subsequent "failure."[66] According to figures published in 1992 by the Lebanese government, 144,240 persons perished in the period 1975–1990 and an additional

[65] Barak (2006, 2009a).
[66] On the Lebanese civil war of 1975–1990, see Owen (1976); Salibi (1976, 1988); Haley and Snider (1979); W. Khalidi (1979); Deeb (1980); D. Gordon (1983); Randal (1983); Azar (1984); Rabinovich (1985); S. Khalaf (1987, 2002); H. Barakat (1988); Shehadi and Mills (1988); Hanf (1993); Picard (1996); Harris (1997); el-Khazen (2000); Barak (2003).

197,506 were wounded. A further 17,000 were deemed to be missing.[67] In addition, about 790,000 Lebanese had to leave their homes, many of them more than once, and damage to property reached an estimated $25 billion.[68] Close to a third of Lebanon's pre-war population of 3.1 million left the country, including an estimated 200,000 professionals.[69] In view of the fact that pre-war Lebanon had been a regional hub for banking and trade, as well as a popular tourist destination, the damage to Lebanon's economy as a result of the conflict was far more significant.

Some students of Lebanon, but also proponents of power-sharing settlements in divided societies, posited that the Lebanese civil war stemmed primarily from external factors,[70] and some Lebanese leaders even spoke of a "war of others" that was being waged on its soil.[71] It is worth noting, however, that, as in previous periods in Lebanon's history, although outside involvement was significant in the conflict, it was not entirely disruptive and had some constructive elements.[72] Moreover, despite Lebanon's weakness, none of the foreign forces that intervened in the conflict managed to establish "special relations"– i.e., a form of hegemony – with it, and all them were compelled to leave its territory unconditionally. Other students of Lebanon have suggested that the underlying causes of the conflict were domestic, pointing out the political and socioeconomic grievances of deprived groups, whose members were overwhelmingly Muslim but included some Christians (especially non-Maronites).[73] As the conflict lingered, many observers noted the deep cultural and ideological fissures in Lebanese society.[74]

The state and its institutions in Lebanon, its pattern of inter-communal relations, and the area of security were inevitably affected by the long and devastating conflict. During its first phase, which became known as the "two years' war" (1975–1976), the state's political, bureaucratic, and security institutions became paralyzed, though none of them disintegrated completely. The political and security vacuum created in Lebanon was filled, at least in part, by new and veteran parties-militias, which took over large swaths of the country, as well as by foreign forces, including the Palestinian armed factions whose members had turned Lebanon into their base, and later by the Syrian and Israeli armies and other foreign forces.

---

[67] *Al-Hayat* (London), March 10, 1992.   [68] Hanf (1993, 342–347).
[69] Labaki (1992, 610).
[70] Lijphart (1984: 40); Buheiry (1987); Cooke (1988); Corm (1988); McGarry and O'Leary (1993, 36); el-Khazen (2000); Seaver (2000).
[71] Barak (2007a, 53).
[72] One can mention the inter-Arab summits in 1976 and the international mediation that facilitated the Ta'if Agreement of 1989, but also other examples. See Sela and Barak (2014).
[73] S. Khalaf (1987); Hanf (1993).   [74] Cf. Salibi (1976, 1988). See also Hourani (1976).

At certain points during the conflict, it appeared that Lebanon would be partitioned and that power sharing between its various communities would not be restored.[75] But these scenarios did not materialize. The state continued to operate, even in a diminished form, and its bureaucratic and security institutions kept in touch with their employees, continued to pay their salaries and, equally important, fostered the idea of the state among their members and the general public.[76] Part of the reason for this outcome was that many Lebanese found their state, no matter how weak and inefficient, to be more appealing than Lebanon's parties-militias, whose members erected roadblocks where they harassed and killed innocents for belonging to the "wrong" community and engaged in extortion and smuggling. These citizens also preferred the state to the various foreign forces that intervened in Lebanon – including states and violent transnational non-state actors – and which tried to exploit its weakness to impose "special relations" on it. Thus, and in the absence of viable and legitimate alternatives to the state, many Lebanese, from all communities, were inclined to support the state, even when it could not successfully claim a monopoly over the legitimate means of violence. Indeed, during the conflict there were almost no attempts to break away from the state and to create new political entities in its place, with the only exception being the "Free Lebanon State" established by Major Saad Haddad, head of the Christian militia in South Lebanon and an ally of Israel (see Chapters 6 and 7). On the contrary, most local actors, as well as many foreign players, sought to preserve Lebanon in its present boundaries, and to be branded an "isolationist" (*in'izali*) was considered to be an insult in Lebanon's political discourse.[77]

In an article from 2006, Iliya Harik criticized the US-based Freedom House Index for categorizing Lebanon as "partially free" (i.e., partially democratic) during the civil war of 1975–1990, when "chaos and violence were the rule of the day ... and formal government was all but a shadow of its former self."[78] But what Harik and many other observers of Lebanon seemed to miss – and Freedom House to capture – was the continued,

---

[75] Kliot (1986); Kedourie (1992).
[76] This message was constantly communicated by the LAF's bulletins, *al-Jundi al-Lubnani* and *al-Jaysh*, in this period. See the discussion in Barak (2009a). It was also conveyed by LAF officers to their subordinates. Personal interview with retired LAF officer, October 2009.
[77] Azar and Haddad (1986); Hanf (1993).
[78] I. Harik (2006, 669). According to Freedom House (2015), Lebanon was "free" (democratic) before the conflict and "partially free" (partially democratic) in the period 1975–1986. It was categorized as "not free" (non-democratic) in the period 1987–1990. In the period 1991–1994, it was again categorized as "partially free," in the period 1995–2004 it was categorized as "not free," but since 2005 it has been categorized as "partially free."

albeit partial, operation of at least some of the state's institutions in Lebanon in this volatile period. These included political institutions such as the presidency, the cabinet, and parliament, whose members met several times during the conflict, elected five presidents, debated and approved important laws, and ratified (and sometimes also annulled) agreements and treaties, including the May 17, 1983, agreement with Israel and, most notably, the Ta'if Agreement, the document of political reforms that paved the way for the termination of the Lebanese conflict.

With regard to Lebanon's pattern of inter-communal relations, although members of all major communities in Lebanon participated in the conflict, not one of them was able to impose a pattern of control over the others. Attempts to achieve dominance through repression (e.g., in the period 1982–1984) also failed (see Chapter 7). In fact, most plans for political reform in Lebanon that were discussed throughout the conflict by the country's leaders and external mediators sought to re-establish inter-communal power sharing. In addition, political and security officials tried to extend this settlement into the area of security, which became even more critical during the conflict. However, the failure of all reform plans in Lebanon before 1989 and the coercive power accumulated by the country's parties-militias, which established their own informal "cantons" in parts of the country, meant that the prevailing pattern of inter-communal relations in this period can best be described as a stalemate.

The area of security in Lebanon, and especially its security sector, mirrored, but also helped reinforce these developments. As far as the LAF, Lebanon's major security agency, was concerned, in the initial phase of the conflict both the civilian and military bodies controlling this institution were predominately Christian, and its officer corps was under Christian, and particularly Maronite, hegemony. In addition, the identity and actual operations of the LAF became contested, especially when its units were mobilized against the Muslim-dominated opposition and its allies, the Palestinian armed factions. It was even accused of being a "Christian army" due to the support it extended to the Maronite-led parties-militias. The results of these grievances were, on the one hand, the first revolt in the LAF's history and, on the other hand, the first coup attempt by a senior army officer who claimed to be acting to preserve the LAF's unity (interestingly, both officers were Sunnis). Consequently, many Lebanese soldiers defected and some LAF units became paralyzed (but only few disintegrated completely).[79]

---

[79] For details, see Lahoud (1976); McLaurin (1984); Kechichian (1985); Barak (2006, 2009a).

However, instead of giving up on the LAF, the Lebanese government attempted to reinvigorate it time and again as part of the efforts to reconstruct the state. Thus, in the second phase of the conflict (1977–1982), the government launched the first attempt to reform the LAF, which included introducing power sharing in its command and in the controlling civilian bodies and establishing Christian–Muslim parity in its officer corps. However, the identity and actual operations of the LAF remained disputed, and the lack of parallel reforms in the political system that could reinstate inter-communal power sharing impinged on the success of these reforms. The regional climate, too, was still unfavorable, and the inability of the LAF to deploy in South Lebanon in the period 1977–1978 (discussed in Chapter 7) was also obstructive.[80] A second attempt to reconstruct the LAF was launched following Israel's invasion of Lebanon in 1982 (see Chapter 7) and the subsequent US involvement. However, in this period the main emphasis was on establishing the LAF's coercive capacities, and although the officer corps remained communally balanced, power sharing in security matters was suspended. This alienated members of Lebanon's Druze and Shi'i communities, especially when the LAF, with US support, entered their regions and fought against their parties-militias – the Progressive Socialist Party (PSP) and the Amal Movement, respectively – leading to mass desertions from the LAF's ranks.[81] Following a fourth phase in the Lebanese conflict (1984–1987), in which attempts to reach a political settlement failed and controversy regarding the area of security and the security sector persisted, several high-ranking officers in the LAF, mostly Christians, led by the commander of the LAF, General Michel Aoun (Maronite), sought to employ the military to "solve" Lebanon's predicament.[82] But although in this period the officer corps and commanding bodies of the LAF were communally balanced, Aoun's program found little support among Lebanon's Muslims, and it also alienated Syria, the main external actor involved in Lebanon in this period. The result was that the inter-communal fissures that already existed within the LAF deepened in the period 1988–1990 and it virtually split into two parts. But even then the LAF, like the Lebanese state itself, did not disintegrate.[83]

In sum, although the area of security in Lebanon in the period of the civil war of 1975–1990 was part of, and also reflected, the volatile situation in the state and the lack of inter-communal agreement, the security sector and its agencies did not disintegrate, and repeated attempts were

---

[80] McLaurin (1984); Kechichian (1985); Barak (2006, 2009a).   [81] Barak (2009a).
[82] Aoun (1988). See also Hoss (1991); Barak (2009a).
[83] McLaurin (1991); Barak (2006, 2009a).

made to reconstruct them, in particular the LAF, as part of the general effort to revitalize the state and reach a new inter-communal settlement. Importantly, the focus on these reforms, particularly in the period 1977–1982, was not only on increasing the LAF's coercive capacities but also on introducing inter-communal power-sharing mechanisms that would make this institution more legitimate in the eyes of all of Lebanon's communities. The success of these attempts is attested to not only by the continued existence of Lebanon's security agencies, and especially the LAF, even in a diminished form, throughout the conflict, but also by the facts that the security sector adopted inter-communal power-sharing mechanisms and the LAF's officer corps achieved Christian–Muslim parity even as the violence raged in the country (see Table 3.3). Moreover, the reforms introduced in the area of security in Lebanon facilitated the political reforms that were later included in the Ta'if Agreement, reforms that were impossible to achieve so long that Lebanon's security sector was dominated by one community.[84]

As mentioned earlier, the main contenders of Lebanon's security sector in this period were the country's militias, or, more accurately, parties-militias, whose power reached its apex during the conflict.[85] Some of these actors were not new: they were political parties that had mobilized their armed members in previous political crises such as the civil war of 1958 but also others. However, even veteran actors sometimes gave rise to new ones. Thus, for example, the Lebanese Forces, commanded by Bashir Gemayel, son of Pierre Gemayel, leader of the Phalanges Party, initially served as the latter's militia but later became an actor in its own right – that is, a party-militia. However, other parties-militias, and especially the Amal Movement and Hizbullah (both Shi'i), were new actors that asserted themselves by mobilizing members of their community and by using violence against other actors, including their intra-communal rivals, and in the case of Amal and Hizbullah (and several other parties-militias) also against the foreign actors that intervened in Lebanon. In this way, these parties-militias managed to penetrate Lebanon's tightly knit political elite, and, ultimately its political system: their leaders were invited to take part in peacemaking efforts, and they were party to various reforms plans.[86] But the price that these newcomers had to pay for joining Lebanon's political elite was assimilation. Moreover, with the notable exception of the Shi'i party-militia Hizbullah, which kept its

[84] Barak (2009a).
[85] On the Lebanese party-militias, see Stoakes (1975); T. Khalaf (1976); Entelis (1979); Snider (1984); Norton (1987); Hanf (1993); J. Harik (1993, 1994); Picard (2000).
[86] On these various plans, see Faris (1994).

military capacities in the postwar era, all of these actors eventually laid down their arms and accepted the authority of the Lebanese state, and many, including Hizbullah, abandoned their radical political platforms and joined the same political system they had initially vowed to eradicate.

At any rate, it was a formal state institution – the Lebanese Parliament, whose members (elected in 1972) represented all of the state's major communities – that discussed and approved the Ta'if Agreement in October–November 1989, enabling the termination of the Lebanese conflict about a year later.[87] The Ta'if Agreement revised and formalized the unwritten National Pact and at the same time sought to promote Lebanon's process of state formation and address the critical area of security. Moving beyond the ambiguous phrases agreed upon by Lebanon's leaders in 1943, the agreement stated that Lebanon was "Arab in its affiliation and its identity" and that it was the "final homeland for all its sons," recognizing the state's expanded borders and rejecting both its contraction and a union with another state. In addition, it defined Lebanon as a democratic parliamentary republic based on respecting general freedoms, and reaffirmed its liberal economy. At the same time, the Ta'if Agreement ratified – and formalized – the power-sharing settlement between Lebanon's major communities and applied it more strictly to the state's political institutions. Executive power was transferred from the President (Maronite) to the cabinet and the Prime Minister (Sunni), and the powers of the Speaker of Parliament (Shi'i) were enhanced. This created a multi-communal troika at the helm, which replaced the old Maronite–Sunni partnership that had been the core of Lebanon's political elite. Power sharing was also manifested in the appointment of the Prime Minister by the President in consultation with parliament and the Speaker of Parliament, thus institutionalizing a long-time custom; of taking cabinet decisions by mutual agreement, and only if this failed, by a vote (requiring a two-thirds majority on key issues); and of regarding the cabinet as having resigned if it lost more than a third of its members.

Hand in hand with institutionalizing power sharing in Lebanon, the Ta'if Agreement described abolishing political sectarianism as a fundamental and national goal, albeit one that must be worked toward according to a staged program (though no timetable was set). Indeed, in 1989, as in 1943, talk was of a plan that would be realized sometime in the future and by agreement. In the meantime, parliamentary seats, whose number was enlarged from 99 to 108 (in 1992 this number was raised to 128),

---

[87] The text of the Ta'if Agreement, see *Tishrin* (Damascus, October 24, 1989). For analysis, see Maila (1992); Hanf (1993); S. Khalaf (2002).

were to be divided equally between Christians and Muslims, replacing the 6:5 ratio from 1943, and proportionally among Lebanon's major communities and geographical regions (see Tables 3.1 and 3.2).

The Ta'if Agreement's major departure from the National Pact, however, was its attempt to transform the triangular relationship between the state, community, and security in Lebanon by enhancing the process of state formation and boosting security. Taking as a lesson the weakness of the state and its institutions before and during the civil war, the agreement aimed to strengthen the government and the security sector and to restrain local and foreign violent non-state actors. At the outset it was determined that any authority that contravened the "pact of coexistence" was illegitimate, thus removing the legality of all "cantons." Lebanon was defined as one united state with a strong central government, and it was declared that all Lebanese parties "agreed on the existence of a strong and capable state founded on national consensus." The Internal Security Forces (ISF) and the LAF were to be strengthened, and a Government of National Reconciliation was to formulate a detailed security plan and gradually impose the state's rule over all of its territory using its own forces but with Syrian assistance. All parties-militias, local and foreign, were to be disarmed and their arms would be handed over to the state within six months of that date. Additional reforms tightened state supervision of education and communications.

As to the question of civilian control of the LAF and the latter's identity and operations, it was decided that the (Maronite) President would continue to be its supreme commander, but that it would be under the authority of the multi-communal cabinet (which, as we have seen, was to be headed by a Sunni). In addition, the cabinet became responsible for declaring a state of emergency, war and peace, and general mobilization, and for supervising all state apparatuses, including the security agencies. Still, the president was to head the multi-communal Higher Defense Council, with the Prime Minister as his deputy. The agreement determined that the LAF's "basic function" was to "defend the homeland," and, when the ISF was unable to do so, to maintain public order, and also to support the latter "in maintaining security in circumstances on which the cabinet would decide." The LAF was to be unified, prepared, and trained so it could fulfill its national responsibility "in the face of Israeli aggression." When the ISF was ready to accept its assignments, the military would return to the barracks.

Last but not least, the Ta'if Agreement included references to Syria's role in Lebanon's reconstruction and to Syria's "distinctive" relations with Lebanon. This part of the agreement reflected Syria's hegemonic role in Lebanon in this period and was actually imposed by Syria's leaders.[88] However, later events proved the extent to which Syria's involvement in Lebanon – which had been invited by Lebanese leaders, agreed to by Israel and the United States and sanctioned by the Arab League in 1976 – remained contingent on favorable domestic and external circumstances.

Postwar Lebanon

On October 13, 1990, a joint Syrian–Lebanese military operation overran the enclave controlled by General Michel Aoun and the LAF units that remained loyal to him, removing the last bastion of resistance to the Ta'if Agreement. This put an end to the Lebanese conflict and opened the way for the state's reconstruction. Until his assassination in 2005, Rafiq al-Hariri (Sunni), a wealthy businessman from Sidon, spearheaded this process. Hariri enjoyed the support of many Lebanese, including members of his own community, and was also close to Saudi Arabia and Syria. Serving as Lebanon's prime minister in the period 1992–1998 and again in 2000–2004, Hariri put much effort into rebuilding the state's institutions and its devastated infrastructure and boosting its image domestically and externally.[89]

However, the end of the conflict in Lebanon did not mean that the country's problems were over. Until the withdrawal of its forces from Lebanon in April 2005, following Hariri's assassination, Syria enjoyed a hegemonic position in Lebanon.[90] Indeed, it was not until 2011, when Syria itself faced a revolt that attracted massive outside involvement, that its destabilizing actions in Lebanon were toned down, although now Lebanon had to cope with the spillover of the Syrian conflict in the form of hundreds of thousands of Syrian refugees sheltering in Lebanon's territory, tensions between supporters and opponents of President Bashar al-Assad's regime, especially in the northern city of Tripoli, and attacks waged by Syrian opposition armed factions against Lebanese villages on the Syrian–Lebanese border.

But on the domestic level, too, the state's reconstruction faced difficulties. First, Lebanon's economy recovered at a slow pace, hindering the ability of the government in Beirut to respond to socioeconomic grievances. This opened the way for some parties-militias in Lebanon, as well as other actors, to provide social services on a wide scale.[91] Second, political corruption in Lebanon in the postwar era was widespread,

---

[88] Maila (1992); Hanf (1993); Harris (1997).
[89] On postwar Lebanon, see Collings (1994); Dagher (2000); S. Khalaf (2002); Barak (2003, 2007b, 2009a, 2012); Volk (2010); M. Young (2010); Larkin (2012); Leenders (2012); el-Husseini (2012); Kingston (2013); Knudsen and Kerr (2013); Cammett (2014).
[90] el-Husseini (2012).   [91] Kingston (2013); Cammett (2014).

although this was by no means a new phenomenon.[92] A third domestic challenge, but with external aspects as well, were the continued activities of Hizbullah, the Shi'i party-militia, which was the only violent non-state actor allowed to retain its weapons in the postwar era for the purpose of "resistance" against Israel's occupation in Lebanon. Hizbullah's armed operations against Israel and its client, the South Lebanese Army (SLA), in the Israeli–Lebanese border area led to occasional fighting there and across the border, which sometimes spilled over to other parts of Lebanon (see Chapter 7).[93] Finally, political consensus in postwar Lebanon was wanting, and, in the wake of Hariri's assassination in February 2005, two opposing political blocs, the March 8 and March 14 camps, named after the mass demonstrations that followed, vied for political power in the state.[94]

Still, and contrary to the expectations of many observers, conflict did not re-ignite in Lebanon in this period. Indeed, most local political actors, including many of the wartime parties-militias and their leaders, joined Lebanon's political institutions, including parliament, which held its first postwar elections in 1992,[95] and the cabinet, which now included members of all of major communities.[96] Moreover, apart from a few exceptions, political actors in Lebanon generally sought to resolve their differences without resorting to violence.

On the external level, too, Lebanon's relations with its close neighbors, which had been volatile before and during the civil war of 1975–1990, gradually stabilized. In the early 1990s, with Syrian backing, the LAF forcefully restrained the Palestinian armed factions throughout its territory, and in May 2000 Israel pulled out its troops from its "security zone" in Lebanon and its proxy, the SLA, disintegrated. As mentioned earlier, in 2005, Syrian troops left after almost three decades of military "presence" in Lebanon, and three years later Syria and Lebanon established diplomatic relations.

When attempting to account for Lebanon's relative stability in the postwar era, which stands out in comparison both to the period of the

---

[92] Leenders (2012). See also el-Husseini (2012, 86–87).
[93] On Hizbullah, see Saad-Ghorayeb (2002); Hamzeh (2004); J. Harik (2004); Sobelman (2004, 2010); Norton (2007).
[94] On the Hariri assassination, see Mehlis Report (2005); Blanford (2006). On the political mobilization in Lebanon in the wake of the Hariri assassination and how it was connected to earlier activities of civil society groups, see the discussion in Barak (2007a).
[95] In the postwar parliament, two seats were reserved for Lebanon's Alawite community.
[96] In addition to members of Lebanon's six largest communities (Shi'is, Sunnis, Druze, Maronites, Orthodox, and Catholics), postwar cabinets have mostly included members of Lebanon's Armenian community, signaling the latter's integration in, and growing influence over, the state.

conflict and to the severe crises that later engulfed many other states in the Middle East since late 2010 (including divided societies such as Syria, Iraq, Libya, and Yemen), two factors are notable. The first is the "chilling effect" of the civil war on many Lebanese, who feared the return of violence to their country. These included the leaders of Lebanon's parties-militias, whose political and economic fortunes improved on account of the conflict (many of them became MPs and cabinet ministers), and who were thus very keen on keeping the peace. The second factor that can be mentioned in this context is the moderating role of several regional and international actors in this period and their ability to restrain domestic and external "spoilers." These actors include Arab states such as Syria, which helped pacify Lebanon in the period 1989–2000 but became a "spoiler" later and was eventually restrained by other regional actors and by the international community, but also Saudi Arabia, Egypt, and Qatar, all of which mediated between rival Lebanese factions and helped defuse political crises. Other outside actors included the United States, France, and the United Nations, which not only expressed their commitment to Lebanon's independence but also provided the government in Beirut with significant material assistance and international support.

But these factors, important as they are when trying to account for Lebanon's relative stability in the postwar era, also raise several questions. First, some local actors, such as the Lebanese Forces, the most powerful Maronite party-militia during the civil war, were dissatisfied with the postwar order in Lebanon, and particularly with Syria's dominant position in the state, and sometimes challenged it, even if unsuccessfully. Other local actors, such as Hizbullah, were also not forthcoming, though most of the violence that the Shi'i party-militia employed in this period was directed outwards, against Israel and later also against the Syrian rebels, and not against its fellow countrymen. Second, not all the external actors involved in Lebanon in this period always exercised restraint: Syria, but also Iran, offered their support to Hizbullah, whereas Israel backed the SLA; Israel launched attacks against Lebanon's infrastructure during its clashes with Hizbullah in the 1990s and in the 2006 War; and Syrian leaders intimidated Lebanese leaders when the latter refused their political dictates. In sum, neither domestic nor external actors always subordinated their particular interests to the goal of Lebanon's reconstruction.

It can be argued that at least part of the reason for Lebanon's relative stability in the postwar era, including during the first years of the "Arab Spring," stemmed from the fact that the state became more legitimate in the eyes of members of Lebanon's various communities. However, unlike the period of the civil war, the support for the state in the postwar era was due not only to it being seen as preferable to all alternatives, but also to the fact that its institutions had become more representative of Lebanese society and offered its major communities a stake in the postwar order that they were fearful of losing.

As we have seen, the Ta'if Agreement created more balance between, and sometimes also within, Lebanon's political institutions, including the presidency, the cabinet, and parliament. To be sure, the leaders occupying the highest positions in these institutions – the President, the Prime Minister, and the Speaker of Parliament, who formed Lebanon's ruling troika – did not always work in concert, and crises erupted between them from time to time. Still, these officials represented Lebanon's three major communities – the Maronites, Sunnis, and Shi'is – which turned these groups into stake-holders in Lebanon's political system.

In addition, and in contrast to the period 1943–1975, new political actors were permitted to join the political institutions, and many seized this opportunity. These included Hizbullah (Shi'i) but also its major intracommunal rival, the Amal Movement (Shi'i); the Future Movement (Sunni); the Free Patriotic Movement (Maronite); and others. Importantly, all four groups were led by individuals who not only had modest socioeconomic backgrounds but who also hailed from the Lebanese periphery – that is, from the outlying areas that were annexed to Mount Lebanon in 1920, or whose family had originated there. These were, respectively, Hassan Nasrallah, whose father came from South Lebanon; Nabih Berri, who was born to a modest family that emigrated from South Lebanon to Sierra Leone, and who would serve as Speaker of Parliament from 1992 onwards; Rafiq al-Hariri, who originated from the city of Sidon in South Lebanon; and Michel Aoun, the former LAF commander who would be elected president in 2016, who was born in the Southern Suburb of Beirut to a family that had moved there from the Jezzine area, also in South Lebanon. In any case, by joining Lebanon's political institutions, all of these actors were compelled to moderate their positions and goals, and became stake-holders in in the state.[97]

As in previous periods in Lebanon's history, the state and the pattern of inter-communal relations were closely linked to the area of security. This was manifested in the fact that Lebanon's security agencies also became more representative in this period. This was achieved by appointing members of different communities as heads of Lebanon's various security agencies. Thus, for example, at the time of writing, the ISF is headed by a Sunni, the General Directorate of General Security is headed by a Shi'i, and the General Directorate of State Security is headed by a Catholic. In

---

[97] On these leaders, see el-Husseini (2012). On Berri, see Norton (1987); Nir (2011). On Aoun see Na'um (1992). On Hariri, see Blanford (2006).

addition, the LAF became more representative. In the wake of the conflict, this institution was unified, strengthened, and enlarged, and its units were restructured on a non-communal and non-regional basis, eliminating excessive links and affiliations between specific units, communities, and regions in Lebanon. Considerable efforts were also made to maintain a communal balance in the LAF's officer corps, where Muslims now had a slight majority of 51.9 percent (Table 3.3). But the LAF's officer corps also became more representative on the regional level. Unlike previous periods in Lebanon's history – especially 1945–1975, when the majority of its officers came from Mount Lebanon – members of Lebanon's periphery became prominent in the LAF, and in the period 1990–2004 only one-quarter of its officers came from Mount Lebanon; the rest came from the outlying territories, including from North Lebanon, South Lebanon, and the Biqa' (Table 3.4).[98] In addition, thousands of Lebanese ex-militiamen, mostly Muslims, were integrated into the LAF, and these were balanced by Christian recruits. At the same time, power sharing was restored in the LAF command and in the controlling civilian bodies, and the LAF began propagating a unifying national and supra-ethnic identity, emphasizing that it was "from all of Lebanon, for all of Lebanon."[99] The LAF's enhanced legitimacy was demonstrated not only in the broad public support enjoyed by this institution, which cut across the lines of community, region, and clan, but also in the election of three consecutive former LAF commanders – Generals Emile Lahoud, Michel Suleiman, and Michel Aoun – as Lebanon's presidents in 1998, 2008, and 2016, respectively.[100]

Table 3.4 *Social background of LAF officers by region*

Period/Region	1945–1958	1958–1975	1975–1990	1990–2004
Mt. Lebanon	40.3	34.2	30.5	26.4
South Lebanon	19	23.3	21.6	20.7
North Lebanon	14.5	16.6	20.8	23.3
Beirut	15.4	15.8	13.4	12.5
Biqa'	10.9	10.1	13.7	17.1

Source: Barak (2006)

[98] This sometimes stemmed from socioeconomic factors, such the lack of other jobs in these peripheral regions. Personal Interview with LAF officer, November 2012.
[99] For details, see Barak (2006, 2009a). See also Taqi al-Din (1987, 1998); Nerguizian (2009); Gaub (2010).
[100] Barak (2009a).

The reforms that were introduced in Lebanon's security sector in the postwar era enhanced its performance and legitimacy. Indeed, during this period, the LAF and the other security agencies in Lebanon proved themselves time and again in curbing attempts by local actors and external players to undermine domestic stability. This role was manifested during major crises that Lebanon witnessed in this period. In the wake of Syria's withdrawal in 2005, the LAF deployed in the areas vacated by the Syrian army, and after the War between Israel and Hizbullah (2006), it deployed in the buffer zone from the Litani River to the Israeli–Lebanese border, alongside an enlarged and strengthened UNIFIL, although Hizbullah operatives also deployed in this area during this period. In 2007, LAF troops positioned themselves between opposing camps in Beirut and prevented escalation, and later that year LAF units waged a three-month-long military campaign against the militant Fatah al-Islam faction in the Nahr al-Bared refugee camp near Tripoli, which earned the LAF widespread domestic and external appreciation. In May 2008, when Hizbullah and its allies staged demonstrations that culminated in their temporary takeover of West Beirut, the LAF did not intervene but Hizbullah was careful not to attack its forces (the LAF's neutrality was, however, criticized by members of the Mustaqbal Movement, whose positions had been overrun by Hizbullah). During the "Arab Spring," too, the LAF managed to mitigate tensions in Lebanon, and especially in Tripoli, where opponents and supporters of the regime of Bashar al-Assad – the former mostly Sunnis, and the latter mostly Alawites – clashed and sometimes targeted the security forces. Finally, LAF units repelled attacks waged by radical Islamic armed factions based in Syria against Lebanon's territory.

However, like previous periods in Lebanese history, the state and its institutions did not enjoy exclusivity in the area of security, but were forced to "coexist" with other actors, external and domestic. One such actor, mentioned earlier, is the Syrian army, which was stationed in Lebanon until 2005. In addition, a more informal "Lebanese-Syrian security system" – that is, a kind of a "deep state"[101] – operated in Lebanon in this period. Former Lebanese Prime Minister Fouad Saniora of the Future Movement later argued that this "security system" "was comprised of a number of individuals and tools that enjoyed close ties with the Syrian security apparatus" and that it abused its power and "hindered the path of justice by failing to tackle past assassinations in Lebanon." He added that following the Hariri assassination in 2005, this "security system" tampered with the Hariri crime scene and began to

---

[101] Cf. Söyler (2013).

target those close to the slain leader, and "even went so far as to fabricate accusations against individuals in order to imprison them."[102]

Another actor that benefited greatly from Syria's dominant role in Lebanon until 2005, as well as from the support extended to it by Iran, Syria's regional ally, was Hizbullah. Some consider the Lebanese Shi'i party-militia, which emerged in Lebanon in the wake of Israel's invasion in 1982, as new type of political actor not only in Lebanon but in the Middle East in general. However, we saw earlier in this chapter that previous periods in Lebanon's history were also characterized by the existence and operation of violent non-state actors – local and foreign – alongside the state's political and security institutions, and from this angle Hizbullah is by no means unique. Indeed, a closer look at the Shi'i party-militia, including from a comparative perspective, suggests striking similarities between this and these other violent non-state actors.[103] The following paragraphs elaborate on this issue, which is critical for comprehending the emergence of Hizbullah, its evolution over the years, and the possibilities and limitations to its role in Lebanon and beyond.

First, Hizbullah has adopted roles and practices that were previously employed by other Lebanese factions. Thus, for example, its claim to wage "resistance" (*muqawama*) against Israel's occupation of parts of Lebanon since the 1980s, as well as its self-appointed role as defender of Lebanon's sovereignty and territorial integrity in the postwar era,[104] are similar both to the Maronite-led Phalanges Party, which also referred to itself as a "Lebanese resistance" and to the Shi'i Amal Movement, whose full name includes the word "resistance."[105] Moreover, like the Phalanges Party, which, as we have seen, was described as being "more than a party and less than a state,"[106] Hizbullah has also been defined in these terms by its members.[107] In late 2016, following a military parade held by Hizbullah in Syria, the party-militia's media department even quoted its deputy chief, Na'im Qassem as saying: "We have become more than a guerrilla movement but less than an army."[108] Another practice

---

[102] Saniora (2015). On the attempt to cover up the crime, see Mehlis Report (2005). See also el-Husseini (2012).

[103] A noted example is 'Imad Mughniya, Hizbullah's military chief, who had previously been a member of Fatah's Force 17 unit. See Baer (2002, 129); Bergman (2009, 157, 165). Baer, who was a CIA operative in Lebanon in the 1980s, mentions that in this period, the Lebanese Forces, a Maronite party-militia, provided Hizbullah with arms and ammunition during the latter's confrontation with the Amal Movement, its major intra-communal rival: Baer (2002, 125).

[104] Iskander (2008). See also M. Young (2010, 94–98).

[105] The full name of the Amal Movement is the Lebanese Resistance Regiments (*Afwaj al-Muqawa al-Lubnaniyya*).

[106] Baqraduni [Pakradouni] (1984, 112).   [107] Koya (2006, 35).

[108] Naharnet (2016).

that Hizbullah has adopted is providing social services to its constituencies in return for political support. This role is reminiscent of some of Lebanon's traditional leaders (*zu'ama'*),[109] of other parties-militias that participated in the civil war of 1975–1990 such as the Druze Progressive Socialist Party (PSP) and the Maronite-led Lebanese Forces,[110] and of some actors which were influential in postwar Lebanon, including Hariri's network which formed the nucleus of the (largely Sunni) Future Movement.[111]

Second, like other Lebanese parties-militias that joined the state's political institutions in the postwar era, Hizbullah has participated in all of Lebanon's parliamentary elections since 1992, and in 2005 it even decided to join the cabinet. Since then, it consistently sought to secure veto power in the latter institution, in accordance with the Ta'if Agreement which, as we have seen, requires a two-thirds majority on key issues and is considered as resigned if it loses more than a third of its members. Moreover, since Lebanon's parliamentary elections are held in multi-member constituencies which are communally diverse, Hizbullah was compelled to form coalitions with other political actors, including its major intra-communal competitor, the Amal Movement, the Maronite-led Free Patriotic Movement, and other factions. This suggests that, in fact, Hizbullah has moved away from its original platform, which rejected Lebanon's "sectarian" politics.[112]

But Hizbullah has also learned much from external (including transnational) violent non-state actors.[113] Thus, for example, Hizbullah's declared goal of deterring and establishing informal "rules of the game" with Israel is reminiscent of the efforts made by the Palestinian armed factions in Lebanon in the early 1980s that resulted in a ceasefire with Israel. While constituting "a milestone in the PLO's struggle for international recognition," this ceasefire lasted only until Israel's invasion of Lebanon in 1982.[114] Even the firing of Katyusha rockets against Israel by Hizbullah is not new, and Palestinian armed factions did this already in the late 1960s.[115] At the same time, Hizbullah has been a source for diffusion of military innovations to other violent non-state actors, such as suicide bombings, which it employed for the first time in Lebanon in 1983.[116] In view of the similarities between Hizbullah and the Palestinian

---

[109] Naor (2014a). On the *zu'ama'*, see, especially, Johnson (1977, 1986).
[110] J. Harik (1994). [111] Cammet (2014). [112] Norton (1987, 2007).
[113] Hizbullah, which is close to Iran, may have been inspired by the latter's model of civil-military relations, which is based on the existence of a parallel military institution, the Revolutionary Guards, alongside the "regular" Iranian army.
[114] Sela (2014, 304). [115] See, e.g., Bartov (2002, 1:176).
[116] M. Horowitz (2010, 34). On Hizbullah's role in 1983, see Baer (2002).

armed factions, it should not come as a surprise that the former tried to provide assistance to the latter during the Second Palestinian Intifada and that senior Israeli officials believed that, in fact, Hizbullah was a Palestinian – and not a Lebanese – faction (see Chapter 7).

In any case, during most of the period under discussion, Hizbullah directed its weapons outwards, toward Israel, and not against other Lebanese actors, and especially the state's institutions. Still, the leaders of the Shi'i party-militia insisted on maintaining their autonomous military capacities in Lebanon, even at the price of escalation. Thus, in May 2008, when the Lebanese government sought to replace the head of security at the international airport and challenged the legality of Hizbullah's independent telephone system, which it considered to be a vital element of its security apparatus, armed members of the Shi'i party-militia took control of parts of West Beirut, signaling that a "red line" had been crossed in the relationship between Hizbullah and the Lebanese state.[117] But even this operation was reminiscent of, on the one hand, the "counter-revolution" staged by the Maronite-led Phalanges Party in the wake of the Lebanese civil war of 1958[118] and, on the other hand, the takeover of West Beirut by Shi'i militiamen in February 1984 during the civil war.[119] In fact, the outcome of Hizbullah's operation was quite similar to these earlier actions: the formation of a national unity government in which Hizbullah and its allies presided over 11 out of 30 cabinet seats, thus according them veto power. However, even if limited in scope, Hizbullah's resort to violence against its compatriots antagonized many in Lebanon, and one report even argued that "[n]ever before had it [Hizbullah] appeared so clearly as a Shiite [sic] militia rather than a resistance movement capable at times of transcending Lebanon's divides."[120]

Since 2011, Hizbullah has been deeply involved in the Syrian conflict, which, according to one of the party-militia's commanders, "is a war not just against us, but against humanity."[121] In addition, five members of the Shi'i party-militia are being tried in absentia for their role in Hariri's assassination,[122] and others, such as 'Imad Mughniya, Hizbullah's military chief, but also others, have been assassinated by Hizbullah's enemies, who sometimes acted in concert.[123] In view of these challenges, as well as

[117] International Crisis Group (2008, 3).
[118] The "counter-revolution" of 1958, which also included mass demonstrations (but not the seizing of offices of rival parties), was launched after the formation of a government that did not adequately represent the Phalanges Party's interests, and ended with the formation of a "conciliation cabinet of four" that included Phalanges leader Pierre Gemayel. See Qubain (1961, 156–159); Entelis (1974, 148–149, 178–181).
[119] Ajami (1992, 206). See also Barak (2009a, 127–129).
[120] International Crisis Group (2008, 5). [121] *Guardian* (2014). [122] Bergman (2015).
[123] Goldman and Nakashima (2015).

the great devastation brought about by Hizbullah in the armed confrontation that it initiated with Israel in 2006, it remains to be seen whether Lebanon's only remaining party-militia will be able to uphold its privileged status in the state.

Conclusion

This chapter discussed the triangular relations between the state, community, and security in Lebanon from the period of the *Mutasarrifiyya* until the post–civil-war era. One element of continuity has been the weakness of the Lebanese state in the coercive-material sense before and, especially, after its expansion in 1920. This stemmed from a deliberate decision made by the country's political and socioeconomic elite, who regarded the state as potentially oppressive and sought to curtail both its coercive and disciplinary powers. On the external level, too, keeping the state weak was seen as the best way to guarantee its neutrality. But despite its weakness in the material sense, Lebanon did elicit the identification of its citizens, including within the outlying regions that were annexed to Mount Lebanon. Indeed, Lebanon's Muslim leaders, who had initially rejected the state's expansion, gradually came to terms with this reality and joined Lebanon's political institutions. This process was heightened by the National Pact of 1943, which installed power sharing domestically and determined Lebanon's foreign policy. But this intercommunal political settlement also had serious shortcomings that, together with external factors, ultimately led to the outbreak of conflict in 1975 and to the state's "failure." The power-sharing settlement could not be updated to reflect changing political and socioeconomic realities, and newcomers could not join the political system, which was dominated by the country's traditional leaders, especially the Maronites and their Sunni allies. This caused growing resentment on the part of these newcomers and, ultimately, encouraged them to try to force their way into the political arena. Another problem was that the state was not the only actor that operated in the area of security, and several parties-militias pursued their own agendas, sometimes challenging the state's monopoly over the legitimate use of violence. During the civil war of 1975–1990, both new and veteran parties-militias presented themselves as protectors of their communities, created autonomous "cantons" under their rule, and forged ties with foreign actors. But none of these violent non-state actors managed to garner support from members of other communities, and this made them inferior to the state's institutions, whose representativeness increased in this period. Lebanon's security sector is particularly telling: Despite its weakness in the coercive-material sense, power-sharing mechanisms were introduced in its agencies, and especially in the LAF, which preceded the introduction of parallel reforms in the political system. The Ta'if Agreement of 1989, which opened the door for the conflict's termination, not only addressed Lebanon's pattern of inter-communal relations but also sought to strengthen the state and enhance its security. The same logic guided the reforms introduced in Lebanon in the postwar era, which simultaneously focused on the state and its institutions, on the pattern of inter-communal relations, and on the area of security, a factor that had a positive impact on their outcome. Still, Lebanon's postwar reconstruction has been only partially successful: political corruption has been widespread, the economy did not make sufficient progress, and both Syria and the Syrian–Lebanese "deep state" undermined domestic stability. Another problem was Hizbullah, the Shi'i party-militia, which eschewed the need to give up its arms by effectively exploiting Israel's continued occupation of South Lebanon, Syria's dominant position in Lebanon, Iran's close ties to Syria, and the feelings of insecurity and social deprivation of many members of Lebanon's Shi'i community. But Hizbullah also faced limitations in its role, stemming from the fact that it, in the end, remained, on the one hand, a communally based movement that found little appeal among other communities, and, on the other hand, a violent non-state actor that did not make the rules but had to play by them.

4 Israel/Palestine: Strong and Illegitimate

This chapter discusses the triangular relationship between the state, community, and security in Israel/Palestine. Its emphasis is on the period after the Israeli–Arab War of 1967, which led to the imposition of Israel's control over the West Bank and the Gaza Strip (as well as other areas) and, ultimately, in the creation of a divided society in Israel/Palestine, albeit informal in nature. However, as was done with regard to Lebanon (in Chapter 3), the period before this watershed event is also addressed in order to identify markers of continuity and change and to assess the impact of the state's expansion on the three above-mentioned spheres and their interplay.

As in the previous chapter, attention is accorded to the political unit in each period and to its ruler, since both have shifted over time. In addition, the major communities in the political unit in each period are identified. Broadly speaking, Israel/Palestine has two major communities – Israeli Jews and Palestinians – but each is quite diverse, and other foci of identity – such as religion (and the level of religiosity) and geographical region – are also significant.[1] In addition, group identities have not been fixed but witnessed considerable change over time, not least because of major events such as the First Arab–Israeli war and the Israeli–Arab War of 1967.[2] Finally, and similar to the discussion of Lebanon, it is important to examine not only the state's formal institutions but also informal settlements, practices, and arrangements.[3]

---

[1] Israeli Jews are secular, national religious, or ultra-religious, but each category is quite broad. Another notable division is between Sepharadi (including Mizrahi) and Ashkenazi Jews, though many Israelis have mixed backgrounds. The Palestinians are also diverse, and include Muslims, Christians, and Druze, all of whom are Arabs, and Circassians, a non-Arab Muslim community. Each of these groups has secular and religious members. Other important foci of identity among the Palestinians are regions (e.g., the Galilee, the Negev/Naqab, the West Bank, and the Gaza Strip, but also smaller areas such as the Hebron area, the Jerusalem area), large families (or clans), and Bedouin tribes. Since 1948, another important distinction is between the Palestinians in Israel/Palestine and the Palestinian refugees in Israel/Palestine and in the diaspora.
[2] This point is emphasized by Shelef (2010). See also Klein (2014).
[3] See, especially, Sharkansky (1999).

In order to address these issues and identify historical trends, the relevant period is divided into five sub-periods: first, the period of British rule in Palestine (1918–1948); second, the First Arab–Israeli War (1947–1949); third, from the end of the latter confrontation to the Israeli–Arab War in 1967 (1948–1967); fourth, from Israel's state's expansion to the outbreak of the first Palestinian Intifada (1967–1987); and fifth, from the first Palestinian Intifada until the present.

Before discussing these periods, however, a note on the major scholarly approaches to Israel/Palestine, with an emphasis on the period since 1967, is in order. With regard to Lebanon, we can find studies dealing with the state and its various communities in different periods, albeit with varying degrees of attention to different groups in each period. Thus, for example, more attention is paid to the Shi'i community and, to an extent, also to the Druze community, in recent decades, as opposed to the emphasis on the Maronites and other Christian communities in earlier periods. However, most studies dealing with Israel/Palestine emphasize one of its communities, either the Israeli Jews or the Palestinians, with very few (mainly recent) works giving equal attention to both communities.[4]

As far as Israel's expansion in 1967 and its implications are concerned, we can identify three major approaches. The first views Israel as an essentially democratic (and Jewish) state, despite its continued occupation of the Territories. Indeed, these works posit that this factor, however significant, has not detracted from the democratic (and Jewish) attributes of Israel's regime, but, rather, is one of several "unsolved problems" the state has grappled with since its independence. In other words, these scholars continue to treat Israel as a nation-state and see its long-term civilian and military presence in the Territories as temporary, while overlooking, or downplaying, its long-term impact. This enables these scholars to consider Israel as an essentially Western state and, moreover, to compare it to Western democracies and more established states in general.[5] However, some of these writers do acknowledge the shortcomings of Israel's democratic regime, which they define as "ethnic democracy," and draw parallels between Israel and less-established democratic states.[6]

A second approach also acknowledges Israel's democratic character but regards its regime as problematic mainly, but not exclusively, on account of its long-term occupation of the Territories since 1967 and its

---

[4] This applies to most works cited below. Exceptions are Sela and Ma'oz (1997a) who brought together a group of leading Palestinian and Israeli scholars of Israel/Palestine and the Israeli–Palestinian conflict. See also Pappe (2006); H. Cohen (2008, 2010); Klein (2014).
[5] Galnoor and Blander (2013). See also Gavison (1999); Nikoleyni (2013); Spruyt (2014).
[6] Smooha (1997, 2002). See also Yoav Peled (2014).

profound impact on many spheres, including politics, society, the economy, and culture. While these scholars, too, compare Israel to more established Western states, their emphasis is on states that experienced major crises on account of their expansion and their attempts to contract in later periods. In particular, they juxtapose Israel to France during the Algerian War (1954–1962), implying that Israel's predicament can also be solved by a general-turned-statesman who would extract it from the Territories.[7] Interestingly, Palestinian writers and political activists also have adopted the Algerian "model," first during the 1960s, when autonomous Palestinian political factions began to emerge emulating the Front de Libération Nationale (FLN), and later during the 1990s, in the course of the Israeli–Palestinian peace process.[8]

Finally, there are those who posit that Israel/Palestine has become (or re-emerged as) a "one-state," albeit informal, on account of the facts on the ground created by Israel in the Territories since the state's expansion.[9] Consequently, some of these authors raise doubts concerning Israel's democratic character – for them, it is, in any case, a formal (or electoral) democracy and not an effective (or liberal) democracy[10] – and some even consider Israel/Palestine to be an "Ethnocracy," i.e., a regime that is non-democratic.[11] Accordingly, some authors compare Israel/Palestine to other divided societies where one community is dominant, in particular South Africa under Apartheid,[12] Serbia,[13] and other territories that witnessed inter-communal conflict and peace, such as Northern Ireland.[14] Others draw parallels between Israel and other post-colonial states, including several Middle Eastern states that have expanded over the years.[15] This book accepts the basic premises of this

---

[7] Lustick (1993, 2001). See also Kimmerling (1989); Zertal and Eldar (2007); Ben-Eliezer (1998a, 2012, 24); Bar-Tal and Schnell (2013). N. Gordon (2008) seems to belong to this category, though his book focuses on the occupation.
[8] On the earlier period, see Abu Iyad (1981, 34); Sela (2014). On the later period, see, e.g., Bishara (2001).
[9] The first to discuss Israel's state expansion was Meron Benvenisti. See Benvenisti (1984, 1986, 1995, 2007). See also Judt (2003); Ron (2003); Tilley (2005); Yiftachel (2006); Klein (2010, 2014); Bhavnani, Miodownik, and Choi (2011); Azoulay and Ophir (2012); Shenhav (2012); Faris (2013). For criticism, see Morris (2009).
[10] According to Heller (2000, 487–488), "formal democracies," or electoral democracies, are states where "[f]unctionally and geographically, the degree of public legality ... remains severely constrained" and "the component of democratic legality and, hence, of publicness and citizenship, fades away at the frontiers of various regions and class, gender and ethnic relations." By contrast, "effective democracies," or liberal democracies, are states where "democratic practices have spread throughout society, governing not only relations between states and citizens but also public relations between citizens."
[11] Yiftachel (2006).
[12] Greenstein (1995); Byrne (1999); Badran (2009); Guelke (2012).   [13] Ron (2003).
[14] Ben-Porat (2006); Byrne (1999); Guelke (2012).
[15] Barak (2005b, 2009b). See also Becke (2014).

third approach and adds to it by providing a detailed comparison between Israel/Palestine and Lebanon.

British Rule in Palestine

Like Lebanon, Palestine was part of the Ottoman Empire until the First World War, when it was occupied by the Allied forces.[16] From then until the departure of the British forces from Palestine on May 14, 1948, this political unit was under direct British rule.[17] Many studies that deal with Palestine start from the period of the British Mandate (1922–1948), which was critical for the development of the futures of both the Israeli state and the Palestinian community.[18] This chapter will follow this path, but will also inquire about the long-term impact of this period on the relationship between the state, community, and security.

Similar to France, which extended its support to the Maronite community in Mount Lebanon and helped its leaders realize their national aspirations in the wake of the First World War, Great Britain, whose leaders made a formal commitment to Zionist leaders in the Balfour Declaration in November 2, 1917, assisted the Jewish community in Palestine (the *Yishuv*) in realizing its national goals. Like in Lebanon, the relations between the colonial power and its local client later deteriorated (an important milestone was Britain's White Paper of 1939, which imposed restrictions on Jewish immigration to Palestine and limited Jewish land purchase[19]), and a Jewish struggle for independence was waged that ended with the departure of the British forces from Palestine in May 1948.

Although in the State of Israel the struggle against the British, and those who took part in it, became part of the national ethos (this occurred also in Lebanon with regard to its struggle for independence from France), the fact of the matter is that, like in Lebanon, British support to the Jewish national project – directly and indirectly – was critical.[20] Indeed, one

---

[16] Gerber (2008) argues that the name "Palestine" (*filastin*) was used during the Ottoman period and identifies the origins of Palestinian identity in the pre-Modern era.

[17] Initially, the area included the eastern bank of the Jordan River but the latter region was separated by the British in 1922 and became the Emirate of Transjordan and, later, the Hashemite Kingdom of Jordan.

[18] On the period of British rule in Palestine, see Porath (1974, 1977); Horowitz and Lissak (1978); Muslih (1988); Kolinsky (1993); R. Khalidi (1997, 2006); Ben-Eliezer (1998b); Segev (2000); Kimmerling (2001, 65–67); Gerber (2003); Migdal (2004, 28); Fieldhouse (2006); H. Cohen (2008); A. Oren (2009); Sternhell (2009); Norris (2013); Klein (2014); Thomas (2014).

[19] H. Cohen (2009, 133).

[20] On Britain's pro-Zionist policy, see B. Smith (1993); Segev (2000); Gerber (2003); Migdal (2004, 28); Norris (2013); Klein (2014).

Israel/Palestine: Strong and Illegitimate 99

needs only to consider the growth of the Jewish community in Palestine (the *Yishuv*) from about 56,000 during the British occupation in 1917, to about 630,000 (which amounted to one-third of the total population) in November 1947, and about 650,000 in May 1948.[21]

David Fieldhouse, who provides a much-needed comparative perspective on the Mandate system in the Middle East, notes the similarities between French support of the Maronites in Lebanon and British support of the Zionists in Palestine, but concludes that "[t]he result in both Lebanon and Palestine was similar: a deeply divided society and civil war."[22] However, there were also marked differences between how the French ruled Lebanon and how the British governed Palestine, and this variation is important not only when assessing the long-term impact of these periods on the evolution of the two political entities, Palestine and Lebanon, but also when asking why the former plunged into inter-communal conflict immediately after it was left to its own devices whereas the latter witnessed three decades of relative stability before it became engulfed in a civil war.

First of all, whereas France established a new state in Lebanon in 1920 and Britain helped the Hashemite princes Abdullah and Faysal to establish their own states in Transjordan and Iraq, respectively, the British did not proclaim a new state in Palestine but ruled it directly.[23] In addition, Britain invested considerable resources in developing the infrastructure in Palestine, mainly because of strategic considerations, and this had a significant impact on the development of the postcolonial state. At the same time, Britain did not attempt to impose a bilateral treaty on Palestine, as it did in Iraq and as the French did in Lebanon.

Second, the British Mandatory authorities neither drafted a constitution for Palestine nor encouraged the indigenous population to do so. This policy was different not only from that of the French, who, as we have seen (in Chapter 3), helped draft a constitution for Lebanon that formalized the principle of communal representation, but also from the policies adopted by the British themselves in Egypt and Iraq, where they imposed constitutions.[24]

Third, apart from several unsuccessful attempts (e.g., in Jerusalem[25]), the British did not establish political institutions that could bring together leaders of the two communities in Palestine. This policy stands in contrast to Lebanon, whose parliament gradually accepted members of all major

---

[21] Morris (2008, 406). See also Kimmerling (2001, 35).   [22] Fieldhouse (2006, 308).
[23] For a different view see Kimmerling (2001, 60), who claims that "Mandatory Palestine was a typical colonial state."
[24] Thompson (2013, 334). It is worth noting, however, that unlike France, Britain itself lacks a codified constitution, as do some of its former colonies, such as New Zealand.
[25] Klein (2014, 117–121).

communities (see Chapter 3), and to Syria, where the parliament helped regulate internal tensions.[26] Part of the reason for this difference is that the British ruled Palestine directly and allowed the Palestinians and the Jews to develop their own separate political, social and, in some cases, security institutions in line with the stipulations of the Mandate.[27] However, some authors note that the Jewish institutions in Palestine were also convenient for the local British authorities, since they assisted them in managing the Mandate's affairs, and that local British officials became dependent on these Jewish institutions for capital, local knowledge, skilled manpower, security, and personnel.[28] At any rate, the result was that three decades of British rule in Palestine "failed to create a viable indigenous government of any sort," and consequently the British "could only evacuate the country and leave its future to be decided by civil war."[29]

In turning to examine British policies in Palestine and their impact on the process of state formation, the relations between the Jewish and Palestinian communities, and the area of security in the new political unit, it appears that, in line with their 1917 commitment to build a "national home" for the Jews in Palestine, Britain was initially forthcoming toward the Jewish community in Palestine (the *Yishuv*). Indeed, in retrospect, the British Mandate served as a sort of "incubator" for the Jewish state-in-the-making. British support for the *Yishuv* was manifested not only in allowing its members to build their own institutions, which were autonomous from those of the colonial power, but also in taking concrete steps, such as the introduction of the Hebrew term *Eretz Israel* ("Land of Israel") to official documents and symbols of the Mandate such as stamps and coins. These actions conveyed Britain's commitment to Zionism and, ultimately, emphasized the Jewish character of Palestine.[30]

But Britain assisted the Jewish community in Palestine (the *Yishuv*) on the material level, too. The institutions of the Mandate, including its security agencies, recruited thousands of Jewish youth,[31] and during

---

[26] Gerber (2003, 37–38).
[27] Palestine Mandate (1922). See also Fieldhouse (2006, 151). On the Jewish community in Palestine (the *Yishuv*), see Horowitz and Lissak (1978); Ben-Eliezer (1998b); Sternhell (2009).
[28] According to Migdal (2004, 28) this practice was similar to the British dependence on the Protestant community in Northern Ireland. See also Fieldhouse (2006, 148).
[29] Ibid., 151.   [30] Wallach (2011a).
[31] According to Klein (2014), the British Mandate employed 2,000 Jewish policemen and 2,000 Arab policemen. The Mandatory police, in coordination with the main Jewish paramilitary, the *Hagana*, also recruited volunteers (known as *Ghafirs*) to guard Jewish settlements, roads, installations, etc. Thomas (2008, 254) posits that by the beginning of July 1938, "more than 5,500 Jewish men had been given some military training, and 1,345 of them were employed as armed guards, largely to defend outlying Jewish

the Second World War they accepted them to the British army. The impact of these measures cannot be overstated. According to Benny Morris, 26,000 Jews received military training during the Second World War,[32] and Yoav Gelber, who collected data on 2,249 Jewish officers who served in the Israel Defense Forces (IDF) during the First Arab–Israeli War and in the IDF's postwar organization period, writes that 724 of these officers (or 32.2 percent) had previously served in the British army (most had previously been members of the *Hagana*, the major Jewish militia in Palestine), and that 258 of the 495 officers who continued to serve in the IDF after 1949 (or 52.1 percent) had previously served in the British army.[33] A recent study on Israel's military elite also suggests that in the period 1948–1957, half of the members of the IDF's general staff had served in the British army, and in the period 1958–1967 their share in the general staff was also significant (37.1 percent).[34]

There are several reasons for British interest in Palestine in this period that help to explain why it received different treatment from other British colonies and Mandates. The first, which seems to be the most important, was strategic: British officials regarded Palestine as their major regional military base in the Middle East.[35] This perception was reinforced during the Second World War, when the British forces fought against the advancing German forces in North Africa and against the allies of the Axis Powers in Iraq, Syria, and Lebanon. Consequently, the British set out to build the military and civilian infrastructure needed to accommodate about 100,000 soldiers with their arms and equipment in Palestine. This included building military bases, airstrips, railways, roads, ports, and oil refineries. Importantly, the infrastructure built by the British in Palestine was concentrated in the coastal areas and not in the hinterland, with the result that in May 1948, following the termination of the British Mandate, the nascent Israeli state took over almost all of these assets. In retrospect, this placed Israel in a better starting point than any of its neighbors in terms of its physical infrastructure.[36]

The other side of the coin, however, was the lack of British support to the Palestinian community, which did not manage to build autonomous political, social, cultural, and security institutions that were comparable to those of the Jewish community (the *Yishuv*).[37] In addition, Britain's pro-Jewish policies encountered resistance from the Palestinians, who felt

---

settlements." He adds that "[s]ecurity force reliance on Jewish auxiliary recruits was never officially admitted, but it was glaringly obvious."

[32] Morris (2008, 28).   [33] Gelber (1986, 552).   [34] Barak and Tsur (2012b, 483–484).
[35] Kolinsky (1993); Fieldhouse (2006, 147).
[36] Segev (2000); Morris (2008, 39); A. Oren (2009); Norris (2013); Sharfman (2014).
[37] Klein (2014, 115–116).

that the *Yishuv* was expanding not only demographically, as more and more Jews, mainly from Europe, arrived in Palestine, but also in terms of its political, social, and economic power. To these apprehensions was added an important religious dimension, as some areas where the Jews settled in Palestine, in particular the city of Jerusalem, had Muslim (and other) holy sites that some Palestinian leaders, especially Mufti Haj Amin al-Husseini, claimed to be in danger.[38] These apprehensions led to rising inter-communal tensions in Palestine, and occasionally to outbursts of violence, most notably during the Palestinian revolt in 1936–1939. It is noteworthy that in this period Palestinian violence was directed not only at the *Yishuv*, but also against the British, who reacted with massive force against the Palestinians.

As mentioned earlier, in the period of the British Mandate in Palestine, both communities, Jews and Palestinians, were encouraged by the local British authorities to build their own institutions. This process was intensified on account of the deterioration of inter-communal relations in Palestine. Thus, the Jewish community in Palestine (the *Yishuv*) built institutions that became increasingly separate from the Palestinian community, and even created its own separate economy. However, the Palestinians were not as successful in their efforts. In addition, both communities attempted to fulfill their collective goals by appealing to the British authorities in Palestine and in London, not by a process of elite accommodation.[39]

It was in this period, moreover, that Jewish leaders in Palestine began to mobilize their community to confront the Palestinians, which many (but not all) Jews came to see as an enemy of their national project, particularly after the Palestinian revolt in 1936–1939, and to build relatively large militias such as the *Hagana* and its regular fighting force, the *Palmach*, but also smaller militias (or parties-militias) such as *Etzel* and *Lehi*, which attracted thousands of Jewish youth.[40] As suggested by several writers, and especially by Uri Ben-Eliezer, however, this process of militarization of the Jewish community in Palestine was not only connected to the objective external threat posed by the Palestinians, but also to intra-communal struggles between rival factions in the *Yishuv*.[41]

In this period, the Jewish security agencies in Palestine began to recruit collaborators from among the Palestinian community, to cooperate with certain sub-groups within that community, such as the Druze, and to exploit religious tensions between Christians and Muslims. These

---

[38] Kolinsky (1993, 220).   [39] Migdal (1996, 189).
[40] Horowitz and Lissak (1978); Pa'il (1979); Gelber (1986); Ostfeld (1994); Segev (2000).
[41] Ben-Eliezer (1998b).

actions, coupled with intra-communal fissures within the Palestinian community, led to a situation where, on the eve of the First Arab–Israeli War, "Palestinian national institutions were ... unable to unite the country's Arabs ... [and] were vulnerable to intelligence penetration by the Zionists, whom each faction and leader helped in his own way in order to harm his opponents." To make things worse, "[t]errorism and counterterrorism" within the Palestinian community "had taken the place of persuasion and national consensus."[42]

Another factor that weakened the Palestinian community in Palestine considerably in the period before 1948 was the massive British response to Palestinian resistance to the British Mandate, especially during the 1936–1939 revolt. Indeed, British sources suggest that the violence their forces in Palestine employed against the Palestinians in this period,[43] by far exceeded the measures taken by the British against the Jewish militias during the violent Jewish–British struggle in 1946–1948.[44] In addition, British coercion became institutionalized during the Palestinian revolt, when they introduced for the first time emergency regulations that permitted their forces to use severe measures against the local population. It should be noted that these same measures, which were codified in 1945, were later incorporated into Israeli law and since 1967 have been imposed by Israel on the Palestinians in the Territories.

Although the majority in the Jewish community in Palestine (the *Yishuv*) was supportive of the Jewish national project, which gained precedence over other considerations (e.g., socialist values and policies),[45] a small group in the *Yishuv* did advocate the idea of a shared political unit between Jews and Arabs in Palestine. The leader of this group was Judah Magnes (1877–1948), who emigrated to Palestine from the United States in 1922 and took part in the establishment of The Hebrew University of Jerusalem, which opened in 1925, eventually becoming its president. Magnes and other members of this group were opposed to a particularly Jewish state in Palestine, and held that this state should be neither Jewish nor Arab. Instead, they advocated a binational state in which equal rights would be shared by all citizens. *Brit Shalom* (Hebrew for Alliance of Peace), the group that Magnes helped found in 1925, promoted this view, and Magnes himself, who was a pacifist and believed in compromise and understanding, continued to work toward these goals until his death in 1948. However, *Brit Shalom* remained a movement of intellectuals and

---

[42] H. Cohen (2008, 229).
[43] The Palestinians also employed violence against the British, including an attack on Lewis Andrews, acting governor of the Galilee district, in September 1937. Ibid., 96.
[44] Levenberg (1993, 74–75); Segev (2000); Gerber (2003); Hughes (2009).
[45] Sternhell (2009).

lacked a mass following in the *Yishuv*, and its ideas did not find much support among the Palestinians either. Still, some groups in both the Jewish and Palestinian communities in Palestine continued to propose the idea of inter-communal coexistence, and there were those within the Jewish community who opposed the ethno-militaristic trends in the *Yishuv* and later in the State of Israel.[46]

In sum, the period of the British Mandate in Palestine was characterized by significant advances in the process of state formation, whether on account of British or Zionist policies, but the main beneficiary of these actions was the Jewish community (the *Yishuv*) and not the Palestinian community. In the Jewish community, state formation efforts included the accumulation of coercive and disciplinary power and national integration. The inter-connected deterioration of Jewish–Palestinian relations, as well as intra-communal power struggles within the *Yishuv*, led to the latter's militarization, and the Palestinian community, too, militarized, although its decision to rebel against the British in 1936–1939 cost it heavily. Since inter-communal relations in Palestine were not institutionalized, and conflict regulation mechanisms, such as a constitution, joint political institutions, and informal political arrangements, were not installed, the relations between the two communities became more strained, and when partition of Palestine was approved by the international community and the British left, the stage was set for inter-communal conflict.

The First Arab–Israeli War

The First Arab–Israeli War, also known as the 1948 War, the Palestine War, the *Nakba* (or Catastrophe), among the Palestinians, and Israel's War of Independence,[47] erupted after the United Nations General Assembly adopted Resolution 181 on November 29, 1947, which recommended partition of Palestine and the creation of two independent states, one Arab and the other Jewish, and the establishment of a Special International Regime for Jerusalem. The war ended almost a year and a half later, in February–March 1949, with the signing of four Armistice agreements between Israel and each of Egypt, Lebanon, Transjordan

---

[46] Heller (2003). See Hermann (2010). See also Morris (2008, 33, 129; 2009). According to Hillel Cohen (2008), some Palestinians supported a compromise with the Zionist movement before 1948. Greenstein (2014) discusses several movements in Palestine and Israel/Palestine that presented visions that were different from, and which defied, the Zionist national vision.

[47] On the First Arab–Israeli War, see Abu Iyad (1981); R. Khalidi (1997); Rogan and Shlaim (2007); Morris (2008); H. Cohen (2008).

(later Jordan), and Syria – but not with the Palestinians, who ceased to be an autonomous political actor on account of the conflict – which put an end to the fighting, but which, significantly, were not formal peace treaties.

At the onset of this period, the relevant political unit was Palestine, which was still under British rule, and the major actors, apart from the local British authorities and the 100,000 troops under their control, were the Palestinian community, which had a solid majority of 1.2–1.4 million, or two-thirds of the total population in Palestine, and the Jewish community (the *Yishuv*), which numbered about 630,000, or one-third.[48] However, when the war came to an end, the area west of the Jordan River was effectively divided between Israel, the nascent Jewish state, which controlled 78 percent of the territory (as opposed to the 56 percent allotted to it in 1947),[49] with the rest divided between Jordan, which controlled and later annexed the West Bank and East Jerusalem, and Egypt, which was in control of the Gaza Strip but did not annex it. Thus, whereas the Jewish community in Palestine (the *Yishuv*) managed to establish its own "place under the sun" – that is, a nation-state according to the Western model – the Palestinian community failed to achieve its national goals and was no longer an autonomous political actor.

During the conflict, about one-half of the Palestinians had either fled their homes or were expelled by the advancing Jewish forces, becoming refugees within Palestine or outside its borders.[50] The first groups of refugees resided in non-recognized settlements within Israel or in several refugee camps that sprang up in the West Bank and the Gaza Strip, whereas the second group resided in the neighboring states, and especially in Jordan, Lebanon, Syria, and Iraq, with each government treating them differently (on Lebanon, see Chapter 6).

The major factor underpinning this one-sided outcome of the conflict was the very divergent levels attained in the process of state formation by the two rival communities in Palestine before the outbreak of intercommunal violence. On the Jewish side, state building, state construction, and national integration efforts all made significant headway, and the population at the end of the period of British rule in Palestine was more than ten times larger than it had been initially. In addition, most members of the Jewish community were highly motivated, not least because they regarded their national struggle against the Palestinians – and later against the Arab states, which intervened in the conflict – as existential. By contrast, commitment to a military struggle against the

---

[48] R. Khalidi (1997, 21, 179, 191); Morris (2008, 7, 81).   [49] Dowty (2012, 112).
[50] R. Khalidi (1997, 21, 179); Morris (2008, 407).

Jewish community on the part of the Palestinians was low, and the political and social fragmentation of this community precluded mass mobilization.[51]

Another factor contributing to the power of the Jewish community was that during the British Mandate period its leaders managed to create political institutions that were not only elected but also representative of the various factions within the *Yishuv*. Indeed, although radical factions, especially on the right of the political spectrum, sometimes operated autonomously and launched violent attacks against Arab and British targets in disregard of the "official" line, they were not the dominant Jewish actors, and the more mainstream factions within the Jewish community managed to co-opt or restrain them when they challenged their authority. By contrast, the Palestinian institutions, notably the Arab Higher Council under the control of Mufti Haj Amin al-Husseini, were neither elected nor representative, and some Palestinian factions were opposed to them and did not accept their authority.[52]

Last but not least, in the area of security, the Jewish community in Palestine (*Yishuv*) built a military force that was better organized, trained, and equipped than its Palestinian counterpart, which was weak and highly factionalized, not only because of its suppression by the British forces in the period 1936–1939, during the Palestinian revolt, but also due to intracommunal factors.[53] Thus, although the Jewish side suffered several military setbacks during the first phase of the conflict (including the loss of the Jewish Quarter in the Old City of Jerusalem and the Gush Etzion settlement bloc in the West Bank), the Jewish militias, which were merged into the IDF in June 1948, not long after Israel's independence, not only managed to overcome the Palestinian militias and the Arab and Muslim volunteers who fought in Palestine, but also repelled the Arab armies who intervened in the conflict after the termination of the British Mandate.

Despite these significant Jewish military gains, however, the leaders of the nascent Israeli state, especially its first prime minister and minister of defense, David Ben-Gurion, were prudent in setting their political goals during the war and in its immediate aftermath. Indeed, although the Jewish militias and later the IDF managed to extend the territory under Israel's control beyond the borders that had been stipulated for the Jewish state in 1947, and despite irredentist claims made by some Jewish actors, mainly on the right of the political spectrum, the leaders of the new state refrained from conquering East Jerusalem (including the Old City), the

---

[51] Ibid.; H. Cohen (2008, 230–258).
[52] Morris (2008, 82). See also R. Khalidi (2006); H. Cohen (2008).
[53] R. Khalidi (2006, 105).

West Bank, and the Gaza Strip, areas that had a clear Palestinian majority and, in the case of East Jerusalem, had important religious sites as well.[54] Thus, and also by preventing the return of Palestinian refugees to Israel after 1949 (Israel officially referred to these refugees as "infiltrators," and many were shot and killed by Israel's security agencies),[55] Israel was able to secure a decisive Jewish majority of 89 percent (see Table 2.2), and most political factions in the state accepted its borders and did not demand their revision.[56]

From Independence to the 1967 War

The first two decades of Israel's independence were characterized by an accelerated process of state formation on all levels.[57] In contrast to Lebanon, where members of the political and socioeconomic elite regarded the state as a necessary evil and did their utmost to curtail its coercive and disciplinary powers, Israel's political elite under the leadership of *Mapai*, the ruling party, openly embraced the principle of statism (*mamlachtiyut*),[58] and its leader Ben-Gurion "worked single-mindedly ... to make the state the dominant and central institution in people's lives."[59]

Drawing on, but also considerably expanding, the institutions that had been established in the period of the *Yishuv*, and making use of the colonial infrastructure that Israel inherited from the British Mandate, the state began to penetrate into all spheres of Israeli society, and attempted to discipline both its Jewish and Palestinian citizens. Importantly, this included the forced disbanding of all Jewish militias that emerged before 1948 and their integration in the IDF.[60] At the same time, the state's leaders sought to unify Israeli society – especially members of the Jewish community, which included not only Jews born in Palestine and later in the State of Israel (*Sabras*), but also hundreds of thousands of Jewish immigrants – around shared national myths, narratives, and symbols.[61]

---

[54] N. Oren (1992); Morris (2008, 163). Some authors mention Jordanian King Abdullah's interests in the West Bank and East Jerusalem in 1948 and a Jewish–Jordanian agreement, or "collusion," concerning these areas. See Shlaim (1988a); Morris (2008).
[55] Ibid., 411.   [56] See Migdal (2001) and the sources he cites.
[57] On the period from Israel's independence until the Israeli–Arab War of 1967, see Lustick (1980); Peri (1983); Horowitz and Lissak (1989); Kimmerling (1993, 2001); Medding (1990); Migdal (2001); Smooha (1997, 2002); Bäuml (2007); A. Oren (2009); Bareli (2014).
[58] Medding (1990, 134–140); Kedar (2003, 2008); Ben-Eliezer (2012).
[59] Migdal (2001, 152).
[60] Horowitz and Lissak (1978, 188–189); Medding (1990, 140–145); Morris (2008).
[61] Zerubavel (1995); Ben-Yehuda (1996); Zertal (2005); Shelef (2010).

What was striking about Israel's process of state formation, however, was the lack of differentiation between the state and (the Jewish) community on both institutional and symbolic levels. Yeshayahu Leibowitz, a professor at The Hebrew University of Jerusalem and a prominent public thinker, later recounted a conversation he had with Prime Minister Ben-Gurion, who told him that he "will never agree to the separation of religion from the State," and that he wanted the latter "to hold religion in the palm of its hand."[62] Apart from the need to preserve the political alliance between Ben-Gurion's party, *Mapai*, and the religious parties, which were members of Israel's ruling coalition, this policy, followed by all Israeli governments since 1948, stemmed from the fact that many components of Israel's process of state formation, including myths, narratives, and symbols, drew on Jewish history and tradition and, as such, required the consent of the major religious actors in the state.[63] But the efforts to promote the process of state formation in Israel also relied on more recent episodes in Jewish history, and especially the Holocaust. Thus, for example, in the early 1960s, the Israeli government, again under Ben-Gurion's leadership, instructed the Mossad, Israel's external security agency, to abduct Adolf Eichmann, the Nazi war criminal, and bring him to Israel, where he was publically tried and executed, thus mobilizing domestic support for the state.[64]

At the same time that the state and its institutions were busy bolstering the state's Jewish character, they did attempt to portray themselves as representing all of Israel's citizens – that is, both Jews and Palestinians – and to provide all Israeli citizens, at least formally, with equal rights and access to the state's institutions, agencies, and services.[65] Thus, the rule of law was established, as were strong legal institutions and other state agencies designed to protect citizens from the government's excesses, including the attorney general and the state comptroller (who also functions as its ombudsman). Indeed, according to Joel Migdal, "[t]he character of the state, even with the encouragement of a markedly Jewish ethos or civil religion and even with the suppression and strong control of the Arab population, was being forged in the years before the 1967 war with strong universal components, premised on the development of a society forged by civic ties."[66] This universal ethos can already be discerned in the Declaration of the Establishment of the State of Israel from May 1948, which proclaimed "the establishment of a Jewish state in *Eretz Israel*, to be known as the State of Israel." According to this document, the new state would

---

[62] Leibowitz (1992, 115).   [63] Kimmerling (2001, 102–104).
[64] For criticism, see Arendt (1963). See also Zertal (2005).   [65] Migdal (2001, 153).
[66] Ibid., 154.

foster the development of the country for the benefit of all its inhabitants; it will be based on freedom, justice and peace as envisaged by the prophets of Israel; it will ensure complete equality of social and political rights to all its inhabitants irrespective of religion, race or sex; it will guarantee freedom of religion, conscience, language, education and culture; it will safeguard the Holy Places of all religions; and it will be faithful to the principles of the Charter of the United Nations.[67]

The document also appealed to the Arab inhabitants of Israel "[t]o preserve peace and participate in the upbuilding of the State on the basis of full and equal citizenship and due representation in all its provisional and permanent institutions."[68] Interestingly, this appeal was made when the Palestinian community had already been defeated militarily.

But in practice the Jewish community in Israel, which comprised about 90 percent of the state's population, and which, moreover, presided over the state's political, bureaucratic and security institutions, effectively employed these agencies to prevent Israel's Palestinian citizens from challenging its hegemony. Indeed, it was in this period that a pattern of inter-communal control over the Palestinians who remained in Israel after the end of the First Arab–Israeli War came into being.[69] At the formal level, the main tool employed for this purpose was the Military Government: a system of laws, regulations, and other measures that were imposed on the state's Palestinian-populated regions in 1949. Until its formal abolition in 1966, the Military Government enabled the state and its institutions to closely monitor Israel's Palestinian citizens and to extract resources (mainly land) from them, which was often done under the pretext of security.[70]

But Jewish control was also maintained informally. Although the Knesset, Israel's parliament, did include several Palestinian members, most of them belonged to "satellite parties" affiliated to Jewish parties, in particular *Mapai*, and were under its influence. Indeed, the only autonomous actor that represented Israel's Palestinian community during this period was the Communist Party, which had both Jewish and Palestinian members, but the security agencies monitored this party closely and sometimes tried to obstruct its activities.[71] Furthermore, and in what would become the norm in Israel, Palestinian and joint Jewish–Palestinian parties were not invited to join the ruling coalition in the Knesset, and Palestinians were only rarely appointed as ministers in the cabinet.[72] Public funds were

---

[67] Declaration of the Establishment of the State of Israel (1948). [68] Ibid.
[69] Lustick (1980); Rouhana (1997); H. Cohen (2010); Robinson (2013).
[70] On the Military Government, see Kemp (2004); Bäuml (2007); H. Cohen (2010); Klein (2014, 171–173). For a Palestinian perspective, see, e.g., Habibi (1974).
[71] H. Cohen (2010); Bäuml (2007, 260–263).
[72] The first minister from among Israel's Palestinian citizens, Saleh Tarif (Druze) from the Labor Party, was appointed only in 2001, and the second, Ghaleb Majadele (Muslim) also from the Labor Party, was appointed in 2007. Both served as ministers without

not equally distributed among Jews and Palestinians, nor were state-sponsored development projects and plans.[73] It should be noted, however, that at least some of the exclusionary practices adopted in this period were also applied to some Jewish actors, especially those on the far-left and far-right of the political spectrum.[74] Indeed, it was Ben-Gurion himself who, during the formation of his first parliamentary coalition, coined the phrase "Without *Herut* and Without *Maki*," suggesting that both *Herut*, the right-wing party, and *Maki*, the Israeli Communist Party, were not legitimate political partners for his own party, *Mapai*.[75]

In their study of the Jewish community in Palestine (the *Yishuv*) during the British Mandate, Dan Horowitz and Moshe Lissak argue that the Jewish political institutions that emerged in that period were characterized by power sharing between the various political factions in the *Yishuv*. This settlement, they posit, stemmed from the outside resources that the *Yishuv* received and from its lack of sovereignty. This pattern of intra-communal relations, in turn, helped regulate conflicts within the Jewish community in Palestine before Israel's independence,[76] and ultimately increased its ability to effectively cope with the challenges posed by the British, the Palestinians, and the Arab states.[77] However, the period immediately after the establishment of the state signaled a departure from this pattern:

[T]he ... disappearance of the open frontiers [of the political unit in 1949] meant that there was no way for the center to acquire new functions and authority except at the expense of the subcenters. This created the background for the struggle between the "movement" orientation, which sought to maintain the autonomous

---

portfolio. Kenig (2014, 184). A third Israeli–Palestinian citizen, Ayoub Kara (Druze) from the Likud Party, was appointed in 2017.

[73] Bäuml (2007, 81–82). See also Kenig (2014, 187) and the sources he cites.

[74] These included former members of the *Etzel* such as Uri Avnery, who published a journal, *Haolam Hazeh*, which challenged the official line. The following anecdote gives a taste of the methods used by the state and by the ruling party, *Mapai*, in this period, but also of the ability to resist them: When my grandfather, Moshe Margalit, started working for *Hamashbir Hamerkazi*, the main wholesale supplier for consumers' cooperatives and labor settlements in Israel, which was affiliated with the *Histadrut*, Israel's Labor Union, he was told by his superior that from now on he would receive *Davar*, the mouthpiece of *Mapai*, because "this is what everyone does here." However, my grandfather, an opinionated man and a long-time reader of the leftist paper *Al Hamishmar*, did not bow to the dictate and a scandal broke out. After some deliberation my grandfather was allowed to continue to receive the newspaper of his choosing.

[75] Medding (1990, 188–189), who quotes this phrase, suggests, however, that in practice there were differences in the level of exclusion of the two parties, and that *Herut*, which was a Zionist party, was more acceptable than *Maki*.

[76] Horowitz and Lissak (1978, 227–230). See also Migdal (2001, 153). Lijphart (1977, 129–134) mentions several Israeli scholars who support this thesis. Cf. Bareli (2014, 23).

[77] Ben-Eliezer (1998b).

authority of the subcenters, and the "statehood" [statism] orientation, which upheld the primacy of the state as a focus of allegiance and as a source of values and entrepreneurial activity. This struggle during the early years of the state ended in a partial victory for the statehood orientation and partial reduction of the authority of the subcenters.[78]

As we will see, the re-opening of Israel's frontiers in 1967, on account of the state's expansion, provided political actors, including those with "communal" agendas, with fresh opportunities that ultimately weakened the dominant "statist" orientation, and this process was soon reflected both domestically and externally.

In addition to the state's institutions, a host of other agencies, including some that had been established during the pre-state period and were not dissolved after independence, also helped preserve Jewish hegemony in Israel and inter-communal control vis-à-vis the subordinate Palestinian community. These included the Jewish Agency and the Jewish National Fund, two institutions engaged in settlement activities designed exclusively for Jews, including in lands that had been confiscated from Palestinian owners who had "abandoned" them during the First Arab–Israeli War. The use of these institutions for national – that is, for Jewish communal – purposes persisted after 1967, but this time also in the Territories, allowing Israeli leaders to wash their hands of their activities.[79]

The area of security in Israel demonstrates quite well this period's intensive state formation process and elaborate pattern of inter-communal relations characterized by control, as well as the close links between all these areas.

In 1949 it was decided that, in view of Israel's volatile security situation, all Jewish citizens, both male and female, would be drafted to the Israeli military, the IDF at the age of 18, with men serving for 30 months[80] and women for 24 months.[81] In the Jewish community, only ultra-religious groups and married women were exempted from military service. But all of Israel's Palestinian citizens were exempted, although small groups within that community, such as the Druze, Circassians, and some Bedouins, were

---

[78] Horowitz and Lissak (1978, 230).
[79] A telling case is the demolition of the three Palestinian villages of Yalu, Beit Nuba, and 'Imwas in the Latrun enclave immediately after the 1967 War and the forced expulsion of their inhabitants. Some of the lands owned by these villages became the Canada Park, which was built with support from the Jewish National Fund in Canada. See M. Benvenisti (1986, 200).
[80] Some conscripts serve in the Border Guard, which is part of the Israeli police. In practice, since 1967, male conscripts have served for 36 months.
[81] Religious Jewish women can serve within the framework of the National Service, which, in recent years, has expanded to include some Palestinian citizens of Israel.

later drafted.[82] This policy effectively fragmented Israel's Palestinian community into its ethnic, religious and tribal elements. In addition, those who were drafted into Israel's security sector were disconnected from Israel's Arab neighbors.[83] But some argue that the exclusion of most of Israel's Palestinian citizens from the military had other purposes as well. In his extensive study of the Military Government, Yair Bäuml contends that this policy, which resulted from opposition not only within the IDF and the Israeli government but also in the Palestinian community itself, allowed the state to achieve three main goals vis-à-vis its Palestinian citizens:

> First, continuously identifying them as enemies of the state, the Jews and Zionism, which justified a tough security policy towards them. Their exclusion from the burden of security, including casualties [related to it], which was the major public, national and social effort of the Jewish population [in Israel], facilitated the second goal, which was to leave them outside the circle of socialization of Israeli society and by this to make it harder for them to penetrate into the labor market, academia and all other Jewish-controlled spheres. The third goal was to deny them various economic benefits (tuition, mortgages, tax benefits, unemployment benefits, and more) which are enjoyed by discharged soldiers.[84]

Two additional mechanisms were adopted in the area of security in Israel that promoted the process of state formation and at the same time reinforced Jewish control as the prevailing pattern of inter-communal relations. First, the IDF was to have a reserve force composed of men and women who had completed their mandatory military service. The reservists, who would undergo periodic military training, could be mobilized during national emergencies. The reserves provided the state with an unparalleled opportunity to influence its citizens after their military service, though in later periods (e.g., during the Lebanon War in 1982) reservists sometimes became a source of opposition to the government's policy and were thus removed from "sensitive" areas. Second, the IDF was to have a small standing force of career officers and noncommissioned officers (NCOs), who would be recruited from among the IDF's

---

[82] A. Peled (1998); Krebs (2006); Bäuml (2007); Kanaaneh (2008); H. Cohen (2010, 159–194); Robinson (2013). In 1956, military service became mandatory for members of Israel's Druze and Circassian communities. Hillel Cohen (2010, 159–160) notes that the state's recruitment efforts in the Druze community were sometimes met with resistance, and that the state used material incentives, including granting gun permits, but also coercion, to achieve this goal. See also Zeedan (2015, 181–188).

[83] H. Cohen (2010, 164). Additional steps were granting the Druze community's spiritual leadership the status of a statutory body in 1961, and passing a law that recognized Druze religious courts and established a separate Druze judicial system in 1962 (ibid., 167). See also Bäuml (2007, 82–88); Robinson (2013). On Israel's policies toward the Bedouins, see Nasasra et al. (2015).

[84] Bäuml (2007, 81–82). Parentheses are in the original.

conscripts.[85] It was decided, however, that military professionals would retire at an early age, and many of them, especially high-ranking officers, were recruited into Israel's large public sector. One of the effects of this policy was the emergence of informal security networks in Israel, which, in addition to accumulating political, social, and economic power, reinforced Jewish hegemony, and inter-communal control, in various civilian spheres.[86]

But it was the practice, and not only the composition, of the state's ostensibly professional institutions, including its security sector, that reinforced Jewish hegemony in Israel. Thus, for example, an official of the General Security Service (*Shin Bet, Shabak*) who served in the Ministry of Education exercised veto power over the appointment of Palestinian teachers that he considered to be too "nationalist."[87] In addition, the security agencies – whose members, like their civilian superiors, perceived Israel's Palestinian citizens primarily as a security threat – employed networks of collaborators and informants that reinforced the pattern of inter-communal control over this community. This practice, which had already begun during the period of the British Mandate, was made all the easier by the economic hardships facing Israel's Palestinian citizens, although, as in the previous period, there were various motives for collaboration.[88] Finally, in addition to these coercive measures, the Israeli state also tried to win the minds, though not necessarily the hearts, of its Palestinians citizens:

> Through tight supervision of speech, the state tried to root out all such language [directed against it]. But this was not sufficient for its goals. It sought to create a pro-Israeli Arab rhetoric and to impel its Arab citizens to act as they spoke, at least in public. In other words, Israel wanted the Arabs to accept the state and its values and to assimilate the broad outline of the Zionist narrative. One prime example of this was the security forces' massive encouragement and inducement of Arabs to celebrate Israel's Independence Day and to disregard the day's pernicious implications for them.[89]

The territorial realm in Israel illustrates the tight-knit relationship between the state, the community, and security since 1948. Many lands owned by Palestinians before independence were now under the state's control, and these confiscated lands were transformed into training areas and military camps for the IDF. Thus, for example, of 89,000 dunams (about 22,000 acres) held by Israel's security sector in 1951, at

---

[85] Horowitz and Lissak (1989, 195–230); Van Creveld (1998, 113–115).
[86] Sheffer and Barak (2013).
[87] H. Cohen (2010, 139–142). See also Sheffer and Barak (2013).
[88] H. Cohen (2010). See also Bäuml (2007, 246–249).
[89] H. Cohen (2010, 132). See also Bäuml (2007, 249). Cf. Wedeen (1999).

least 33,352 dunams (about 8,200 acres, or 37 percent) had previously belonged to Palestinians. But the presence of Israel's security agencies in these areas was not only for security reasons. Amiram Oren, in a pioneering study on the relations between territory and security in Israel in this formative period, writes that at the end of 1951, the IDF's Operations Department directed its Training Command to hold military training in the areas of the Military Government in the Triangle and the Galilee, which were populated by Palestinians, "to enhance the status of the state and the status of the IDF in the eyes of their Arab inhabitants."[90] Indeed, inter-communal relations in Israel in this period were at times characterized by "demonstrations" of the state's coercive capacities, a practice that would be repeated in later periods. The most violent episode, however, occurred in October 1956, during the Suez War, when members of a unit of Israel's Border Guards under the IDF's command killed almost 50 Palestinian citizens after they allegedly defied a curfew, in what became known as the Kafar Qassem Massacre.[91]

In sum, during this period Israel witnessed an intensive process of state formation that engendered a strong state in terms of its coercive capacities, which penetrated into the lives of its citizens and attempted to discipline them. At the same time, the sub-process of national integration, which drew on Jewish myths, narratives, and symbols, was mainly directed at the Jewish community dominating the state, although some efforts were also directed at the subordinate Palestinian community. Although in this period Israel was considered to be a democracy – albeit formal and not effective – its Jewish community, which enjoyed an overwhelming majority in the state, presided over its political, bureaucratic, and security institutions and used these and a host of informal practices to maintain its privileged position. Israel's leaders justified their policy of inter-communal control by arguing that their state faced an existential threat from the neighboring Arab states, which, these leaders posited, prepared for a "second round" against Israel, as well as from members of its Palestinian community, which were liable to join their brothers during wartime. However, it was Israel, and not the Arab states, that launched the next Israeli–Arab confrontation, the Suez War, in 1956, and the latter scenario never materialized: the Arab states, and especially Egypt, mainly encouraged attacks by violent non-state actors, the Fidayin, and did not risk another all-out war with Israel. By 1966, the Military Government over Israel's Palestinian citizens was abolished, but Israel's exclusionary

---

[90] A. Oren (2009, 243). See also Bäuml (2007); H. Cohen (2010).
[91] Bäuml (2007); H. Cohen (2010, 135–136); Robinson (2013, 160–175).

policies toward members of this community persisted, as did the collective grievances that emanated from the state's actions.

From Israel's Expansion to the First Palestinian Intifada

In 2001, following the collapse of the Israeli–Palestinian peace process and the outbreak of the Second Palestinian Intifada (or the al-Aqsa Intifada), Baruch Kimmerling posited that "[d]e facto, since 1967, Israel has ... been transformed into a binational Jewish-Arab state."[92] This section discusses the period from the Israeli–Arab War of 1967 to the outbreak of the first Palestinian Intifada in December 1987, which was the formative period of the divided society that emerged in Israel/Palestine following the state's expansion.[93]

As mentioned earlier (see Chapter 2), some writers have suggested that Israel's expansion into the West Bank and the Gaza Strip in 1967 was not a premeditated act, but rather stemmed from the dynamics of that particular conflict. In addition, the political unit that was created on account of the 1967 War, referred to herein as Israel/Palestine, has remained informal, and not one state, including Israel itself, has recognized it. Indeed, even the most ardent supporters of a "Greater Israel" west of the Jordan River have, until recently, objected to the formal annexation of the Territories that Israel occupied – or, in their view, were "liberated" - preferring to create additional "facts on the ground," which they considered to be more beneficial and less costly on both the domestic and external levels.[94]

Still, the continued denial of the state's expansion by most political actors in Israel, by many Palestinians in the Territories, and by the majority of outside actors, cannot obscure the actual existence of Israel/Palestine as a single political unit throughout the period under discussion, and also later, or the profound implications that the state's expansion has had on the triangular relationship between the state, community, and security throughout Israel/Palestine.[95] These issues will now be discussed.

---

[92] Kimmerling (2001, 79).
[93] On the Israeli–Arab War of 1967, see M. Oren (2003); Gluska (2007); Segev (2007); Louis and Shlaim (2012); Bowen (2013). On the period from the 1967 War to the first Palestinian Intifada, see M. Benvenisti (1986); Pedatzur (1996); S. Gazit (2003); Gorenberg (2006).
[94] M. Benvenisti (1986, 173). Two recently declassified official Israeli documents from the period 1967–1968 reveal Israel's efforts to evade the characterization of its rule in the Territories as "occupation" so as to prevent Israel's conduct there from being subject to the Fourth Geneva Convention (1949) which deals with the protection of civilians in time of war. See Berger (2016b).
[95] Kimmerling (2001, 75); Migdal (2001).

Israel's stunning military victory over the Arab states in the 1967 War attested to the considerable progress that it had made in the material-coercive aspects of its process of state formation. However, the period immediately before the war, the dynamics of the conflict, and especially its aftermath highlighted the blurred boundaries between the state and its dominant Jewish community and also between its civilian and security spheres. Indeed, one of the most significant outcomes of the 1967 War was that acting and retired security officials in Israel, as well as new political actors with "communal" agendas, managed to break loose from the grip of the state and its leaders, and began to cooperate in and toward the Territories, often hiding behind one another's backs and sometimes enlisting the support of government ministers.[96] In the triangular relationship between state, community, and security, emphasis thus began to shift away from the state and toward security and the community.

Already before the 1967 War, the capacity and legitimacy of Israel's civilian leaders to make decisions on matters of war and peace had become contested. During the "waiting period" that preceded the conflict, and on account of the massive pressures from members of the IDF's general staff, Israeli Prime Minister Eshkol, who also served as defense minister, was compelled to surrender the latter portfolio to Lieutenant General (res.) Moshe Dayan, a former chief of staff of the IDF and one of the architects of the Suez War in 1956.[97] Later, when the war began, the IDF operated quite autonomously from the state's civilian leaders, who were not always notified about its advances. When the war ended, the popularity of the IDF in Israel skyrocketed, and its generals, who were seen as national heroes, overshadowed the state's civilian leaders. This allowed acting and retired security officials, in particular Dayan and Yigal Allon, who served as ministers in the government, to operate autonomously in and vis-à-vis the Territories, which were placed under Israeli Military Government, like the Arab territories in Israel after the First Arab–Israeli War.[98] Major General (ret.) Shlomo Gazit, who was appointed as the first Coordinator of Israel's Operations in the Territories, argued later that "the most practical and important expression of our presence in the Territories was a gradual process of turning Israel and the Territories into one unit, with free movement from and to the Territories, for both Jews and for Arabs."[99]

[96] For details, see Sheffer and Barak (2013, 102–114). See also Kimmerling (2001, 78).
[97] Gluska (2007); Segev (2007). On Dayan's role in 1956, see Sheffer (1996); Golani (2001).
[98] Pedatzur (1996); Gorenberg (2006); Sheffer and Barak (2013); Ranta (2015); Elad (2015, 97).
[99] S. Gazit (2016, 168).

At the same time, the opening of the state's boundaries in 1967 allowed various actors, mainly on the center-right and far-right of Israel's political spectrum, who, as we have seen, had been marginalized in the period 1949–1967, to assert themselves since it provided them with new areas – material and symbolic – to operate. The harbinger of this change was the inclusion of *Herut*, a party with clear communal undertones, in Israel's first National Unity Government, which had been formed on the war's eve.[100] Later, the state's expansion led to the imposition of Israel's control for the first time since 1948 over sacred spaces such as the Western Wall in East Jerusalem, Rachel's Tomb in Bethlehem, and the Cave of the Patriarchs (or the Ibrahimi Mosque) in Hebron, which, in turn, enhanced the communal identity of many Israelis and strengthened "communal" entrepreneurs within its Jewish community.[101]

The cumulative effect of these processes was that the autonomy of Israel's civilian leaders to make decisions about the Territories decreased, and other actors, claiming to speak in the name of security and/or the community, sought to determine the state's policies in and toward the outlying territories. Initially, the impact of these other actors was largely informal, through competing security networks that effectively bypassed the state's political institutions.[102] However, it was not long before the state's institutions – the cabinet, the Knesset, the bureaucracy, and even the court system – endorsed these activities and, moreover, accorded them legitimacy.[103]

Let us examine Israel's policies in the Territories since 1967 on both the material and discursive-symbolic levels and assess their overall impact. Despite their official rhetoric, according to which the Territories were a "deposit" that could be returned in exchange for peace with the Arabs, successive Israeli governments sought to radically transform these areas so as to make the state's contraction more difficult. Although this policy fell short of formal annexation of the Territories, except for East Jerusalem, where Israel's jurisdiction was imposed in 1967 (see Chapter 1), it did make significant parts of them practically indistinguishable from pre-1967 Israel. Thus, the term "East Jerusalem," which had been employed since 1949, was annulled, and Jerusalem, whose area was significantly enlarged, began to be referred to as one "unified" city.[104] The West Bank and the Gaza Strip were now called

---

[100] Kimmerling (2001, 78).
[101] For a useful discussion of this process in a regional perspective, see Owen (2000).
[102] Sheffer and Barak (2013).
[103] Kretzmer (2002, 2–3); N. Gordon (2008, 26–33). See also Sasson (2005).
[104] In Arabic, the unified city was officially referred to as *Urshalim-al-Quds*, combining the city's Hebrew and Arabic names. See M. Benvenisti (1986, 196). For criticism, see R. Khalidi (1997, 14).

"Judea, Samaria and the Gaza District."[105] In addition, Israeli officials referred to these areas as an integral part of the Jewish homeland, and some even described them as "the cradle of the Jewish people."[106] Importantly, the state's institutions, including its security sector, government ministries, and schools, as well as leaders' statements, state media broadcasts, and official documents, began to use these terms only when referring to the Territories, thus signaling Israel's ownership of these areas and helping disseminate these terms domestically and externally.

In addition, nearly all Israeli maps published after 1967 omitted the Green Line, Israel's pre-1967 border, and many ignored the Palestinian cities and towns lying beyond it.[107] The long-term impact of these measures was apparent in 2006, when Israel's Minister of Education Yael Tamir of the Labor Party attempted to include the Green Line in Israeli school textbooks: About half of Israel's Jewish citizens objected to this move.[108] But private firms, too, have abided by this "code" and, as we have seen (in Chapter 1), an Israeli coffee chain whose advertised map of its branches accidentally left out the Territories was compelled to issue a public apology and provide a new and "correct" map that included these areas.[109]

But it was not only the official discourse in Israel that made the state's expansion more concrete. It was also, and perhaps even more so, the actual steps taken by successive Israeli governments in and vis-à-vis these areas since 1967. According to Ron, in the period 1967–1987, "Israel consolidated its infrastructural regime of power over Palestine by sealing the enclave's external borders, crushing internal armed resistance, rationalizing its mechanisms of control, and integrating its economy."[110] Some of the mechanisms that Israel employed for this purpose had been used with regard to its Palestinian community in the period 1949–1966. These included the "securitization" of both the Palestinian Territories and their population,[111] which justified the imposition of the Military Government in these areas and the massive confiscation of Palestinian lands.[112] However, the political context in which these measures were applied – a military occupation over territories lying outside Israel's borders – was novel.

The state's institutions also attempted to physically erase the boundaries separating Israel and the territories, such as by redrawing the

---

[105] Weizman (2012); Tsur (2013).   [106] Sharon (2003).
[107] Lustick (1993, 358–359); Zertal and Eldar (2007, xiii); N. Gordon (2008, 7). See also Klein (2010, 2014). On the role of maps in the Israeli–Palestinian conflict, see M. Benvenisti (1986, 191–202); Wallach (2011b).
[108] Yaar and Herman (2006). See also Kashti (2014).   [109] Kristal (2014).
[110] Ron (2003, 128). See also N. Gordon (2008); Klein (2014, 139–170); Ranta (2015).
[111] Sheffer and Barak (2013, 102–124); Klein (2014, 264–265, 273–274).
[112] N. Gordon (2008, 29–30, 107–108). See also Harel (2015); Elad (2015, 315–318).

municipal boundaries in Jerusalem to include the eastern part of the city and several Arab villages, and by imposing Israel's jurisdiction over this area but without granting Israeli citizenship to its Palestinian inhabitants.[113] Israel also built numerous military bases and civilian settlements in the Territories, first in areas that its leaders deemed strategically important but later also in other areas, including in and around the major Palestinian cities and towns. In addition, Israel built roads and other infrastructures in the Territories, which mostly served the military units and the Jewish settlers (many of these roads were, or eventually became, closed to Palestinians). As done within Israel since 1949, the main tool used for this purpose was the massive confiscation of Palestinian lands due to "security considerations." Israel also assumed control over all land and water resources in the Territories, as well as over their residents' relations with the outside world.[114] As a result of these actions, the number of Jewish settlers in the West Bank steadily increased: 4,400 in 1977; 16,200 in 1981; 35,300 at the end of 1984; and almost 60,000 by the end of 1987.[115]

Unlike Israel's Palestinian community, whose members became Israeli citizens after the state's independence, the Palestinian community in the West Bank and the Gaza Strip was not offered Israeli citizenship and thus was effectively excluded from Israel's political system. Only the Palestinians living in post-1967 Jerusalem became Israeli residents, but they could not vote for the Knesset and most of them boycotted the municipal elections since, to them, participation in these elections implied recognition of the Israeli occupation.

At the same time, the Israeli government, at the initiative of Defense Minister Moshe Dayan, encouraged Palestinian laborers to work in Israel and in the Jewish settlements springing up in the Territories and offered various incentives to Israeli firms that invested in these areas.[116] However, Israel did not permit the Palestinians in the Territories to identify with the Palestinian national movement, and its security agencies forcefully prevented Fatah, the major Palestinian armed faction, and also smaller groups, from taking root in the Territories. It did this by clamping down on these groups' political and armed activities or by assisting or tolerating their competitors, including Islamic organizations that would later establish their own armed factions (e.g., Hamas).[117] Indeed, one of

---

[113] For maps of the "unified" or "Greater" Jerusalem, see the website of the Ir Amim organization at www.ir-amim.org.il/en (accessed November 17, 2016).
[114] Efrat (2006, 59–70); N. Gordon (2008, 127–128); Elad (2015, 318–319).
[115] B'Tselem (2002, 18).
[116] Pedatzur (1996); Gorenberg (2006); N. Gordon (2008); Sheffer and Barak (2013).
[117] Mishal and Sela (2000); N. Gordon (2008, 94–95); Sela (2014).

the major causes for Israel's invasion of Lebanon in 1982 was to crush the PLO, the umbrella organization of the Palestinian armed factions, thus removing the major obstacle to Israel's expansion (see Chapter 7).[118] In addition, Israel did not allow the Palestinians to use their national symbols – for example, referring to the Palestinian flag as the "PLO flag" and removing it whenever its security personnel encountered it in the Territories.

In 1968, only a year after Israel's expansion, a leading Israeli public thinker, Yeshayahu Leibowitz, voiced his concern over the possible transformation of the Israeli state, its pattern of inter-communal relations, and its security, if it were to hold onto the Territories occupied in 1967:

> The Arabs would be the working people and the Jews the administrators, inspectors, officials, and police – mainly secret police. A state ruling a hostile population of 1.5 to 2 million foreigners would necessarily become a secret-police state, with all that this implies for education, free speech and democratic institutions. The corruption characteristic of every colonial regime would also prevail in the State of Israel. The administration would suppress Arab insurgency on the one hand and acquire Arab Quislings on the other. There is also good reason to fear that the Israel Defense Force[s], which has been until now a people's army, would, as a result of being transformed into an army of occupation, degenerate, and its commanders, who will have become military governors, resemble their colleagues in other nations.[119]

In 2012, when Israel's expansion reached its forty-fifth anniversary, a former director of Israel's General Security Service, Yuval Diskin, openly admitted that he "agreed with every word" in Leibowitz's statement.[120]

Diskin knew what he was talking about. Since 1967, one of the main institutions entrusted with controlling the Palestinians in the Territories, besides the IDF, was the General Security Service, which until then had mostly dealt with domestic security, including vis-à-vis Israel's Palestinian citizens. Avraham Shalom, a senior official in the General Security Service in the period after 1967 who later served as its director, later recounted:

> We began working in the [West] Bank and the [Gaza] Strip, in the area of anti-terrorism, without exactly knowing what it is because terrorism was not developed. The population was not hostile ... Meanwhile, in the [General Security]

---

[118] Tessler (1994, 519); N. Gordon (2008, 111–114); Bregman (2014, 122–130).
[119] Leibowitz (1992, 225–226).
[120] Quoted in the film *The Gatekeepers* (2012). In the film, directed by Dror Moreh, six former directors of the General Security Service narrate their efforts to suppress the Palestinians' resistance to Israel's rule in the Territories since 1967. For a critical review of the film, see Bar-Tuvia and Barak (2014).

Service, we had a group of people, who went from Arab to Arab in the [West] Bank and talked to them. The goal was to understand what drives this business, the Palestinians. Originally we wanted to make peace with Jordan, not with the Palestinians. Because who thought that the Jordanians will not return? Then the idea popped up of a Palestinian state. This idea was not conceived by the Arabs. It was us ... I was excited about it, although it was not in my domain as Head of Operations. ... But how do you say in a cynical way, "luckily" terrorism increased bit by bit ... and all of a sudden we had something to do. Once you take care of something specific you forget about the strategy. So we stopped dealing with the Palestinian state. Once we stopped dealing with the Palestinian state and were preoccupied with terrorism, terrorism became more sophisticated, and we also became more sophisticated.[121]

As suggested by Shalom and several other officials in the General Security Service, this cycle of Palestinian resistance and Israeli suppression led to the increased penetration of the Territories by Israel's security sector. Indeed, in the same way that the General Security Service had helped reinforce Jewish control over the Palestinian community in Israel, it now sought to impose a pattern of control over the Palestinians in the Territories. The problem, however, was that the latter group was significantly larger than the former group (Table 2.2), and the political options offered to the latter were far more limited than those that were available to the former. Consequently, Shalom and his successors, as well as Israel's security sector in general, were caught in a vicious cycle of suppression and resistance, facing essentially the same predicament time and again.[122]

Part of the reason why Israel failed to accommodate the Palestinians in the Territories was that, despite its long-term occupation of these areas, its leaders continued to regard their inhabitants as an external element. According to Adrian Guelke, "It suited Israel to present the threat to its security primarily in external terms, justifying the role of its army and thereby also portraying the conflict as a David and Goliath struggle between Israel and the Arab world rather than a conflict within a deeply divided society, between Israelis and Palestinians."[123] By contrast, British leaders "wished the outside world to view the conflict in Northern Ireland as an internal one."[124] This perception had, of course, important implications for how these two conflicts were dealt with by the two states. Thus, for example, during the first Palestinian Intifada (1987–1993), there were 1,204 Palestinian deaths compared to 179 Israeli deaths, and of the latter

---

[121] Quoted in *The Gatekeepers* (2012). On the role of the General Security Service in the Territories, see also T. Friedman (1989, 354); Ronen (1989); N. Gordon (2008, 24); Elad (2015, 81–87); Ranta (2015, 72–76); S. Gazit (2016, 169–170, 173–174).
[122] Bar-Tuvia and Barak (2014). On the shift to coercive measures in Israel vis-à-vis the Territories, see Ron (2003); N. Gordon (2008); Bregman (2014).
[123] Guelke (2012, 69).   [124] Ibid. See also M. Benvenisti (1995, 207–208).

only 4.7 percent were security personnel. By contrast, 28.4 percent of the 3,379 casualties in the conflict in Northern Ireland in the period 1969–2010 were security personnel.[125] In addition, this perception affected the two conflicts' very different historical trajectories.

We see, then, that during the first two decades after Israel's expansion, what emerged in Israel/Palestine was a political unit that was similar to pre-1967 Israel in some respects but very different in others. First, this expanded state did not have clear boundaries that enjoyed international recognition and were accepted by Israel's neighbors.[126] Second, Israel's civilian leaders were not autonomous in making decision about the "fate" of the outlying territories, in particular the West Bank and East Jerusalem, and they had to share power with, and were often bypassed by, other actors including security networks and "communal" entrepreneurs that exploited Israel's open frontiers to defy the more "statist" orientation. Third, the Palestinian community in the Territories was significantly larger than the Palestinian community in Israel, did not enjoy the political rights and opportunities available to the latter, and was, moreover, considered to be an external and not a domestic actor by Israel's leaders. The pattern of inter-communal relations in Israel/Palestine, too, was markedly different. Some of its manifestations were not new: detention of Palestinian suspects without trial; large-scale confiscation of Palestinian land "for security considerations"; the frequent use of permits to supervise the Palestinians; and the use of vast networks of collaborators and informants and other means of intelligence gathering that penetrated deep into – and, ultimately, helped weaken – this community. But their scale was much larger than before and the relationship itself was repressive, especially when Israel's actions encountered Palestinian resistance.[127]

Despite all of this, however, until the outbreak of the first Intifada in December 1987, Israel's leaders and large segments of its general public were not aware of or ignored the full magnitude of the profound changes that had taken place in Israel/Palestine since 1967, and many believed that the "status quo" would persist indefinitely. Indeed, some even suggested that what they referred to as the "enlightened occupation" was not only in Israel's interest but also in the interest of the Palestinians themselves. They were thus surprised to discover that this was not the case.[128]

---

[125] On the First Intifada, see B'Tselem (n.d.). On Northern Ireland, see Guelke (2012, 62–63).
[126] This was reflected in the repeated military confrontations between Israel and Egypt until the signing of the peace treaty in 1979.
[127] N. Gordon (2008, 42–44, 95).
[128] T. Friedman (1989, 360); N. Gordon (2008, 148).

The First Intifada and Its Aftermath

Four episodes that took place in Israel/Palestine since late 1987 have captured the most attention of its inhabitants and outside observers: the first Palestinian Intifada that erupted in the West Bank (including East Jerusalem) and the Gaza Strip in December 1987; the Israeli–Palestinian peace process that took place in the period 1993–2000; the Second Palestinian Intifada (or the al-Aqsa Intifada), which began in September 2000; and Israel's unilateral withdrawal (the Disengagement Plan) from the Gaza Strip in August 2005. But beyond these dramatic episodes, deeper processes and developments were at work in Israel/Palestine, and these further entrenched the expanded-state-turned-divided-society that had emerged there since 1967.

First, the number of Jewish settlements and settlers in the Territories increased steadily throughout this period. By 1992, the number of Jewish settlements in the West Bank and the Gaza Strip had already reached 120, and this figure remained more or less the same until the end of 2013, when there were 125 formal (that is, government-sanctioned) settlements in the West Bank (those in the Gaza Strip were evacuated and demolished in 2005).[129] However, by that time there were also about one hundred "unauthorized outposts" throughout the West Bank. These informal settlements began to emerge in the 1990s during the Israeli–Palestinian peace process, when the Israeli government imposed limits on building new settlements in the Territories. The "unauthorized outposts" were smaller than the formal settlements and were not government-sanctioned. However, an official Israeli report from 2005 suggests that they were often built with the knowledge and assistance of at least some of the state's agencies. Moreover, apart from a few exceptions, these "unauthorized outposts" were not dismantled, and continuous attempts were made to sanction them.[130] To these formal and informal Jewish settlements in the Territories one can add 12 Jewish neighborhoods that were built in the Palestinian areas that Israel annexed to the Jerusalem Municipality in 1967, as well as several Jewish enclaves built within Palestinian neighborhoods in East Jerusalem and Hebron, with aid from the Israeli government and, in East Jerusalem, also from the Jerusalem municipality.[131]

---

[129] B'Tselem (2015).
[130] Sasson (2005). This report mentions 105 outposts in the Territories (ibid., 21), adding that "[t]he method for establishing outposts is mostly by bypassing procedures and breach of the law, misrepresentation towards some of the state's authorities, and the participation in the blatant violation of the law of other authorities" (ibid., 24).
[131] B'Tselem (2015). See also the website of the Ir Amim organization, at www.ir-amim.org.il/en (accessed November 17, 2016).

As a consequence of Israel's ongoing settlement project in the Territories, the number of Israeli citizens living there increased from 60,000 by the end of 1987 to 100,000 by 1992, 110,900 by the end of 1993, and 191,600 by the end of 2000. This suggests that, in fact, the number of Jewish settlers in the Territories had almost doubled in the period of the Israeli–Palestinian peace process, which, among other things, was supposed to determine the "fate" of these areas.[132]

Israel's Disengagement Plan in 2005 consisted of a unilateral withdrawal from the Gaza Strip, including the dismantling of all 21 Jewish settlements built there, and from four small settlements in the West Bank (however, the area of the latter settlements remained under Israeli control), and the evacuation of 8,000–9,000 settlers, who, at that time, amounted to 3.7 percent of the total number of Jewish settlers in the Territories.[133] However, apart from these four settlements, not one formal settlement that Israel built in the West Bank since 1967 was dismantled. Thus, by the end of 2013 about 350,010 Jewish settlers lived in the West Bank, and at the end of 2012 an additional population of 196,890 lived in the Jewish neighborhoods in East Jerusalem, suggesting that the total number of Israeli Jews in the Territories occupied in 1967 at that time reached 547,000.[134] By the end of 2015, the number of Israelis in the Territories stood at 585,900: 385,900 in the West Bank, where they comprised 13 percent of the total population,[135] and an additional 200,000 in East Jerusalem, with Jews constituting 62 percent of the expanded city's total population.[136]

We see, then, that successive Israeli governments, regardless of their political inclination and actual policies toward the Palestinians, were quite adamant in maintaining the state's hold over the Territories and sought to further buttress it. However, the major difference between the period after 1993 and the previous one was that Israel's control over the Territories became more indirect. Thus, for example, Israeli troops were not always present in all areas but controlled them by sealing their "borders" with Israel, by erecting barriers and checkpoints within these

---

[132] B'Tselem (2002, 18).
[133] Rice (2011, 382). The figure of 8,000 is mentioned by Bar-Siman-Tov (2009, 11). The figure of 9,000 is mentioned by Even (2015, 75) and by Israel's Ministry of Foreign Affairs. See Ministry of Foreign Affairs, "Israel's Disengagement from Gaza and North Samaria (2005)," n.d., at http://mfa.gov.il/MFA/AboutIsrael/Maps/Pages/Israels%20Disengagement%20Plan-%202005.aspx (accessed November 12, 2016). According to B'Tselem (2015), there were 234,820 Jewish settlers in the West Bank at the end of 2004. If one adds to this number the 8,000–9,000 settlers evacuated from the Gaza Strip in 2005, the total number of settlers in the Territories (excluding East Jerusalem) at the end of 2004 was 242,820–243,820. The settlers evacuated in 2005 were, thus, only 3.3–3.7 percent of the total number of settlers.
[134] B'Tselem (2015). [135] Peace Now (2016a). [136] Peace Now (2016b).

areas themselves, and by launching military operations after which the security personnel returned to their bases. In other words, and using Ron's distinction (see Chapter 1), what were initially Palestinian "ghettos" were effectively transformed into "frontiers" so as to facilitate Israel's continued control over them. The same goal was attained by delegating the task of controlling the Territories to other actors, including Palestinian forces, especially after the establishment of the Palestinian National Authority in 1994, but also militias set up by Jewish settlers. These militias sometimes cooperated with Israel's security sector, but at other times acted autonomously, challenging the state's claim to a monopoly over the legitimate means of violence.[137] This process of "frontierization" reached its pinnacle during the Second Palestinian Intifada, when, following a wave of Palestinian suicide bombings against Israel, the Israeli government decided on the construction of a massive 708-kilometers long "separation barrier" that was built mainly on Palestinian lands and not on the "Green Line,"[138] and with Israel retaining its military and civilian presence on both sides of the barrier.

The shift to informal control over the Territories was also manifested in the state's settlement policy. In a lengthy report from 2005, which dealt with the "unauthorized outposts" in the Territories, Talia Sasson, an official in Israel's State Attorney's Office, stated:

In fact, the unauthorized outposts phenomenon is a continuation of the settlement project in the Territories. But whereas in the distant past the settlement project had gained, in some years, the formal recognition and encouragement of the Israeli government, in the mid-nineties it changed its face. Israeli governments were no longer *formally* involved in establishing the outposts, presumably due to Israel's international situation and the negative position of most states against the settlement project. This is not the case with regard to public authorities and institutions of the state, which played a major role in their establishment along with others, in part inspired by the political echelon, some by looking the other way, some by encouragement and support, but without a decision by the political echelon which is *authorized* by the state [to make such decisions].[139]

Other methods of inter-communal control that Israel employed in Israel/Palestine in this period included monitoring Palestinian groups and individuals by its security agencies, especially the IDF and the General Security Service. In addition to the methods that these two agencies had employed in the past, Israel made extensive use of observations, overflights, unmanned drones, and naval vessels in, over, and around the

---

[137] Ron (2003, 169–170); N. Gordon (2008).
[138] B'Tselem (2011); Ben-Eliezer (2012, 178).
[139] Sasson (2005, 19). Emphases are in the original.

Territories.[140] At times, Israel also launched commando raids against ships and convoys headed to the Territories in order to prevent the smuggling of arms and other supplies to the Palestinian armed factions and also to enforce a sea and land blockade on the Gaza Strip after Israel's withdrawal from that area. One important consequence of the increase in the number of Jewish settlements and settlers in the Territories and Israel's deepening control over these areas was the increased geographical and political fragmentation of the Palestinian community. Indeed, during this period, East Jerusalem, the West Bank, and the Gaza Strip, as well as smaller regions within them, became distinct and loosely connected enclaves, and the Palestinians who resided in these regions were subject to different security, legal, and economic measures.[141] This process was accelerated after the establishment of the Palestinian National Authority, Israel's "closure" policy, the construction of the "separation barrier," and Hamas' takeover of the Gaza Strip in 2007. At the same time, the Palestinian economy continued to be highly dependent on Israel, and this was only increased during the Israeli–Palestinian peace process.[142] In addition, Israel continued to dominate other spheres, such as water, land, natural resources, and the environment, and its leaders could withhold tax revenues from the Palestinian National Authority to exert pressure on its leaders.

It is quite clear, then, that in this period, the state's expansion in Israel/Palestine was further buttressed. It is against this backdrop that we can better assess the aforementioned episodes, which, essentially, were attempts to transform this situation.

The first Palestinian Intifada, which erupted in December 1987, was a popular uprising that stemmed from the political, social, and economic grievances of the Palestinians in the West Bank and in the Gaza Strip after two decades of Israeli occupation.[143] Previously, resistance to Israel's expansion within this community had taken the form of guerrilla operations launched by Palestinian armed factions in the Territories and across Israel's borders with its neighbors, mainly Jordan and Lebanon.

---

[140] This process is documented in the film *The Gatekeepers* (2012). In 2014, 43 Israelis who had served in the IDF's signals intelligence unit (Unit 8200), including several officers, sent an open letter to Prime Minister Netanyahu and senior military officials, in which they stated that Israel's intelligence gathering "harms innocents and serves for political persecution and sowing discord in Palestinian society" and that they "refuse to take part in actions against Palestinians and refuse to continue serving as tools in deepening the military control over the Occupied Territories." See G. Cohen (2014); Pfeffer (2014).

[141] M. Benvenisti (2007, 178).   [142] Selby (2003).

[143] On the First Palestinian Intifada, see Lockman and Beinin (1989); Schiff and Ya'ari (1989); Peretz (1990); Hiltermann (1991); Hunter (1993); M. Benvenisti (1995); Sela and Mishal (2000); Ron (2003); Alimi (2007); N. Gordon (2008, 147–168); Sela (2014).

However, Israel's security sector effectively suppressed these "separatist" acts, and sealed the border between Israel/Palestine and Jordan, not least because of the close security cooperation between the Israeli and Jordanian states. Moreover, in 1982, during the Lebanon War, Israel forcefully expelled the Palestinian armed factions from that country (see Chapters 6–7). At the same time, efforts to launch an Israeli–Palestinian peace process did not lead to tangible results: Successive Israeli governments refused to negotiate with the PLO, which was recognized in 1974 as the sole legitimate representative of the Palestinian people, and all attempts to reach an agreement with Arab states such as Jordan or with local elements in the Territories that were not associated with the PLO came to naught.[144] For the Palestinians in the Territories marking the 20th anniversary of Israel's occupation, the only way left open was to take matters into their own hands.

In retrospect, what the Palestinians in the Territories tried to achieve in 1987 was similar to what Egyptian President Anwar al-Sadat and Syrian President Hafez al-Assad had attempted to do on October 6, 1973, when they launched a surprise attack against Israel's forces in the occupied Sinai Peninsula and the occupied Golan, respectively. Like Egypt and Syria, the Palestinians sought to break Israel's "psychological barrier" regarding the Territories, after both small-scale violence and diplomacy had proven to be futile, and after consecutive governments in Israel led to further entrenchment of the state in these areas. It should be noted, however, that the Intifada was also different from the Arab–Israeli War of 1973 in that it was, at least initially, non-violent.

But the Palestinian reasoning in 1987 was problematic. Unlike the conflict between Israel and Egypt, which was an inter-state conflict that was terminated when both sides managed to attain at least part of their interests, the Israeli–Palestinian conflict became, especially on account of Israel's expansion and the creation of a divided society in Israel/Palestine, an intercommunal conflict. In this conflict, moreover, the identity of both sides, and not just their material interests, became significant. This explains why Israeli leaders and other members of the Jewish community in Israel/Palestine, who regarded the Territories as crucial not only for Israel's security but also for their collective identity, perceived the Palestinian Intifada as an "existential threat," and not as an attempt to put an end to two decades of Israel's occupation of the Territories. This is also why Israel's National Unity Government, which included members of both the center-left Labor Party and the center-right Likud Party, considered the Intifada as a "test of will" and instructed Israel's security sector to suppress it.

[144] Sela (2014).

However, the Palestinian Intifada also indicated that coercion alone could not compel the Palestinians in the Territories to acquiesce to Israel's rule. The same was true with regard to the material incentives that Israel offered to members of this community and the efforts to stymie its national mobilization. In other words, the Intifada suggested that the pattern of inter-communal control in Israel/Palestine, which had been established in 1967, was untenable, although, as mentioned earlier, Israeli leaders later came up with new, informal, and indirect ways to maintain their community's dominant position in Israel/Palestine. Finally, in the area of security, Israel's security agencies, including the IDF and the General Security Service, regarded the Palestinian actions, whether violent or not, as "terrorism" and conceived of their own actions in the Territories as "counterterrorism" and not as policing. But this policy, which, in Israeli eyes, justified the use of massive violence against the Palestinians in the Territories, and sometimes also within Israel itself, alienated the Palestinians, who sometimes replied in the same token. At any rate, the growing violence in Israel/Palestine led at least some Israeli scholars to acknowledge that the state's expansion in 1967 had ushered in a fundamental change in its security sector, and that the IDF became, for all intents and purposes, an internal policing force. In 1993, Baruch Kimmerling observed that Israel's military became "essentially the same as the tribal armies of various African states, that assures the hegemony of one part of a collectivity's population and the subjugation of all of the other parts."[145]

After more years of political deadlock and several international and regional developments such as the end of the Cold War, the Gulf War, and the Madrid Conference in 1991, and following the victory of the Labor Party led by Yitzhak Rabin in the parliamentary elections of 1992 and further violence between Israelis and Palestinians, including within Israel itself, the Israeli government and the PLO launched secret talks in Norway that led to the signing of the Oslo Agreement on September 13, 1993.[146] For many Palestinians, including the PLO leadership, the Israeli–Palestinian peace process was supposed to achieve the same goals as the Intifada, in the same way that the Egyptian–Israeli peace process, which culminated in the Camp David Accords and the Egyptian–Israeli peace treaty (1979), followed from the Arab–Israeli War of 1973. Indeed, Palestinian leaders, especially Yasser Arafat, repeatedly called on Prime Minister Rabin to agree to a "Peace of the

---

[145] Kimmerling (2012, 137). The original piece appeared in 1993.
[146] On the Israeli–Palestinian peace process, see Harkabi (1995); Sela and Ma'oz (1997a); Lustick (1997c); Barnett (1999); Said (2001); Barak (2005a); Sela (2009, 2014).

Brave," implying that the Israeli former general-turned-statesman should follow President Charles de Gaulle's footsteps and instigate a full Israeli withdrawal from the Territories.[147]

But these expectations, which some Israelis, especially on the center-left of the political spectrum, shared, did not come to fruition. First, as it turned out, the Israeli government was not autonomous with regard to the West Bank and East Jerusalem (and, to a lesser extent, the Gaza Strip), as it was with regard to the Sinai Peninsula. This became clear when Israel's moves toward the Palestinians in the period 1994–1995, which included partial withdrawals in the Territories, elicited mass protests by actors to the right and far-right of the political spectrum, culminating in Prime Minister Rabin's assassination in 1995. Part of the reason for this had to do with the proximity of the West Bank to Israel's population centers and lack of trust toward the Palestinians and their leaders by many Israelis. But the significance of the Territories for the identity of many Israeli Jews also played an important role.[148] Second, it was not at all clear that Israel's leaders themselves intended to play the role that their Palestinian counterparts expected them to play. In early 1993, Prime Minister Rabin stated that the problem with the Territories was that Israel could not use its full force there, adding: "I hope that we will find a partner which will be responsible in Gaza for the internal Palestinian problems. It will deal with Gaza without the problems of the High Court of Justice, without the problems of *B'Tselem* and without the problems of all kinds of sensitive souls and all kinds of mothers and fathers."[149] From this angle, Arafat and the PLO appeared to be convenient: They could rule over the Palestinians in the Territories and enjoy the spoils of government like their counterparts in the Arab states and, if needed, restrain anti-Israeli actions just like these Arab leaders were doing in their own states. At the same time, Israel, the stronger party, would ensure that Arafat and the PLO would play along, while washing its hands of their actions.[150]

The main problem with this scenario, however, was that by that period the Israeli–Palestinian conflict had already become an inter-communal conflict and not an inter-state conflict.[151] As we have seen, Israel's expansion and its subsequent actions in the Territories created a divided society

---

[147] See, e.g., Arafat (1994).
[148] Barak (2005a); Ben-Eliezer (2012, 38–42). See also Mitzen (2006).
[149] Quoted in Kretzmer (2002, 2). See also N. Gordon (2008, 170–171); Seliktar (2009). B'Tselem, the Israeli Information Center for Human Rights in the Occupied Territories, is an Israeli NGO that monitors human rights violations in the Territories.
[150] Kimmerling (2001, 236). See also Harkabi (1995); N. Gordon (2008, 169–196); Cf. Barnett (1999).
[151] Barak (2005a).

in Israel/Palestine, and this meant that the Israeli–Palestinian conflict had become even less like the inter-state conflicts between Israel and Arab states such as Egypt, Jordan and Syria. Thus, it was not at all clear that the inter-state "tool-kit" that had been successfully used to achieve Egyptian–Israeli peace in 1979 (and, in 1994, also Jordanian–Israeli peace)[152] was relevant to Israel/Palestine and to the conflict between its communities.

The Oslo Agreement reflected this inter-state paradigm and its limitations. The agreement called for a limited withdrawal of Israeli forces from the Gaza Strip and Jericho, for the creation of a Palestinian National Authority, and for Palestinian elections in a "transitional period" of five years. At the same time, it postponed the most difficult issues in the relationship between Israelis and Palestinians – Jerusalem, the Palestinian refugees, the Jewish settlements, and the Palestinian state and its borders – to the "permanent status" negotiations. Thus, all of the issues that could suggest that the Israeli–Palestinian conflict was, in fact, an inter-communal conflict and not an inter-state conflict became taboos that could not be openly addressed. The issue of Jerusalem could have implied that the Israeli–Palestinian conflict was, or had become, an identity-based conflict, in addition to its being a territorial dispute. The issue of the refugees was liable to evoke the conflicting narratives of the First Arab–Israeli War and the needs of the Palestinian refugees in Israel/Palestine and in the diaspora. Finally, the two issues of Jewish settlements in the Territories and a Palestinian state could have revealed the magnitude of the former and how it effectively obstructed the latter – namely, that Israel's expansion since 1967 has created a divided society in Israel/Palestine and caused its two communities to become intertwined.

Importantly, the taboo surrounding the discussion of these four issues in the "transitional period" did not apply to Israeli and Palestinian opponents (or "spoilers") of the peace process. Thus, in Israel, the right-wing opposition, led by Benjamin Netanyahu of the Likud Party, called to preserve Jewish rule over the entire "Land of Israel," and openly challenged the legitimacy of the Rabin government, arguing that its majority in the Knesset rested on non-Jewish MPs (that is, Israeli–Palestinian citizens). In 1994, a Jewish settler, Baruch Goldstein, massacred 29 Palestinian worshippers in Hebron in order to derail the peace process, and in 1995, another extremist, Yigal Amir, assassinated Prime Minister Rabin and accomplished just that.

But on the Palestinian side, too, the Oslo Agreement was met with considerable opposition, including from Islamic and leftist factions but

---

[152] Stein (1999).

also from some members of Arafat's Fatah. Some groups, most notably Hamas, tried to obstruct the peace process by launching armed attacks against Israelis on both sides of the Green Line, and were quite successful. One of the major problems in this period was that the Palestinian National Authority, while representing a first autonomous Palestinian foothold in the Territories and having certain attributes of a state, was nevertheless not a sovereign state, although it was encouraged to perform as one by Israel, the United States, the European Union, and other actors. Rather, it was "an archipelago of disconnected enclaves separated by [Israeli] checkpoints ... bent on reminding Palestinians who's in charge."[153]

Thus, and despite some progress made in the Israeli–Palestinian peace process, the Palestinians in the Territories came nowhere near an independent state, and instead found themselves trapped in a "transitional period" that was extended time and again by the more powerful side: Israel. The inability to gain tangible results through negotiations eventually prompted some Palestinians to resort to violence against Israel, or to turn a blind eye to it, perhaps in order to induce the Algerian model and bring about the state's contraction, but also to preserve their own fragile intra-communal consensus. At the same time, Israeli hopes that Arafat and his lieutenants would impose law and order in the Territories without the normative constraints imposed on Israel's security sector were fulfilled only in part.[154]

Following several years of political impasse in the Israeli–Palestinian peace process, under the governments of Shimon Peres and Netanyahu (1996–1999), a new government, led by Ehud Barak – who, like Rabin, was a former chief of staff of the IDF – was formed, and hopes for Israeli–Palestinian peace were renewed. However, a summit held in Camp David in July 2000 between Prime Minister Barak, PLO Chairman Arafat, and US President Clinton – an event which, in itself, epitomized the interstate logic of the Israeli–Palestinian peace process – ended in failure, and after a provocative visit by Knesset Member Ariel Sharon of the Likud Party to Al-Haram al-Sharif/Temple Mount in Jerusalem, the peace process collapsed. Mass Palestinian demonstrations in the Territories and in Israel were met with massive Israeli violence, and "[t]he violence of the other side justified each side's escalation of violence to defeat the other."[155]

In the course of the Second Palestinian Intifada (or the al-Aqsa Intifada),[156] thousands of Palestinians and Israelis were killed and

---

[153] Shipler (2002). [154] Sela (2014, 294). [155] Kriesberg (2002, 563).
[156] On the Second Palestinian Intifada (or al-Aqsa Intifada), see Ron (2003); Dor (2004); Peri (2006); Levy (2007); N. Gordon (2008, 197–222); Ben-Ari et al. (2010); Grinberg (2010); Ben-Eliezer (2012); Sela (2014). See also Sheffer and Barak (2010).

wounded, with both sides killing more civilians than combatants. Uri Ben-Eliezer writes that between September 30, 2000 and October 31, 2005, a total of 3,729 Palestinians were killed by Israel and nearly 25,000 were wounded, and that less than one-third of the Palestinians who died had taken part in the fighting. On the Israeli side, 1,064 were killed, of whom 70 percent were civilians, and an additional 7,462 were wounded.[157] In addition, many thousands, especially Palestinians, lost their homes and their property. Attempts to renew the peace process between the two rival communities in Israel/Palestine in subsequent years, especially during the period of Ehud Olmert's premiership (2007–2008), as well as several other initiatives, have all failed to break the impasse.[158]

In August 2005, following mounting domestic and external pressures, Ariel Sharon, who succeeded Barak as Israel's prime minister in 2001, decided on the Disengagement Plan, according to which all settlements in the Gaza Strip and four small settlements in the West Bank, together with 8,000–9,000 Jewish settlers, were evacuated. However, Israel's unilateral withdrawal from the Gaza Strip, which according to Dov Weisglass, Sharon's senior adviser, was specifically designed to freeze the peace process with the Palestinians,[159] did not lead to the delineation of an international border between Israel and the Gaza Strip, and Israel imposed a land and sea blockade on this region. Two years later, in 2007, Hamas took over the area from the Palestinian National Authority, and since then, Hamas, which has been the de facto ruler of the Gaza Strip, fought Israel several times – most notably in 2008–2009, 2012, and 2014 – with each confrontation being more bloody and devastating than the one before.[160]

We see, then, that all attempts to dismantle the expanded state in Israel/Palestine since 1967 have ended in failure, and that Israel's hold over the outlying territories has become even more entrenched over the years. In an op-ed published in the daily *Haaretz* in May 2015, a leading Israeli political scientist, Zeev Sternhell observed that "[a]fter half

---

[157] Ben-Eliezer (2012, 213).   [158] Podeh (2015, 304–357).
[159] In a press interview in October 2004, Weisglass added: "[W]hen you freeze that process, you prevent the establishment of a Palestinian state, and you prevent a discussion on the refugees, the borders and Jerusalem. Effectively, this whole package called the Palestinian state, with all that it entails, has been removed indefinitely from our agenda. And all this with authority and permission. All with a [US] presidential blessing and the ratification of both houses of Congress." Quoted in Shavit (2004). On Israel's unilateralist steps toward the Palestinians as attempts to deal with the threats to its identities as a Jewish and democratic state, but also to the state's identity as a security provider, see Lupovici (2012).
[160] Ben-Eliezer (2012, 214–219).

a century of control of the territories, most Israelis view the colonial rule as obvious and the denial of Palestinian rights as part of the natural order of things."[161] While this might indeed be the case, the question remains of why so many Israelis have come to see things in this light, despite the considerable human, political, economic, and moral costs of the occupation. The next paragraphs try to account for this question by focusing on several long-term developments that have taken place in the Jewish community in Israel/Palestine since 1967, and which helped reinforce the state's expansion rather than bring about its contraction.

As we have seen, during the period of British rule in Palestine, the Jewish community (the *Yishuv*) developed its own political and security institutions that included members of the various factions in this community, and these proved to be quite effective in excluding, and, later, in defeating, the rival Palestinian community, which lacked such mechanisms. Later, when the boundaries of the Israeli state became closed and the "statist" orientation in the political center became dominant, Ben-Gurion's *Mapai* and its allies were hegemonic in the Jewish community in Israel and the state imposed a pattern of inter-communal control over its Palestinian community. However, in 1967, when the state expanded and its boundaries re-opened, both the pattern of intra-communal power sharing and the inter-connected pattern of inter-communal repression began to resurface.[162]

The first indication of this change was the formation of the National Unity Government on the eve of the 1967 War, which included members of *Herut*, which, as we have seen, had been excluded from Israel's ruling coalition since independence. After *Herut* left the government in 1970, Israel was led by the Labor Party (1970–1977) and then by the Likud Party (1977–1984). But in 1984, in the wake of Israel's invasion of Lebanon and the political, social, and economic crisis that followed, National Unity Governments, which, in Israel, serve as an important mechanism of intra-communal power sharing, ruled the state until 1990.[163] But later, too, this conflict regulation mechanism was adopted in order to maintain the intra-communal consensus within the Jewish community in Israel/Palestine and at the same time to allow the latter to cope with major challenges, and particularly the first and second

---

[161] Sternhell (2015).
[162] Other parallels with the period of the *Yishuv* are the emergence of Jewish militias in the Territories which were independent from the political center and posed a challenge to the state's authority, and of "unauthorized outposts," which were reminiscent of the illegal Jewish settlements built during the British Mandate, though the former enjoyed the support of government agencies. See also Chapter 7.
[163] T. Friedman (1989, 270–271).

134   State Expansion and Conflict

Palestinian Intifadas, which Israel sought to forcefully suppress. At the same time, minority Israeli governments found it difficult to govern. In the early 1980s, the Likud government of Menachem Begin faced a mounting crisis in the Territories, which it tried to "solve" by invading Lebanon in 1982 (see Chapter 7). Later, in the period 1990–1992, the government of Yitzhak Shamir faced mounting domestic and external pressures on account of its intransigent position with regard to the Territories, and in 1992–1995 the Rabin government faced an organized campaign of de-legitimization from the Israeli right. The governments of Peres (1995–1996) and Netanyahu (1996–1999), though attempting to broaden the basis of their support – the former adopted a conciliatory policy toward the Israeli right and launched a military operation in Lebanon in 1996 ("Operation Grapes of Wrath"), and the latter signed the Wye River Memorandum with the Palestinians in 1998 – also found it difficult to govern, and both leaders were defeated in subsequent elections (though Netanyahu was appointed prime minister later, in 2009, 2013, and 2015). It can thus be argued that, in Israel, "national unity" – that is, intra-communal consensus – meant a freeze of peacemaking efforts and a resort to inter-communal repression.

Another factor that can be mentioned in this context is that the Territories offered political opportunities for various actors in the Jewish community in Israel/Palestine, and especially those in the center-right and far-right of the political spectrum. Reversing Ben-Gurion's idea that the state should hold religion in the palm of its hand, these actors viewed the state as an instrument of the Jewish community, whose interests, as they interpreted them, stood above, rather than below, raison d'état.[164] But the Territories also offered these actors material incentives: from the mid-1980s, and following a major socioeconomic crisis, Israel underwent a rapid process of economic liberalization, which led to severe cuts in the benefits that it distributed to its citizens. At the same time, the Territories offered inexpensive land and housing, low utility bills, and opportunities for employment in the government and in various agencies affiliated with it. Thus, in tandem with the shrinking welfare state in Israel, an alternative welfare state gradually emerged in the Territories, whose beneficiaries had a clear interest in its preservation.[165]

But it was not only the Jewish settlers in the Territories who acquired new privileges and political and material assets that they were fearful of losing. Other groups within the Jewish community in Israel/Palestine, too, had made considerable headway since 1967, which turned them into

[164] This process is discussed in Migdal (2001, 157–161).
[165] Newman (1995); Zertal and Eldar (2007).

stake-holders in the expanded state. Whereas in the first decades of Israel's independence, the state and its institutions were dominated by Ashkenazi Jews, who immigrated from Eastern Europe, in later years, these institutions opened up to other groups, and especially Mizrahi Jews who originated from Arab and Muslim countries.[166] The increasing social representativeness of Israel's institutions is attested to by a number of recent studies on the social makeup of the Israeli cabinet,[167] the Knesset,[168] the military elite,[169] the IDF's combat units,[170] and the Israeli economy.[171] Together, these studies suggest that the Israeli state has, in time, become more representative of the dominant Jewish community in Israel/Palestine and the various groups within it, thus increasing not only the stakes of these groups in the state but also their sense of ownership toward it. In particular, these newcomers include peripheral groups, such as residents of Israel's north and south (including many Mizrahi Jews), immigrants from the former Soviet Union, and the younger generation among the national religious Jews, particularly Gush Emunim (Bloc of the Faithful), the movement that was one of the main initiators of the construction of Jewish settlements in the Territories in the wake of the 1973 War.[172] For all of these groups, a profound political change in Israel/Palestine, such as the one envisaged by the Rabin government and its supporters in the 1990s, but also later, could jeopardize their newly acquired position in the state. This is not to say that all members of these peripheral groups supported Israel's expansion. What is important is that many of these newcomers had a vested interest in the political, social, and economic status quo in Israel/Palestine since 1967.

Let us focus on one of these studies, which deals with the social background of Israel's military elite in the period from Israel's independence in 1948 until 2011.[173] This group is significant not only because it includes the commanders of the IDF, including those high-ranking officers who had governed the Territories since 1967, but also because its members were sometimes appointed as heads of other security agencies in Israel, as ministers of defense and other cabinet members, and as prime ministers. In addition, members of this group represent the core of Israel's security networks, which expanded into the Territories in the wake of the 1967 War and played a key role in

---

[166] Migdal (2001, 155–157); Kimmerling (2001, 130).   [167] Kenig (2014).
[168] Rahat and Malka (2012).   [169] Barak and Tsur (2012b).   [170] Levy (2012).
[171] Dahan (2013).
[172] Horowitz and Lissak (1989, 246); Shafir and Peled (2002, 171); Pedahzur (2012, 48–50).
[173] Barak and Tsur (2012b).

securitizing these areas and facilitating Israel's continued rule there.[174]

According to the study on Israel's military elite, this group has in recent decades attracted members of various groups within the Jewish community in Israel/Palestine, including some from the social and geographical periphery. At the same time, members of Israel's Palestinian community, including Druze and Circassians, who tend to identify with the state and serve in the IDF, have been largely excluded from this group (women were also excluded, except during the period 2011–2014).[175] Israel's military elite, in other words, has become more and more representative on the intra-communal level, but at the same time functioned as a quite effective mechanism of inter-communal exclusion. It can also be argued that the gradual and incremental change in the social background of Israel's military elite, in itself, has been an important source of stability for the IDF as an institution and for the Israeli state in general, especially in view of the IDF's pivotal role in its security and civilian spheres. But because this change was by and large limited to the Jewish community in Israel/Palestine, it was a factor that helped reinforce the latter's dominant position vis-à-vis the Palestinian community in Israel and, ultimately, in all of Israel/Palestine.

Conclusion

This chapter focused on the triangular relationship between the state, community, and security in Palestine, Israel, and Israel/Palestine in the last century or so, emphasizing the close inter-linkages between these three spheres. As it argued, Israel's process of state formation can be traced to the period of the British Mandate, which served as a sort of incubator for the Jewish community and its state-in-the-making; at the same time, it weakened its main rival, the Palestinian community, and built the infrastructure that would serve the independent State of Israel for years to come. On the inter-communal level, the British did little to institutionalize the relations between Jews and Palestinians, and it was up to both communities to create their own institutions and structures. Very early, the issue of security became paramount, and there, too, each community responded by building its own security sector, with the Jews having an advantage due to their close relations to the British and their more effective state formation

---

[174] Sheffer and Barak (2013). An Israeli document from July 15, 1970, which has recently been released, suggests that Israel expropriated Palestinian land in the Territories for ostensibly military purposes when the true intent was to build civilian settlements. See Berger (2016a). This is also admitted by S. Gazit (2016, 179).

[175] Only one Druze officer was appointed as major general in this period.

process. The Jews emerged victorious from the First Arab–Israeli War, in which one-half of the Palestinians became refugees, and this was reflected in the state that was built in its aftermath, where a pattern of inter-communal control was institutionalized. Israel's security sector, and especially the IDF, which played a pivotal role in the process of state formation, reinforced this pattern of inter-communal relations on account of its composition, command, identity, and actions. In 1966, the Military Government that had been imposed on Israel's Palestinian citizens was abolished, but more informal aspects of Jewish control persisted. Then, in 1967, during the Israeli–Arab War, Israel expanded into all of Israel/Palestine, creating a divided society, albeit of a new kind. This political unit has borne some of the markers of pre-1967 Israel, but is different from it in several crucial respects. Although all Israeli governments refrained from formally annexing the Territories, the state's expansion became more entrenched on account of Israel's settlement policy, which was launched by the settler movement but was facilitated by Israel's security networks and was endorsed by the state's institutions. This policy demonstrated the conflation between the non-separation of Israel's civilian and security spheres, on the one hand, and between the state and the Jewish community, on the other hand. Settling the Territories thus became Israel's primary national project, and the number of settlements and settlers, as well as the infrastructure that linked them and connected them to Israel, grew rapidly. On the inter-communal level, Israel imposed a pattern of control over the Palestinians in the Territories, but the latter's growing grievances led to its collapse two decades later, with the outbreak of the first Palestinian Intifada, and to inter-communal repression. In the 1990s, Israeli and Palestinian officials held peace talks which culminated in the Oslo Agreement. But this agreement, for all its importance, overlooked the fact that, by then, the Israeli–Palestinian conflict has become an inter-communal conflict within a single political unit. Thus, although an autonomous Palestinian National Authority was set up in the Territories, it was weak in the coercive sense and lacked broad legitimacy, and Israeli leaders' hopes that it would solve their predicament as a state that is powerful in the coercive sense and weak in terms of the broad identification with it were unfulfilled. The Israeli–Palestinian peace process broke down in 2000, and more violence occurred between the two sides. In 2005, following mounting domestic and external pressures, Israel withdrew from the Gaza Strip and evacuated four small settlements in the West Bank. But this partial and limited move did not fundamentally change the relationship between the state formation process, the pattern of inter-communal relations, and the area of security in Israel/Palestine, which remained a divided society.

5 Lebanon and Israel/Palestine Compared

This chapter compares Lebanon and Israel/Palestine, focusing on the triangular relations between the state, community, and security. As we have seen in the previous chapters, the Maronites and the Jews are two communities that experienced major collective traumas, and, consequently, actively sought to promote their collective security by expanding the borders of their political unit with formal or tacit support from the great powers. However, instead of creating the nation-state their members had yearned for, both communities found themselves within a divided society in which they already lost, or were on their way to losing, their majority. Still, in both cases, this undesired outcome of the state's expansion did not lead to its contraction. Greater Lebanon has been around for almost a century, and Greater Israel or Israel/Palestine is marking its semi-centennial. Although both national projects seem paradoxical, both have, thus far, defied all attempts to undo them.

State Formation in Lebanon and in Israel/Palestine

Lebanon and Israel/Palestine have exhibited marked differences in their process of state formation. As far as the sub-processes of state building and state construction are concerned, Lebanon's political and socioeconomic elite, which included members of all of its major communities, was apprehensive of the state and sought to curtail its power. The result was that the state accumulated limited coercive capacities and its attempts to ingrain itself in its citizens' minds were restricted. Thus, during most of its independent history, and apart from relatively short periods of time (especially in 1958–1964, during Fouad Chehab's presidency), the state was merely one among several political actors in Lebanon – including communities, large families, and geographical regions – and it had to compete with them for power and allegiance. But national integration efforts in Lebanon, too, were limited: each community presided over its own schools, the security sector was small and weak, the media was fragmented, and state-based efforts to foster a national identity were, necessarily, restricted. Still, the vision of a Maronite Christian nation-state was largely abandoned in 1943, when the National Pact, the intercommunal power-sharing settlement between Lebanon's leaders, acknowledged the state's multi-communal character, enabling all of its citizens, and not just the Christians, to identify with the state, although each also had other foci of identity. In later decades, the material capacities of the Lebanese state did not increase significantly, and it could thus not respond to growing social and economic disparities, not only between its communities but also between center and periphery. This resulted in mounting socioeconomic grievances that were at the bottom of the political upheaval in Lebanon, culminating in the civil war of 1975–1990. However, although they became paralyzed during the conflict, the state's institutions – its political system (the presidency, the cabinet and parliament), bureaucracy, and security sector (especially the LAF) – did not disintegrate, and when the Ta'if Agreement was reached in 1989, these institutions were reformed in a manner that was designed to win them support from all communities. This facilitated the end of the conflict and opened the way for Lebanon's reconstruction. In the postwar era, the state's institutions became even more representative of Lebanese society: the largely Muslim population in the outlying territories, but also Christians from these areas, joined these institutions and thus signaled their acceptance of the state in its present form. At the same time, communally based networks, new and old, continued to provide social services to Lebanon's population.

In Israel/Palestine, by contrast, state building and state construction made considerable headway in Israel before 1967, not least because of the "statist" orientation of its exclusively Jewish political elite before and after independence. Thus, in the first decades of statehood, Israel's political, bureaucratic, and security institutions penetrated into all spheres, and they did their utmost to accumulate coercive power, transform the citizens' perceptions, and win their loyalty and identification. At the same time, non-state actors that challenged the state's monopoly over the legitimate use of violence were restrained. Instead of competing with the dominant Jewish community, the state embraced it and made effective use of its inventory of myths and symbols, which were modified to fit the state's interests. But this also meant that members of Israel's Palestinian community found it difficult (though not impossible) to identify with the state. However, after 1967, when Israel imposed its control over all of Israel/Palestine, the state's institutions – and especially the security sector, which presided over the outlying regions and which enjoyed broad public support – put their best efforts into adapting the multi-communal reality in Israel/Palestine to fit the vision of the Jewish nation-state. Israel's leaders, which coveted the Territories but did not wish to integrate the Palestinians, expected the latter to be content with the improvement in their standard of living. In the meantime, successive Israeli governments built settlements, outposts, military bases, roads, and other installations in the Territories, and sought to erase the Green Line in official maps, textbooks, and in the public discourse. However, two decades after the state's expansion, and despite's Israel's efforts to control them, the Palestinians in the Territories demanded their political rights, and the state had no institutional mechanism with which to accommodate them. After Israel's security sector failed to quash the first Palestinian Intifada, and following several external developments (the end of the Cold War and the Gulf War of 1991), as well as development within the PLO, the major Palestinian political–military actor, Israel abandoned its official policy of non-negotiation with the latter. But the Oslo Process (1993–2000) ignored the transformation of Israel/Palestine since 1967 and the fact that, by now, the Israeli–Palestinian conflict had become an intrastate conflict between two rival communities. After the peace process failed to bring about the state's contraction, a second and more violent Palestinian Intifada erupted. Claiming that this was an "existential" struggle – a continuation of Israel's War of Independence[1] – Israel tried to forcefully suppress the Palestinians, who responded in the same token. Some Israeli leaders, especially from the center-right and far-right, sought to reinforce the state's Jewish character by a spate of nationalist laws, and also to boost the Jewish identity of the state's institutions, including the educational system, the security sector, and other areas. Still, and despite a limited Israeli withdrawal from the Gaza Strip in 2005, which turned this area into a "frontier," neither of the two sides could dramatically change the situation in Israel/Palestine, and its divided society remained in place.

As the preceding chapters have shown, the different ways that Israel/Palestine and Lebanon have coped with the effects of the state's expansion can be traced to their different historical legacies. In Lebanon, the seeds of inter-communal power sharing were sown in the political institutions that were established in the periods of the *Mutasarrifiyya* and under the French Mandate, whereas in Israel/Palestine the British Mandate encouraged the creation of separate institutions for each of the two communities and did not foster inter-communal accommodation. These policies were followed by the two states of Lebanon and Israel after they became independent. Another factor that can be mentioned in this context is the markedly different

---

[1] Lieutenant General Moshe Ya'alon, chief of staff of the IDF, as quoted in Shavit (2002).

economic policies of the two states in their early decades. In Lebanon, curtailing the state's power was closely inter-linked to establishing a free market economy, whereas Israel's large and intrusive state apparatus supported its centralized state-run economy, although it, too, later moved toward a free market economy. A third factor concerns the changes that took place in the international system and how they helped reinforce domestic processes in both cases. Greater Lebanon was established before the fixation of international borders in 1945, whereas Israel/Palestine came into being after the annexation of outlying territories had become taboo. This meant that whereas those in Lebanon who wished to preserve the expanded state could receive crucial external support on both the regional and international levels, supporters of Greater Israel – or, for that matter, Greater Palestine – could not depend on such backing.

In sum, the process of state formation in Lebanon and Israel/Palestine led to different results. In Lebanon, it engendered a weak state in the material sense, but one that members of all of its communities gradually – and sometimes grudgingly – came to identify with. Indeed, ownership of the state and its political, bureaucratic, and security institutions by all of Lebanon's communities, which was attained by modifying these institutions' composition, leadership, identity, and behavior, accorded them legitimacy *despite* their limited effectiveness. In Israel/Palestine, by contrast, the process of state formation produced a materially strong state that possessed considerable coercive capacities, but this was a state that only its Jewish community could identify with unreservedly. As the Israeli–Palestinian conflict lingered, the state's Jewish character did not diminish but was further emphasized, as were Palestinian grievances toward it. One striking similarity between the two cases does, however, stand out: the rising power of peripheral actors and their quest to for attaining veto power over the state's institutions. In Lebanon, this has mainly been Hizbullah, the Shi'i party-militia, which sought to protect its unique position in postwar Lebanon; in Israel/Palestine, these have been the Jewish settlers in the Territories which penetrated the political center and sought to prevent the state's contraction. Interestingly, however, neither of these two actors has thus far managed to move beyond this veto power to transform the state to reflect its values, interests, and goals. Moreover, these actors' relentless quest for power, in itself, has antagonized many in both political entities.

The process of state formation in Lebanon and Israel/Palestine is presented in Table 5.1.

Table 5.1 *Strong and weak states: Lebanon and Israel/Palestine*

Broad identification / Coercive power	Strong	Weak
Strong	Israel (1949–1967)	Israel/Palestine (1967–)
Weak	Lebanon (1943–1975, 1991–)	Lebanon (1975–1990)

Inter-Communal Relations in Lebanon and in Israel/Palestine

Since the state's expansion, Lebanon and Israel/Palestine have exhibited different patterns of inter-communal relations. Following its establishment, Greater Lebanon witnessed a period of inter-communal control by its Christians, particularly the Maronites, over the Muslims (including the Druze), but this period also witnessed several developments that ultimately facilitated inter-communal power sharing in later periods. Then, after Lebanon became independent, a power-sharing settlement was reached between its major communities. In the late 1960s and early 1970s, inter-communal relations began to deteriorate and again acquired some markers of control. In addition, this period was at times characterized by intra-communal struggles that turned violent, particularly during elections. The power-sharing settlement in Lebanon collapsed in 1975 with the outbreak of the civil war, giving way to a stalemate, though in certain phases of the conflict, inter-communal relations were characterized by repression at both the inter- and intra-communal levels. However, the attempts to restore inter-communal power sharing in Lebanon persisted throughout the conflict. Following the Ta'if Agreement in 1989 and the end of the conflict a year later, Lebanon returned to a new and reformed power-sharing settlement, but one in which Syria, Lebanon's more powerful neighbor, was accorded a central role. However, this role diminished by 2005, when the Syrian forces withdrew from Lebanon, and the outbreak of the Syrian conflict in 2011 reduced it further. Although Hizbullah, the Shi'i party-militia, managed to acquire veto power in Lebanon's political system, and especially in the cabinet, it did not manage to dominate the state in the postwar era. In sum, Lebanon has throughout its history known mostly inter-communal power sharing and stalemate, whereas the periods of control and repression, including by external actors, were relatively short and untenable.

Israel/Palestine, by contrast, has been characterized by inter-communal control, first in Israel and then also in the West Bank and the Gaza Strip in the first two decades after the state's expansion.

However, the first Palestinian Intifada resulted in the collapse of Jewish control in the Territories occupied in 1967, which gave way to Israeli repression and, ultimately, to inter-communal violence, but not to a stalemate like in Lebanon. This pattern has persisted ever since, except for the period of the Israeli–Palestinian peace process in the 1990s, but it, too, was marked by inter-communal (and occasionally intra-communal) violence. At the same time, power sharing was not considered as a solution to the Israeli–Palestinian conflict, and Israel was powerful enough to prevent a stalemate and also partition of the shared land. The result was that Israel/Palestine continued to oscillate between Jewish attempts to impose control over the Palestinians, who resisted these efforts, and by Jewish repression that, too, was opposed by the Palestinians, including by force.

Why did Lebanon move back and forth between power sharing and a stalemate, whereas Israel/Palestine oscillated between control and repression? First, as mentioned earlier, the state in Lebanon was weaker than that in Israel/Palestine, and it did not have the capacity to effectively control all of its territory and seal its borders. This meant that the state in Lebanon could not prevent violent non-state actors – those from within Lebanon (i.e., its parties-militias) or transnationals who entered its territory – from creating their own autonomous enclaves (referred to as "cantons," a "state within a state," etc.). The state in Israel/Palestine, by contrast, had the power to control the borders of the political unit before and after its expansion, and to prevent internal fragmentation, although some violent non-state actors – Palestinian and Jewish – occasionally challenged its monopoly over the legitimate use of violence. One consequence was that the Lebanese conflict (1975–1990) was far more bloody and devastating than the conflict in Israel/Palestine since 1987 (but not when compared to earlier military encounters such as the First Arab–Israeli War). Another was that in Lebanon no single community could employ the state to control or repress other communities, whereas in Israel/Palestine the dominant group could do so, albeit at the price of the state's legitimacy in the eyes of most members of its subordinate community, some members of its dominant group and external actors.

But historical factors are also significant in both contexts. The legacy of inter-communal power sharing in Mount Lebanon and the institutions established in the period of the French Mandate made it easier for Christian and Muslim leaders to forego their maximalist visions less than a quarter-century after the state's expansion, and to agree on the National Pact. In Israel/Palestine, by contrast, there was no legacy of inter-communal power sharing, and many Israelis and Palestinians continued to believe that they would somehow manage to realize their maximalist national visions without having to concede to the other side. Indeed, it seems that only a major shift within the two communities in Israel/Palestine, reinforced by a parallel shift in the external arena – as occurred, for example, in other divided societies such as South Africa, Northern Ireland, and Lebanon – could move them closer to inter-communal power sharing. However, if anything, regional and international actors, like many Israeli and Palestinians, still consider partition, and not power sharing, as the preferred solution for Israel/Palestine, though some, like US Secretary of State John Kerry, have warned that "Israel and the Palestinians are moving in the direction of a binational state rather than a Palestinian state alongside Israel and are also headed toward war," adding that if the international community is interested in putting a halt to these developments, "Either we mean it and we act on it, or we should shut up."[2]

Comparing the pattern of inter-communal relations in Israel/Palestine and Lebanon suggests an important distinction between two types of intrastate conflicts: conflicts that are waged *about* the state and conflicts that are waged *over* the state. The first type of conflict revolves around the question of whether the state should exist in its present form or be replaced by a different type of political unit. Secession, which is an attempt to change the boundaries of the polity,[3] falls under this category, although, as we have seen, leaders of a dominant community might perceive, or portray, attempts to bring about such a move as an existential threat to the state and use extreme measures to thwart them. The second type of conflict is waged over the state, wherein each side wishes to have more control over power and resources but without challenging the state's boundaries. These conflicts may include infighting among rival communal elites over the spoils of government and rebellions waged by disenfranchised groups whose members wish to participate in the state's institutions.[4] But here, too, a dominant elite (but sometimes also a subordinate one) is liable to present the conflict as an attempt to undermine the polity. Indeed, it seems that both types of intrastate conflict are not entirely exclusive, and there are cases, such as Iraq since 2003 and Syria since 2011, where conflicts over the state have evolved into conflicts about the state. Still, this distinction seems useful when thinking about the two conflicts in Israel/Palestine and in Lebanon, including their causes, dynamics, and the possible ways to ameliorate them.

In Lebanon, the state was in most periods not party to the inter-communal conflict but, rather, constituted part of the spoils. In Israeli/Palestine, by contrast, the Jewish community effectively mobilized not only

[2] Quoted in Ravid (2016).   [3] Wimmer, Cederman, and Min (2009, 322).   [4] Ibid.

the state's institutions, but also a host of informal, including cultural, means against the Palestinian community, which, at least as far as the Palestinians in the Territories were concerned, rejected the state and its right to rule over it. This factor can explain why the Lebanese conflict could be terminated successfully when members of all communities reached a new compromise on how to govern the state, whereas in Israel/Palestine, the state remained dominated by the Jewish community, and as such could not serve as a "meeting place" for all of its communities, and especially for the Palestinians in the Territories. The demands made by Israeli leaders, and especially Prime Minister Benjamin Netanyahu, that Israel – which has effectively ruled Israel/Palestine since 1967 – would be recognized as a "Jewish State" by the Palestinians, on the one hand, and these leaders' exclusionist discourse toward Israel's Palestinian citizens, on the other hand, are telling in this regard.

This basic difference between the two conflicts in Lebanon and Israel/Palestine also helps explain why the parties themselves, as well as outside forces, adopted markedly different strategies for coping with them. In Lebanon, there were almost no attempts to break away from the state and form new political entities in its place. On the contrary, most local actors and the majority of foreign players that were involved in the Lebanese conflict sought to preserve Lebanon in its present form. In Israel/Palestine, by contrast, the mainstream Palestinian leadership in the Territories sought to establish an independent Palestinian state in the West Bank (including East Jerusalem) and the Gaza Strip, although more radical Palestinian armed factions such as Hamas and the Islamic Jihad propagated the establishment of a state in all of Israel/Palestine (in 2011, Hamas did signal a change in this position[5]), and the Palestinian community in Israel openly called for power sharing within the Israeli state.[6]

But for many Israelis, the Palestinian Intifadas were not attempts to bring about the contraction of Israel/Palestine – but rather represented an existential threat to Israel itself. Moreover, many in Israel regarded the struggle over the Territories as only one facet of the "overall" conflict between Israel and the Arabs (and even Muslim) worlds, arguing that this conflict would not abate even after an Israeli withdrawal from the Territories. This explains why Israel's repressive actions toward the Palestinians, especially after the breakdown of the Oslo Process, were designed not only to prevent their separation from Israel, but also to completely dissuade them from trying to achieve their "real" goals.

[5] Bronner (2011).
[6] See, especially, "The Future Vision of the Palestinian Arabs in Israel" published in 2006 by the National Committee for the Heads of the Arab Local Authorities in Israel. On the document, see Barak (2016).

At the same time, Israeli leaders accelerated the sub-process of national integration within Israel itself, including with regard to its dominant Jewish community, resulting in what might be termed "ethno-militarism," or "ethno-securitism,"[7] and attempts to suppress political dissent.

A comparison of the Ta'if Agreement (1989) and the Oslo Agreement (1993), the two major attempts to ameliorate the conflicts in Lebanon and in Israel/Palestine, respectively, provides an opportunity to assess peacemaking efforts in both cases. On the one hand, in Lebanon, an agreement was reached not only with regard to the state and its identity, but also on power sharing as the preferred pattern of inter-communal relations. The area of security, too, was addressed, including the dismantling of the militias (although, as the case of Hizbullah suggests, this goal was not fully attained), the strengthening of the security sector, and the imposition of effective civilian control over the security agencies (though this was also not fully achieved). Although the agreement stipulated "special relations" between Lebanon and Syria, these proved to be temporary: Syria withdrew its forces from Lebanon in 2005, and six years later Syria itself became engulfed in a bloody conflict. At the same time, the Ta'if Agreement was not conceived as a "final" or "permanent" settlement to the Lebanese conflict, but provided the necessary tools for regulating inter-communal relations within its divided society. The agreement was, moreover, not dependent on a particular leader, group, or community, but sought to encompass all relevant actors in Lebanon. One consequence was that sensitive issues, such as Lebanon's turbulent history and the question of "who did what to whom and when" in the conflict of 1975–1990 were not formally addressed, but were left by default to Lebanon's civil society. Indeed, some years later, several civil society groups in Lebanon produced another document called the "Beirut Declaration," which addressed these very issues.[8]

The Oslo Agreement, on the other hand, was not an inter-communal agreement regarding a particular political entity (Israeli, Palestinian, or both) or concerning a specific pattern of inter-communal relations. Rather, it was an attempt to impose an inter-state model of peacemaking on the Israeli–Palestinian conflict, ignoring the fact that, since 1967, the

---

[7] For a vivid illustration of this brand of militarism, see the novel *The Road to Ein Harod* by Israeli writer and former *Lehi* member Amos Kenan (1984). See also Bar-Tal, Halperin, and Magal (2009). For various approaches to, and aspects of, militarism in Israel, see Sheffer and Barak (2010). Cf. Kohn (2009).

[8] Beirut Declaration (2004). See also Barak (2007a).

two communities were part of a divided society. Thus, for example, the critical issue of security was addressed only partially, through the establishment of the Palestinian Police in the Territories (but not a Palestinian military, which was anathema to Israel) and the initiation of joint Israeli–Palestinian patrols in parts of these areas. At the same time, the most important issues in Israeli–Palestinian relations – Jerusalem, the Palestinian refugees, the Jewish settlements in the Territories, and the Palestinian state and its borders – were postponed to the permanent status negotiations, which did not follow. Another problem was that the Oslo Agreement did not reflect a broad consensus in both the Israeli and Palestinian communities, but hinged primarily on two leaders, Israeli Prime Minister Rabin and PLO leader Arafat, who were expected to enforce the agreement in their respective communities but were only partially successful even before Rabin's assassination. In 1999, when Ehud Barak became Israel's prime minister, the drive toward a "final settlement" to the Israeli–Palestinian conflict became pronounced, culminating in the Camp David summit in 2000. However, the result was not the replication of the successful Camp David summit between US President Carter, Egyptian President Sadat, and Israeli Prime Minister Begin in 1978, but, rather, an outcome that was reminiscent of Alfred Hitchcock's film *Vertigo*.

We see, then, that of the two agreements that sought to ameliorate the conflicts in Lebanon and in Israel/Palestine, only the Ta'if Agreement, which acknowledged the fact that Lebanon was a divided society, corresponded to the nature of the conflict and dealt with the major issues pertaining to the relations between its communities. The Oslo Agreement, for its part, ignored the existence of a divided society in Israel/Palestine, as well as the issues emanating from this reality. As a result, it is not surprising that only the peace process in Lebanon, which culminated in the Ta'if Agreement, managed to regulate the conflict, even if imperfectly.

The patterns of inter-communal relations in Israel/Palestine and Lebanon are presented in Table 5.2.

Table 5.2 *Inter-communal relations in Lebanon and Israel/Palestine*

	No communal domination	One community is dominant
Not explicitly violent	Power sharing: Lebanon (1943–1975, 1991–)	Control: Israel (1948–); Israel/Palestine (1967–1987)
Massively violent	Stalemate: Lebanon (1975–1990)	Repression: Israel/Palestine (1987–)

Security in Lebanon and Israel/Palestine

When Lebanon and Israel/Palestine turned out to be divided societies and not Western-style nation-states, their dominant communities – the Maronites and the Jews, respectively – pursued quite different paths to address their collective security. However, a closer examination suggests that at least some of the outcomes of the policies that both states adopted in the area of security were not as different as one might expect.

From an early stage of its development, the Jewish community in Palestine underwent a rapid process of militarization, which was seen as crucial for coping with the threat to its security posed by the Palestinian community and the Arabs more broadly. This process, which continued after Israel's independence, included building a large and powerful security sector that could defend Israel's borders, although during major confrontations with the latter's Arab neighbors (e.g., in 1956, 1967, and 1973) Israel's leaders did seek support from the great powers. In order to provide the manpower needed to uphold this military, Israel resorted to mandatory conscription, but most of its Palestinian citizens were exempted, and the Israeli military, the IDF has been characterized by Jewish dominance. In addition, Jews presided over the security sector's command and the civilian controlling bodies. The identity of the IDF and of the security sector as a whole was, from the outset, a Jewish identity, and this identity was only accentuated in later periods, and especially since 2000. The IDF also played a major role in the process of state formation in Israel, performing civilian tasks such as settlement, education, and immigrant absorption. In 1953, Israel adopted an offensive-defensive military strategy designed to defuse existential threats to the state. This strategy proved useful during the Arab–Israeli Wars in 1956 and 1967. However, this process of militarization did not come to a halt after the state's expansion in 1967, and in some respects it even intensified. This was because keeping hold of the Territories constituted a major security challenge, and, as some critics had foreseen, consumed considerable material and human resources. In any case, Israel's powerful security sector – specifically, the IDF and the General Security Service, which administered the Territories after 1967 – did not win it support in the eyes of the Palestinians, and Israel's coercive power needed to be repeatedly asserted. Furthermore, and as will be demonstrated in the next two chapters, the primary goal of Israel's foreign policy became to preserve the state's expanded borders, which were seen as crucial for its security, and this led to additional conflicts with the Arab states, in 1969–1970 (the War of Attrition), 1973, and 1982. The result of this policy was Israel's deepening international isolation, which its leaders tried to solve by forging close ties with the United States and other powers (especially Britain and Germany but also others such as China, India, and Russia). They also fostered close relations with states and other actors that had similar security predicaments, including South Africa and Singapore, both of which are divided societies that faced existential threats. Another process – which intensified following the 1967 and 1973 wars and was connected to Israel's rule over Territories (and later over South Lebanon) – was the increased power and influence of its security networks. Indeed, since 1967, these became highly influential actors in security and other crucial areas in Israel.

In Lebanon, by contrast, the solution that the state's leaders came up with for its security problems was strict de-militarization. Accordingly, Lebanon's security sector – especially the Lebanese Armed Forces (LAF), which was from the outset an all-volunteer force – was kept weak and small, mainly engaging with policing and in most periods unable to defend the state's borders against outside threats. However, because of the weakness of other state institutions in Lebanon, and especially its political ones, the LAF, which included members of all communities and was more cohesive than other state institutions, became increasingly involved in politics as a mediator, arbitrator, and holder of the balance. Lebanon's leaders could not agree on formal neutrality, mainly on account of their obligations to the other Arab states, but in practice they sought to steer their state away from the Arab–Israeli conflict and from other regional and international disputes. However, this policy sometimes opened the door for Lebanon's neighbors and for violent transnational non-state actors to become involved in its affairs. In some cases, such as the civil war of 1958, but also later, it was these leaders themselves who invited these foreign actors. Before 1975, the foreign actors that were involved in Lebanon included Egypt and Syria – and from 1967, the Palestinian armed factions, which turned Lebanon into their major base of operations (see Chapter 6). But on the domestic level, too, the state's weakness opened the way for the emergence of violent non-state actors such as the Phalanges Party, which, as we have seen, was not only a party-militia but also saw itself as "more than a party and less than a state." During the civil war of 1975–1990, many of Lebanon's neighbors, including Syria, Israel, the Palestinians, Libya, Iraq, and Iran, were involved, and in the postwar period it was Hizbullah, the Shi'i party-militia, that asserted itself, including in the area of security. We see, then, that de-militarization on both the domestic and external levels was not very successful in attaining security in Lebanon. As for the composition of Lebanon's security sector, although initially there was a Christian majority in the LAF's officer corps, it gradually opened its ranks to members of all communities, including from Lebanon's peripheral areas. Indeed, it was during the second civil war, and as part of the efforts to reconstruct the state, that parity was attained for the first time among the LAF's Christian and Muslim officers. As for as command and control of the security sector, Christian (especially Maronite) dominance in early decades gave way to multi-communal command and civilian controlling bodies in later periods, which promoted power sharing in this critical area. With regard to its identity, the security sector sought to promote a national identity that highlighted the role of the military as a meeting place for members of all communities. However, this succeeded only in part. Finally, concerning the actual operation of Lebanon's security sector, after 1958, a security network composed of security officials, especially from within the LAF's Intelligence Branch, and civilian supporters of President Chehab managed Lebanon's affairs from behind the scenes. But in the early 1970s the LAF was effectively marginalized by its traditional opponents. When the LAF was called in to suppress the opposition after the outbreak of the civil war in 1975, this resulted in widespread defections from its ranks and in its paralysis. Still, the LAF did not disintegrate: Attempts were made to rebuild it on a more equitable basis and, as mentioned earlier, to introduce power sharing in its command and in the controlling civilian bodies. In the postwar era, the LAF became the mainstay of the political order in Lebanon, sometimes inserting its units between rival factions; however, it had to coexist with a sizable Syrian military presence and a joint Syrian–Lebanese "deep state" (until 2005), as well as with a local violent non-state actor, the Shi'i party-militia Hizbullah.

In sum, Lebanon and Israel/Palestine exhibit important differences in the area of security, which are closely related to their particular process of state formation and pattern of inter-communal relations. Israel's security sector was far more powerful and efficient than its Lebanese counterpart, but its close association with the Jewish community in Israel/Palestine ensured that it would enjoy legitimacy mainly within that group and not among the Palestinians in the Territories, who, since 1967, considered it to be an army of occupation. At the same time, Lebanon's security sector, and especially the LAF, adopted the principle of inter-communal power sharing, which accorded it broad legitimacy but could not prevent a stalemate in periods of internal conflict. Both security sectors had to share power with other actors and this impinged on their autonomy: in Lebanon, these were the Syrian army, the Syrian–Lebanese "deep state," and the Shi'i party-militia Hizbullah, and in Israel/Palestine these were the Jewish settlers in the Territories which organized their own militias and, ultimately, occupied key positions in the Israeli state. In addition, in both cases attempts to achieve effective, and not merely formal, civilian control

Table 5.3 *The security sector in Lebanon and Israel/Palestine*

	Israel/Palestine	Lebanon
Composition	Mostly Jewish	All major communities
Command & Civilian Control	Exclusively Jewish	All major communities (since 1989)
Identity & Missions	National identity but emphasis is on Jewish identity	National identity, supra-communal
Operations	Attempts to reinforce position of dominant Jewish community	Preserving inter-communal balance, not always efficient

over the security sector were unsuccessful: In Lebanon, this stemmed from the failure to establish "objective control" – that is, to create distinctive civilian and security spheres and establish effective control of the latter by the former; in Israel this resulted from the failed attempt to establish a "nation in arms" characterized by porous boundaries between the state's civilian and security spheres that facilitate civilian control,[9] although, as we have seen, a pattern of "ethno-securitism" or "ethno-militarism" – which was characterized by a lack of effective civilian control of the security sector – did emerge in this case. This outcome suggests that applying Western models of civilian control of the security sector to non-Western states, and particularly divided societies, is problematic.

The area of security in Lebanon and Israel/Palestine is presented in Table 5.3.

State, Community, and Security in Israel/Palestine and in Lebanon

We turn now to consider the type of relationship that emerged between the state, community, and security in Israel/Palestine and Lebanon in the aftermath of the state's expansion. In Lebanon, the state was not only weak in the material-coercive sense, but, in most periods, it was not dominated by a single community. As for security, it was provided mainly by ensuring the weakness of Lebanon's security sector, which prevented it from being used as a tool of repression by any single community. As in other weak states, however, the result was that when security in Lebanon deteriorated, as occurred in the late 1960s and early 1970s, the country's various communities had to look after their own security, including by

---

[9] On the two models, see Burk (2002).

militarizing and ultimately by resorting to inter-communal (and, occasionally, intra-communal) violence. This trajectory is similar to the intrastate "security dilemma" identified by Barry Posen and others,[10] although one should also note the pivotal role of political entrepreneurs, such as Lebanon's parties-militias, in securitizing the domestic crises. Furthermore, myths, symbols, and historical narratives, as well as apprehensions and fears, fueled the violence. As we have seen, the peace process in Lebanon did address at least some of these problems: the settlements reached by the country's leaders, first in the area of security and then in other spheres, made the state's political, bureaucratic, and security institutions more representative. This provided Lebanon's various communities with stakes in the state and at the same time soothed their mutual apprehensions. This factor, in addition to the external guarantees that Lebanon received from the Arab states and the international community after the end of the conflict, opened the way for desecuritization of its inter-communal relations, though this process remained incomplete (Figure 5.1).

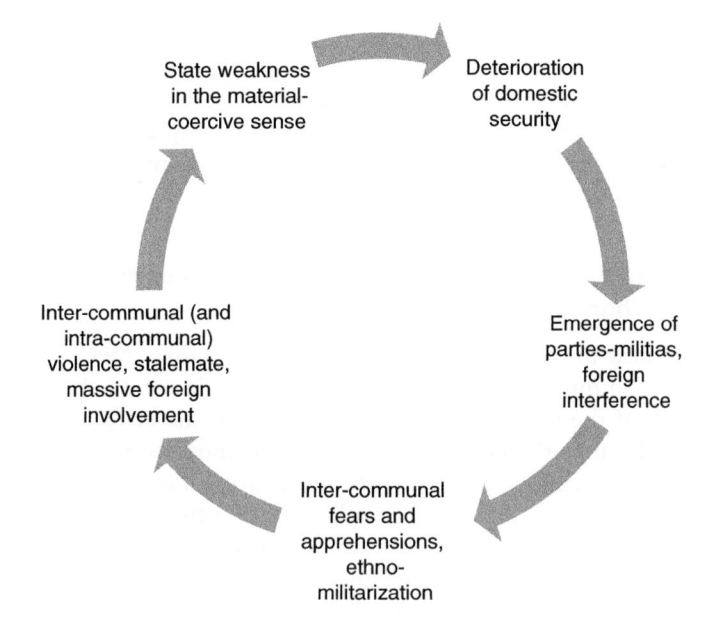

Figure 5.1: State, community, and security in Lebanon

[10] Posen (1993). See also Barak (2007a) and the sources cited therein.

In Israel/Palestine, on the other hand, the institutions of the Israeli state have, since 1948, accumulated material-coercive power and engaged in successful national integration efforts, mainly on behalf of the dominant Jewish community. At the same time, they fostered a more universal ethos that appealed to at least some of the state's Palestinian citizens but also to others outside its borders. However, following the state's expansion in 1967, the role of the state as a tool of the dominant Jewish community was reinforced, as well as the emphasis accorded to security. Indeed, instead of better differentiating the civilian and security spheres in Israel, on the one hand, and the state and the Jewish community, on the other hand, all of these spheres became closely intertwined. As in the period before Israel's independence, this relationship became even more intimate in 1987, when the Palestinians in the Territories openly challenged the state's expansion. Instead of accommodating the political demands of the subordinate Palestinian community, these demands were effectively securitized, and Israel's response was ethno-militarization that resulted in inter-communal violence and, ultimately, in further increasing the state's coercive capacities (Figure 5.2).

We see, then, that in the wake of the state's expansion, Lebanon and Israel/Palestine witnessed different "vicious cycles" that pushed them toward conflict, in 1975 and in 1987, respectively, and that only in

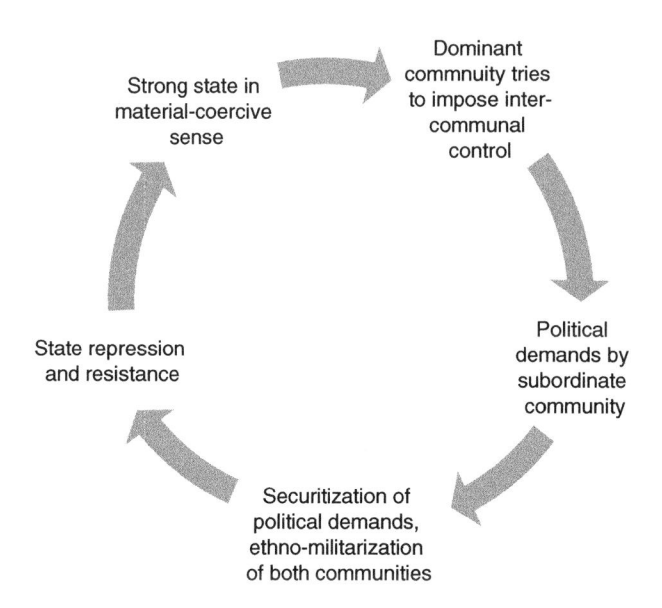

Figure 5.2: State, community, and security in Israel/Palestine

Lebanon did a "virtuous cycle" emerge during the peace process that facilitated the end of the conflict in 1990. However, even in Lebanon there were problems in the relations between the state, community, and security that beleaguered the state in later periods and which sometimes spilled over across its borders.

Conclusion

This chapter has compared Israel/Palestine and Lebanon, with an emphasis on the triangular relationship between the state, community, and security in the wake of the state's expansion. What emerges from this comparison are two distinct types of relationships between the state, community, and security, which can be described as two different kinds of "vicious cycles": one characterized by a strong state in the material sense, inter-communal control, subordinate grievances, securitization of these grievances by the dominant community, and periods of repression and resistance (in Israel/Palestine), and the other marked by a weak state, the decline of inter-communal power sharing, communal mobilization and outside meddling in the state's affairs, violence, and a stalemate (in Lebanon). The next two chapters will explore the possible connections and inter-linkages between these two vicious cycles – and between Lebanon and Israel/Palestine more generally – by considering the fact that these are not only expanded states that turned out to be divided societies but also close neighbors whose mutual relations have witnessed periods of relative stability and conflict.

6 The Deterioration of Israeli–Lebanese Relations

This chapter explores the impact of Israel's expansion and creation of a divided society in Israel/Palestine on the relations between Israel and Lebanon, which were relatively stable from the signing of the Israeli–Lebanese Armistice Agreement in 1949 but deteriorated in the wake of the Israeli–Arab War of 1967. This discussion is motivated by an increasing body of research in the field of International Relations and in other areas[1] that has shifted focus from "objective" actions and relations of states to the state's identity, which is formed in relation to other states and which shapes and is shaped by the state's interaction with various "others" that it encounters.[2] Drawing on these studies, one can expect the state's expansion – which, as suggested in the previous chapters, influences the triangular relations between the state, community, and security, and which, as we have seen, produced "vicious cycles" of violence and conflict in Lebanon and in Israel/Palestine – to also have an impact on the state's relations with various "others," which, in turn, will affect the expanded state's identity.[3] Furthermore, since Israel/Palestine and Lebanon are close neighbors, we can explore possible inter-linkages between these two "cycles." Along with casting new light on Israeli–Lebanese relations, the current discussion addresses a significant lacuna in the study of state expansion (and contraction), which more often than not overlooks its external effects.[4] At the same time, it adds to those works that deal with the domestic sources of Israel's foreign relations, including its political system,[5] economy,[6] society,[7] culture,[8]

---

[1] See, especially, Said (1979).
[2] Wendt (1999); Barnett (1999); Telhami and Barnett (2002); Lupovici (2013).
[3] Arendt (1973 [1951]) describes this process with regard to European Imperialism and its devastating impact on the European nation-states.
[4] Lustick (1993); Migdal (2001); O'Leary et al. (2001).
[5] Merom (2002); Freilich (2012).   [6] Laron (2015).   [7] Levy (2007); Sela (2007).
[8] Brecher (1972). Bar-Yosef (2007) deals with Israeli perceptions of Africa in early decades and how they reflected domestic, and especially cultural, processes in Israel since its independence. Ram (2009), who focuses on Israeli perceptions of Iran, suggests that Israelis have come to view their neighbors, including Iran, not only objectively but also as a reflection of social and political phenomena within Israel itself.

military strategy,[9] and security networks.[10] After surveying existing works on Israeli–Lebanese relations, the discussion will turn to the period before and after 1967, leading up to Israel's more intensive involvement in Lebanon in the late 1970s and early 1980s, which will be examined in Chapter 7.

Israeli–Lebanese Relations: Approaches and Gaps

The relations between Israel and Lebanon are unique among Israel's relations with its Arab neighbors in that they shifted from relative stability prior to the Israeli–Arab War of 1967 to growing instability and open conflict in later decades, especially in the Lebanon War of 1982 but also in a number of more limited confrontations in 1978, 1993, 1996, and 2006.[11] By contrast, Egyptian–Israeli relations shifted from conflict to peace in 1979; Israeli–Jordanian relations changed from secret and tacit cooperation, disrupted by the 1967 War and the Battle of Karameh in 1968, to peace since 1994; and Israeli–Syrian relations have remained tense since 1948, including open military confrontations in 1967, 1973, and 1982, although the two sides did hold (unsuccessful) peace negotiations in the 1990s.

As argued earlier (in Chapter 3), when Lebanon's leaders reached the National Pact in 1943, they received the consent of their Arab neighbors for their state's expansion more than two decades earlier. Indeed, even Syria, Lebanon's neighbor, which had irredentist claims toward it, later established diplomatic relations with Lebanon. But Israel's expansion in 1967 was rejected by all of its neighbors, and thus needed to be asserted time and again. The result was a series of armed confrontations between Israel and Egypt (in 1969–1970 and 1973), Israel and Syria (in 1973 and 1982), and Israel and Jordan (in 1968), as well as conflicts between Israel and the Palestinians (in 1987 and 2000). At the same time, Israel reached peace agreements with Egypt (in 1979) and Jordan (in 1994), but two other peace processes, with the Palestinians and Syria, were not successful (a third process, with Lebanon in 1983, also failed). We see, then, that the state's expansion in Lebanon and in Israel/Palestine has had different outcomes on the external level.

Studies on Israeli–Lebanese relations before 1967 focus on the period before Israel's independence,[12] on the early decades of Israel's

---

[9] Oren, Barak, and Shapira (2013). See also Handel (1994).
[10] Sheffer and Barak (2013).
[11] Two states that are not close neighbors of Israel (and are also non-Arab) and with which Israel's relations have deteriorated are Iran and Turkey.
[12] Eisenberg (1994).

statehood,[13] or on both periods.[14] Interestingly, one of the questions underlying many of these works is whether Israel's massive involvement in Lebanon in later decades, and especially in the Lebanon War of 1982, can be traced to early Israeli–Lebanese encounters, particularly between Jewish Zionist activists in the United States, on the one hand, and members of the Maronite-led Phalanges Party, on the other hand, during the First Arab–Israeli War.[15] Another question is whether Israel's involvement in Lebanon since the late 1970s can be traced to debates among political and military leaders in Israel concerning its policy toward Lebanon in the period 1954–1955.[16] Interestingly, the latter debates, which became public knowledge since the late 1970s and early 1980s, have also left their mark on the political discourse in Lebanon and in Syria. Thus, for example, Georges Corm, Lebanon's finance minister (1998–2000), argued in the wake of the War between Israel and Hizbullah (2006) that Israel disapproved of the coexistence of Christians and Muslims in Lebanon and thus wanted to sabotage it, thereby justifying its own existence as an ethnic entity in the Middle East.[17] Syrian President Hafez al-Assad made a similar argument three decades earlier, in July 1976, when he explained the causes for Syria's involvement in Lebanon.[18] However, as we shall see, the relations between Israel and Lebanon were actually quite stable in the period 1949–1967, despite certain "communal" ideas floated by some Israeli leaders.

At the same time, studies on Israeli–Lebanese relations before 1967 have accorded insufficient attention to the formal interaction between the two states, and especially to the Israel–Lebanon Mixed Armistice Commission (ILMAC). This body was established in accordance with the Armistice Agreement of 1949 and helped stabilize the two states' relations in the period 1949–1967.[19] Moreover, with the exception of a few works,[20] the discussion of ILMAC is limited to the period up to the Lebanese civil war of 1958, although ILMAC was not officially disbanded until after the Israeli–Arab War of 1967, and despite the fact that Israeli

---

[13] Morris (1984); Zisser (1995). [14] Schulze (1998); Erlich (2000).
[15] Morris (1984); Parker (1993); Zisser (1995); Eisenberg (2009). In 1996 I interviewed Shulamith Schwartz-Nardi, the Zionist official who had met Phalanges Party official Elias Rababi at that time, in her home in Jerusalem. What struck me in the meeting was a huge poster of Pierre Gemayel, leader of the Phalanges Party, which hung on her apartment wall.
[16] Morris (1984); Rokach (1986); Shlaim (1988b); Parker (1993); Shultze (1998).
[17] Corm (2006).
[18] Assad (1976). See also Baqraduni [Pakradouni] (1984); Rabinovich (1985); Tlass (1985).
[19] Hof (1985); McDermott (1996). [20] Foley (2005); Barak (2010); Kaufman (2013).

and Lebanese military officers continued to hold meetings in later periods.[21]

Turning to the period after 1967, most studies dealing with Israel's growing involvement in Lebanon in the late 1960s and early 1970s, but also later, do so mainly in the context of the general Middle East conflict.[22] Accordingly, Israel's involvement in Lebanon from the latter's "failure" in the period 1975–1976 until Israel's withdrawal from its self-declared "security zone" in South Lebanon in May 2000 is often presented as an attempt to address Israel's regional security dilemma – that is, from a "realist" perspective.[23] Some studies deal with specific actors in Israel who shaped its relations with Lebanon before and during the 1982 War, including members of the political and military elite,[24] the leaders of the Likud Party (Menachem Begin and Ariel Sharon, who, together with IDF Chief of Staff Rafael Eitan, initiated Israel's invasion of Lebanon),[25] and Israel's security networks, which presided over the Israeli–Lebanese border area from the mid-1970s until Israel's withdrawal from Lebanon in 2000.[26] To these one can add works that focus on particular Lebanese actors, including Maronite groups that established close ties with Israel before and during the 1982 War, in particular the Phalanges Party;[27] the Shi'i party-militia Hizbullah, which emerged as Israel's major Lebanese opponent in the wake of that conflict;[28] and the SLA, Israel's proxy in South Lebanon.[29] Other works emphasize cultural aspects of Israel's relations with Lebanon, including Israeli and Lebanese mutual perceptions,[30] the social construction of Israel's deterrence vis-à-vis Hizbullah,[31] the role of ambiguity in Israeli–Lebanese relations,[32] and the role of revenge.[33] However, these studies are the exception and they,

---

[21] McDermott (1996, 104–105). The Israel State Archives (hereafter, ISA) contains numerous reports on meetings held between LAF and IDF officials in the period after 1967. Interestingly, these meetings continued also after the LAF's paralysis in 1976, including with representatives of the Lebanese Arab Army, the breakaway faction from the LAF. See ISA, Ministry of Foreign Affairs, 267/3-A, MFA to Embassies and General Consulates in the US, August 8, 1976. See also Gur (1998, 76). In 1996, after Israel's military operation against Hizbullah in South Lebanon("Operation Grapes of Wrath"), these meetings were held within the framework of the Israel–Lebanon Monitoring Group, which included representatives of the United States, France, Lebanon, Israel, and Syria, but not of Hizbullah or the UN. See Waldman (2003); Tamir (2005).
[22] Eisenberg (1997, 2009, 2010); Zisser (2009); Khashan (2009). Kaufman (2013) focuses on the Syria–Lebanon–Israel border region.
[23] Yaniv (1987); Evron (1987); Gilboa (2015).   [24] Aronson and Horowitz (1971).
[25] Schiff and Ya'ari (1984); Shilon (2012).
[26] Hamizrachi (1988); Sela (2007); O. Gazit (2011); Sheffer and Barak (2013, 115–124).
[27] Randal (1983); Schulze (1998); Nisan (2004).
[28] Saad-Ghorayeb (2002); Hamzeh (2004); J. Harik (2004); Norton (2007); Sobelman (2004, 2010).
[29] Hamizrachi (1988); O. Gazit (2011).   [30] Eisenberg (2000).   [31] Lupovici (2009).
[32] Barak (2010).   [33] Löwenheim and Heimann (2008).

too, do not identify possible links between Israel's state expansion and its policy toward Lebanon. There have also been studies done on the many films produced on Israel's experience in Lebanon, but their focus, like the films they analyze, is on Israel and not on Lebanon.[34] In this sense, these Israeli films are similar to many Lebanese films, including those dealing with the civil war of 1975–1990, which make only passing references to Israel or ignore it altogether.[35] Still, some of these Israeli films (e.g., *Waltz with Bashir*) do suggest that Israel's invasion of Lebanon in 1982 was closely connected to the Palestinian issue. These films are discussed in Chapter 7.

A recurring theme in most works on Israeli–Lebanese relations is that as long as Lebanon was politically stable and its regime democratic, Lebanon's relations with Israel, its southern neighbor, were also stable, but that Lebanon's weakening and "failure" in the mid-1970s impinged on its relations with Israel and, ultimately, led to Israel's increased involvement in Lebanon's affairs.[36] One problem with this argument is that despite the fact that the Lebanese conflict ended in October 1990 and reconstruction of the state made considerable headway in later years (see Chapter 3), Israeli–Lebanese relations remained volatile and in some respects even deteriorated. But a closer examination of the period 1949–1967 – that is, when Israeli–Lebanese relations were the most stable – suggests that in fact Lebanon's stability was closely linked to its neighbors' behavior toward it.[37] These included not only Israel, which, as suggested below, exercised considerable restraint toward Lebanon before 1967, but also Syria, which in the first two decades and a half since its independence was too weak to exert effective pressure on Lebanon.[38] Another, more distant neighbor was Egypt, which some leaders in Beirut, such as Prime Minister Riad al-Sulh (Sunni), referred to as Lebanon's "Big Sister" in 1943, and which sometimes meddled in Lebanon's affairs and at other times helped stabilize it.[39]

---

[34] Almog (2009); Shohat (2010); Morag (2012, 2013); Benziman (2013); Niv (2014).

[35] A notable exception is *The Kite* (*Le cerf-volant*, 2003) by Randa Chahal-Sabbag, who also directed *Civilisées* (1999), which is one of the most critical films made on the Lebanese civil war of 1975–1990. See Barak (2007a, 60). *The Kite* depicts a young Lebanese women, presumably a Druze, who lives in a village on the Lebanese side of the Israeli–Lebanese border and falls in love with a young Israeli soldier on the other side of the fence. The entire film is a meditation on the absurdity of borders between states and the triumph of those who defy them. See also Khatib (2008, 145–146).

[36] Atzili (2010, 2011); Eisenberg (2010); Eiran (2013).

[37] This finding is commensurate with studies on sovereignty in the field of International Relations that emphasize its mutually constitutive nature. See, especially, Jackson and Rosberg (1982); Robert Jackson (1990); Wendt (1999); Van Benthuysen (2015).

[38] Rabinovich (1985, 36).

[39] See al-Sulh (1943). The signing of the Cairo Agreement in Egypt and under President Nasser's auspices is a case in point.

The major problem with most studies on Israeli–Lebanese relations, however, is that their main emphasis, including after 1967, is on Israel and Lebanon and not on Israel/Palestine and its relations with Lebanon. In other words, these studies do not "factor in" the effects of Israel's expansion on its foreign relations, including with Lebanon. This weakness has sometimes led to "essentialist" arguments regarding Lebanon as either a peaceful or a conflict-prone political unit. One of the goals of the discussion that follows is to challenge this deficiency by "bringing in" Israel's expansion and its effects – that is, to discuss the complex relations between Israel/Palestine and Lebanon, and not only between Israel and Lebanon.

Relative Stability

> If only the other borders had been as quiet!
> – Lt. General E.L.M. Burns, Chief of Staff of UNSTO (1962)

Before the First Arab–Israeli War, close ties existed between some Maronite leaders in French-controlled (and, later, independent) Lebanon and Jewish leaders in Mandatory Palestine. This relationship motivated some leaders and groups in the two communities to envision the establishment of peaceful relations between them and the political units that they wished to establish.[40] However, by 1943, when Christian and Muslim leaders in Lebanon reached the National Pact, the inter-communal settlement that paved the way for Lebanon's independence (see Chapter 3), it became clear that most members of the Maronite community in Lebanon had opted for accommodation with their Muslim compatriots and the Arab states, and Maronite–Jewish ties became marginal.[41]

During the crisis in Palestine that culminated in the First Arab–Israeli War, Lebanon was divided between those who advocated a more active role in Palestine and those who preferred to keep a safe distance from the conflict. The former included, on the one hand, some Muslims who volunteered to fight on behalf of the Palestinians,[42] and, on the other hand, Christian leaders, especially Maronites, who supported the partition of Palestine and the establishment of a Jewish state.[43] However, most

---

[40] Eisenberg (1994). [41] Kimche (1991, 130–131); Erlich (2000).
[42] These included Fawzi al-Qawuqji (Sunni), leader of the Arab Liberation Army, and several LAF officers who joined the Arab volunteers, such as Shawkat Shuqair (Druze), who later became the chief of staff of the Syrian army, and Muhammad Zughayyeb (Shi'i), who was killed in battle.
[43] These included the Maronite Patriarch Antoine Arida, former President Emile Eddé (Maronite), and Ignatius Mubarak, the Maronite Bishop of Beirut. The latter even disputed the Arab claims to Palestine and Lebanon.

Lebanese leaders,[44] although voicing their objection to the partition of Palestine and their support to the all-Arab position regarding this issue, nonetheless tried to minimize Lebanon's role in the crisis. These internal divisions, and also the weakness of the LAF in this period, prompted Lebanon's leaders to decide that the LAF would not intervene in Palestine after the termination of the British Mandate but, rather, would limit itself to a defensive role on Lebanon's border with Palestine, a position that was accepted by the other Arab states. Indeed, throughout the First Arab–Israeli War there was little fighting between Lebanon and Israel – the LAF waged only one battle against the Israel Defense Forces (IDF), in Malikiyya, a village on the border between Israel and Lebanon, on June 5–6, 1948 – though some Lebanese volunteers joined the Arab Liberation Army (ALA), which operated from Lebanon's territory.[45]

In 1949, when the First Arab–Israeli War came to an end, Lebanon was the second Arab state to sign an Armistice Agreement with Israel.[46] By then, 100,000–110,000 Palestinians, especially from the north of Palestine, had found refuge in Lebanon and settled mainly in camps near its major cities: Beirut, Tripoli, and Sidon.[47] The LAF, which controlled the Israeli–Lebanese border and the adjacent area, removed the Palestinian refugees from that region, and in the following years the Palestinians in Lebanon remained under the close supervision of the LAF's Intelligence Branch.[48] Most of the Palestinian refugees were excluded from Lebanese politics, society, and economy, not least because of the potential challenge that their continued presence in Lebanon posed to its pattern of inter-communal relations.

As mentioned earlier, from 1949 until the Israeli–Arab War of 1967, Israel's relations with Lebanon were the most stable among all of Israel's

---

[44] These included President Bechara al-Khoury (Maronite), Prime Minister Riad al-Sulh (Sunni), LAF Commander Fouad Chehab (Maronite), Foreign Minister Hamid Frangieh (Maronite), and Lebanon's representative in the UN, Camille Chamoun (Maronite).
[45] Barak (2001, 2009a). See also Hughes (2005); Morris (2008, 45–46, 258–260).
[46] Ibid., 378–380.
[47] Sirriyeh (1976); Abu Iyad (1981); R. Khalidi (1986); Brynen (1990). The figure 100,000 is mentioned in Brynen (1990, 19) and the figure 110,000 appears in R. Sayegh (1994, 21). A British document from 1949 mentions more than 80,000 Palestinian refugees in Lebanon. PRO, Foreign Office, 371/75317. Houstoun Boswall to Bevin, April 14, 1949.
[48] ISA, Ministry of Foreign Affairs, 2432/71, Information for the Delegations Abroad, Israel Armistice Commission, July 26, 1949; ISA, Ministry of Foreign Affairs, 2433/2, Report on ILMAC Meeting No. 145 on August 5, 1953, August 10, 1953. See also Burns (1962, 122). According to an Israeli source, it was the Lebanese parliament that decided on the removal of the Palestinian refugees from the border area. See ISA, Ministry of Foreign Affairs, 2433/3, Tekoa to the Foreign Minister, August 13, 1954. See also ISA, Ministry of Foreign Affairs, 2433/3, Salant to Staff Officer for the Armistice Commission, April 20, 1954.

relations with its Arab neighbors. Whatever problems occurred in the two states' relations were dealt with effectively by the Israel–Lebanon Mixed Armistice Commission (ILMAC), formed in 1949, which included representatives of the two armies and a UN observer.[49] The main problems on the Israeli–Lebanese border until the mid-1960s stemmed from bands of smugglers who operated in the area, but also from attempts made by Palestinian refugees to return to their lands and homes in Israel. However, both sides usually addressed these issues through ILMAC. Sometimes understandings were reached in ILMAC that were not acceptable to the Lebanese government but appeared necessary to the LAF officers who conducted the talks with Israel. This behavior on the part of the Lebanese side can be explained not only by the considerable autonomy enjoyed by the LAF in security matters in Lebanon since its independence,[50] but also by the fact that for the government in Beirut and for most members of Lebanon's political elite, South Lebanon was a peripheral area that was only secondary in importance. Israel, for its part, did not hesitate to demand from the Lebanese side that Lebanon honor its obligations according to the Armistice Agreement, and usually got what it requested. Therefore, Israel generally practiced restraint in its policy toward Lebanon, particularly compared to the volatile situation with its other neighbors in this period. The following example is telling. On February 12, 1964, a special meeting of ILMAC was held in Naqoura at Lebanon's request after its representatives had received an unsigned letter from the Israeli side that alerted the Lebanese to the fact that "certain elements intend to embarrass Lebanon and Israel by using Lebanese territory as a way for infiltrating [Palestinian] fidayin or for other hostile acts, in connection with the Israeli irrigation plan," and informed the Lebanese that if this were to occur, "[w]e shall then be obliged to hold the Lebanese authorities for any act of this kind in the future." In the meeting, the Lebanese representative, an LAF officer at the rank of colonel, stated:

I always said and I repeat it again, the Lebanese side abides and will always abode by the clauses of the Armistice [Agreement] and thanks to this Commission [ILMAC], the relations between Israel and Lebanon are as correct as between the friendlier States. Even friendly states cannot get on better together, thanks to this Commission, which always succeeds in settling the disagreements coming between us. Lebanon never initiated problems along the border; on the contrary, it used all its means to settle all incidents to the satisfaction of both parties.

[49] Burns (1962, 120–122); Hof (1985, 63–69); Morris (1993); Pelcovits (1993, 48–49); McDermott (1996). This section is also based on my reading of the protocols of the meetings of ILMAC), which are found at the Israel State Archives (ISA).
[50] Barak (2009a, 37).

To which the Israeli representative, an IDF lieutenant colonel, replied: "I do agree with SLD [Senior Lebanese Delegate] that there are friendly relations between the two representatives of the two parties. I go further, we are married by Catholic marriage. We can separate, but cannot divorce. These are facts of life between our two countries."[51]

Nathan Pelcovits, who studied the Armistice regime between Israel and its neighbors in the period 1949–1960, explains the relative success of ILMAC:

First, the ADL [Armistice Demarcation Line between Israel and Lebanon] coincided with the prewar frontier between Palestine and Lebanon. Both sides accepted it. No residue of territorial claims, no "galling innovation" of armistice lines drawn on a map complicated the armistice relationship. There was no demilitarized zone in which sovereignty and territorial rights were disputed, as they were on the Syrian frontier. Second, both sides had parallel security interests. Border trouble was therefore eschewed. UNTSO [the United Nations Truce Supervision Organization] attributed the stability in large part to Beirut's perception of its comparative military weakness. It therefore had an interest in avoiding confrontation, snuffing out signs of [Palestinian] fedayeen activity based in the refugee camps during the early years, and refraining from exacerbating incidents.[52]

But it was not only the representatives of both sides that preferred to sort their differences through ILMAC – that is, on a state-to-state basis: their superiors, too, favored this over other alternatives. Indeed, an examination of official statements, memoirs, and other texts authored by officials who were involved in determining Israel's relations with Lebanon in this period suggests that two competing approaches existed in Israel with regard to Lebanon – the "statist" approach and the "communal" approach – and that the former was dominant before 1967.

Employing the terms discussed in the previous chapters, it can be argued that on the domestic level, these two approaches, which were not entirely exclusive, represented different positions toward the triangular relationship between the state, community, and security in Israel. The "statist" approach held that the state, which is the most important actor, presides over the community and security – namely, that raison d'état should be given precedence over security considerations and communal agendas. The "communal" approach, for its part, suggested that the community and its interests should be paramount. On the external level, the "statist" approach favored state-to-state or inter-state relations, including between Israel and its neighbors, whereas the "communal"

---

[51] ISA, Ministry of Foreign Affairs, 6546/6, Verbatim Record of the Special Meeting held at Naqoura on February 12, 1964.
[52] Pelcovits (1993, 49).

approach preferred to reach out to particular groups within these states – ethnic, national, tribal, etc. – sometimes without the knowledge of their government.[53]

With regard to Lebanon, the "statist" approach in Israel viewed it, first and foremost, as a neighboring state with which Israel should maintain a stable relationship, and, if possible, reach a formal peace treaty in continuation of the Armistice Agreement of 1949. The "communal" approach, in its turn, emphasized the community as the major actor in Lebanon, and perceived the latter as a country with a prominent Maronite Christian community that was purportedly friendly to Israel, a factor that could open the door for Israel's involvement in its northern neighbor's affairs.

The "statist" approach, shared mainly by Prime Minister and Foreign Minister Moshe Sharett (1954–1955) and members of Israel's Ministry of Foreign Affairs, can be discerned in a consultation on the practices of Israel in the Middle East held on August 24–25, 1953, which was attended by senior Israeli ambassadors. During this meeting, Reuven Shiloah, former head of the Mossad and Israel's Chargé d'Affaires in Washington, observed: "There is nothing to say about Lebanon. The situation in the border with Lebanon is generally adequate. From time to time the Lebanese wish to demonstrate their nationalism, and then an incident occurs ... But the relations with Lebanon are generally not our utmost concern."[54]

About two years later, Sharett, Israel's prime minister and foreign minister, was asked by *Newsweek* which country held the best prospects for peace with Israel, to which he replied: "Lebanon is the 'first candidate to be the second' Arab state that would sign a peace treaty with Israel."[55] For Sharett, the same logic that had prompted Lebanon to be the second Arab state to sign an Armistice Agreement with Israel in 1949 could lead to its signing a second peace treaty with Israel, thus formalizing the two states' relations.

---

[53] There is some overlap between the "statist" and "communal" approaches, as identified here, and the distinction made by Gabriel Sheffer between the "moderate" and "activist" camps within *Mapai*, Israel's ruling party, in the 1950s. Sheffer (1996). See also Kimche (1991, 130–131); Erlich (2000). Cf. Laron (2015).

[54] ISA, Ministry of Foreign Affairs, 2408/10, Report on Consultation on the Practices of Israel in the Middle East, August 24–25, 1953. About a decade later, Israel's Foreign Minister, Golda Meir, told US President John F. Kennedy that "Israel has never had real trouble with Lebanon. Cows occasionally wander over the border from Lebanon and are sent back... Girls in the Israeli army may get lost and wander across the Lebanese border, but they are very politely returned. None of the incidents are serious." Quoted in Foley (2005, 47).

[55] *Newsweek*, May 30, 1955.

With regard to the "communal" approach, Sharett, in his personal diary, wrote that on two occasions when he was Israel's prime minister and foreign minister, David Ben-Gurion (who had resigned his posts as prime minister and defense minister on January 1954, and resumed the latter in February 1955) suggested that Israel encourage the establishment of a Maronite Christian state in Lebanon, and that in the second instance Ben-Gurion, now in his capacity as defense minister, was joined by the IDF's chief of staff, Lieutenant General Moshe Dayan. On February 27, 1954, Sharett wrote in his diary:

Then he [Ben-Gurion] passed on to another issue. This is the time to encourage Lebanon – that is, the Maronites in it – to proclaim a Christian State. I said that this was an illusion. The Maronites are divided. The partisans of Christian separatism are weak and will dare do nothing. A Christian Lebanon would mean giving up Tyre, Tripoli, the Biqa'. There is no force that could bring Lebanon back to its pre-World War I dimensions, and all the more so because in that case it would lose its economic raison d'etre. Ben-Gurion reacted furiously. He began to enumerate the historical justification for a reduced Christian Lebanon. If such a fact were to be created, the Christian Powers would not dare oppose it. I claimed that there was no actor that would create such a fact, and that if we were to spur and encourage it we would get ourselves into an adventure that will place nothing but shame on us. Here came a wave of rebukes regarding my lack of daring and narrow-mindedness. We ought to send envoys and spend money. I said there was no money. The reasonable answer was that this is nonsense, the money must be found, if not in the Treasury then at the Jewish Agency (!). For this purpose it is worthwhile throwing away one hundred thousand, half a million, a million dollars because if this were to it happen, a radical change will come in the Middle East, and a new era will start. I got tired of struggling against a whirlwind.[56]

About a year later, on May 16, 1955, during a joint meeting of senior officials from the Ministry of Defense, the Ministry of Foreign Affairs, and the IDF, Ben-Gurion, now defense minister, again raised the idea that Israel do something about Lebanon, this time in the context of a possible Iraqi invasion of Syria or a unification of these two states. This time, Ben-Gurion was supported by the IDF Chief of Staff Dayan, who argued:

The only thing that is necessary is to find an officer, even at the rank of Major, and to either win his heart or buy him with money, in order to make him agree to declare himself the savior of the Maronite population. Then, the IDF will enter Lebanon, will occupy the relevant territory, and will create a Christian regime which will ally itself with Israel. The territory from the Litani southward will be totally annexed to Israel and everything will be all right. If we were to accept the advice of the Chief of Staff we would do it tomorrow, without awaiting a signal from Baghdad, but in view of the circumstances the Chief of Staff is prepared to

[56] Sharett (1978, 2: 377). In translating this passage I also relied on Rokach (1986, 22).

wait patiently until the Iraqi government will fulfil our wish and occupy Syria. Indeed, Ben-Gurion quickly emphasized that his plan was to be implemented only if Syria were to be occupied by Iraq. I did not want to enter into a long and deep argument with Ben-Gurion on his imaginary and adventurous plan – which is surprising in its detachedness and crudeness – in the presence of his officers, and limited myself to saying that this might mean not the strengthening of Christian Lebanon, but war between Israel and Syria ... At the same time I agreed to Ben-Gurion's proposal to set up a joint commission composed of officials of the Ministry of Foreign Affairs and the IDF to deal with issues related to Lebanon.[57]

A committee was indeed set up, but it made little headway, not least because of Sharett's negative stance,[58] which stemmed from his "statist" approach.

We see, then, that in this period, the "communal" approach in Israel with regard to Lebanon, which was represented by Ben-Gurion and Dayan, was effectively overruled by the "statist" approach, represented by Sharett. Indeed, we have seen earlier that in 1955 Sharett openly favored peace between the two states.

The prevailing view in Israel before 1967 was thus that Lebanon was, first and foremost, a sovereign state, and that there was no real dispute between it and Israel, as there was between Israel and other Arab states. Some Israeli leaders hoped that if the circumstances permitted, a formal peace treaty between Israel and Lebanon could be attained. In the meantime, the main channel between the two states was ILMAC, which was quite effective not least because of the support that it enjoyed from Israel's political and military leaders.

More broadly, the "statist" approach with regard to Israel's relations with Lebanon reflected the way that Israeli leaders perceived their own state before 1967: a sovereign state where, as we have seen (in Chapter 3), the principle of statism (*mamlachtiyut*) was paramount. Although it was Ben-Gurion, one of the main advocates of statism, who in the period 1954–1956 suggested that Israel act in a "communal" manner that was not commensurate with this principle, neither he nor Dayan tried to implement their ideas during the Suez War of 1956, which underscored the limits to Israel's military power,[59]

---

[57] Sharett (1978, 4: 966). In translating this passages I also relied on Rokach (1986, 26). On May 28, 1955, Moshe Sharett wrote: "The Chief of Staff [Moshe Dayan] supports hiring some [Lebanese] officer who will agree to serve as a puppet leader so that the IDF may appear as responding to his appeal to 'liberate' Christian Lebanon from its Muslim oppressors. This will, of course, be a crazy adventure and it's a good thing that a joint committee was formed so that we could prevent dangerous complications through it. The committee must be charged with research tasks and prudent actions directed at encouraging Maronite circles who do not bow to Muslim pressures and agree to lean on us." Ibid., 4:1024. See also Erlich (2000); Eisenberg (2009).
[58] Erlich (2000); Eisenberg (2009, 2010).
[59] Erlich (2000, 365–391). In the consultations that preceded the eve of the Suez War in 1956, Ben-Gurion raised the idea of downsizing Lebanon and Israel's expansion up to

and the Lebanese civil war of 1958. Indeed, in a government meeting on July 17, 1958, Ben-Gurion spoke very differently about Lebanon than before: "We are interested in having weak neighbors around us. We are interested in Lebanon. I am not scared of Lebanon, although [President Camille] Chamoun was always an Israel hater [*soneh Israel*]. In deepest secret we helped them [during the civil war of 1958]. I don't see any danger in him."[60]

In the meeting, moreover, Ben-Gurion recounted a meeting he had with a Soviet official in which he told the latter that "in general, our policy is not to intervene in the policy of our neighbors or any other state, and of course we would like Lebanon to be independent."[61]

In sum, Israel's relations with Lebanon in the period 1949–1967 were dealt with mainly from a "statist" approach, which, at the time, was dominant among Israel's leaders, and this factor is significant when trying to account for the two states' stable relations throughout this period. As we shall see, the weakening of the "statist" approach in Israel since 1967 due to the state's expansion, and the subsequent strengthening of the "communal" approach, especially after 1977, can help account for the deterioration of these relations in later periods.

Deterioration

> When the War of Independence was over, we signed the Armistice agreements with the Arabs. We were smart enough to understand that these Armistice agreements were not peace treaties, namely, that they are temporary. But we were not smart enough to understand that the Armistice agreements, which were under the auspices of the UN, and which were actually reached by the UN, and which the great powers recognize ... are very serious agreements, which create something that has political value of its own.
> – Lieutenant General (ret.) Moshe Dayan (November 1976)[62]

---

the Litani River, but did not find support for his plan, including among his French interlocutors (ibid., 379).

[60] Israeli Government (1958). On Israel's limited role in the Lebanese civil war of 1958, see Hamizrachi (1988); Erlich (2000).

[61] Israeli Government (1958). Ben-Gurion added, "I will not tell America to trust Lebanon" because of the "family competition" among its Christians, which "supersedes any other issue." Drawing a parallel with Israel's domestic politics, Ben-Gurion added that "they [the Christians] think that Israel's existence is their only support. They have no courage. They behave like *Herut* [Israel's right-wing party] and support *Maki* [the Israeli Communist Party; a possible reference to the Arab states], they do not like *Maki* but they support it, and in this way they hurt *Mapai* [Israel], or as they say, the head of *Mapai* [Ben-Gurion]." See also Erlich (2000).

[62] Quoted in Tal (1997). See also Maoz (2009, 102–103).

The Israeli–Arab war of 1967 ushered in a profound change in Israel's relations not only with Egypt, Syria, and Jordan, the three Arab states that Israel had fought against, and conquered territories from, in the conflict, but also with Lebanon and the Palestinians, although neither actor was directly involved in the fighting.[63] At the same time, the war gave rise to profound changes in Israel itself, and especially the strengthening of the communal identity of its citizens at the expense of statism. These changes were not only due to the opening of the state's borders and the acquisition of new territories, but also on account of the rising power of the IDF and the sphere of security in general as well as the emergence of new "communal" entrepreneurs (see Chapter 4). This section focuses on the impact of the profound change that took place in Israel/Palestine, especially the state's expansion, on Israeli–Lebanese relations.

The Palestinian armed factions were among the first actors in the Middle East to assert themselves in the wake of the Arab defeat in the 1967 War. Indeed, while a Palestinian national identity had existed before the war, there is little doubt that its outcome gave it a new impetus. This was soon manifested in the growing activities of the Palestinian armed factions, and especially Fatah, the major Palestinian armed group that emerged in this period, but also others (e.g., the PFLP and the DFLP). These actors sought to become autonomous from the Arab states, which had dominated the Palestine issue before 1967. By 1968, Yasser Arafat, the leader of Fatah, and his comrades managed to wrest control of the PLO, the political wing of the Palestinian national movement, which had been under Egyptian dominance, and from then onwards the Palestinian armed struggle was complemented by political action.[64]

However, the attempts by the Palestinian armed factions to establish a territorial foothold for themselves after 1967 proved to be more challenging. Israel, which sought to impose its control over the newly acquired West Bank and Gaza Strip, forcefully prevented the Palestinian armed factions from becoming entrenched there (see Chapter 4). In addition, Israel pressured Jordan to clamp down on the Palestinian armed factions across the Jordan River, including by launching Israeli military raids against Jordan's territory. It is noteworthy that during one of these raids, which led to the Battle of Karameh in 1968, the Jordanian army fought alongside the Palestinian armed factions and against the IDF. However, Israel's mounting pressures, on the one hand, and provocative actions by some Palestinian armed factions in Jordan, on the other hand,

---

[63] On Lebanon's role in the 1967 War, see Barak (2009a, 217 n.77).
[64] Abu Iyad (1981); Brynen (1990); R. Khalidi (1997); Y. Sayigh (1997); Meier (2014); Sela (2014).

led to growing Jordanian–Palestinian tensions, and Jordan became engulfed in a civil war (1970–1971). This conflict, which later became known as "Black September," ended when King Hussein, who presided over a powerful, homogenous, and loyal military and, moreover, was backed by the United States and Israel, forcefully suppressed the Palestinian armed factions and ousted them from the kingdom.[65]

The subsequent sealing of the border between Jordan and Israel and the successful clampdown on their armed activists on both sides of the Jordan River[66] forced the Palestinian armed factions to take their revolution elsewhere. One place that seemed appropriate was the Israeli–Lebanese border area, where the Palestinian armed factions could operate in a relatively autonomous manner. Thus, and although some of these factions, such as Fatah, had operated in and from Lebanon's territory before 1967, the scope of their activities in this region increased manifold, and Lebanon gradually emerged as the Palestinians' primary base of operations.[67] Indeed, according to an Israeli report from March 1972, by that time there were at least 4,000–5,000 Palestinian "terrorists" in South Lebanon.[68]

Eager to establish themselves as a political actor to be reckoned with, the Palestinian armed factions began to launch armed operations against Israel's northern region from Lebanon's territory and to fire rockets at Israeli towns. However, despite the casualties and the physical damage that Israel sustained in this period, its leaders remained immovable and would not accept the Palestinian armed factions, or, for that matter, the PLO, as legitimate partners. Indeed, it was during this period that Prime Minister Golda Meir, leader of the Labor Party, argued that "there is no Palestinian people,"[69] and Foreign Minister Abba Eban, from the same party, referred to Israel's pre-1967 borders as the "Borders of Auschwitz" (see Chapter 2). Other Israeli officials, too, related to the Palestinians either as "terrorists" or as "refugees," and some, like Deputy Prime Minister Yigal Allon, even held that the "Arab terrorist organizations" – that is, the Palestinian armed factions – "are not a serious problem for us."[70] In September 1969, after a Palestinian Katyusha hit Kiryat Shmonah, David Elazar, head of the IDF's Northern Command, told the northern town's residents: "If the [armed] activity from Lebanon

---

[65] Abu Iyad (1981); Ajami (1992); Nevo (2008); Rubinovich (2010).
[66] On Israel's actions against Fatah in the West Bank after the 1967 War, see Ronen (1989); Elad (2015, 363–372). See also the recollection of Avraham Shalom quoted in Chapter 4.
[67] Salibi (1976: 28); Sirriyeh (1976); Hof (1985, 74); Bartov (2002, 1:165–184); Kaufman (2013, 112).
[68] ISA, Ministry of Foreign Affairs, 7037/4-A, MFA to Brussels and other delegations, Observers on the Lebanon Border, March 19, 1972.
[69] Quoted in Zertal and Eldar (2007, 278–279).   [70] *Haaretz* (1969).

170 State Expansion and Conflict

continues, this activity will endanger the state of Lebanon. The IDF will do everything to remove the danger from Kiryat Shmonah – but the town must stand firm, because victory is assured us."[71]

However, Israel's unyielding position only made the Palestinian armed factions more determined to prove that they could not be ignored. This was done by increasing the scope of their armed operations from Lebanon (and elsewhere). Thus, during the 1970s, a vicious cycle began of Palestinian incursions into Israel, which included the taking of civilians as hostages in order to compel Israel to negotiate with them and release Palestinian prisoners; Israeli refusals to "capitulate to terrorism" and the launching of Israeli commando operations to free the hostages, which sometimes ended in bloodshed;[72] mounting Israeli pressures on Lebanon to curb the Palestinian armed factions in its territory; and Israeli punitive raids across the border with Lebanon that resulted in more casualties and physical damage, this time on the Lebanese side.[73] Importantly, the Palestinian attacks against Israel in this period did not represent a major threat to its security: indeed, certain Israeli leaders, such as Eban, even argued, in retrospect, that Israel's anti-terrorist actions in this period shifted its leaders' attention from the war preparations in Syria and Egypt before 1973.[74] However, the impact of these attacks on Israel's leaders cannot be overstated. For years to come, including after the removal of the bulk of the Palestinian fighters from Lebanon in 1982, Israel's political and military leaders continued to insist on a permanent Israeli military "presence" (that is, occupation) in Lebanon to prevent the recurring of such events.[75]

[71] Quoted in Bartov (2002, 1: 176).
[72] In 1970, when the first Israeli citizen, Shmuel Rosenwasser, a civilian guard from the town of Metula, was abducted by the Palestinian armed factions, the IDF launched a raid into Lebanon's territory and abducted ten Lebanese soldiers to secure his release, but to no avail; Bergman (2009, 24). Later, Israel tried to pressure Lebanon to show "good will" in preventing hostile activity in the border in return for the release of its soldiers. ISA, Ministry of Foreign Affairs, 5251/14, Staff Officer for Liaison with the UN to Deputy Head of Operations of the IDF, Meeting of Major General [Mordechai] Gur and Brigadier [Antoun] Saad, March 22, 1971.
[73] The most well-known cases of Palestinian armed incursions into Israel in this period occurred near Avivim (1970), in Kiryat Shmona (1974), in Ma'alot (1974), in Nahariyya (1979), and in Misgav Am (1980). Other Palestinian armed operations that originated from Lebanon's territory were the attack on the Savoy Hotel in Tel Aviv (1975) and on Israel's Coastal Highway (1978). On this period, see Gur (1998); Eitan (2001). See also Eisenberg (2010). In a meeting of the Knesset's Foreign Affairs and Security Committee in March 1975, following the attack on the Savoy hotel, Defense Minister Shimon Peres stated that the goal of the "terrorists" was to negotiate "from the heart of Tel Aviv" and thus gain international attention, but that "we did not intend to negotiate." See Foreign Affairs and Security Committee (1975).
[74] Eban (1978, 2: 474).
[75] Luft (2000); Sela (2007); Kaufman (2013, 116–117). According to Uri Lubrani, the Coordinator of Israel's Operations in Lebanon in the period 1983–2000, Rabin was

We see, then, that in the period after the 1967 War and following Israel's expansion, Lebanon, and particularly the Israeli–Lebanese border, gradually emerged as the major arena for waging the struggle over Israel/Palestine between its two rival communities – the Israelis and the Palestinians. For the Palestinian armed factions, which were defeated in Israel/Palestine and later also in Jordan, Lebanon was a safe haven, and its proximity to Israel/Palestine enabled the Palestinian fighters to access its territory through the Israeli–Lebanese border, which, at that time, was mostly porous.[76] Lebanon's relative weakness in the coercive sense (in this period, the LAF was four times weaker than its Jordanian counterpart[77]) made it difficult for its security sector to suppress the Palestinian armed factions, and the legitimacy of its security sector, too, was at stake: unlike Jordan, some groups in Lebanon, especially among the Muslim communities and leftist and pan-Arab organizations, openly sympathized with the Palestinian cause and regarded the Palestinian armed factions as a force for change in the Arab states and in Lebanon. We have also seen (in Chapter 3) that in this period Lebanon's political elite effectively barred newcomers from joining the political system, and for these actors, the Palestinians, whose coercive power and all-Arab legitimacy were on the rise, could open the door to political participation. It is worth remembering, however, that not all of the Lebanese viewed the rise of the Palestinian armed factions in Lebanon in a positive light. Christian groups (e.g., the Maronite-led Phalanges Party) voiced concerns about their increasing role in Lebanon and the state's inability to curb them. These apprehensions were reinforced in November 1969, when, following a major crisis between the Palestinian armed factions and the Lebanese government, Fatah leader Arafat and the commander of the LAF, General Emile Boustani, signed the Cairo Agreement, which accorded legitimacy to the Palestinian armed presence in Lebanon, albeit under certain limits.[78]

---

fearful for the "fate" of Israel's border settlements and thus supported the creation of a "security zone" under the control of the IDF and the SLA that would physically separate the Galilee from Lebanon. Quoted in Barnea (2000). In November 1997, for example, Israeli Defense Minister Yitzhak Mordechai mentioned some of these past attacks as a factor that should prevent Israel's unilateral withdrawal from Lebanon. Quoted in Rabin, Alon, and Segev (1997); see also Goren, Hilleli, and Bender (1997).

[76] Kaufman (2013, 113); Meier (2014). A retired Israeli officer, Brigadier General Uzi Eilam mentions that in the early 1970s he proposed to the head of the IDF's Northern Command to build a sophisticated fence on the Israeli–Lebanese border, but the plan was rejected for budgetary reasons. Eilam (2009, 150–151). According to Kaufman (2013, 118) the "fence system" on the Israeli–Lebanese border was built in 1972.

[77] Barak (2009a, 24). See also Chamberlin (2012, 201–202, 213–214).

[78] Hof (1985); R. Khalidi (1986); Brynen (1990); Kaufman (2013, 112). Interestingly, the LAF presented the Cairo Agreement as an achievement, arguing that the LAF had again

Israel's leaders, who were alarmed by the Palestinian armed presence in Lebanon, made it clear to Lebanon's leaders that it was their responsibility to impose the state's authority over all of its territory, especially in the Israeli–Lebanese border area. Indeed, there is evidence that the Lebanese side did respond to Israel's demands by erecting roadblocks, arresting Palestinian fighters, dismantling rockets before they could be fired at Israel's territory, and even firing at Palestinian armed activists.[79] However, for Israel's political and military leaders, who were enraged by the vocal support of some Lebanese leaders (e.g., Sunni Prime Minister Abdullah Yafi) for the Palestinian armed factions and by what they regarded as Lebanon's "capitulation" to Palestinian "terrorism" in the Cairo Agreement, this was insufficient.[80] Indeed, numerous Israeli official documents from this period, including reports on meetings between IDF and LAF officers, portray Lebanon and its military as not firm enough in carrying out their duties. In May 1968, for example, an Israeli official argued that "the government of Lebanon has ... joined with Arab governments in pursuing a policy of active belligerency against Israel" since it "allowed the use of its territory by terror organizations through which the Arab states continue to wage warfare against Israel."[81] Therefore, and since, in the words of Israeli Prime Minister Meir, "regretfully, our neighbors do not understand only when we talk to them with words,"[82] Israel began to apply more and more military pressure on Lebanon to act more decisively against the "terrorists."

managed to preserve Lebanon's domestic equilibrium, and Lebanese President Charles Helou added that Lebanon had managed to buy time and that Egyptian President Nasser would guarantee that the deal would be honored. But other actors, and especially the Maronite-led parties, maintained that the agreement was a grave mistake and demanded that it be annulled or revised, since it reinserted Lebanon into the Arab–Israeli conflict and opened the way for massive Israeli retaliations against Lebanon. Barak (2009a, 88).

[79] See, e.g., ISA, Ministry of Foreign Affairs, 7428/23-A, MFA to New York, May 29, 1968; ISA, Ministry of Foreign Affairs, 6554/26, Ben-Aharon to MFA, February 19, 1969; ISA, Ministry of Foreign Affairs, 4471/11, Staff Officer for Liaison with the UN to Head of Operations, the IDF, Meeting with Major Hamdan [on], December 29, 1971. During a meeting between Lebanese and Israeli officers in 1971, the Lebanese representative delivered a message from LAF Commander Jean Nujeim, which stated that "you [the Israelis] know that we have so far acted as a special police for you against the terrorists." He protested that Israeli forces fired on the LAF, severely wounding one of its officers. See ISA, Ministry of Foreign Affairs, 7428/22-A, MFA to New York, June 10, 1970. An Israeli representative later apologized to the Lebanese for the "misunderstanding." ISA, Ministry of Foreign Affairs, 7428/22-A, MFA to New York, June 11, 1970. See also Kaufman (2013, 119).

[80] See, e.g., ISA, Ministry of Foreign Affairs, 6593/22, MFA to New York, May 14, 1968; ISA, Ministry of Foreign Affairs, 7037/4-A, MFA to Brussels and other delegations, Observers on the Lebanon Border, March 19, 1972.

[81] See, e.g., ISA, Ministry of Foreign Affairs, 6593/22, New York to MFA, May 15, 1968.

[82] ISA, Ministry of Foreign Affairs, 7428/22-A, MFA to Washington, June 3, 1970.

The main tool for communicating Israel's messages to Lebanon in this period were the aforementioned meetings between IDF and LAF officers, which sometimes were friendly but at other times were confrontational. In addition, Israel sent messages to Lebanon via third parties, launched military raids into Lebanon's territory, and shelled "terrorist camps" there, actions that were sometimes coordinated with the LAF or which received its commanders' tacit consent.[83] In addition, and in what would become a routine in later decades, Israeli warplanes penetrated Lebanon's airspace and Israeli warships entered its waters, thus violating its sovereignty.[84] All in all, in the period 1968–1974, there were more than 3,000 Israeli incursions into Lebanon's territory (an average of 1.4 - per day), which left some 880 civilians dead and thousands wounded, and which forced one-fifth of the 150,000 inhabitants of the Israeli–Lebanese border area to flee northward.[85] As for Israel, in the period 1970–1982 it lost 54 soldiers and 40 civilians, and about 700 were wounded in attacks from Lebanon.[86]

However, for the Palestinian armed factions and their supporters in Lebanon, Israel's retaliatory raids against Lebanon's territory only proved that the government in Beirut and the LAF had abandoned the Palestinians to the mercy of the Israelis. Thus, when the LAF tried, at the behest of some of the Maronite parties, to act forcibly against the Palestinian armed factions so as to further limit their armed operations

---

[83] On Israel's position, see ISA, Ministry of Foreign Affairs, 7428/23-A, New York to MFA, May 15, 1968. On the meetings in this period, see, e.g., ISA, Ministry of Foreign Affairs, 7428/23-A, MFA to New York, May 17, 1968; ISA, Ministry of Foreign Affairs, 7428/22-A, MFA to New York, June 1, 1970; ISA. See also report on a meeting between the head of the IDF's Intelligence Branch, Major General Aharon Yariv, and the LAF's Deputy Chief of Staff for Operations, Colonel Musa Kan'aan: ISA, Ministry of Foreign Affairs, 7033/9-A, MFA to Delegation in New York, January 17, 1972. Prior to the meeting, a lower-level meeting was held between Israeli and Lebanese officers, during which the Israeli side delivered a "harsh warning" to Lebanon, stating that Israel asks that "the terrorist activity from Lebanon would be ended completely or else we would have to maintain a permanent presence in the area in some form or another" and this "may lead to the plight of civilians from villages which is certainly against our wish." Yariv, too, warned his Lebanese interlocutor that if Israel was fired on from Lebanon's territory "we would have to respond by fire on the terrorists' bases in the villages and civilians (might) be hurt." Parentheses are in the original. On the coordination of Israeli incursions into Lebanon's territory in this period, see, e.g., ISA, Ministry of Foreign Affairs, 7428/22-A, MFA to New York, June 2, 1970; ISA, Ministry of Foreign Affairs, 7428/22-A, MFA to New York, July 20, 1970. On the Coordination of Israeli shelling of positions in Lebanon, see ISA, Ministry of Foreign Affairs, 7428/22-A, MFA to New York, June 11, 1970.
[84] See, e.g., ISA, Ministry of Foreign Affairs, 4470/3, MFA to New York and Washington, October 28, 1971; ISA, Ministry of Foreign Affairs, 4470/3, MFA to New York and Washington, December 14, 1971.
[85] *Al-Anwar* (Lebanon), July 1, 1975; Frieha (1980, 198); Hof (1985, 74); Brynen (1990, 67).
[86] Sela (2007, 65).

from Lebanon, this aroused opposition from many Muslims (especially Sunnis) as well as others, culminating in the aforementioned Cairo Agreement.[87] Lebanon accused Israel of abrogating the Armistice Agreement from 1949 and ILMAC, claiming that this prevented an impartial investigation of Israel's claims regarding Palestinian cross-border actions. In addition, Lebanese spokesmen sometimes accused Israel of expansionist aims and aggressive intentions toward Lebanon.[88] Indeed, when reading the primary and secondary sources on this period, one is struck by the absence of an effective conflict regulation mechanism such as the one that had existed in the Israeli–Lebanese border area in the period 1949–1967.

Israel's insistence, after 1967, that the Armistice Agreement with Lebanon from 1949 was null and void is telling in this regard. In the wake of Israel's military victory, its leaders argued that the Armistice agreements between Israel and all of its neighbors, including Lebanon – which, as mentioned earlier, did not participate in the war – were no longer valid, and Israeli officials rejected the role played by the UN on the Israeli–Lebanese border. This, Israel's leaders posited, was because Lebanon had been hostile to Israel before and during the 1967 War, and because the war itself made all of the Israeli–Arab Armistice agreements irrelevant.[89] However, this claim – which even Meir Rosen, legal adviser to Israel's Ministry of Foreign Affairs, in a detailed opinion from 1972, called "not well founded" and "not very convincing"[90] – was rejected by Lebanon, whose leaders continued to argue that the Armistice Agreement was valid and acted accordingly. The result was that in meetings held between Israeli and Lebanese military officers after 1967, the Lebanese side would insist they were working within the framework of the Armistice Agreement and ILMAC, whereas the Israeli side would reject the Lebanese claim and even refuse to receive messages through the UN.[91]

[87] Chamoun (1977, 145–156); Abu Iyad (1981). See also S. Khalaf (2002); Sela (2014).
[88] ISA, Ministry of Foreign Affairs, 7428/23-A, New York to MFA, May 20, 1968.
[89] Israeli Government (1967); *Jerusalem Post* (1969). See also Blum (2007, 325, n. 2).
[90] ISA, Ministry of Foreign Affairs, 5251/4, Rosen to Foreign Minister, April 12, 1972. According to this document, the most serious step that was taken by Lebanon was the signing of the Cairo Agreement with the PLO in 1969.
[91] Kaufman (2013, 119). Following the Litani Operation (1978), Israel's foreign minister, Moshe Dayan, informed UN Secretary-General Kurt Waldheim that Israel "is considering agreeing to reinstate the Lebanese-Israel General Armistice Agreement of 1949" if Lebanon would reaffirm that it abides by all of its provisions. Moshe Dayan to Kurt Waldheim, August 3, 1978, UN Archives (1978). Lebanese officials were pleased with Israel's position. See Sélim Tadmoury to Kurt Waldheim [August 1978], ibid. Elie Salem, who served as Lebanon's foreign minister under President Amine Gemayel in the 1980s, writes that Dayan's letter contradicted Israel's position during the military

The significance of these changes in Israel's policy toward Lebanon can better be appreciated when comparing it to the period before 1967. In the 1950s, Israeli officials began to hold the neighboring Arab states responsible for all armed actions planned or carried out from their territory, including by Palestinian fedayin, claiming that it was these states' duty to prevent them. Indeed, during the 1950s and 1960s, numerous Israeli retaliatory raids were launched against Jordan, Egypt, and Syria. But Israel's policy toward Lebanon was different. As mentioned earlier, the two states handled problems in their relations mainly through ILMAC, and Israel refrained from launching armed reprisals against Lebanon's territory.[92] Now, however, Israeli leaders interpreted Lebanon's conundrum as an inability, and even an unwillingness, to impose its authority over all of its territory, and Israel began to employ its military to address its security concerns.[93] Moreover, Israeli officials and observers began to contemplate more severe policies toward Lebanon. Thus, in a meeting between IDF and LAF officers on March 2, 1970, Major General Mordechai Gur, head of the IDF's Northern Command (and the IDF's future chief of staff), told his Lebanese counterpart, Brigadier Antoun Saad, that "militarily, if we were just told to do so, we would enter deep into Lebanon and would restore order." Citing the example of Jordan, Gur added:

The Jordanians had to leave the territory [near the border with Israel/Palestine] and today there are no infiltrations. We can reach a [situation of] scorched earth, this could solve the problem if there is no other way and I can assure you that in such a situation there will be no bases for the fidayin ... Along the Jordanian border, all the inhabitants had to leave everything, there is nothing, everything is dead.[94]

In an op-ed published on May 24, 1970, about two weeks after a major Israeli operation in South Lebanon ("Operation Uproar 2"), in which the LAF, like its Jordanian counterpart in the Battle of Karameh, resisted the Israeli invaders, Ze'ev Schiff, the well-connected military commentator of the Israeli daily *Haaretz*, suggested that Israel turn South Lebanon into

talks held between Israel and Lebanon in Naqoura in 1984, according to which the Armistice Agreement was null and void. See Salem (1993, 185). On Israel's position in the talks, see Sela (2007, 64). Before the Madrid conference in 1991, Lebanese President Elias Hrawi insisted that the two states' relations would be subject to the Armistice Agreement, but during the conference Israel's representatives, Yosef Hadas and Uri Lubrani, reiterated Israel's claim that it was Lebanon that breached the agreement. See *Haaretz* (1991); Eldar and Nir (1991).

[92] Morris (1993).
[93] See, e.g., ISA, Ministry of Foreign Affairs, 7033/9-A, Instructions for Response to Lebanese Representatives, n.d. [early 1970s].
[94] ISA, Ministry of Foreign Affairs, 4473/1, Staff Officer for Liaison with the UN to Comay of the MFA, March 3, 1970. See also ISA, Ministry of Foreign Affairs, 4473/1, New York to MFA, February 4, 1970; Hof (1985, 73); Kaufman (2013, 114).

a "no man's land" and wage the fighting against "terrorists" there and not in Israel's territory.[95] It is noteworthy that when he described this period later, in 1981, Gur chose to emphasize Israel's restrained policy toward Lebanon, which, moreover, sought to preserve it as an independent state and refrain from undermining it.[96]

But Israel's shift away from a "statist" policy toward Lebanon in this period was not only the result of "objective" security considerations. It also stemmed from Israel's changing perception of itself, of its Arab neighbors, and of its relations with them, which, in turn, reflected deeper processes that were at work in Israel/Palestine after 1967. Thus, for example, the UN, which had demonstrated its "defeatist" behavior during the crisis that preceded the 1967 War, was no longer accepted by Israel as an impartial mediator with its Arab neighbors, and the mechanisms that had been installed in 1949 under the UN's auspices, including ILMAC, were now seen as a liability rather than an asset by Israel's political and military leaders.[97] This was evident, for example, in Israel's outright rejection of Lebanon's proposal to the UN Security Council to deploy international observers on the Israeli–Lebanese border in the early 1970s, a position that Israel's Ministry of Foreign Affairs explained as follows:

The main problem on the border with Lebanon is to prevent the terrorists from attacking Israel. Taking care of this problem in Lebanon is the responsibility of the Lebanese government. Deploying [International] observers will not solve the problem and will only serve as an excuse for the Lebanese government [to argue] that it did all that it could. Our experience from 24 years [i.e., since 1948] is that in no place in no period UN observers had succeeded in preventing any kind of operation that the Arab side was interested in carrying out [against Israel] and on the other hand that when an Arab state decided to prevent operations against Israel it knew very well how to do it.[98]

---

[95] Schiff (1970). The article is found at ISA, Ministry of Foreign Affairs, 5182/2-G. On the operation see Kaufman (2013, 114–115).

[96] Gur (1981, 42–43).

[97] See, e.g., a message by Yitzhak Rabin, Israel's ambassador to the United States, in which he argued that the UN Security Council was a "hostile and one-sided element" and refused to submit a complaint to it on a Palestinian attack. ISA, Ministry of Foreign Affairs, 4473/1, Washington-MFA, May 22, 1970. Israel's deep distrust of the UN was also manifested later, in the establishment of the Multinational Force and Observers (MFO) – a non-UN military force – in the Sinai Peninsula as part of Israel's peace treaty with Egypt in 1979. See Tabory (1986). David Kimche describes ILMAC as "discredited" and "ineffective"; see Kimche (1991, 164). It was only later, in the late 1990s, that Israel would return to UN Security Council Resolution 425 in order to facilitate its withdrawal from Lebanon.

[98] ISA, Ministry of Foreign Affairs, 270/10, Information, March 31, 1972. See also ISA, Ministry of Foreign Affairs, 5202/12, Panama to MFA, March 16, 1972. For a similar Israeli position toward the UN, see ISA, Ministry of Foreign Affairs, 6818/9, Staff Officer for Liaison with the UN to Head of Operations, the IDF, Lebanon – Meeting with General [Bengt] Liljestrand, January 12, 1975.

What is interesting in this passage is how the entire period 1949–1967, including the role of ILMAC, which was chaired by UN observers, was presented in a negative light. Earlier, in January 1969, when a similar idea was floated by the United States, an Israeli official argued that "this would not help make the border quiet and would create complexities concerning the counter-operation that are necessary to combat terrorism" – namely, that the presence of international observers on the Israeli–Lebanese border was liable to hinder Israel's freedom of action toward Lebanon.[99]

The abolishment of the Israeli–Lebanese Armistice Agreement, and the Armistice regime in general, attests to Israel's changing perception toward Lebanon after 1967 and, inter-connectedly, to the transformation of Israel itself following its expansion. Israel's formal position, as expressed in 1970, was that "since June 1967 ... the entire Armistice regime has collapsed and is no longer valid because of the Arab belligerency that led to an open and declared war with the purpose of annihilating Israel." In August 1970, Israel posited, moreover, that from June 1967, its relations with the neighboring countries "[we]re founded on the ceasefire and the international obligation to establish a permanent peace."[100] Now, if the Armistice regime were to remain in effect even on one Arab–Israeli front – namely, between Israel and Lebanon – then this could lead to the restoration of this regime in other fronts, thus challenging Israel's expansion.[101] Israel's decision was, therefore, to renounce all Armistice agreements, including with Lebanon, and there was nothing that prevented it from doing so. As a result of this policy, the main mechanism for regulating Israeli–Lebanese relations, which had proven its utility before 1967, was jettisoned, and no effective mechanism was installed in its place.

But Israel's new policy toward Lebanon, which, as we have seen, rested on shaky legal foundations, was also questionable from a utilitarian perspective. In a meeting between senior LAF and IDF officers in May 1969, Brigadier General Antoun Saad, a former head of the LAF's Intelligence Branch, explained to his Israeli interlocutor that "if Israel were to return to make contacts" with the Lebanese "within the framework of ILMAC" then the Lebanese "would be able to claim that they are acting [against

---

[99] ISA, Ministry of Foreign Affairs, 3871/4, Eliav to North America Department, Deployment of Observers on the Israel–Lebanon Border, January 15, 1969.
[100] ISA, Ministry of Foreign Affairs, 6603/16, Comay to Remez, August 26, 1970.
[101] See, especially, Hof (1985, 66–68). Even on Israel's border with Lebanon, retaining the Armistice regime could cause problems for Israel: in September 1971, for example, Lebanon claimed that Israel had built a road inside Lebanon's territory and called upon ILMAC to investigate the matter, but Israeli officials did not allow the UN investigation to commence, which resulted in heated exchanges between UN and Israel. See ISA, Ministry of Foreign Affairs, 4471/11, Bunworth to Nevo, September 23, 1971.

the Palestinian armed factions] within the framework of an agreement – and an agreement must be honored."[102] But Israel would not budge, and it spared no effort to make it clear that both the Armistice Agreement with Lebanon and ILMAC were null and void.

But, as with regard to the Territories occupied in 1967, the decline of the "statist" approach in Israel with regard to Lebanon was the most blatant in Israel's military actions against it, and especially its attacks on national symbols of the Lebanese state. On December 28, 1968, an IDF commando unit led by Rafael Eitan, who a decade later would be appointed as the IDF's chief of staff and in this capacity would be one of the architects of the 1982 War, launched an attack on Beirut International Airport that destroyed about a dozen commercial planes belonging to Lebanon's national carrier, Middle East Airlines. In his account of the attack, Eitan mused: "The raid on a respectable place, an airport that served for landing aircraft from around the world, necessitated, in my view, an appropriate appearance: With 'class A' uniforms [service dress], polished shoes and caps on our heads, we looked filled with pride and honor, angels of destruction 'class A.'"[103]

Indeed, as suggested by the title of the relevant chapter in Eitan's memoires, "To let [them] know that we were here – Beirut," as well as by other sources, Israel's operation was specifically designed to compel the Lebanese to act forcefully against the Palestinians. Thus, for example, after being informed by a US official that "fear and nervousness continue to prevail in Beirut" in the aftermath of Israel's operation, an Israeli official replied that "if such an apprehension exists in Lebanon which compels them to act against the Fatah concentrations in their territory then this is a positive outcome and one can only hope that it will continue."[104]

It is noteworthy, in this context, that the Israeli attack was launched not in response to a Palestinian armed attack from Lebanon but following Palestinian attacks on El Al planes in Athens and the hijacking of an El Al plane to Algiers. The latter event was particularly embarrassing for Israel, since, contrary to its official policy of "not capitulating to terrorism," it was compelled to release several dozen Palestinian prisoners (ostensibly uninvolved in "terrorist" action, but in reality quite active) in return for the hostages.[105] In his autobiography, Defense Minister Moshe Dayan

---

[102] ISA, Ministry of Foreign Affairs, 3871/4, Staff Officer for Liaison with the UN to Head of Operations, the IDF, Lebanon–Meeting of Brigadier [Antoun] Saad and Head of Northern Command, May 14, 1969.
[103] Eitan (2001, 178–179).
[104] ISA, Ministry of Foreign Affairs, 6554/26, Ben-Aharon to Research, January 8, 1969.
[105] Bergman (2009, 28–29).

writes that when he spoke to the Israeli soldiers that embarked on the operation against Beirut International Airport in 1968, he told them:

> Our objective in this operation is to make clear to the Arabs of Lebanon that they have to stop employing Fatah to act against our airline services. The plane that brought the Fatah people to Athens took off from Lebanon. The terrorists trained in this country. If the Lebanese authorities enable Fatah to train in their territory, they have to pay the consequences ... The result of the operation has to be such that the Lebanese will think twice before they take actions against our planes.[106]

Lebanon, which allegedly employed Fatah against Israel, was thus seen as responsible for the presence of the Palestinian armed factions in its territory, whereas the Palestinians themselves, who had humiliated Israel, were ignored.[107] It is also noteworthy that Dayan, who, as we have seen, had advocated the creation of a pro-Israeli Christian regime in Lebanon in the mid-1950s, now considered the Lebanese to be Arabs.

In the wake of the events of "Black September" in Jordan, Israel became even more determined to compel Lebanon to suppress the Palestinian armed factions in its territory, and Israeli officials pressured their Lebanese counterparts time and again to follow Jordan's "example." However, the LAF officers who met with their Israeli counterparts, while showing little sympathy for the Palestinian armed factions, alerted their interlocutors to the major differences that existed between Lebanon and Jordan, which made Israel's "suggestion" impractical. Thus, for example, in a meeting held in March 23, 1971, the Lebanese representative argued that "clashes between the [Lebanese] army and the fedayin are a very sensitive point for us," and when asked by his Israeli interlocutor if this was the case "even after what happened in Jordan," he replied "they [the Jordanians] are the sons of the prophet and I am not." This alludes to Jordan's more homogenous societal makeup compared to Lebanon, but also to the religious legitimacy claimed by King Hussein and the Hashemite family.[108] As a result of these differences between Jordan

---

[106] Dayan (1976, 544). See also Bartov (2002, 1: 167).
[107] The same "creative solution" was adopted in 1970, when Shmuel Rosenwasser, the guard from Metula (see above), was abducted by Fatah. See Bergman (2009, 23–24).
[108] See, e.g., a report on meeting between Major General Mordechai Gur, head of the IDF's Northern Command, and Brigadier [Antoun] Saad of the LAF, ISA, Ministry of Foreign Affairs, 5251/14, Nevo to Deputy Head of Operations, March 23, 1971. See also ISA, Ministry of Foreign Affairs, 6805/6, MFA to New York and Washington, May 17, 1973. See also a report on a meeting between Israeli Prime Minister Yitzhak Rabin and Secretary of State Henry Kissinger on June 21, 1974, in which PM Rabin said: "I do not understand why Lebanon does not follow the path of Syria, Egypt and Jordan in handling the terrorists. It can do much more than it is doing today." On Jordan's effective use of an Islamic discourse to de-legitimize the Palestinian armed factions in the period 1970–1971, see Ajami (1992, 176–178).

and Lebanon – and contrary to Israel's expectations – Lebanon did not act as forcefully as Jordan against the Palestinian armed factions, and Israel's pressures only weakened the state and its institutions, not only in the coercive sense but also in terms of their legitimacy. This factor, as well as the growing support to the Palestinian armed factions in Lebanon and other Arab states, particularly in Syria and Egypt, made it even harder for Lebanon to restrain them, leading to the continued deterioration of security and stability in the Israeli–Lebanese border area.[109]

But Israel did not give up. In April 1973, a second Israeli commando raid, this time against prominent Palestinian leaders, was launched in the heart of Beirut, Lebanon's capital, and in other parts of Lebanon. Major General Eli Zeira, head of the IDF's Intelligence Branch, who would soon be removed on account of his role in Israel's military debacle in the 1973 War, explained to members of the Knesset's Foreign Affairs and Security Committee that the first and "strategic" goal of the operation in Beirut was to "start a process that would ultimately lead ... to Lebanon not only preventing terrorist activity through its borders in the direction of Israel, but also refraining from being a base for organization, planning and activities abroad." However, Zeira admitted that this goal was "pretentious" and "long-term" and that more Israeli actions were needed in order to realize it.[110]

The result of the Israeli operation was, indeed, a major crisis between Lebanon and the Palestinian armed factions, including an attempt by the LAF to redefine these factions' position in Lebanon by besieging the Palestinian refugee camps in Beirut and launching a military offensive that included artillery fire and aerial bombing. However, the Arab states – especially Syria, Lebanon's neighbor – exerted massive pressure on Lebanese President Suleiman Frangieh, and, as a result, representatives of the LAF and the Palestinian armed factions met and signed a protocol to the Cairo Agreement. To the chagrin of Israel's leaders, the new agreement neither led to more supervision by Lebanon of the

In a conversation held on August 31, 1978, between Prime Minister Menachem Begin and opposition chairman Shimon Peres, both leaders expressed their wish that Jordan, and not the Palestinians, would be Israel's partner for an agreement, because, in Peres' words, "they [Jordan] can do to the PLO things that we can never do." Quoted in Weitz (2016).

[109] Kaufman (2013, 117–118); Sela (2014, 305).
[110] ISA, Minutes of the Knesset's Foreign Affairs and Security Committee, April 13, 1973. Already in 1970, Zeira's deputy, Brigadier General Aryeh Shalev, head of the research department of the IDF's Intelligence Branch, argued that "if the regime in Lebanon would like to continue to exist, it will have no other choice besides a direct confrontation between the Lebanese Army and the terrorists. In this respect, it would be better to do this as early as possible." ISA, Ministry of Foreign Affairs, 4473/1, Shalev to IDF Attaché in Washington, Proposed Arguments concerning Lebanon, May 27, 1970.

Palestinian armed factions, ended the "state within a state" the latter had set up in Lebanon, nor reasserted the latter's sovereignty over all of its territory.[111] The result was more Israeli military incursions into Lebanon as well as increased efforts by Israeli officials to denounce Lebanon as a "source of Arab terrorism." One official Israeli document, prepared during the 1973 Lebanese–Palestinian crisis, even stated:

> Lebanon still enjoys the pretension of a small, ostensibly peace-seeking state that is well-intentioned. This while there is non-stop evidence in the international media and even the Arab media, from viewing and hearing witnesses, on the activities of the terrorist organizations in Lebanon and on the coexistence between the Lebanese state and the terrorist state. This evidence demonstrates that the terrorist organizations carry their weapons and exercise their "sovereignty" openly in Lebanon.[112]

As the 1973 crisis and its outcome had suggested, Syria had become an influential actor in the relations between Israel/Palestine and Lebanon. Indeed, since the consolidation of the Baath regime in Damascus in the early 1970s under President Hafez al-Assad, Syria adopted a more assertive policy toward Lebanon, which effectively countered whatever pressures Israel could apply on the latter. Thus, for example, a LAF officer argued that 3,000–4,000 Palestinian fighters armed with cannons and tanks had crossed the border from Syria into Lebanon during the crisis of 1973, and as part of its efforts to pressure Lebanon during that crisis, Syria closed its border with Lebanon, cutting it off from the outside world.[113] Indeed, when asked by his Israeli interlocutor why the Lebanese did not "continue the operations against the terrorists to the end like the Jordanians," a LAF officer replied, "We have the military capacity to get rid of the terrorists, but the problem is a political one and not a military one. We are facing pressure by the Arab states and there are also internal problems."[114]

Syria's role in Lebanon increased after the 1973 War, in which Syria participated and Lebanon did not (Lebanon did, however, operate its radar system "in the service of the Syrian aggression," according to an Israeli document, resulting in its destruction by the Israeli air force[115]). Later, Israeli leaders were apprehensive of Syria and its aspirations in

---

[111] R. Khalidi (1986); Brynen (1990). See also Bartov (2002, 1: 240–242); Naor (2013).
[112] ISA, Ministry of Foreign Affairs, 6803/5, Eliav to Director-General of the MFA, April 30, 1973.
[113] ISA, Ministry of Foreign Affairs, 5251/14, MFA to New York and Washington, DC, May 9, 1973.
[114] ISA, Ministry of Foreign Affairs, 6805/6, MFA to New York and Washington, DC, May 17, 1973.
[115] ISA, Ministry of Foreign Affairs, 6803/5, MFA to New York, October 12, 1973.

Lebanon, which they attributed to a drive to create a "Greater Syria,"[116] but, quite tellingly, without mentioning their own irredentist policies in Israel/Palestine. However, it seems that Syria's goals in Lebanon in this period, but also later, were more modest: first, to protect itself against an Israeli attack via Lebanon; second, to prevent the latter from becoming a base for actors hostile to Syria; third, and following Israel's rapprochement with Egypt in the mid-1970s, to exert control over Lebanon and the Palestinians, Syria's weaker neighbors (and also over Jordan), and prevent their "defection," which could worsen Syria's isolation. Lebanese leaders differed in their positions toward Syria: Some, like President Frangieh (Maronite), were close to the Assad regime, but others, such as Kamal Junblat (Druze), were more apprehensive. It is noteworthy that among the Palestinian armed factions, too, there were those who were suspicious of Syria, which continuously sought to curb their autonomy in Lebanon, but also those who regarded it as an ally, particularly after Egypt's "defection" in the late 1970s.[117]

Statelessness

Following the outbreak of the civil war in Lebanon in 1975 and the ensuing paralysis of the state's institutions, Israel's political and military leaders came to the conclusion that Lebanon would not be able to follow Jordan's "example" and forcefully suppress the Palestinian armed factions in its territory. This prompted the Israeli government, led by Prime Minister Rabin, to shift its attention away from the Lebanese state toward, on the one hand, Christian parties-militias that emerged in the Israeli–Lebanese border area, whose members began to reach out to Israel, and, on the other hand, the Syrian regime led by Hafez al-Assad, which was gravely concerned by what it regarded as Lebanon's possible disintegration and the takeover of most of its parts by violent non-state actors hostile to Syria, and which gradually moved toward direct military intervention in the crisis.

Although he later argued that "Israel felt a natural affinity to the Christian community in Lebanon," Rabin's view was that "under no circumstances could we undertake political or military responsibility for its fate." Indeed, many sources suggest that Rabin's position in this period

---

[116] The following two works are telling: Tlass (1985); Avi-Ran [Erlich] (1991). The former, by Syria's defense minister, emphasizes Israel's historical schemes with regard to Lebanon, whereas the latter, by an Israeli official who was involved in shaping Israel's policy toward Lebanon, stresses Syria's historical schemes concerning Lebanon.

[117] On Syria's relations with Lebanon, see Junblat (1987); Seale (1988); Y. Sayigh (1991); Sela and Ma'oz (1997b); Sela (1998, 2014).

was that Israel should help the Christians help themselves – that is, provide their parties-militias with humanitarian assistance and with military aid and training, but no more.[118] Thus, and at the initiative of Defense Minister Shimon Peres, Israel adopted a policy called the "Good Fence," a name that in itself suggested that porous boundaries between Israel and Lebanon were now the best way to guarantee Israel's security.[119] According to this policy, which was endorsed by Israel's Ministry of Foreign Affairs,[120] Israel offered humanitarian aid to Lebanese villagers in the Israeli–Lebanese border area, and provided weapons and military training to Christian parties-militias in this region and, later, also in other parts of Lebanon. Indeed, according to an Israeli report, by June 1, 1976, when Syrian forces intervened in Lebanon, Israel provided these Lebanese parties-militias with 15 armored cars, 114 artillery pieces, 385 anti-tank weapons, 9,725 small arms, 31 pieces of electronic equipment, 188,600 artillery shells and mortar rounds, 11,900,000 small-arms ammunition rounds, and 10 tons of explosives. The total value of these materials was $15 million, and Israel's ambassador in Washington was instructed that "in view of the volume of the assistance and the sum and the fact that this is a continuous matter," he should arrange for "American compensation" to Israel.[121] Interestingly, the US government was not opposed to Israel's provision of arms to the Christian militias in Lebanon since, in the words of Secretary of State Henry Kissinger, in March 1976, "it helps maintain the balance."[122] At any rate, in the period 1976–1982, during the height of Israel relations with the Lebanese Christians, most of whom were Maronites, Israel provided their parties-militias with weapons and training worth $118.5 million.[123]

At the same time, and despite the apprehensions of some Israeli political and military leaders toward Syria, which attacked Israel only a few

---

[118] Rabin (1996, 281). See also Kimche (1991, 132); Eisenberg (2010); Navot (2015, 125). Rabin did, however, criticize the Christian countries for failing to come to the support of the Christians in Lebanon. See Douglas (1975). Douglas's article is found in ISA, Ministry of Foreign Affairs, 6711/3. See also an interview with Foreign Minister Yigal Allon in the Israeli Radio, September 20, 1975, ibid.
[119] Peres (1978, 85–88); Hof (1985, 80–81); Parker (1996).
[120] A MFA official argued that "this issue is one of the most positive that could be conceived at this moment and that every effort should be made to exploit it for public relations." ISA, Ministry of Foreign Affairs, 267-3-A, Washington to MFA, Humanitarian Activities on the Israel–Lebanon Border, July 20, 1976.
[121] ISA, Ministry of Foreign Affairs, 267/1-A, MFA to Washington, Aid to the Christians in Lebanon, June 17, 1976. See also Randal (1983); Schiff and Ya'ari (1984); Kimche (1991, 132); Eitan (2001, 217–221).
[122] Document 284, FRUS (2010, 1015–1019).   [123] Shilon (2012, 507 n. 14).

years earlier, in the 1973 War, the Rabin government agreed to Syria's direct military involvement in Lebanon. Such a step was also looked on favorably by the United States, although the latter, particularly Secretary of State Kissinger, was fearful of a Syrian–Israeli clash in Lebanon that could lead to Soviet involvement on behalf of its client.[124] Indeed, in this period there emerged a consensus among the United States, Syria, Jordan, and Israel that the Palestinian armed factions, which were the major force that fought alongside the Muslim-led opposition in Lebanon, needed to be restrained as a prerequisite for a political solution to the Lebanese crisis and, possibly, also for the launching of a regional peace process in the Middle East.[125] Kissinger even observed, in a high-level conversation in Washington in March 24, 1976, that "[i]f Syria could go in [to Lebanon] quickly and clean it out, it would be good. They would leave the PLO in the same condition as in Jordan."[126] But as Kissinger and his colleagues in the United States were weighing the pros and cons of Syria's role in Lebanon, as well as of a direct US involvement in the crisis, King Hussein of Jordan, whose army had defeated the Palestinians armed factions in 1970–1971, told US President Gerald Ford in a visit to the United States in March 1976 that "Syria has an excellent opportunity to finish the job now."[127] Hussein then set out to mediate a secret understanding between Syria and Israel regarding Syria's involvement in Lebanon, which was communicated to President Assad in a letter by

---

[124] Israel's apprehensions can be discerned from a consultation between its senior political and military officials held on March 23, 1976, following Syria's increased involvement in Lebanon. In the meeting, Foreign Minister Yigal Allon, said: "From Yom Kippur [the 1973 War] we have slowly rehabilitated our army and regained our senses, although not sufficiently in the public, but more so in the army and this is a big asset. I would not want the Syrians, of all others, to also think that this [the IDF] is a paper tiger." ISA, Prime Minister's Office, 7019/1-A, Protocol of Consultation on the Situation in Lebanon, Jerusalem, March 23, 1976. In a meeting in Washington, DC, on the same day, US Secretary of State Henry Kissinger described Israel's position toward Syria, as communicated to him by Israel's ambassador in the United States, Simcha Dinitz, as follows: "Their position is that they cannot trust the Syrians. They are not at all sure that the Syrians would leave [Lebanon] if they go in, so that if they do go in, the Israelis would then quietly take over strategic points in Southern Lebanon and in effect hold them hostage till the Syrians leave." Document 75, FRUS (2010, 955). On Israel's apprehensions, see also Eitan (2001, 217–219). See also a special report prepared by the Ministry of Foreign Affairs' Research Department, entitled "Possible Deteriorations from Developments in South Lebanon," at ISA, Ministry of Foreign Affairs, 6711/3, Jerusalem, February 3, 1975.
[125] Michael Kerr (2009).
[126] Document 269, FRUS (2010, 960). See also Document 283, FRUS (2010, 1013).
[127] Document 284, FRUS (2010, 1015). Kimche argues that King Hussein played a role also in the Cairo Agreement of 1969 between Lebanon and the PLO, which opened the way for the suppression of the Palestinian armed factions in Jordan. See Kimche (1991, 127).

Prime Minister Rabin and Foreign Minister Allon.[128] Rabin later wrote that he agreed to Syria's operation in Lebanon but that his government had set a "red line ... running directly east from Sidon to the Lebanese-Syrian border," which Syria's troops were forbidden to cross.[129] In addition, Syria could not use its air force in Lebanon, thus preserving Israel's air supremacy.[130] According to Allon, Israel's veto on Syria's advancement to South Lebanon was because "whereas there are various ways to act in order to prevent the activity of the terrorists [i.e., the Palestinian armed factions], the Syrian penetration [into South Lebanon] is in our view more serious than the action of the terrorists and has long-term strategic meaning."[131]

The result of Israel's two-pronged policy toward Lebanon in this period, however, was a basic contradiction that would impinge on the two states' relations for decades to come. On the one hand, Israel approved of Syria's efforts to pacify Lebanon, a position that seemed to suggest that Israel adhered to a "statist" approach with regard to Lebanon, with Syria playing the role of a surrogate for the "failed" Lebanese state. On the other hand, the "red line" that Israel drew in this period effectively barred the Syrian forces, and later also units of the reconstructed LAF, from approaching the Israeli–Lebanese border area, which, in a paradox that became evident to many observers (including Rabin himself),[132] enabled the continued presence of the Palestinian

---

[128] Bechor (1995). Whether the exact details of this secret Israeli–Syrian understanding was fully shared with the United States government is not entirely clear. On June 22, 1976, about three weeks after Syria's intervention in Lebanon, US Secretary of State Kissinger remarked that Syria's "action in Lebanon resembles our action in Vietnam – the idea that if you do something incompetently, it takes the moral curse off." Thomas Pickering, the US Ambassador to Jordan, observed that "He [Syrian President Hafez al-Assad] seems to be captured by the restrictions we've put on him, all the signals we gave him to 'watch it,'" to which Kissinger replied "Because the Israelis changed signals on us without telling us." Alfred Atherton, the Assistant Secretary for Near Eastern and South Asian Affairs, added "They've [the Israelis] defined the 'red line' for us – and redefined it several times. They'd have gone to war by now (if they stuck to their original definition of the 'red line.')," to which Kissinger replied "And they never gave us a different concept ... we never knew a goddamn thing about what Israel was doing." Document 290, FRUS (2010, 1039). Parentheses in the original. See also ibid., 1046.
[129] Rabin (1996, 280). See also S. Gazit (2016, 296–297).
[130] Evron (1987, 56). On the significance of this factor, see Gur (1981).
[131] ISA, Ministry of Foreign Affairs, 267/5-A, MFA to Washington, South Lebanon – Towards Your Talk with the Secretary, December 3, 1976. See also ISA, Ministry of Foreign Affairs, 267/5-A, MFA to Washington, South Lebanon, November 30, 1976.
[132] Rabin (1996, 280). Uri Avnery, an Israeli journalist and former Knesset Member, later recounted that Prime Minister Rabin told him that he was opposed to the "red line" and that he preferred to have the Syrian and Israeli armies facing one another on the Israeli–Lebanese border instead of creating a "no man's land" in Lebanon, but that Defense Minister Shimon Peres and his men, who raised the specter of a Syrian threat from Lebanon, compelled him to agree to the "red line." See Avnery (1995). However,

armed factions – and other violent non-state actors – there. What is striking, however, is that many Israeli leaders regarded this contradictory policy as serving Israel's interests.

At any rate, the opening of Israel's border with Lebanon in the period 1975–1976 – like the opening of Israel's boundaries with the Territories in 1967 – allowed for an increased Israeli involvement in the Israeli–Lebanese border area, which eventually became known as the "South Lebanon Area" (in Hebrew: *ADAL*). This included, at first, Israeli support to the local Lebanese militia commanded by Major Saad Haddad (Catholic), a LAF officer who appeared to preserve the semblance of state authority in this area, particularly vis-à-vis the Palestinian armed factions, but whose Israeli-backed actions against the Lebanese state and the UN, especially in the wake of Israel's Litani Operation (1978), constantly undermined it, effectively preserving it as a zone of statelessness.[133]

Conclusion

Israel's policy toward Lebanon gradually shifted from one that sought to achieve a formal peace treaty between the two states in the 1950s to one that, following the 1967 War, tried to compel Lebanon to forcefully suppress the Palestinian armed factions that arrived in its territory and turned it into its primary political and military base. However, despite Israel's diplomatic and military pressures, the Jordanian "model" did not repeat itself in Lebanon. Israel (and the United States) then acquiesced to Syria's efforts to crush the PLO in 1976, but at the same time set limits to Syria's involvement in Lebanon. Meanwhile, Israel began to endorse local violent non-state actors in the Israeli–Lebanese border area, which became its clients. The result of this basic contradiction in Israel's policy was that the zone of statelessness in South Lebanon was reinforced, with the Palestinian armed factions becoming more entrenched there. Moreover, in view of Lebanon's weakness, on the one hand, and Israel's military incursions into Lebanon's territory, on the other hand, the Palestinians could claim that their armed activities were legitimate because they acted in self-defense, a pattern that would repeat itself in later periods with the

---

to his US interlocutors, Rabin argued, in February 1977 (like Foreign Minister Allon in 1976), that "Israel preferred that the vacuum in southern Lebanon be filled by the terrorists rather than the Syrians" but that "there should be a truly Lebanese force as soon as possible" and he "would prefer that Lebanon take on the responsibility for the forces in south Lebanon." Document 7, FRUS (2013, 49–50).

[133] On the making of Israel's "security zone" in South Lebanon, see Hamizrachi (1988); Danguri (1998); Eitan (2001, 221–223); Sela (2007). For Lebanese views, see Lahad (2003); C. Barakat (2011). For US perspectives, see Lewis (1998, 83); FRUS (2013).

Lebanese party-militia Hizbullah. Underlying the significant changes in Israel's policy toward Lebanon were the developments that had taken place in Israel/Palestine after 1967. This was manifested in Israel's attempts to suppress the Palestinian armed factions – the main actor actively resisting Israel's expansion – first in the Territories and later in Jordan, which compelled them to move to Lebanon; and it was also seen in Israel's attempt to do away with the Armistice regime, which had effectively regulated Israeli–Lebanese relations but which Israeli leaders now considered to be a liability. But Israel's efforts backfired: Syria's veto and domestic factors prevented Lebanon from suppressing the Palestinians in its territory, and Israel's military raids into Lebanon's territory exposed Lebanon's weakness and helped undermine its legitimacy. Together with other factors, this contributed to the "failure" of the Lebanese state in the same way that Israel's "statist" policy toward Lebanon had helped stabilize it in earlier periods. As Israel's "statist" approach to Lebanon weakened, parallel to its decline in Israel/Palestine, the Israeli–Lebanese border was opened, similar to the opening of Israel's other boundaries after 1967. New political entrepreneurs, Lebanese and Israeli, then further shifted the balance away from the state toward the community and security, paving the way for new political–military alliances and adventures.

7 Two Conflicts Intertwined

This chapter focuses on the period 1977–2006, which was the most volatile in the relationship between Israel/Palestine and Lebanon. This period witnessed three major military confrontations: the Litani Operation (1978), the Lebanon War of 1982, and the War between Israel and Hizbullah (2006), in addition to several smaller-scale military encounters. The emphasis in this chapter, however, is not just on these particular episodes, but also on how they were connected to significant developments that took place both in Lebanon and in Israel/Palestine, especially the efforts made by Israel's leaders to consolidate the expanded state that they had created in 1967. The chapter also considers Israel's changing perceptions of Lebanon, which influenced Israeli actions toward its neighbor and which were also linked to the developments in Israel/Palestine. The first part of the chapter looks at the period 1977–1982, when Israel's involvement in Lebanon intensified, culminating in its invasion of Lebanon. In the second part, the image of Lebanon as a quagmire, which began to emerge in Israel after the Lebanon War of 1982, as well as the impact of this perception on Israel's behavior toward Lebanon in later decades, is addressed. The emphasis then shifts to examining the inter-linkages between the two conflicts in Israel/Palestine and Lebanon, which were further reinforced after 1982, even as the scope of Israel's involvement there became more limited.

Great Expectations

> The fighting in Lebanon will stop soon. Then, once we have made absolutely sure that the enemy will not be able anymore to shed the blood of our men, women and children we will withdraw our forces from Lebanon. We don't covet an inch of its territory. We want a peace treaty between Israel and Lebanon on the basis of the international boundary between our two countries. For nineteen years it was the most tranquil of borders; it then became the bloodiest one. It can again become as

pastoral as it once was, when only sheep would transgress the boundary
to be returned by one neighbor to another.
– Prime Minister Menachem Begin to Egyptian President Hosni
Mubarak (June 9, 1982)[1]

In my distant childhood I was raised on following saying: "It is not clear
who will be the first Arab state to make peace with Israel. But Lebanon
will undoubtedly be the second ... " Today it is clear who the first was.
According to the above, it was Lebanon's turn. We waited a year.
We waited for two years. Lebanon refused to fulfill its duties. How
many years can a Jew accept the fact, that he is not correct in his
predictions? So we went in. To make peace. Henceforth they will learn
not to challenge Israeli truths.
– B. Michael, *Haaretz*, July 2, 1982

Israel's invasion of Lebanon in June 1982[2] demonstrates the extent to which the "communal" approach in Israel, which had strengthened considerably in the wake of the 1967 War, superseded the "statist" approach, which prevailed in the first two decades after Israel's independence but weakened after the state's expansion (see Chapter 6). Indeed, for the first time in Israel's history, its military, the IDF, occupied significant parts of a neighboring state and laid a siege on its capital. But this was not the only innovation in that conflict. Underpinning Israel's invasion of Lebanon was a secret alliance between two "communal" entrepreneurs, one Jewish and the other Maronite: The Likud Party under the leadership of Prime Minister Menachem Begin and Defense Minister Ariel Sharon, and the Lebanese Forces, the militia of the Phalanges Party, led by Bashir Gemayel. The Phalanges and the Likud Party had both previously been on the margins of the political systems in Lebanon and Israel, respectively, although their leaders were sometimes brought on board during major crises such as the Lebanese civil war of 1958 and the crisis that culminated in the Israeli–Arab War of 1967. But now they were in power (the Likud Party in Israel) or on the verge of acquiring it (the Phalanges Party in Lebanon). This section focuses on the period leading up to the Lebanon War of 1982, highlighting the close inter-linkages between the changes that took place in Israel/Palestine, on the one hand, and Israel's relations with Lebanon, in particular Israel's emerging alliance with the Maronite-led parties-militias, on the other hand.

We have seen (Chapter 6) that after the outbreak of civil war in Lebanon in 1975 and the state's "failure," Israel, under Prime Minister

---

[1] ISA, Ministry of Foreign Affairs, 4178/4-A, Prime Minister Menachem Begin to President Hosni Mubarak, June 9, 1982.
[2] On the Lebanon War of 1982, see Schiff and Ya'ari (1984); Tlass (1985); R. Khalidi (1986); Evron (1987); Yaniv (1987); Kimche (1991); Shultz (1993); Parker (1993); Salem (1993); Zipori (1997); Eitan (2001); Merom (2003); Maoz (2009); Kaufman (2010a, 2010b); Freilich (2012); Shilon (2012); Darwish (2013); Navot (2015).

Rabin's Labor government, extended humanitarian aid and military support to Major Haddad's Christian militia in South Lebanon and, later, also to Maronite-led parties-militias in other parts of the country, and especially the Phalanges Party led by the Gemayel family. At the same time, Israel gave consent to Syria's direct involvement in Lebanon but imposed a "red line" that limited its scope. This contradictory policy was not untypical of the leaders of the Labor Party and many members of Israel's military elite who identified with it, who oscillated between "statist" and "communal" approaches toward Israel/Palestine – including the Territories but also Israel itself – and toward its neighbors.[3]

The victory of the Likud Party in Israel's 1977 elections, however, ushered in a significant change in the balance between these approaches in both respects. Unlike the Labor Party, the Likud Party had a clear "communal" agenda that its leaders, especially Begin, Israel's new prime minister, sought to implement. This was soon manifested in a more assertive settlement policy in the West Bank and the Gaza Strip, which was presided over by Major General (ret.) Sharon, who served as minister of agriculture and head of the ministerial committee for settlement. Consequently, the number of Jewish settlers in the Territories increased from about 4,400 in 1977 to 16,200 in 1981, and to 35,300 at the end of 1984 – a growth of about 800 percent in seven years (see Chapter 4).

The first Begin government (1977–1981) was initially preoccupied with the Egyptian–Israeli peace process, and some of its members, such as Foreign Minister Moshe Dayan and Defense Minister Ezer Weizman, both retired army generals, played a moderating role in this and other aspects of Israeli–Arab relations. The United States, then under the Carter administration, also did not approve of a more militant Israeli policy toward Lebanon, and its overall goal was to launch a regional peace process in the Middle East.

However, the second Begin government (1981–1983) was markedly different. It was more "communal" and militant in its orientation, particularly after Ariel Sharon's appointment as defense minister in

---

[3] For a penetrating critique of the Labor Party and its policies, see Strenhell (2009). See also an insightful lecture by Lieutenant General (ret.) Mordechai Gur, who later joined the party's ranks (Gur 1981). For more examples, see Sheffer and Barak (2013). The Labor Party's ambiguous policy toward Israel's Palestinian citizens is telling. On the one hand, the party's leaders encouraged this community to participate in Israeli politics and until 2017 the Labor Party was the only Israeli party to appoint Israeli Palestinians as ministers in the cabinet. At the same time, it was during this party's reign that the worst atrocities were committed against this community: the Kafar Qassem Massacre in 1956, the killing of 6 demonstrators during the Land Day demonstrations in 1976, and the killing of 13 demonstrators in the October 2000 Events.

August 1981.[4] Indeed, it was in this period that the thesis regarding the "irreversibility" of Israel's occupation of the Territories was first put forward by Meron Benvenisti (and also criticized),[5] with some government ministers regarding this as proof that things were moving in the right direction.[6] By 1980, Israel had imposed its jurisdiction over the occupied East Jerusalem, and in 1981, the new government decided to do the same in the occupied Golan, an action that was designed to punish Syria for deploying anti-aircraft missiles in the Biqa' in Lebanon in response to Israel's downing of two Syrian helicopters there after Maronite leaders called upon Israel for help.[7] With regard to Lebanon, too, the balance in Israel had shifted from the "statist" approach toward the "communal" approach.

Indeed, Israel's "communal" approach toward Lebanon in this period was demonstrated, first and foremost, in the strengthening of its ties with Maronite-led parties-militias, specifically the Phalanges Party. Prime Minister Begin perceived the Christians in Lebanon as similar to the Jews who were persecuted in Europe, and he believed that by supporting them Israel could demonstrate not only its military power but also its moral high ground, especially vis-à-vis the Western states, but also toward other international actors, including those that challenged Israel's expansion.[8] Nachum (Nachik) Navot, a Mossad official who attended many of the meetings held in Israel before the 1982 War, later wrote:

The policy of "we will help the Christians help themselves" of the Rabin government gave way to a moral perception, stemming from Begin's historic awareness. Israel's prime minister, who had just been elected, saw a moral duty in substantial help by Israel, the strongest regional power, to the Christians, the minority that was groaning under the military pressure in Lebanon. Begin's political directive was consolidated into an operational plan.[9]

---

[4] Tzipori (1997); Shilon (2012, 356–257); Weitz (2014).
[5] On the thesis and criticisms thereof, see Benvenisti (2007, 199–203); Lustick (1993, 11–20).
[6] See, e.g., a comment made by Gideon Pat during the government meeting in 1983, during which its members discussed their reaction to the report of the Kahan Commission of Inquiry regarding the Sabra and Shatila Massacre (Israeli Government, 1983).
[7] Shilon (2012, 360–361).
[8] Ibid., 366. See also the minutes of a meeting between Prime Minister Begin and US President Carter from July 1977, Document 52, FRUS (2013, 339). In the meeting, Begin told Carter: "We do not want any Lebanese territory ... we do not want war ... [and] we will not let down our Christian allies. We have been a minority in the past, but we are not one now ... we will not let the Christian minority be destroyed. That is our main concern." See also Document 81, ibid., 436; Document 19, FRUS (2014, 54). Samuel Lewis, the US ambassador to Israel, argued that this view was shared by members of the Reagan administration, and especially Secretary of State Haig. See Lewis (1998, 152–156).
[9] Navot (2015, 125). See also Schiff and Ya'ari (1984, 25); Hof (1985, 74).

Another important change that took place in Israel in this period, which also had an impact on its relations with Lebanon, was the adoption of a preventive strategy toward real or perceived threats to Israel's security.[10] Already in March 1975, following an attack by Fatah, the major Palestinian armed faction, on the Savoy Hotel in Tel Aviv that left eight citizens and three Israeli soldiers dead, Begin, who was then a member of the Knesset's Foreign Relations and Defense Committee, posited that Israel should take the initiative and destroy the Fatah command in Beirut, and that it should not leave the initiative in the enemy's hands.[11] In June 1981, when he was in power, Begin ordered the bombing of Iraq's nuclear reactor, thus establishing what would later be known as the "Begin Doctrine," which held that Israel would not allow any other state in the Middle East to develop nuclear weapons, thus preserving its superiority in this realm.[12]

With regard to Lebanon, the harbinger of the change in Israel's policy was the Litani Operation in March 1978, the first large-scale Israeli invasion into Lebanon's territory since the First Arab–Israeli War. During the operation, Israel occupied the area from the Israeli–Lebanese border up to the Litani River, with the exception of the city of Tyre and its surroundings, causing a temporary retreat northward of the Palestinian armed factions and massive destruction in South Lebanon.[13] In a letter to the Secretary-General of the UN Kurt Waldheim on August 3, 1978, after the Israeli forces had withdrawn from Lebanon, Prime Minister Begin stated:

Israel is not party to the internal strife in Lebanon. We want peace on our northern border just as we have, indeed, a moral commitment to the Christian minority [in Lebanon] not to allow its destruction. May I respectfully say in this connection, Mr. Secretary-General, that I sometimes wonder how the United Nations, after all the experiences of our times, can show such indifference in face of the real and direct threat confronting a persecuted religious minority.[14]

However, the Litani Operation, which led to UN Security Council Resolution 425 and to the deployment of the United Nations Interim

---

[10] Shilon (2012, 366); Naor (2015, 463).
[11] Foreign Affairs and Security Committee (1975).
[12] Maoz (2009, 351–353); Shilon (2012, 345); A. Cohen (2013, 224).
[13] On the Litani Operation, see Hof (1985, 87–93); Parker (1996); Gur (1998); Eitan (2001, 206–207, 221); Kaufman (2010b, 2013, 122–124); S. Gazit (2016, 299–303).
[14] Menachem Begin to Kurt Waldheim, August 3, 1978, UN Archives (1978). See also a letter from Prime Minister Begin to US President Carter: ISA, Ministry of Foreign Affairs 267/7-A, September 29, 1977. In a meeting between Begin and the US Ambassador to Israel on November 10, 1977, Begin stressed that "we will do what is necessary to defend the Christians and protect our civilian population," adding that "we could clear up the whole southern Lebanon in one night." ISA, Ministry of Foreign Affairs 267/7-A.

Force in Lebanon (UNIFIL) as a barrier between the Palestinian armed factions and Israel, did not prevent further Palestinian attacks on Israel's north, and Israel's involvement in Lebanon intensified. Moreover, UNIFIL did not deploy in the Christian enclaves on the Lebanese side of the Israeli–Lebanese border area, which became consolidated following the Israeli operation and which Israel handed over to its local ally, Major Haddad. Thus, what began with limited Israeli humanitarian and military support to the Christians in South Lebanon, so as to allow them to defend themselves against attacks by the Palestinian armed factions and their Lebanese allies, evolved into a full-fledged alliance between Israel and a Christian-dominated "South Lebanon Area," the precursor of Israel's self-declared "security zone," which would be established in 1985. Importantly, the area's leader, Major Haddad, no longer accepted the authority of the government in Beirut and the LAF command, and in 1979 even proclaimed the creation of a "Free Lebanon State" under Israel's auspices.[15]

An Israeli official later explained that the decision to back Major Haddad in the wake of the Litani Operation was a result of a clash between two different "factors" in Israel's political and military hierarchy, which correspond to the aforementioned "statist" and "communal" approaches toward Lebanon, but also more generally:

One factor was more political and was represented by [Defense Minister] Ezer Weizman ... [who] said, essentially, what does it matter to us if the Lebanese Army enters [the Israeli–Lebanese border area], since it is under UNIFIL's command, it will help UNIFIL achieve its objectives ... it is in the Israeli interest to rehabilitate the Lebanese Army, it is in the Israeli interest not to clash with the United States on a trivial matter, and similar considerations.... The second factor was the pro-Haddad factor ... [and it was characterized by] suspicion that if the Lebanese Army went down to the South and the situation returned to normal, Haddad would not have an enemy and he would cease to exist ... There were Israeli actors who said that it is more important for us in the long run what Haddad wants, and we will therefore support Haddad.[16]

Indeed, it was during this period that the "communal" approach, adhered to also by several members of Israel's security networks, who had been operating in South Lebanon since the mid-1970s, gained the upper hand with respect to the "statist" approach in Israel. These actors would

---

[15] Hof (1985); Hamizrachi (1988). See also Barak (2009a).
[16] Quoted in Parker (1996, 557). Major General (ret.) Shlomo Gazit, then head of the IDF's Intelligence Branch, later argued that at the time he suggested that the Syrian army, together with an LAF force, would deploy in the Israeli–Lebanese border area, but that Prime Minister Begin rejected the idea. Gazit (2016, 300–303).

continue to shape Israel's policy in and vis-à-vis Lebanon until Israel's unilateral withdrawal from Lebanon in May 2000.[17]

Encouraged by Israel's support, Major Haddad felt confident enough to forcefully resist the deployment of LAF in his area in July 1978, causing embarrassment to the Lebanese state, which at that time sought to reassert its authority over all of its territory.[18] It should be noted that the possibility of the LAF's deployment in South Lebanon had already been raised in late 1977, but while Israel did not object to this move in principle its leaders did insist that the Palestinian armed factions first stop firing at Israel and then withdraw from the area so as to allow for the LAF's deployment. In any case, Israel's political and military leaders were quite skeptical of the LAF and its capacities, and the head of the IDF's Intelligence Branch, Major General Shlomo Gazit, even told US ambassador to Israel Samuel Lewis, "[B]etween us ... there is no Lebanese army. Let's forget about it. They have hardly a peace keeping police force if there is quiet. And the quiet is not between us and them, it is between [the] Christian militia and [the] Palestinians."[19] Richard Parker, who served as the US Ambassador to Lebanon in this period, later argued that Israel's decision to keep the LAF out of the South in 1978 "was a fateful move that blocked Lebanon's efforts to reassert its sovereignty over its own territory and ensured further trouble and loss of life for all concerned."[20] It is noteworthy that in this period Syria, too, sought to dispatch its army to the Israeli–Lebanese border area, but Israel considered this a breach of the "red line" and prevented Syrian troops from advancing southward.[21]

At the same time that Israel and Major Haddad (and also the Palestinian armed factions) obstructed Lebanon's attempts to reassert its authority in the Israeli–Lebanese border area, effectively buttressing the zone of statelessness in this region, Israel's clandestine ties with Lebanon's Maronite parties-militias (chiefly Pierre Gemayel's Phalanges Party and Camille Chamoun's National Liberal Party) intensified. This was manifested in weapons supply, military training of Christian militiamen in Israel, and intelligence cooperation.[22] In particular, Israeli officials forged ties with the younger generation of

[17] Sheffer and Barak (2013). See also Sela (2007); O. Gazit (2011). The following publication is also telling: Gilboa (2015).
[18] Hof (1985, 92–93); Parker (1996, 556–558); Gur (1998, ch. 7). See also Kurt Waldheim to Menachem Begin, August 1, 1978, UN Archives (1978).
[19] ISA, Ministry of Foreign Affairs 267/5-A, Meeting between Minister of Defense Gen. E[zer] Weizmann and US Ambassador to Israel Mr. S[amuel] Lewis, October 14, 1977. On this period, see also Hof (1985, 82–84).
[20] Parker (1996, 558). [21] Ibid.
[22] Eitan (2001, 222–223). See also Hof (1985, 97); Parker (1996).

Maronite leaders, particularly with Bashir Gemayel (son of Pierre Gemayel) and Dani Chamoun (son of Camille Chamoun). To their Israeli interlocutors, these leaders appeared to be more forthcoming to open relations with Israel, unlike their fathers, who as members of the "1943 generation" had qualms about severing the Christians' and Lebanon's ties with the Arab states. David Kimche, a Mossad official who later served as director-general of the Ministry of Foreign Affairs, and who played an important role in forging Israel's relations with these Maronite leaders, writes of a "special bond" that "developed between the Israelis and the young Lebanese, with both sides feeling the common interest of our two nationalist entities, both of whom were fighting to maintain their own special identity in a region peopled by a Muslim majority."[23] However, the hopes of Prime Minister Begin and his associates for the establishment of a formal relationship with the Maronites in Lebanon were dashed: first, after Bashir Gemayel's election as Lebanon's president in August 1982, when he refused to negotiate a peace treaty with Israel, and then also following his assassination in September and the election of his brother, Amine, as president in his place.[24]

But the developments in Israel/Palestine in this period were no less important in pushing Israel toward a more militant policy in Lebanon. The Israeli–Egyptian peace process, which was launched after President Anwar al-Sadat's visit to Jerusalem in 1977, culminated in the Camp David Accords between Israel and Egypt in 1978 and in the first peace treaty signed between Israel and an Arab state in 1979. In addition to a full withdrawal from the Sinai Peninsula, including the dismantling of all Israel settlements there, Israel agreed to granting autonomy to the Palestinians in the Territories. However, the talks on autonomy, held between Israeli and Egyptian representatives, that began in 1980 made little progress, mainly on account of Israel's unyielding position. In the meantime, Israel faced serious obstacles in its attempt to consolidate its control over the Territories. After the municipal elections held in the West Bank in 1976 resulted in the victory of nationalist candidates (i.e.,

---

[23] Kimche (1991, 132).
[24] On Bashir Gemayel's position after his election, see Kimche (1991, 157–158); Shilon (2012, 400–401). On Pierre Gemayel's position, see e.g., the minutes of his meeting with Israeli officials from the Ministry of Foreign Affairs and the Mossad in early 1983, in which he stated: "Israel is a homogenous state. Lebanon is a heterogeneous state. We must appease everyone," and added that if Lebanese President Amine Gemayel were to dismiss the Muslim prime minister and appoint a Christian in his place, "this would be the end of Lebanon." ISA, Ministry of Foreign Affairs 6848/8, Conversation with Pierre Gemayel. On the Chamoun family's positions, see ISA, Ministry of Foreign Affairs 6848/8, Conversation with Camille Chamoun and Dani Chamoun, January 10, 1983.

those affiliated with the PLO and not with Jordan, which objected to this move[25]) and became a major site of Palestinian resistance to Israel's occupation, Israel's leaders decided to step up inter-communal repression: Israel banned Palestinian organizations, arrested and deported Palestinian activists, and prohibited the publication of Palestinian newspapers.[26] In addition, in 1981 Israel established the "Civil Administration" in the Territories, which replaced the Military Government and took on some of its prerogatives. However, the new body, ostensibly designed to empower the Palestinians in the Territories, actually increased Israel's control over these areas, and was more often than not a cover for the IDF and the General Security Service, which were the most influential actors there (besides, of course, the Jewish settlers, whose number was on the rise). In this period, Israel also established the "Village Committees," – groups of Palestinians with rural backgrounds who were supposed to serve as a counterweight to the urban-based national current in the Territories. Neve Gordon writes that the Village Committees, whose members were trained and armed by Israel and which formed their own small militias, were a sort of "subcontractor" for Israel's security sector in the Territories, and some even regarded them as having parallels with Major Haddad's militia in South Lebanon. But this initiative, too, ended in failure, demonstrating – and not for the last time – the PLO's veto power in the Territories.[27]

For some Israeli leaders, the conclusion to be drawn from these setbacks was that in order to uphold the state's expansion there was an urgent need to crush the Palestinian armed factions, which had built themselves a "state within a state" in Lebanon by exploiting the ongoing conflict there and also Israel's "red line" in South Lebanon. Indeed, the Oranim plan, prepared by the Operations Branch of the IDF general staff in April 1982, specified the goal of the Israel operation in Lebanon as follows:

The IDF will destroy terrorists and infrastructure until the "Awali," Hasbaiya, Kawkaba, "Jabal Wastani" until the "zero" [hour] plus 24 h[ours], will team up with the Christians in the Beirut area until the "zero" [hour] plus 48 h[ours], will occupy Beirut by the "zero" [hour] plus 96 h[ours] [and] will be ready to destroy the Syrian army in the Biqa'[28]

---

[25] Milson (1984, 36). [26] N. Gordon (2008, 106); Elad (2015, 437–447).
[27] S. Gazit (2003, 228–232); N. Gordon (2008, 93–115); Bregman (2014, 122–130).
[28] ISA, "Operation Peace for Galilee," at: http://www.archives.mod.gov.il/Exhib/shlomha galil/Pages/ExhibitionsDocs.aspx?ExhbId=41 (accessed November 29, 2016).

Writing in 1985, Frederic Hof, a US official who, among others, had served as military attaché in Lebanon and later served at the Department of Defense and the Department of State, observed:

> By destroying Arafat's military apparatus, thereby dislodging him from the "state within a state" in Beirut and southern Lebanon, the PLO's claim to be the independent, legitimate representative of all Palestinians could not possibly remain valid. The scattered remnants of the PLO would be snatched up by competing Arab states, and the Arabs of the Occupied Territories would finally realize the inevitability of permanent Israeli rule.[29]

Three decades after the publication of Hof's book and after the main protagonists of the Lebanon War of 1982 – Prime Minister Begin, Defense Minister Sharon, and IDF Chief of Staff Rafael Eitan – had passed away, Navot, the former Mossad official, wrote:

> Years later it became clear to me why Begin authorized Operation Peace for Galilee [the Lebanon War of 1982]: In Camp David Begin gave his consent to the granting of autonomy to the Palestinians. It seems that, as time passed, he regretted and was deeply sorry about his agreement, because he was apprehensive that autonomy would lead to a Palestinian state. Therefore, it was easy to persuade the prime minister that in order to prevent the establishment of Palestinian state in the West Bank the Palestinian leadership in Lebanon should be expelled from Lebanon and removed from the region.[30]

---

[29] Hof (1985, 98). See also Lewis (1998, 214, 220).

[30] Navot (2015, 127–128). Military correspondent Ron Ben-Yishai later recounted that "the main goal of the initiators of that war – Defense Minister Sharon and Chief of Staff Eitan – was to establish, politically and militarily, forever, our hold on the West Bank. Their initial intent was to expel the PLO from Lebanon thereby liquidating the hope and aspiration of the Palestinians to regain the territories that they had lost during the Six Day War." Ben-Yishai added: "I know this with confidence because I heard this personally from Sharon and Raful [Eitan] long before that war. At that time, I was the military correspondent of the Israeli Broadcast Authority and they assumed that I could never and would not want ... to publish it"; Ben-Yishai (2012). Uri Avnery also recounted that "nine months before the Lebanon War, he [Sharon] disclosed to me his Grand Plan for a new Middle East of his making. He allowed me to publish it, provided I did not mention him as the source ... The [Israeli] army would invade Lebanon and drive the Palestinians from there to Syria, from whence the Syrians would drive them into Jordan. There the Palestinians would overthrow the king and establish the State of Palestine. The [Israeli] army would also drive the Syrians out of Lebanon. In Lebanon Sharon would choose a Christian officer and install him as dictator. Lebanon would make official peace with Israel and in effect become a vassal state"; Avnery (2014). Avnery adds that Sharon even asked him to arrange a meeting with PLO leader Arafat to discuss his plan "to help the Palestinians to overthrow the Jordanian monarchy, and turn Jordan into a Palestinian state, with Arafat as its president." Sharon added: "Once Jordan becomes Palestine, there will no longer be a conflict between two peoples, but between two states. That will be much easier to resolve. We shall find some form of partition, territorial or functional, or we shall rule the territory together." According to Avnery, his friends "submitted the request to Arafat, who laughed it off"; ibid. See also T. Friedman (1989, 268–269); Lewis (1998, 214).

It should be noted that in a meeting of Israel's National Unity Government on June 18, 1967, a few days after the end of the Israeli–Arab War and Israel's occupation of the West Bank and the Gaza Strip, Begin, then a minister without portfolio, warned that "the concept of autonomy leads to a Palestinian state in the iron logic of things," and that "[i]f we say autonomy, this is an invitation to an independent Palestinian-Arab state," adding that this was not in Israel's favor.[31] Interestingly, in the first part of that meeting, Begin claimed that in 1967 Lebanon had annulled the Armistice Agreement because it declared war on Israel, which was also the view of Prime Minister Levi Eshkol, but not of other ministers, including Defense Minister Dayan, who in 1978 would propose the reinstatement of the 1949 agreement with Lebanon.[32] But after he became prime minister, too, Begin preferred to grant the Palestinians in the Territories (whom he consistently referred to as "Palestinian Arabs" or simply as "Arabs") a limited non-territorial "administrative autonomy," leaving to Israel the right to claim sovereignty over these areas in the future.[33]

It should be emphasized that for Prime Minister Begin and his colleagues in 1982, the PLO was more than an obstacle to Israel's expansion. It was a terrorist organization that threatened Israel's very existence since, in Begin own words, its goal was to commit "genocide" against Israel's citizens.[34] Thus, in September 1981, following a meeting with US President Ronald Reagan, who, unlike his predecessor, considered Israel to be a US ally in the global struggle against the Soviet Union – a factor that Israeli leaders also emphasized – Prime Minister Begin told Israeli Major General Avigdor Ben-Gal that the solution to the rockets fired by the PLO at Israel's north from Lebanon's territory would be to "go into Lebanon, catch the bearded man [Arafat], get him out of his bunker, and put him on trial in Jerusalem. Just like Adolf Eichmann."[35] During the Lebanon War of 1982, too, Begin referred to the PLO using similar terms.[36] By siding with the Maronite parties-militias in Lebanon, whose leaders also saw the Palestinian armed factions as an obstacle for the fulfillment of their vision – the imposition of Maronite control over the state's other communities – Israel's long-term goal was at last to be realized.[37]

[31] Israeli Government (1967). See also M. Oren (2003, 314).
[32] Israeli Government (1967). On Dayan's position in 1978, see Chapter 6, n. 91.
[33] Begin's plan from 1977, see Laqueur and Rubin (2001). On his discussions after the elections, see Rubinovich and Steinberg (2012); Naor (2015, 472).
[34] See, e.g., protocol of a meeting between Prime Minister Begin and Romanian leader Nicolae Ceauşescu on August 28, 1977, ISA, at https://docs.google.com/a/mail.huji.ac.il/file/d/0B_wZ8qKsEas2YnhZYTJMU0VDb1E/edit (accessed September 3, 2015).
[35] Shilon (2012, 358).   [36] Zertal (2005, 195).   [37] Kimche (1991, 132–133).

At about the same time that Israel's leaders became convinced that the PLO needed to be eliminated, some of them began to think that Syria, which had fought alongside Egypt in the 1973 War but, unlike the latter, did not make peace with Israel in its aftermath, also needed to be defeated in order to guarantee Israel's security, which, in the eyes of these leaders, hinged on Israel's continued rule over the occupied Golan. Chief of Staff Eitan, for one, believed that Syria's military presence in Lebanon was not, as suggested by Prime Minister Rabin, aimed to pacify Lebanon or to make Syria "uncomfortable" by forcing it to deploy its army on two fronts. It was, first and foremost, the continuation of the 1973 War by other means. After the signing of a peace treaty between Israel and Egypt, the time seemed to be ripe to deal with this threat.[38] The rising tensions between Israel and Syria in this period, especially after Israel shot down two Syrian aircraft in Lebanon and Syria responded by deploying SA-6 anti-aircraft missiles in the Biqa', were manifested during Israel's 1981 elections, one of the most turbulent in its history, when Prime Minister Begin publically warned: "Assad beware! Yanush [Avigdor Ben-Gal] and Raful [Rafael Eitan] are waiting for you."[39]

In contrast to the challenge the PLO and Syria posed to Israel as an expanded state, the Maronites in Lebanon – who presented themselves to Israeli officials as the sworn enemies of the Palestinians in Lebanon and who in this period had a falling out with Syria after it came to their aid but, as it turned out, had no intention of leaving Lebanon anytime soon – were seen as potential allies of Israel.[40] Indeed, in this period some Israeli officials regarded the Maronite parties-militias as resembling the Jewish parties-militias under the British Mandate in Palestine before 1948, and sometimes even cast themselves as the pro-Zionist British officers who helped the Jewish community in Palestine (the *Yishuv*) and its military forces.[41] For some of these Israeli officials, imposing permanent Jewish

---

[38] Eitan (2001, 217). Cf. Rabin (1996, 280). See also Freilich (2012). Other Israeli observers shared this view. See, e.g., two reports prepared in August 1977 by an Israeli expert on Syria, Professor Moshe Ma'oz from The Hebrew University of Jerusalem, who advocated a more intensive Israeli involvement in South Lebanon and warned of Syria's war preparations against Israel. ISA, Ministry of Foreign Affairs, 267/5-A, Prof. Moshe Ma'oz to Members of the Subcommittee on South Lebanon of the Knesset's Foreign Relations and Security Committee, August 21, 1977, Prof. Moshe Ma'oz, "Syria's Motives for War against Israel," August 31, 1977.
[39] Shilon (2012, 349).   [40] Baqraduni [Pakradouni] (1984, 112); Parker (1996).
[41] A telling example is Yehuda Danguri, an Israeli officer who served in South Lebanon in the late 1970s and 1980s. In his memoirs, Danguri recounts how he was named "Abu Layl" (Father of the Night) by his Lebanese allies, and how this name immediately reminded him of Orde Wingate, a British captain who trained and led *Hagana* troops in counterinsurgency operations during the Palestinian Revolt (1936–1939); Danguri (1998, 128–129). On Wingate, see Morris (2008, 54–55). Another former Israeli officer,

control over all of Israel/Palestine was to be paralleled by establishing Maronite control in Lebanon. Mordechai Zipori, a minister in Begin's second government, later argued that "Begin wanted to help the Christians to establish in Lebanon a state where they will be the rulers."[42] Other Israeli officials, especially in the Mossad, also subscribed to this view, although others in this agency were more skeptical about the Maronites in general and the Phalanges Party in particular.[43]

But the Jewish–Maronite alliance that was forged toward 1982 also stemmed from practical considerations. Some in Israel were impressed by the Maronite parties-militias, especially by the Phalanges Party, which was seen, in Israel and abroad, as the most powerful local military force in Lebanon.[44] In 1981, Itamar Rabinovich, a professor at Tel Aviv University and a leading Israeli specialist on Syria and Lebanon, argued that "if, by some magic wand, the Palestinians and the Syrians were to disappear from the Lebanese arena, there is no doubt that, according to the conditions that prevail today, the Christian camp would take control over Lebanon within a short time."[45] Indeed, it was in this period that Israeli leaders and security officials, including high-ranking IDF officers and senior Mossad officials, who held numerous meetings with Maronite leaders, adopted the view that the Israeli–Maronite alliance, with its combined military power and legitimacy, could attain the goal that both

---

Knesset Member and government minister, Colonel (ret.) Yuval Ne'eman, likened the attempts made by the Gemayel family in 1980 to unify the militias under its command to *Altalena*, the arms-carrying ship that *Etzel* tried to bring to Israel during the First Arab–Israeli War, which was sunk by the IDF under Ben-Gurion's orders; Ne'eman (1981, 71). Major General (ret.) Avigdor Ben-Gal, who served as head of the IDF's Northern Command in the period before the Lebanon War of 1982, later explained that Israeli generals and many ministers in that period "believed [the Christians because] they loved those young fighters, the Phalange[s], because it reminded them when they were young, and when they were patriots during the War of Independence, from the *Hagana*, *Palmach*, the IDF and the different forces and before the IDF, and I've seen a certain chemistry between those who were the age of 50 or 50 plus [the Israelis] and those who were age of 28 [the Lebanese]"; quoted in Morselli (2015, 192). It is noteworthy that some Israeli officials who had been active in settling the Territories in the period after 1967 also made references to the period of the British Mandate. Thus, for example, Yigal Allon argued: "Once [under British rule] we built an army camouflaged as settlements . . . Now we'll build settlements camouflaged as an army"; quoted in Gorenberg (2006, 121). See also S. Gazit (2016, 177).

[42] Quoted in Navot (2015, 160). See also Zipori (1997) and the accounts of Israeli officers and soldiers who served in Lebanon during the Lebanon War of 1982 as they appear in Gal and Hammerman (2002).

[43] A major supporter of Israel's Maronite "option" was David Kimche, deputy director of the Mossad and later the director-general of the Ministry of Foreign Affairs. One of the major opponents of this policy was the director of the Mossad, Major General (ret.) Yitzhak Hofi. Kimche (1991); Bergman (1997); Shilon (2012, 367).

[44] Entelis (1973); Stoakes (1975).

[45] Rabinovich (1981, 38). See also Kimche (1991, 133).

Lebanon and Syria had failed to achieve before: crushing the Palestinian armed factions in Lebanon. In this way, they would remove not only the major threat to Israel's north and to Lebanon's south, but also the main obstacle to Jewish and Maronite inter-communal control in their respective states.[46]

By the early 1980s, then, the stage was set for a military showdown between Israel and its Maronite allies, on the one hand, and the Palestinian armed factions and the Syrian forces in Lebanon, on the other hand. For Prime Minister Begin, Defense Minister Sharon, and Chief of Staff Eitan, the regional and global climate seemed to be forthcoming for such a confrontation: Egypt, the most powerful Arab state, had left the Arab fold following the peace treaty of 1979, and the new US President, Ronald Reagan, was seen as supportive of Israel's intentions. Indeed, in talks between Prime Minister Begin and US Secretary of State Alexander Haig in April 1981, the latter conveyed the goal of the new US Administration to create a regional anti-Soviet alignment to "contain at all cost Syria and its President [Hafez al-] Assad, who appeared, and not only in Washington, as the source of evil in our region." Following these talks, some ministers in the Israeli government concluded that the time was ripe for a military operation in Lebanon.[47] Two additional meetings held with Secretary of State Haig in May 1982, first by Defense Minister Sharon and then by Israel's ambassador to Washington, Moshe Arens, convinced Israel's leaders that they had received what amounts to a "green light" from the United States to invade Lebanon.[48] However, Haig himself, in a letter to Begin from May 28, 1982, expressed his "concern about future Israeli military actions in Lebanon" adding that "[w]e want to make it very clear that we sincerely hope Israel will continue to exercise complete restraint and refrain from any action which could further damage the understanding underlying the cessation of hostilities. Israeli military actions, regardless of size, could lead to consequences none of us can foresee at this time."[49]

Toward 1982, Israel extended considerable material support to the Maronite-led armed factions in Lebanon, especially to the Lebanese

---

[46] This view is reflected in Kimche (1991). [47] Zipori (1997, 266).
[48] Schiff (1983, 80). See also Kimche (1991, 145).
[49] ISA, Ministry of Foreign Affairs, 4178/4-A, Secretary of State Alexander Haig to Prime Minister Menachem Begin, May 28, 1982. Begin was upset by Haig's letter and replied: "You know there is in Lebanon a neo-Nazi terrorist organization which constantly proclaims its design to kill our people. ... the man has not yet been born who will ever obtain from me consent to let Jews be killed by a bloodthirsty enemy and allow those responsible for the shedding of this blood to enjoy immunity, to say nothing of luxury ... I do hope that there will never be a Prime Minister of the Jewish State who will ever succumb to such a demand." ISA, Ministry of Foreign Affairs, 4178/4-A, Prime Minister Menachem Begin to Secretary of State Alexander Haig, May 30, 1982.

Forces, the militia of the Phalanges Party, which Bashir Gemayel had forcefully consolidated in the period 1978–1980 by crushing his Maronite opponents. In addition, Israeli leaders, again especially Prime Minister Begin, further underscored Lebanon's Christian identity and the "historic ties" between Israel and Lebanon, signaling the prevalence of Israel's "communal" approach to Lebanon. On June 8, 1982, following the launching of "Operation Peace for Galilee," the official name chosen for Israel's massive invasion of Lebanon, Prime Minister Begin stated in the Knesset:

> From time to time our people have a meeting with history. Well, now our soldiers are in Tyre ... We remember the two chapters in the Book of Kings, which tell of the friendship between Hiram King of Tyre and our King David, and the alliance that our King Solomon forged with the King of Tyre when he built the First Temple. We cannot provide to Tyre with what Solomon had provided it, but we will give her security, peace and quiet; provided that peace and quiet will also be given to Nahariya, which for years was bombarded from Tyre by Katyusha shells [sic]. No more.[50]

At the same time – and although in this period Israel/Palestine, too, was becoming more entrenched as a divided society – some Israeli leaders did their best to disassociate themselves from Lebanon's multi-communal character. A telling example is opposition leader Shimon Peres, who, like his colleagues in the Labor Party, openly supported the Lebanon War of 1982. During the same debate in the Knesset, Peres recounted:

> In a meeting of the council of the Socialist International, which took place in Helsinki, there was a representative of Lebanon. She asked me: Why don't you agree to a secular state [in Israel/Palestine], where Jews and Arabs, Muslims, Christians and Druze will live together? My reply was very short: We don't want to be Lebanon. We don't want to be like you.[51]

Whereas Lebanon's Christians, and especially Maronites, were extolled by Israeli officials, other communities in Lebanon, and especially Shi'is, who could "spoil" Lebanon's image as an essentially Christian and pro-Israeli state, received far less attention. Yossi Sarid, who, at the time, was a Knesset Member of the Labor Party, later recounted:

[50] Israeli Knesset (1982). According to Merom (2003, 196), "Israel's Chief Rabbinate, under Rabbi Shlomo Goren (a retired Chief Rabbi of the IDF) argued that the war was not simply a 'just war' but also a *mitzvah* war – that is, a war of religious prescription." Parentheses in the original. Merom adds that "the military rabbinate distributed, maps of Lebanon with the Biblical names of villages. And the zealots of the Gush Emunim movement, who settled in the occupied territories, were more than happy to find Biblical references suggesting that current Lebanese territories had belonged in the past to the ancient kingdom of Israel."
[51] Israeli Knesset (1982).

When the first Lebanon War started and quickly became complex and interminable, I had an opportunity to exchange some words with the deputy prime minister at the time, Simcha Erlich. "What did you see in this tragic foolishness," I asked him privately. "Yossi, believe me, nobody told us there were so many Shi'is in Lebanon. They talked to us all the time about Christians and more Christians."[52]

Indeed, when one looks at speeches, official statements, and other Israeli documents related to the Lebanon War of 1982, one can easily note the omission not only of the Shi'is in Lebanon but also of its other non-Christian communities, including the Druze, who were one of the first to feel the brunt of the Maronites' attempt to impose inter-communal control throughout the country.[53] Even when, in the wake of the 1982 War, Israeli officials "discovered" Lebanon's Shi'is – and also the Druze, who forcefully resisted the Lebanese Forces' takeover of the Druze stronghold in the Chouf area – these officials failed to reach out to members of these communities, some of which had opposed the PLO's actions in Lebanon before 1982. The IDF even engaged in punitive actions against the Shi'is on account of their connections with the Palestinian armed factions, actions that some in Israel, including senior officials in the General Security Service, later regretted.[54] But it was Israel's lingering occupation in South Lebanon that elicited the most resistance within the Shi'i community, leading to the rise of party-militias that began targeting the Israeli forces and their local proxy: Major Haddad's Christian militia.

In sum, Israel's declared goal of removing the security threat to its north could not conceal the true purpose of the Lebanon War of 1982, which was to buttress the state's expansion by delivering a fatal blow to the Palestinian armed factions, the main resistors to Israel's actions in the Territories, as well as by forcefully removing Syria from Lebanon and shattering its resistance to Israel's occupation of the Golan. It was thus ironic that one of the outcomes of the conflict was the Reagan Plan, which, reiterating the Camp David Accords, spoke of the legitimate rights of the Palestinian people and their just requirements; called for "full autonomy" to the Palestinian inhabitants of the Territories during a five-year "interim period" and, although rejecting the idea of an independent Palestinian state in the Territories, supported "self-government by the Palestinians of the West Bank and Gaza in association with Jordan"; and called for an immediate "settlement freeze" by Israel.[55] Instead of bolstering Maronite and Jewish control over the expanded states

---

[52] Sarid (2006).   [53] Parker (1993, 169).
[54] See, especially, Hof (1985, 99); Ajami (1986); Norton (1987); Kimche (1991, 133); Barnea (2000); Goulding (2003, 64–74); Bergman (2009, 273).
[55] Reagan Plan (1982). See also Kimche (1991, 157); Shilon (2012, 399–400); Naor (2015, 478–479). On Begin's disappointed reaction, see Lewis (1998, 215–216).

of Lebanon and Israel/Palestine, respectively, the divided character of both political units was ultimately underscored.

The Quagmire

> We wanted to be like Syria, we wanted to rule Lebanon. We did not realize that this is an impossible mission: We cannot be an occupying people.
> – Uri Lubrani, Coordinator of Israel's Operations in Lebanon (2000)[56]

On September 14, 1982, Israel's major Lebanese ally, President-elect Bashir Gemayel, was assassinated by a member of the SSNP, a small Lebanese party-militia that advocated the creation of a "Greater Syria" and was close to Syria. A few days later, members of Gemayel's militia, the Lebanese Forces, perpetrated the Sabra and Shatila Massacre in the Palestinian refugee camps in Beirut, with IDF units stationed nearby and with some Israeli troops firing flares that facilitated this atrocity.[57] But Israel's political and military debacle in Lebanon would come to an end only 18 years later, in May 2000, when Prime Minister Ehud Barak and his government decided to withdraw Israel's forces from Lebanon, under the pressure of Hizbullah, the Lebanese Shi'i party-militia, and to deploy them on the "Blue Line."[58]

When attempting to explain Israel's continued occupation in Lebanon, and also its involvement there in later periods, one important factor that does not always receive sufficient attention is the perception of Lebanon as a "quagmire" (or "mud"). This image became entrenched in the public discourse in Israel and among its political and security leaders after the Lebanon War of 1982 and, in retrospect, helped shape Israel's policy toward Lebanon and, no less importantly, to justify this policy both domestically and externally.

As suggested earlier, in the period leading up to the 1982 War, some Israeli officials viewed Lebanon in almost romantic colors. For them, Lebanon was to be the place where Israel, the regional power, would establish a "new order" under the leadership of Israel's Maronite allies, who would not only dominate Lebanon but also sign a second peace treaty with Israel and in this way enhance Israel's security. But the image of Lebanon that emerged in Israel during the war, and was further

---

[56] Quoted in Barnea (2000).
[57] Several accounts of Israeli soldiers who served in the Lebanon War of 1982 contradict Israel's official position regarding the massacre. See Gal and Hammerman (2002). The firing of flares by the IDF during the massacre is mentioned in *Waltz with Bashir*, the animated documentary directed by Ari Folman, another veteran of the 1982 War.
[58] O'Shea (2004).

reinforced in its aftermath, was that of a "quagmire": A zone of endemic disorder and perpetual violence that emanated from Lebanon's internal divisions – and especially among its communities – where actors played by different rules and norms that foreigners, including Israelis, could not comprehend and which, in view of the "unbridgeable gap" between Lebanon and Israel, lay outside the latter's sphere of responsibility. Indeed, according to Asher Kaufman, "the Lebanon quagmire became not one that Israel concocted for itself, but a Lebanese swamp into which it may very well have been a mistake to sink in 1982."[59]

As in previous periods in Israeli–Lebanese relations, this Israeli image of Lebanon stemmed in part from an objective assessment of the latter, which was indeed quite chaotic at the time, not least due to the attempts of Maronite parties-militias to exploit Israel's invasion of Lebanon (and, later, the massive US involvement there) to impose a pattern of intercommunal control vis-à-vis the Druze and Shi'i communities, which was resisted, respectively, by the Progressive Socialist Party (PSP) and by the Amal Movement and Hizbullah.[60] But the image of Lebanon as a quagmire also attested to the growing disillusionment of some Israelis, especially on the center-left of the political spectrum, with regard to their own state, including its political and military leaders, democratic institutions, the moral high ground that it claimed to represent, and its peace-loving character. In particular, criticism was leveled at the name "Operation Peace for Galilee," chosen for Israel's invasion of Lebanon in 1982. Amos Oz, one of Israel's most acclaimed novelists, wrote: "'Peace for the Galilee' is a deceptive phrase. War, even when it is fully justified, should not be called 'peace'. Only in the world of brainwashing and tyranny described by George Orwell do such slogans as 'War is peace,' 'Slavery is freedom,' and 'Ignorance is power' prevail."[61] This growing disillusionment, in turn, gave rise to mass protests against the war by new civil society groups, and to numerous books, songs, plays, and films that criticized the war and Israel's militaristic tendencies.[62]

This new image of Lebanon as a quagmire is manifested in the Israeli films produced on Israel's experience in Lebanon since 1982. The first wave of these films began in the mid-1980s, during the war, and a second wave began in the first decade of the twenty-first century, after the Second

---

[59] Kaufman (2010a, 214–215).
[60] On this period, see Norton (1987); Salem (1993); Parker (1993); Baer (2002); Barak (2009a).
[61] Oz (2012 [1989], 33). Many Israelis, from both left and right of the political spectrum, shared this view. See, e.g., Zipori (1997, 283). Mordechai Zipori was a minister in Begin's government in 1982.
[62] Kenan (1984); Hermann (2009); Kaufman (2010a).

Palestinian Intifada and the War between Israel and Hizbullah in 2006.[63] A discussion of these films is important not only because popular culture reflects societal values and perceptions, but also because public culture, especially films, can shape public attitudes, especially when they attract large audiences, as was the case with some of the films discussed in this chapter.[64]

The first Israeli film to deal with Lebanon was *Ricochet* (1986), largely filmed in Lebanon by the IDF, which sought to educate its soldiers about the dilemmas confronting the Israeli soldiers in dealing with a civilian population in wartime.[65] Interestingly, the IDF had for some time confronted similar dilemmas in its occupation in the Territories, but addressing these sensitive issues in the context of Israel's "presence" (that is, occupation) in Lebanon seemed to be more acceptable than in the context of the state's expansion. In the film, a young Israeli officer who arrives in Lebanon to command a military unit stationed in the Sidon area finds his worldview challenged by the prevailing chaos he encounters. In one of the film's most powerful scenes, the officer meets the unit's cook, who is busy preparing *Shakshouka*, a Mediterranean dish that is made by mixing eggs in a sauce of tomatoes, peppers, onions and spices, and which, in this context, symbolized the Lebanese "mess." As the cook prepares the dish, he introduces the newcomer to the realities of Lebanon as he has come to know them from an expert:

They brought us some doctor, an orientalist, and he lectured us about the structure of this country. Now I get it. Okay, so it goes like this. The Christians hate the Druze and the Shi'is – the Sunnis and Palestinians as well. The Druze hate the Christians ... Yes ... No ... The Druze hate the Christians, the Shi'is and the Syrians. Why? The Shi'is, they "screwed" them for generations, so they hate everybody. The Sunnis hate whoever their bosses tell them to hate, and the Palestinians hate not only all the others, but also each other ... They all have one thing in common. Everybody hates – and how they hate – us, the Israelis. They would have totally "screwed" us, if only they could.

Significantly, the Christians, Israel's allies during the Lebanon War of 1982, are also mentioned among those who hate the Israelis and would like to "screw" them. Ella Shohat, who discusses this scene, observes that "[s]uch a caricatured presentation of sociopolitical dynamics in Lebanon leads to identification with the 'rational' Israelis whose presence there is implied, in obedience to official discourse, as uniquely serving to maintain order" and adds, "The reasons for hating the Israelis are dehistoricized,

---

[63] On these films, see Almog (2009); Shohat (2010); Yosef (2011); Morag (2012, 2013); Benziman (2013); Niv (2014).
[64] Shapiro (2009); Birkenstein, Froula, and Randell (2010).   [65] T. Friedman (1986).

and the spectator inevitably identifies with the nice young Israelis who wish no one any harm ... attempts to comprehend why the soldiers are hated can lead in only one direction: Arabs are fanatical and irrational."[66]

Another Israeli film from the first wave, *Time for Cherries* (1991), presents a similar image of Lebanon and, ultimately, of Israel as well. Shulamit Almog, in an insightful piece that discusses the absence of law from Israeli war films, writes:

Time for Cherries emphasizes and intensifies the image of Lebanon as an anomalous enclave in which everything is possible and that nothing taking place within its borders can be subject to the usual standards of judgment. Immediately after a soldier of the [Israeli] unit is shot and killed by a sharpshooter, one of the soldiers who are interviewed says: "Everything in our state [Israel] is considered sacred, here [in Lebanon] nothing is considered so." The film presents the gap between Israel – "our state" – and "Lebanon," and the significance of the gap in practical terms. In Lebanon one does things that one would never consider doing in Israel.[67]

This gap between "civilized" or "law-abiding" Israel, on the one hand, and "uncivilized" or "lawless" Lebanon, on the other hand, which suggests an Orientalist Israeli perspective toward Lebanon, can also be observed in other spheres in Israel. One such sphere is the books published by Israeli scholars on Lebanon, which, though dealing with relatively stable periods in the state's modern history, nonetheless carry titles suggesting that Lebanon is, perhaps inherently, disordered. Examples include *The Fractured Cedar: Lebanon's Road to Statehood*, which deals with Lebanon in the period 1926–1939, when the state's political institutions crystalized;[68] *The Lebanon Tangle*, which, quite interestingly, surveys the comparatively stable period of Israeli–Lebanese relations before 1958;[69] and *Lebanon: Blood in the Cedar*, which discusses the period after the end of the Lebanese civil war, when the state's reconstruction commenced.[70]

Israeli practitioners who have written about their experience in Lebanon also seem to prefer to highlight the major differences – and not the possible similarities – between the two states. David Kimche, one the architects of the Israeli–Maronite alliance in 1982, speaks of the "sense of hopelessness and a frightening disregard for the human life" produced by the Lebanese civil war, adding that "I have witnessed pleasant, cultured and seemingly civilized Lebanese speak with incredible savagery and lust

---

[66] Shohat (2010, 234).   [67] Almog (2009, 41–42).
[68] Zamir (2002). The title of the English version of the book is different. Cf. Zamir (1997).
[69] Erlich (2000). The book's author, a retired Colonel in the IDF, served as deputy to Uri Lubrani, the Coordinator of Israel's Operations in Lebanon. See Erlich (1997).
[70] Zisser (2009).

for the blood of their fellow countrymen of a different religion, sect or faction." "The Lebanese morass," he reckons, "proved to be too strong for us."[71] A more recent book by another former Mossad official depicts Israel's Christian allies in Lebanon as "drug dealers and whores,"[72] and the book *Labyrinth in Lebanon,* also by a former Mossad agent who operated in Lebanon, effectively casts its author as a neutral "traffic cop" amidst the Lebanese "chaos," adding that Israelis and Lebanese have different moral norms and that "there is (still) an unbridgeable gap between us and them."[73] Another book, by a former IDF officer who served in the South Lebanon Area (ADAL) in the 1970s and 1980s, describes his first encounter with Lebanon as follows:

> I could not help but think what a shame it is that people are destroying their lives with their own hands in a region that is so beautiful, while repeating to myself the basic characteristics of the population of Lebanon, which is made up of a wide variety of sects and descendants of many peoples, who have made their mark on the country in the course of its history ... in this state, what divides the population is a social and political problem that arises from its being a state of minorities where an imbalance between the sects is still the focus of a problem that leads to political instability ... We, the Israelis, are actually "walking between the raindrops."[74]

These Israeli perceptions of Lebanon are significant not least because they guided Israel's decisions and actions toward it since 1982. Major General (ret.) Yossi Peled, who served as head of the IDF's Northern Command in the period 1986–1991 and in this capacity was one of the architects of Israel's "security zone" in South Lebanon, observed in 1997:

> Most of us wrongly think we have a problem with the state called Lebanon. But we have a Lebanese problem in which there is no state, and this is a complicated problem that many ignore ... We are dealing with a chaos ... We are not dealing with a state but with a large disturbance, and in Lebanon there is still no body that is strong enough to initiate processes that will change this reality.[75]

What followed from this view is that Israel needed to secure its own interests in Lebanon, including by maintaining a permanent "presence" (i.e., an occupation) in its territory. This view was shared by many of Israel's political leaders. Yitzhak Shamir, who in 1983 replaced Menachem Begin as prime minister and served in this post until 1984 and also later (in the period 1986–1992), was asked in 1997 about his opinion in the debate that waged in Israel at the time regarding a possible unilateral withdrawal from Lebanon, to which he replied: "I once said to

---

[71] Kimche (1991, 160, 182).   [72] Navot (2015, 161).
[73] Tsafrir (2006, 114). Parentheses are in the original.   [74] Danguri (1998, 118–199).
[75] Yossi Peled (1997, 29–30).

one of the Americans that Lebanon is not a state, and he looked at me as if I am insane. We should search for solutions but I'm afraid there is no way out."[76]

It is noteworthy that both Shamir's statement and Peled's observation were made seven years after the end of the civil war in Lebanon. Indeed, during this period, Israel looked with great suspicion at Lebanon's reconstruction, including the efforts to rebuild the LAF and deploy it throughout its territory. Moreover, at least some of Israel's actions – its continued occupation of the "security zone" in South Lebanon and its support of the South Lebanese Army (SLA); its assassination of Hizbullah's leader Abbas Musawi in 1992; the deportation of Hamas operatives to Lebanon in the same year; and its repeated incursions into Lebanon's airspace and waters – had a negative effect on these efforts.

Let us conclude with the view of another Israeli leader, Shimon Peres, who, as we have seen, played a key role in formulating Israel's "Good Fence" policy in 1976. Under his leadership, the Labor Party supported the Lebanon War of 1982, and in 1996 his government ordered the launching of "Operation Grapes of Wrath" against Hizbullah, which came to an abrupt end after the IDF killed more than one hundred Lebanese civilians in the Lebanese village of Qana. A decade later, during the War between Israel and Hizbullah, Peres served as Israel's deputy prime minister, and following the latter confrontation, Peres told the Winograd Commission of inquiry, whose members were appointed to look into the latter conflict: "We also know that Lebanon is an ungoverned country, ridden with mines and organizations, and there murder is a daily thing, among themselves, among the sects, among the groups."[77] The possible connection between this state of affairs and Israel's policy toward Lebanon, including in the periods when Peres was at the helm, was not mentioned.

In sum, following Israel's political and military debacle in Lebanon in 1982, many Israelis came to view Lebanon as a quagmire: A place of chronic disorder and endemic violence, not least because of its multicommunal character. This image stands in stark contrast to the way that many Israelis have come to see their own state before 1982: Western, civilized, democratic, homogenous, and peace-loving. Moreover, since violence and chaos were seen as endemic to Lebanon, using violence against it, even on a massive scale, seemed justified. Importantly, the image of Lebanon as a "failed state" in this period was not entirely

---

[76] Shalev (1997). See also Shamir (1994, 137). In 1996, Israel's annual intelligence estimate held that Lebanon is "a state that is practically non-existent, which is ruled by Syria in all parameters"; quoted in Benn (1996).
[77] Peres Testimony (2006).

inaccurate, especially until the end of the civil war of 1975–1990; and others besides Israel, including some students of Lebanon, also embraced it (see Chapter 3). But what is striking about this image is how it persisted even after the Lebanese civil war came to an end and reconstruction of the state began, and how Lebanon was repeatedly contrasted with Israel, despite the fact that both Lebanon and Israel/Palestine were, ultimately, divided societies engulfed in inter-communal conflict.

Two Conflicts Intertwined

Writing about Israel's military confrontation with Hamas in 2006 and the War between Israel and Hizbullah in the same year,[78] Hew Strachan posited that, for Israel and its Western allies, "two separate conflicts, waged at the opposite ends of the Israeli state, were conflated into one existential crisis."[79] However, at least for Israel, the close inter-linkages between the two political entities – Israel/Palestine and Lebanon – did not disappear in the wake of the Lebanon War of 1982, but were actually reinforced by it. This section attempts to trace this increasing inter-linkage between Israel/Palestine and Lebanon from the Lebanon War of 1982 to the War between Israel and Hizbullah in 2006. However, as before, the emphasis is not only on the actual connections between the two cases, but also on how these links were perceived, especially in Israeli eyes but also in the eyes of Hizbullah, the Shi'i party-militia which became Israel's major Lebanese adversary in this period.

In August 1982, most members of the Palestinian armed factions left Beirut under Israel's military pressure, and after a pro-Syrian rebellion in Fatah and another military showdown, this time between Arafat's loyalists and the Syrian army in Tripoli, most Palestinian activists left Lebanon and settled in Tunisia. There, PLO leaders placed a greater emphasis on diplomacy, although some did not yet give up the armed struggle against Israel. At any rate, although the Palestinian armed factions remained active in Lebanon in later years, especially in the Palestinian refugee camps in South Lebanon, this state ceased to be their main base of operations.

But the removal of the Palestinian armed factions from Lebanon did not mean that the linkage between Lebanon and Israel/Palestine, reinforced by Israel's expansion in 1967 and its ramifications, as well as by the Lebanon War of 1982, was a thing of the past. Israel's political and

---

[78] On the War between Israel and Hizbullah, see Harel and Issacharoff (2008); Lupovici (2009); Porter (2009); Barak (2009a, 2010); Tidy (2012).
[79] Quoted in Porter (2009, 176).

military leaders continued to regard the Lebanese and Palestinian "fronts" as closely connected, and some violent non-state actors in Lebanon, especially Hizbullah, also adopted this view, which served their interests. On the Israeli side, the main reason seems to be that, in the period after the 1982 War, Israeli political and military leaders were apprehensive that the Palestinian armed factions might return to Lebanon and launch military incursions into Israel's territory, as they did before the war. Indeed, in addition to preserving Israel's local client, the South Lebanese Army (SLA) – reorganized in 1984 under a retired Lebanese officer, General Antoine Lahad (Maronite) – this was the logic behind the "security zone" that Israel maintained in South Lebanon from its partial withdrawal from Lebanon in 1985 until its full withdrawal in 2000.[80]

But the inter-linkage between Lebanon and Israel/Palestine was also manifested in the policies that Israel adopted in and vis-à-vis these two regions. In the period 1985–2000, the official in charge of Israel's "security zone" in South Lebanon was the Coordinator of Israel's Operations in Lebanon, who reported to the minister of defense. This role was similar to the Coordinator of Israel's Operations in the Territories, though the former was, in most periods, a civilian and the latter was an army officer. In addition, both officials presided over "civilian administrations": the Civil Support Administration in Lebanon" and the "Civil Administration in the Territories."[81]

But on the tactical level, too, Israel operated in both regions in a similar fashion: Brigadier (ret.) General Moshe Tamir, an Israeli officer who served in South Lebanon in the 1990s, later recounted how the IDF, which was accustomed to using counterterrorist tactics against the Palestinian armed factions in the Territories, failed to implement these tactics in the Israeli–Lebanese border area, where the IDF and the SLA waged a different kind of struggle, a guerrilla war, against the Shi'i party-militia Hizbullah. According to Tamir, the use of these tactics in Lebanon resulted in many casualties for Israel and its local client, which led to the development of new tactics that would be more appropriate to this struggle.[82] A similar problem was mentioned in the wake of the War between Israel and Hizbullah (2006).[83] But this aspect of the inter-linkage between Israel/Palestine and Lebanon was not always one-directional: Reuven Hazak, Deputy Director of the General Security Service, which played a critical role in imposing Israel's rule over the Territories after 1967 (see Chapter 4) and that was made responsible for

---

[80] Luft (2000); Sela (2007). [81] Bergman (1995); Erlich (1997).
[82] Tamir (2005, 274–275). See also Ron (2003, iv). [83] Porter (2009, 183).

South Lebanon following Israel's occupation of this area in 1982,[84] later observed: "It was a country that has no laws. We [the General Security Service] had no choice but we entered this game too with our gun drawn, and this, one way or another, also affected what happened on the bus. The ability to operate aggressive weapons of war probably went to someone's head."[85] Here, Hazak referred to the Bus 300 Affair, which involved the execution by several General Security Service operatives of two Palestinians who had kidnapped an Israeli bus in 1984 and were captured alive by Israel's security forces. This scandal shook the General Security Service after it became known.

One reason for the persistence of these inter-linkages between Israel's policies in Lebanon and in Israel/Palestine was that many government officials, including experts that served as advisers on the Territories and on Lebanon, were either the same people, had a similar background or were members of the same social networks. Many of these officials were graduates and faculty members at academic departments and research centers on Islamic and Middle Eastern Studies in Israel's universities, and some (but not all) of them held Orientalist views toward "the Arabs" that they sought to implement both in the Territories and in Lebanon. The role of these experts in according "scientific" credence to Israel's policies in both areas cannot be overstated.[86] In addition, at least some Israeli officials might have believed that there was no real difference between Lebanese armed factions such Hizbullah and the Palestinian armed factions such as Fatah, and that, in the end, they were all "terrorists."[87] In 2006, Yossi Sarid, who had served as Knesset Member and government minister, recounted the following anecdote about a meeting between members of the Four Mothers movement, a civil society group that advocated an Israeli withdrawal from Lebanon in the late 1990s, and former IDF Chief of Staff Rafael Eitan, who had also served as a government minister:

Many muddy years went by in the Lebanese quagmire, and the Four Mothers came to solicit my support for the withdrawal from Lebanon. They insisted on telling me a story. "You've got to hear this," they begged. "A few days ago we went to see Raful (Rafael Eitan)." "Suddenly, in the middle of the meeting, we

---

[84] Bergman (2009, 271).
[85] Quoted in the documentary *Alef Eliminate Them – The Order that Shook the General Security Service* (2012).
[86] Eyal (2002). See, for example, the account of Israel's assassination of Hizbullah leader Abbas Musawi in 1992. Bergman (2009). See also Porter (2009).
[87] This is reminiscent of Israel's decision to hold the PLO responsible for the attempt made by Yasser Arafat's arch-rival, Abu Nidal, to assassinate Israel's ambassador in London, Shlomo Argov, which Israel used as a pretext to launch the Lebanon War of 1982. Schiff and Ya'ari (1984, 98); Shilon (2012, 374–375).

realized Raful thought that Hezbollah was a Palestinian organization. Would you believe it?" I would.[88]

Another reason for this mix-up was that, since the mid-1980s, Hizbullah itself embraced some of the tactics that had been employed by the Palestinian armed factions in Lebanon in the period before 1982, including firing Katyusha rockets against Israel's territory, reaching ceasefires with Israel, and abducting Israeli soldiers in order to compel the Israeli government to agree to prisoner swaps. This was because, like the Palestinian armed factions before it, Hizbullah realized that these tactics would increase its standing domestically and regionally. This development was, however, not without irony: In 1982, Israel invaded Lebanon in order to win the struggle for Israel/Palestine; but from 1985, it was Hizbullah that was using its "resistance" against Israel and exploiting the Palestinian issue to win the struggle over Lebanon. Two differences between Hizbullah and the Palestinian armed factions were, however, that Hizbullah did not infiltrate Israel's territory before October 2000, and even then it launched an operation in Shebaa Farms, a contested zone that Israel occupied from Syria in the 1967 War.[89] Since 1992, moreover, Hizbullah has participated in Lebanese politics, first in parliament and later also in the cabinet.

But these were not the only inter-linkages between Lebanon and Israel/Palestine. In May 1985, Israel released 1,150 Palestinian prisoners in return for three Israeli soldiers who were captured during the Lebanon War of 1982 by a Palestinian armed faction, Ahmad Jibril's Popular Front for the Liberation of Palestine-General Command. Some in Israel, as well as Jibril himself, later argued that this gave a boost to the Palestinians in the Territories and was, moreover, one of the causes of the first Palestinian Intifada in 1987.[90] This perception – whether true or false – caused many Israelis to be apprehensive about any future concession in Lebanon, especially regarding a unilateral withdrawal from the "security zone," which was liable to reflect negatively on Israel/Palestine.

But the inter-linkage between Israel/Palestine and Lebanon sometimes worked in the opposite direction. James Ron notes the difference between Israel's relatively moderate response to the wave of suicide bombings launched against it by the Palestinian group Hamas in 1996 compared to its massive response against the hostile action of the Lebanese party-militia Hizbullah's later that year ("Operation Grapes of Wrath"), and attributes this difference to Israel's divergent policies toward these two

---

[88] Sarid (2006). This anecdote was confirmed to me by a former member of the movement.
[89] Kaufman (2013).   [90] Schiff and Ya'ari (1989, 214–215).

territories – "ghetto" and "frontier" respectively.[91] However, it is also possible that, as in many instances before and after 1996, Israel's responses on both fronts were closely inter-linked. Indeed, Ron himself notes, "In a pattern that repeated itself throughout the 1980s and 1990s, Israel used more intense methods in Lebanon, even though its real target was Palestinians in the West Bank and Gaza."[92] Thus, for example, Israel's assassination of Abbas Musawi, the secretary-general of Hizbullah, on February 16, 1992, took place only a day after Palestinian activists affiliated with the Islamic Jihad (an organization that, like Hizbullah, had close ties with Iran) armed with knives, axes, and a pitchfork infiltrated an army camp in Israel and killed three soldiers, an attack that angered Israel's political leaders and created an "aura of revenge" in the IDF.[93] Ronen Bergman, who provides a detailed account of Musawi's assassination, recounts that what began as exercise for this leader's possible abduction in order to exchange him with an Israel MIA turned into a targeted assassination that resulted in the first use of Katyusha rockets against Israel by Hizbullah, a series of attacks against Israeli targets in Turkey, and the bombing of the Israeli embassy in Argentina.[94] Later that year, Israel created a new link between Israel/Palestine and Lebanon when the newly formed Labor government headed by Rabin decided to deport 400 Hamas operatives from the Territories to South Lebanon. This enabled these activists to forge ties with Hizbullah and to become acquainted with military know-how, including suicide bombings, which Hamas later employed in its struggle in Israel/Palestine.[95] What is also interesting in this case is how two years after the end of the Lebanese conflict, and after the LAF had deployed in many parts of the state and asserted its authority, Israeli leaders still perceived Lebanon as a "non-state" and simply assumed that it would accept the Palestinian deportees. However, this assumption proved to be false, and Israel later had to return the deportees to the Territories.

In May 2000 Israeli troops left Lebanon, and later that year the Second Palestinian Intifada (or al-Aqsa Intifada) erupted in the Territories. For many inside and outside Israel, including both supporters and opponents of Israel's withdrawal from Lebanon, the Second Palestinian Intifada demonstrated the close inter-linkage between Lebanon and

[91] Ron (2003, 2–4).   [92] Ibid., (180).
[93] Following the assassination of Musawi, Israeli Defense Minister Moshe Arens argued that Musawi's death was not incidental and that "this is a message to all terrorist organizations, that those who open an account with us – we will settle the account"; *Haaretz* (1992).
[94] Bergman (2009, 348–371).   [95] Mishal and Sela (2000, 65–66).

Israel/Palestine.[96] Indeed, Shlomo Ben-Ami, who served as a minister in the Israeli government and was a member of the negotiating team with the Palestinians, later claimed that "the second Intifada ... was born on the night of our hasty withdrawal from Lebanon."[97] This inter-linkage was further emphasized by later developments such as the abduction of three Israeli soldiers in the contested Shebaa Farms area in October 2000 by Hizbullah, whose bodies were later returned to Israel in January 2004 in exchange for Lebanese and Palestinian prisoners, thus setting an important precedent, as well as by the Shi'i party-militia's pro-Palestinian discourse and, occasionally, also its covert cooperation with Palestinian armed factions inside Israel/Palestine.[98]

Six years later, in 2006, Israel's decision on a massive response against Hizbullah, after members of the Shi'i party-militia abducted two Israeli soldiers, this time within Israel's territory, was also connected to events in Israel/Palestine: About a year earlier, in August 2005, Israel had withdrawn from the Gaza Strip, a move that many in Israel regarded as a sign of weakness on its part. Then, in June 2006, an Israeli soldier, Gilad Shalit, was abducted by the Palestinian group Hamas in a cross-border raid. These two events, especially the latter, which humiliated the IDF, encouraged some Israeli political and military leaders to think that the time had come to "rehabilitate" Israel's deterrence by inflicting a blow to Hizbullah, which was seen – and which sometimes portrayed itself – as an inspiration to the Palestinians in the Territories. But Hizbullah, too, created a clear linkage between Israel/Palestine and Lebanon: After the Shi'i party-militia abducted the two Israeli soldiers on July 12, 2006, its leader, Hassan Nasrallah, declared that he would not reject the use of multiple channels in negotiating for the release of the two Israeli soldiers held by his organization and for Shalit, held by Hamas. Some Israeli security officials interpreted this as attempt by Hizbullah "to gain control of the Palestinian track and lead the occupied territories to a more radical line."[99]

Writing about the second "wave" of Israeli films on the Lebanon War of 1982, Raya Morag observes that they "involve a two-fold process of displacement: from the *intifada* to the First Lebanon War and from the figure of the victimized Palestinian to that of the (heroic) victimized Israeli soldier."[100] But the close inter-linkages between Israel/Palestine and Lebanon in the period since 1982 were already evident in the earlier

---

[96] Pipes (2001); Erlich (2011, 60). See also Beilin (2001, 117–118); Gerges (2001); Sher (2001, 112).
[97] Ben-Ami (2004, 73). See also Harel and Issacharoff (2004, 64–65).
[98] Sobelman (2004, 84–88); Alagha (2011, 163). [99] Harel and Issacharoff (2008, 83).
[100] Morag (2013, 23).

wave of Israeli films on Israel's experience in Lebanon. The Israeli soldiers who police the villages in South Lebanon in *Ricochet* (1986), for example, do not seem too different from their peers who patrolled the villages and towns in the West Bank and the Gaza Strip before the first Intifada – except, perhaps, for the level of violence in both regions at that time. Another film, *Cup Final* (1991), portrays an Israeli soldier who is captured by a group of Palestinian fighters in Lebanon. Turning to the second wave of Israeli films on Lebanon, in *Waltz with Bashir* (2008), an Israeli who had served as a soldier in the Lebanon War of 1982 attempts to discover where he was and what he did during the Sabra and Shatila Massacre. Most of this film is animated, with the exception of the massacre itself, which is presented using footage filmed in the Palestinian refugee camps in Beirut following the killings. The Israeli soldier – and, by extension, Israel – who had invaded Lebanon to crush the PLO and help Bashir Gemayel become Lebanon's president, is thus confronted with the Palestinian issue that he tried so hard to suppress, and the entire campaign acquires a new and disturbing meaning.

But the inter-linkage between Lebanon and Israel/Palestine is also reinforced by what is more often than not absent from these films, especially those belonging to the second wave – namely, the Lebanese themselves. In the film *Beaufort* (2007), the Israeli soldiers, who are stationed in a desolate Crusaders' fortress that had been presented as symbol of Israel's victory over the PLO in the Lebanon War of 1982, are continuously bombarded, presumably by Hizbullah, but the attackers are nowhere to be seen. Similarly, in the film *Lebanon* (2009), the country itself is seen only through the lens of the targeting device of an Israeli tank that advances into its territory during the first day of the Lebanon War of 1982. When a Lebanese finally enters the Israeli "space," this is a cunning and treacherous Christian militiaman who, by his diabolic existence, only serves to exonerate the Israeli soldiers in the same way that the Lebanese "quagmire" has "transformed" Israel/Palestine into a peaceful and ordered place.

The most extreme depiction of the inter-linkage between Israel/Palestine and Lebanon to date, however, is found in the Israeli zombie film *Battle of the Undead* (2013). In the film, an Israeli military unit, whose four members represent the major sub-groups in the Jewish community in Israel/Palestine (Secular, Ethiopian, Russian, and National Religious), is sent on a top-secret mission into Lebanon to capture a senior Hizbullah operative who allegedly developed a secret weapon that threatens Israel. However, immediately after crossing the Israeli–Lebanese border, the soldiers encounter bleeding corpses, and upon entering the Lebanese village where their target resides, they are assaulted by blood-thirsty zombies. Of all the Lebanese that the Israeli soldiers encounter, only one is not a zombie: A Christian woman who wears a cross around her neck, an item that she later drops when crossing the border to Israel. The Israeli unit then discovers that the new weapon – which, as it turns out, Israel, and not Hizbullah, had developed – has gotten out of hand and is turning all of Lebanon's inhabitants into zombies. The Israeli soldiers fight their way back to safety, but are pursued by the ever-increasing number of blood-thirsty Lebanese. After they manage to cross the border back to Israel, the soldiers discover, to their horror, that their state, too, has been contaminated. In his book *Theories of International Politics and Zombies*, Daniel Drezner posits that "[p]opular culture often provides a window into the subliminal or unstated fears of citizens, and zombies are no exception."[101] Indeed, the film *Battle of the Undead* seems to suggest that, at least for some Israelis, Lebanon has completed its transformation from the focus of Israel's hopes to the sum of all of its fears.

Conclusion

The main goal of Israel's invasion of Lebanon in 1982 was to finish off the Palestinian armed factions that challenged Israel's expansion in the West Bank and the Gaza Strip and to deal a blow to Syria and cement Israel's occupation of the Golan. The third goal was to reinforce the dominant position of the Maronites in Lebanon, which was supposed to become the second Arab state to make peace with Israel. But none of these goals were attained. Instead of disappearing, the Palestinian issue resurfaced in the Reagan Plan, and the PLO turned its efforts to the diplomatic arena. Syria, for its part, managed to thwart Israel's plans in Lebanon, exploiting the grievances of its non-Christian communities, especially the Shi'is and the Druze. Maronite actors, for their part, failed in their quest to dominate Lebanon, and their power in the state began to wane, particularly after the US and Israeli withdrawals and the internecine struggles among their leaders. But this apparent failure of the "communal" approach in Israel did not signal a return to the "statist" approach toward Lebanon or back in Israel/Palestine. Instead of leaving Lebanon and buttressing the latter's sovereignty, Israeli troops remained stationed there for an additional 18 years, and the Israel Defense Forces (IDF), together with its local proxy, the SLA, was bogged down in a guerrilla war with Hizbullah, which exploited it to its advantage. The Israeli perception of Lebanon as a quagmire thus became a self-fulfilling prophecy, and the blurred boundaries between Israel/Palestine and Lebanon further reinforced the inter-

---

[101] Drezner (2011, 4).

linkages between the two political entities. When examining the period 1985–2000 – from Israel's partial withdrawal from Lebanon and the creation of its "security zone" in South Lebanon until Israel's final withdrawal from Lebanon – the main questions to ask are why Israel persisted in its policy toward Lebanon despite the fact that the Palestinian armed factions had left this state in 1982, and how a Lebanese actor, the Shi'i party-militia Hizbullah, gradually took their place and waged a successful "resistance" against Israel's occupation. As this chapter has suggested, at least part of the answer to these questions has to do with the close ties and linkages created between Israel/Palestine and Lebanon, which were manifested in, but also shaped by, political decisions, military tactics, and popular culture.

Conclusion

Lebanon and Israel/Palestine are two expanded states that came into being when smaller political units, the autonomous district of Mount Lebanon and the State of Israel, respectively, incorporated territories that lay outside their borders, with open or tacit backing from powerful outside forces but without the consent of these territories' inhabitants. Whereas Greater Lebanon, which later became the independent Republic of Lebanon, was ultimately accepted by most of its inhabitants and recognized by most outsiders, not one state, including Israel itself, has recognized the existence of a Greater Israel or an Israel/Palestine, and many of its inhabitants, including most Palestinians and many Israelis, oppose it and seek to undo it. Still, all attempts to bring about the contraction of these two expanded states have, thus far, been unsuccessful, and this fact encourages us to take these two cases – and possibly others – very seriously and to analyze them as one does with regard to other political phenomena.

As shown in the previous chapters, in both Lebanon and Israel/Palestine, the state's expansion, whether formal or informal, engendered a divided society in place of a relatively homogenous political unit that seemed to be on its way to becoming a nation-state according to the Western model. This new political reality, which signaled a departure from the national vision that underpinned the state's creation, had to be dealt with one way or the other. In subsequent decades, political leaders in Israel/Palestine and Lebanon adopted quite different methods of coping with their conundrums, and their policy choices have led to outcomes that were sometimes similar and at other times different, and which, moreover, conflated for certain periods of time.

In both cases, political stability was established in the aftermath of the state's expansion, whether on account of inter-communal power sharing (in Lebanon) or control (in Israel/Palestine). But in both political entities, political stability was later undermined by mounting political and socio-economic grievances, communal mobilization, securitization, and conflict. Still, the difference in the capacities of the state in both cases and its varying levels of legitimacy, as well as the different scope of international involvement, produced two distinct "vicious cycles." Whereas in Lebanon, the conflict was mainly waged over power, positions, and resources but did not challenge the expanded state's existence, in Israel/Palestine the conflict was waged over the expanded state itself. This basic difference allowed for a relatively successful peace process in Lebanon, culminating in the Ta'if Agreement of 1989, but resulted in a largely unsuccessful peace process in Israel/Palestine in the period 1993–2000, which led to even more violence following its breakdown.

But developments in Israel/Palestine and Lebanon, and particularly the state's expansion in the former case and the weakening of the state in the latter case, also affected the relations between these two political units. As we have seen, contrary to the popular image of Israeli–Lebanese relations as being inherently volatile and conflict-prone, the two states of Israel and Lebanon have actually known periods of relative stability along their mutual border. Indeed, in the period 1949–1967, these relations were more stable than Israel's relations with Egypt, Syria, or Jordan. In this period, problems in the two states' relations were dealt with mainly by the ILMAC, which included representatives of both armies and a UN observer. As a result, Israel generally practiced restraint toward Lebanon.

After the 1967 war, however, Israeli–Lebanese relations began to deteriorate. In the wake of Israel's expansion, the Palestinian armed factions were pushed out of the Territories and later also expelled from Jordan, and they found refuge in the Lebanese–Israeli border area, where they could organize and launch attacks against Israel's territory. Israel, for its part, retaliated first in order to compel Lebanon to subdue the Palestinian armed factions, like Jordan did in 1970–1971, and then set out to address its own security concerns. But Israel's policy toward Lebanon in this period was not only shaped only by objective factors; it also stemmed from the profound changes that had taken place in Israel/Palestine, and especially the state's expansion and the decline of the dominant "statist" orientation in Israel, both domestically and in Israel's relations with its neighbors and beyond.

The outbreak of Lebanon's civil war in 1975 and the emergence of the Phalanges Party as the major Maronite party-militia in Lebanon offered Israeli leaders, especially those who adhered to the "communal" approach – including leaders of the center-right Likud Party and members of Israel's security networks – an opportunity to deal a fatal blow to the Palestinian armed factions, to defeat Syria, and to transform Israel's relations with Lebanon. But this attempt to break the two "vicious cycles" of conflict in Lebanon and in Israel/Palestine in one swift stroke backfired. Indeed, although Israel did manage to drive the PLO out of Lebanon and

Conclusion 221

to inflict heavy losses on Syria, Bashir Gemayel, Israel's main Lebanese ally, was assassinated; Israel was blamed for the Sabra and Shatila Massacre perpetrated by its Maronite ally, the Lebanese Forces militia; and the Palestinian issue, instead of disappearing, became even more pronounced.

When Israel later encountered guerrilla attacks, this time by Lebanese party-militias, it decided on a partial withdrawal from Lebanon in 1985 and the establishment of a "security zone" in the Israeli–Lebanese border area, to be run by its proxy, the SLA. However, the result, according to one Israeli military commander, was that "Hizbullah transformed from a rejected terrorist organization, which acts against the wish of the central government in Lebanon, into a legitimate resistance movement of the Lebanese people to the Israeli occupation."[1] Only in 2000, almost a decade after the end of the civil war in Lebanon, did Israel decide on a full withdrawal from its "security zone." However, by then the two conflicts in Lebanon and in Israel/Palestine had become intertwined, as demonstrated in the War between Israel and Hizbullah in 2006 but also in previous military incidents.

Let us conclude this book by considering some of the broader conclusions and implications of the discussion of each of Lebanon and Israel/ Palestine, of how they stand in relation to one another, and of their mutual relations.

The first observation is that the processes of state formation, intercommunal relations, and security in Lebanon and in Israel/Palestine, as well as the inter-linkages between these three spheres, have been markedly different from the Western "model." This suggests that cases from non-Western regions, including the Middle East, might be more relevant when attempting to better comprehend these two cases, but also when asking about the broader relevance of the findings from their analysis.

In terms of their process of state formation, Lebanon and Israel/ Palestine are similar to other postcolonial states where foreign, especially European, influences enmeshed with local factors and gave rise to hybrid political entities. The majority of Middle Eastern states fall within this category. In particular, the two cases are comparable to non-Western states that have expanded before or after 1945, whether formally or informally, such as Morocco and Western Sahara, China and Tibet, Turkey and North Cyprus and, most recently, Russia and the Crimean Peninsula. Historical cases include Jordan and the West Bank (1949–1967), Indonesia and East Timor (1975–1999), and Syria and Lebanon (1976–2005). In all of these cases, it would be interesting to ask

[1] Tamir (2005, 65).

how the state's expansion (and, where relevant, also its contraction) has affected its process of state formation and its various dimensions. At the same time, the continued existence of the expanded state in Israel/ Palestine and in Lebanon makes these two cases markedly different from Western states that expanded but later contracted, such as France and Algeria and Great Britain and Ireland; from multi-communal states that disintegrated, such as Yugoslavia and the Soviet Union; and from states where the solution to an inter-communal conflict was partition, such as Ethiopia and Eritrea and Sudan and South Sudan.

As for their patterns of inter-communal relations, Israel/Palestine and Lebanon are comparable to other divided societies that witnessed periods of power sharing, control, repression, and stalemate, as well as to cases that have shifted from one pattern to another. Singapore, Jordan, Turkey, and South Africa under Apartheid are relevant cases of inter-communal control, though some of them have also witnessed periods of repression. South Africa, however, later established a more equitable pattern of inter-communal relations. Syria and Iraq have oscillated between control and repression: In 2003, following the US-led invasion of Iraq, a new regime, which adopted some markers of power sharing but was considered by many Iraqis (especially Sunnis) as characterized by inter-communal control, was installed in Baghdad, but a rebellion ("insurgency") broke out and the result has been a stalemate and the rise of violent transnational non-state actors such as the Islamic State which engaged in repression. In Syria, protests against the Alawi-dominated regime of President Bashar al-Assad in 2011 were met by repression on the part of the regime and its security sector, and the result, too, was a stalemate. Importantly, in both cases the state failed to exercise control over its borders, and this allowed violent transnational non-state actors to enter its territory. Indeed, since 2011, these two conflicts, separated by a porous border, have also become intertwined.

Finally, in the area of security, Lebanon and Israel/Palestine can be juxtaposed to other "small states" that attempted to cope with domestic and external challenges to their security. In particular, they can be compared to small states where one community has dominated the security sector – including its composition; its command and controlling bodies; its identity; and its actual operation – and to states where the security sector is shared by all communities. As far as Israel is concerned, it has been compared to South Africa under Apartheid and to Singapore, but it – and even more so Israel/Palestine – can also be compared to other relevant cases, such as Turkey, Iraq, and Syria. In the former case, Turks have presided over the security sector and employed it to suppress the Kurds; in Iraq, Sunnis dominated the security sector until 2003 but were nearly excluded from it after the US-led invasion, when it became dominated by Shi'is and Kurds; and in Syria, Alawites have dominated the security sector since the early 1970s and are currently struggling to preserve its cohesion in the face of a largely Sunni rebellion.

The triangular relationship between the state, community, and security in Lebanon and in Israel/Palestine is also comparable to other cases. The Lebanese case can be compared to other places where the weakening of the state led to communal mobilization and conflict (e.g., in the former Yugoslavia), whereas Israel/Palestine is comparable to cases where the state resorted to repression in the face of communally based grievances (e.g., in Serbia, South Africa, Syria, and Iraq before 2003), but also to cases where the state attempted to remain aloof from the inter-communal conflict (e.g., Britain in Northern Ireland). At the same time, it seems worthwhile to compare Lebanon and Israel/Palestine to cases where peaceful settlements were reached, such as Northern Ireland and South Africa, but also to cases where peace processes were less successful (e.g., Cyprus). While certain comparisons between some of these cases have been made, more systematic multi-case comparisons that focus on the triangular relationship between the state, community, and security – but that also consider the inter-connected question of how the states have related to one another – are still wanting.

Indeed, on a more general level, this book has demonstrated that in addition to asking how particular states or other political actors are related to each other, a question that is generally answered by comparing them and identifying similarities and differences, it is also worthwhile to think how the main characteristics of these cases are reflected in the ways these actors relate to one another, including their perception of themselves and of the other, as well as their actual behavior toward one another. In this way, the gap between comparative politics and International Relations – both of which deal with states' relations – can be reduced.

As far as Israel/Palestine and Lebanon are concerned, it is quite clear that the main features of the two cases, which changed over time, affected their mutual relations both in the more stable periods and in the more volatile ones. It would be interesting to examine the relations between Israel and its other neighbors – Arab and non-Arab – including detailed comparisons between Israel and these other cases and an examination of their relations, and to see whether this strategy can help better comprehend them. But examining other states' relations – that is, how they are related to each other and how they actually relate to each other, as well as the linkages between these two types of relations – also seems promising.

What can be done to stop the vicious cycle of conflict in Israel/Palestine and, inter-connectedly, in the convoluted relations between Israel/

Palestine and Lebanon? The underlying premise of Lebanon's pattern of peacemaking, which has parallels elsewhere (e.g., in Northern Ireland and South Africa), is the acknowledgment by all sides of the existence of a divided society. This must also be applied to Israel/Palestine, where, as mentioned earlier, many Israelis and Palestinians still believe they can realize their maximalist national visions without conceding to, or even recognizing, the other side. Once the existence of a divided society has been acknowledged by all sides, different ways of regulating intercommunal relations can be devised, including by learning from the experience of others, such as Lebanon. However, the continued denial of the existence of a divided society in Israel/Palestine – as seen, for example, in the Oslo Agreement and in later peacemaking efforts, all of which ended in failure – seems less likely to break the "vicious cycle" of Israeli suppression and Palestinian resistance.

Turning to the relations between Israel/Palestine and Lebanon, this book has shown that the period 1949–1967, which was the most tranquil in Israeli–Lebanese relations, was characterized by mutual respect of the states' sovereignty, as well as by abiding by the Armistice Agreement and operating within the framework of ILMAC. Therefore, it seems useful to resort to such "statist" mechanisms to stabilize the two states' relations. At the same time, Israeli and Lebanese leaders can seek outside help in finding mutually accepted solutions to contentious issues such as the Shebaa Farms, which violent non-state actors such as Hizbullah have managed to exploit. While none of these measures can guarantee peace and stability in the two states' relations, the historical record suggests that they are preferable to all other options.

Beyond the attempts to cope with, and alleviate, the conflicts in Israel/Palestine and between the latter and Lebanon, efforts – by the two states and by international actors – should focus on disentangling these two issues, which, as suggested earlier, have become closely intertwined, not least because of the self-interested actions of political actors on both sides. Such a separation might also benefit other situations (e.g., Iraq and Syria) where intrastate conflicts have become inter-linked with relations between neighboring states, a situation that has provided ample opportunities for violent transnational non-state actors.

Many Israelis, Palestinians, and Lebanese, as well as numerous other families in the present-day Middle East, are currently unhappy in their own way. But by learning more about one another's experience both in the past and at present – including possible similarities and differences between them – the future of these families can, perhaps, be less bleak.

Bibliography

Films

Alef Eliminate Them – The Order that Shook the General Security Service (Levi Zini and Gidi Weitz, 2012).
Battle of the Undead [Hebrew title: *Cannon Fodder*] (Eitan Gafny, 2013).
Beaufort (Joseph Cedar, 2007).
Civilisées [English title: *A Civilized People*] (Randa Chahal-Sabbag, 1999).
Cup Final (Eran Riklis, 1991).
Lebanon (Samuel Maoz, 2009).
Ricochet [Hebrew title: *Two Fingers from Sidon*] (Eli Cohen and the Film Unit of the IDF Spokesman Unit, 1986).
The Gatekeepers (Dror Moreh, 2012).
The Kite [French title: *Le cerf-volant*] (Randa Chahal-Sabbag, 2003).
Time for Cherries (Haim Buzaglo, 1991).
Waltz with Bashir (Ari Folman, 2008).

Documents and Reports

Abou Lteif, Eduardo W. 2015. "What Iraq's Army Can Learn from Lebanon." *Daily Star* [Beirut], February 9, at: www.dailystar.com.lb/Opinion/Comment ary/2015/Feb-09/286826-what-iraqs-army-can-learn-from-lebanon.ashx (accessed July 9, 2015).
Al-Sulh, Riad. 1943. "Speech by Prime Minister Riad al-Sulh, Delivered in the Lebanese Chamber of Deputies, October 7, 1943." In *The Arab States and the Arab League: A Documentary Record*, ed. Muhammad Khalil. Beirut: Khayats, 1962, 2 Vols., 1:105–109.
Arafat, Yasser. 1994. "Nobel Lecture," at: www.nobelprize.org/nobel_prizes/pe ace/laureates/1994/arafat-lecture.html (accessed May 30, 2015).
Assad, Hafez. 1976. "Hafez al-Assad Speech, 20 July 1976," at: http://en.wikisource .org/wiki/Hafez_al-Assad_speech,_20_July_1976 (accessed June 10, 2015).
Avnery, Uri. 1995. "Is This What We Are Dying For?" *Maariv*, April 10 [Hebrew].
Avnery, Uri. 1997. "The Real War." *The Other Israel*, July–August, at: www.hag alil.com/israel/GuShalom/other_israel/uri-trw.htm (accessed June 11, 2015).
Avnery, Uri. 2014. "The Imperator." *Washington Report on Middle East Affairs*, March/April, at: www.wrmea.org/2014-march-april/two-views-ariel-sharon-1 928–2014.html (accessed November 23, 2016).

Bibliography

Barnea, Nachum. 2000. "Uri Lubrani Gets Out of Lebanon." *Yedioth Ahronoth*, June 23 [Hebrew].
BBC News. 2014. "Ukraine Crisis: Putin Signs Russia-Crimea Treaty." BBC News, March 14, at: www.bbc.com/news/world-europe-26630062 (accessed May 18, 2015).
Bechor, Guy. 1995. "Let the Syrians Restore Order." *Haaretz*, April 10 [Hebrew].
The Beirut Declaration. 2004. *The Daily Star*, July 9, at: www.dailystar.com.lb/News/Middle-East/2004/Jul-09/63458-the-beirut-declaration.ashx (accessed February 7, 2015).
Benn, Aluf. 1996. "AMAN's Estimate: Saddam Hussein's Regime Is Still Stable." *Haaretz*, January 8 [Hebrew].
Ben-Simon, Daniel. 2008. "Delusions of Lebanon." *Haaretz*, April 10 [Hebrew].
Ben-Yishai, Ron. 2012. "Barrages of Fire and Barrages of Rice: 30 Years to the First Lebanon War." *Ynet*, June 4, at: www.ynet.co.il/articles/0,7340,L-4234086,00.html (accessed June 9, 2015) [Hebrew].
Berger, Yotam. 2016a. "Secret 1970 Document Confirms First West Bank Settlements Built on a Lie." *Haaretz*, July 28, at: www.haaretz.com/israel-news/.premium-1.733746 (accessed November 27, 2016).
Berger, Yotam. 2016b. "Secret Documents Reveal How Israel Tried to Evade International Scrutiny of Occupation." *Haaretz*, September 20, at: www.haaretz.com/israel-news/.premium-1.742757 (accessed November 25, 2016).
Bergman, Ronen. 1995. "Under Hizbullah's Nose." *Haaretz*, October 27 [Hebrew].
Bergman, Ronen. 1997. "The Gamble." *Haaretz*, January 3 [Hebrew].
Bergman, Ronen. 2015. "The Hezbollah Connection." *New York Times*, February 10, at: www.nytimes.com/2015/02/15/magazine/the-hezbollah-connection.html (accessed May 29, 2015).
Bronner, Ethan. 2011. "Hamas Leader Calls for Two-State Solution, but Refuses to Renounce Violence," *New York Times*, May 5, at: www.nytimes.com/2011/05/06/world/middleeast/06palestinians.html (accessed November 18, 2016).
Browne, Walter L., ed. 1976/7. *The Political History of Lebanon, 1920–1950*. 2 Vols. Salisbury, NC: Documentary Publications.
B'Tselem. n.d. "Fatalities in the First Intifada," at: www.btselem.org/statistics/first_intifada_tables (accessed May 27, 2015).
B'Tselem. 2002. *Land Grab: Israel's Settlement Policy in the West Bank*. Jerusalem, at: www.btselem.org/download/200205_land_grab_eng.pdf (accessed January 8, 2015).
B'Tselem. 2011. "The Separation Barrier," at: www.btselem.org/separation_barrier (accessed March 1, 2015).
B'Tselem. 2015. "Statistics on Settlements and Settler Population." May 11, 2015, at: www.btselem.org/settlements/statistics (accessed May 26, 2015).
Chamoun, Camille. 1955. "Presidential Decree by President Camille Chamoun Granting Amnesty to the Hermel Tribesmen as per General Chehab's Request." August 18, 1955, at: www.fouadchehab.com/doc/doc/off/amnsty55.jpg (accessed May 5, 2015) [Arabic].

Cohen, Gili. 2014. "Reservists from Elite IDF Intel Unit Refuse to Serve over Palestinian 'Persecution.'" *Haaretz*, September 12, at: www.haaretz.com/news/diplomacy-defense/1.615498 (accessed May 30, 2015).

Corm, Georges. 2006. "Lebanon: No 'Civil War' This Time." *Le Monde diplomatique*, September, at: http://mondediplo.com/2006/09/02lebanon (accessed February 13, 2015).

The Declaration of the Establishment of the State of Israel. May 14, 1948. At: www.mfa.gov.il/mfa/foreignpolicy/peace/guide/pages/declaration%20of%20establishment%20of%20state%20of%20israel.aspx (accessed February 7, 2015).

DellaPergola, Sergio. 2011. *Jewish Demographic Policies: Population Trends and Options in Israel and in the Diaspora*. Jerusalem: Jewish People Policy Planning Institute, at: http://jppi.org.il/uploads/Jewish_Demographic_Policies.pdf (accessed November 14, 2016).

Douglas, Ted. 1975. "Christian Apathy Assailed." *Detroit News*, October 28.

Eban, Abba. 1969. Interview with *Der Spiegel*, January 27, at: www.spiegel.de/spiegel/print/d-45861331.html (accessed June 11, 2015) [German].

Eglash, Ruth. 2015. "Does Israel Actually Occupy the Gaza Strip?" *Washington Post*, July 2, at: www.washingtonpost.com/news/worldviews/wp/2015/07/02/does-israel-actually-occupy-the-gaza-strip/?utm_term=.038a59cf9212 (accessed December 7, 2016).

Eldar, Akiva, and Ori Nir. 1991. "Israel Is Ready to Discuss a Withdrawal in Conditions of Peace." *Haaretz*, December 11 [Hebrew].

Foreign Affairs and Security Committee. 1975. Protocol No. 121 of Meeting of the Foreign Affairs and Security Committee, Israeli Knesset, March 6, 1975, 16:00, Israel State Archives (ISA), at: https://drive.google.com/a/mail.huji.ac.il/file/d/0B2Ly-x55KRNqdmtqdDY0VUJDNDQ/edit (accessed June 30, 2015) [Hebrew].

Freedom House. 2014. *Freedom in the World 2014*, at: http://freedomhouse.org/sites/default/files/Freedom%20in%20the%20World%202014%20Booklet.pdf (accessed September 25, 2014).

Freedom House. 2015. "Individual Country Ratings and Status, FIW 1973–2015," at: https://freedomhouse.org/report-types/freedom-world#.VTqRr9JViko (accessed April 24, 2015).

Friedman, Thomas L. 1986. "The Israeli Army Films Its Troubles in Lebanon." *New York Times*, June 11.

FRUS (*Foreign Relations of the United States*). 2010. 1969–1976, Vol. 26, Arab–Israeli Dispute, 1974–1976, ed. Adam M. Howard. Washington: Government Printing Office.

FRUS (*Foreign Relations of the United States*). 2013. 1976–1980, Vol. 8, Arab–Israeli Dispute, January 1977–August 1978, ed. Adam M. Howard. Washington: Government Printing Office.

FRUS (*Foreign Relations of the United States*). 2014. 1977–1980, Vol. 9, Arab–Israeli Dispute, August 1978–December 1980, ed. Alexander R. Wieland. Washington: Government Printing Office.

Gilad, Amos. 2011. "Israeli Official Warns from the Threat of 'Hizbullastan.'" *Naharnet*, April 11, at: www.naharnet.com/stories/en/5165 (accessed May 5, 2015).

Goldman, Adam, and Ellen Nakashima. 2015. "CIA and Mossad killed senior Hezbollah figure in car bombing," *Washington Post*, January 30, at: www.washingtonpost.com/world/national-security/cia-and-mossad-killed-senior-hezbollah-figure-in-car-bombing/2015/01/30/ebb88682-968a-11e4-8005-1924ede3e54a_story.html?utm_term=.dc137edcca36 (accessed December 3, 2016).

Goren, Yehuda, Yonatan Hilleli, and Arie Bender. 1997. "If We Withdraw Unilaterally from Lebanon the Terrorists Will Reach the Border Fence." *Maariv*, February 12 [Hebrew].

Guardian. 2014. "Syria Conflict Pits Shia Against Sunni as Hezbollah Says This Is 'War We Must Win.'" *The Guardian*, January 1, at: www.theguardian.com/world/2014/jan/01/syria-shia-sunni-hezbollah-war (accessed June 11, 2015).

Harel, Amos. 2015. "How Israel Keeps Palestinians Off a Third of All West Bank Land." *Haaretz*, September 25, at: www.haaretz.com/news/diplomacy-defense/.premium-1.677426 (accessed September 29, 2015).

Haaretz. 1969. "Allon: I Would Not Like to See Lebanon in Jordan's Situation." *Haaretz*, January 26 [Hebrew].

Haaretz. 1991. "Lebanon Demands from the U.S. a Commitment for Israel's Withdrawal." *Haaretz*, September 26 [Hebrew].

Haaretz. 1992. "Arens: 'Musawi's Death Was Not Incidental. This Is a Message to All Terrorist Groups." *Haaretz*, February 17 [Hebrew].

Harkabi, Yehoshafat. 1995. Interview of Yehoshafat Harkabi by Pinhas Genosar and Zaki Shalom (January 14, 1994). *Iyunim Bitkumat Israel* 5: 1–20 [Hebrew].

Herlitz, Ester. 2012. "'Palestinians' – Unmentionable." August 17, *Haaretz*, at: www.haaretz.co.il/opinions/letters/1.1803579 (accessed June 5, 2015) [Hebrew].

International Crisis Group. 2008. *Lebanon: Hizbollah's Weapons Turn Inward.* Middle East Briefing N°23. Beirut/Brussels, May 15, at: www.crisisgroup.org/middle-east-north-africa/eastern-mediterranean/lebanon/lebanon-hizbollah-s-weapons-turn-inward (accessed April 22, 2017).

Iskander, Abdullah. 2008. "Bashir Gemayel and Hassan Nasrallah." *Al-Arabiya News*, May 15, at: www.alarabiya.net/views/2008/05/15/49884.html (accessed July 10, 2015).

Israeli Knesset. 1982. 95th Meeting of the 10th Knesset, June 8, at: http://knesset.gov.il/tql/knesset_new/knesset10/HTML_27_03_2012_05–50-30-PM/19820608@19820608001@001.html (accessed February 7, 2015) [Hebrew].

Israeli Government. 1958. Protocol of Meeting of the Israeli Government, July 17. ISA [Hebrew].

Israeli Government. 1967. Protocol of Meeting of the Israeli Government, June 18, at: www.archives.gov.il/archives/#/Archive/0b0717068031be30/File/0b07170680348bd6/Item/0907170680348cff (accessed April 22, 2017) [Hebrew].

Israeli Government. 1983. ISA, 4282/A-2, Protocol of Meeting of the Israeli Government, February 8, at: www.archives.gov.il/archives/#/Archive/0b0717068031be30/File/0b07170682943130/Item/0907170682e16c71 (accessed April 22, 2017).

Israeli Government. 2011 [1973]. Protocol of Meeting of the Israeli Government, October 6, at: www.haaretz.co.il/hasite/images/yk%206%2010%2008%2005%20.pdf (accessed April 22, 2017) [Hebrew].

Jerusalem Post. 1969. "Israel, Lebanon, Meet to Discuss Cease-Fire." January 7.

Kashti, Or. 2014. "The Study of History in the Service of the National Effort." *Haaretz*, August 22 [Hebrew].
Kristal, Meirav. 2014. "Anger at the Coffee Chain: Published a Map with the '67 Borders." *Ynet*, October 1, at: www.ynet.co.il/articles/0,7340,L-4576874,00.html (accessed February 7, 2015) [Hebrew].
Laqueur, Walter, and Barry M. Rubin, eds. 2001. *The Israel-Arab Reader: A Documentary History of the Middle East Conflict*. New York: Penguin.
Lebanese Constitution. 1960. Beirut: American University of Beirut.
Lewis, Samuel L. 1998. Interview by Peter Jessup, August 9. The Association for Diplomatic Studies and Training Foreign Affairs Oral History Project, at: www.adst.org/OH%20TOCs/Lewis,%20Samuel%20W.toc.pdf (accessed November 23, 2016).
Luttwak, Edward N. 2013. "Keep Syria in a Stalemate." *International Herald Tribune*, August 24–25.
Mehlis Report. 2005. *Report of the International Independent Investigation Commission Established Pursuant to Security Council Resolution 1595 (2005)*, 19 October, at: www.un.org/News/dh/docs/mehlisreport (accessed April 26, 2015).
Merhav, Reuven. 1993. "A Late Perspective." *Haaretz*, November 17 [Hebrew].
Naharnet. 2016. "Hizbullah Denies Qassem Said Party Has 'an Army'," November 16, at: www.naharnet.com/stories/en/220413-hizbullah-denies-qassem-said-party-has-an-army (accessed November 16, 2016).
New York Times. 2008. "Syria and Lebanon Establish First Full Diplomatic Relations." *New York Times*, August 13, at: www.nytimes.com/2008/08/13/world/africa/13iht-syria.4.15257847.html (accessed May 29, 2015).
Palestinian Central Bureau of Statistics [PCBS]. 2003. *Palestinians at the End of Year 2003*. Ramallah: Palestinian Central Bureau of Statistics, at: www.pcbs.gov.ps/Portals/_PCBS/Downloads/book1027.pdf (accessed January 8, 2015) [Arabic].
Palestinian Central Bureau of Statistics [PCBS]. 2013. *Palestinians at the End of Year 2013*. Ramallah: Palestinian Central Bureau of Statistics, at: www.pcbs.gov.ps/Portals/_PCBS/Downloads/book2028.pdf (accessed January 16, 2015) [Arabic].
Palestine Mandate. 1922. At: http://avalon.law.yale.edu/20th_century/palmanda.asp (accessed December 16, 2014).
Peace Now. 2016a. "Population," at: http://peacenow.org.il/en/settlements-watch/settlements-data/population (accessed November 13, 2016).
Peace Now. 2016b. "Jerusalem," at: http://peacenow.org.il/en/settlements-watch/settlements-data/jerusalem (accessed November 13, 2016).
Peres, Shimon. 2006. "Testimony of Mr. Shimon Peres, the Winograd Commission," at: www.vaadatwino.gov.il/pdf/%D7%9E%D7%A1%D7%9E%D7%9A%20%D7%91-%20%D7%A9%D7%9E%D7%A2%D7%95%D7%9F%20%D7%A4%D7%A8%D7%A1.pdf (accessed February 13, 2015) [Hebrew].
Pfeffer, Anshel. 2014. "Unit 8200 Refuseniks Shed Light on Ethics of Israel's Intel Gathering." *Haaretz*, September 15, at: www.haaretz.com/news/diplomacy-defense/.premium-1.615811 (accessed May 30, 2015).

Pipes, Daniel. 2001. "Israel's Lebanon Lesson." *Jerusalem Post*, May 23.
Rabin, Eitan, Gideon Alon, and Amira Segev. 1997. "Major General Levin Is the Official Who Supported a Withdrawal from Lebanon," *Haaretz*, November [Hebrew].
Ravid, Barak. 2015. "Kerry at Saban Forum: Current Trends Are Leading to a One-state Reality," *Haaretz*, December 5, at: www.haaretz.com/israel-news/1.690205 (accessed November 24, 2016).
Ravid, Barak. 2016. "Israel and Palestinians Are Headed for Binational State, World Must Act or Shut Up," *Haaretz*, September 25, at: www.haaretz.com/israel-news/.premium-1.744060 (accessed December 19, 2016).
Reagan Plan. 1982. "The Reagan Plan: U.S. Policy for Peace in the Middle East." September 1, Council of Foreign Relations Essential Documents, at: www.cfr.org/israel/reagan-plan-us-policy-peace-middle-east/p14140 (accessed June 30, 2015).
Saniora, Fouad. 2015. "Saniora before STL: I am Not in Position to Say that Hizbullah Assassinated Hariri." *Naharnet*, March 25, at: http://m.naharnet.com/stories/en/173027-saniora-before-stl-i-am-not-in-position-to-say-that-hizbullah-assassinated-hariri (accessed April 26, 2015).
Sarid, Yossi. 2006. "No Answers, and No Questions Either." *Haaretz*, December 27, at: www.haaretz.com/print-edition/opinion/no-answers-and-no-questions-either-1.208306 (accessed February 7, 2015).
Sasson, Talia. 2005. *Opinion Concerning Unauthorized Outposts*. at: www.pmo.gov.il/SiteCollectionDocuments/PMO/Communication/Spokesman/sason2.pdf (accessed May 27, 2015) [Hebrew].
Schiff, Ze'ev. 1970. "South Lebanon: A No-mans' Land." *Haaretz*, May 24 [Hebrew].
Schiff, Ze'ev. 1983. "The Green Light." *Foreign Policy* 50: 73–85.
Shalev, Hemi. 1997. "Shamir Bombards." *Maariv*, February 21 [Hebrew].
Sharon, Ariel. 2003. "An Interview with PM Sharon." *The Daily Telegraph*, July 12.
Shavit, Ari. 2002. "The Enemy from Within," *Haaretz*, August 29, at: www.haaretz.com/the-enemy-within-1.35604 (accessed November 18, 2016).
Shavit, Ari. 2004. "Top PM Aide: Gaza Plan Aims to Freeze the Peace Process." *Haaretz*, October 6, at: www.haaretz.com/print-edition/news/top-pm-aide-gaza-plan-aims-to-freeze-the-peace-process-1.136686 (accessed May 29, 2015).
Sheffler, Gil S. 2010. "'Jews now a minority between the River and the Sea'." *Jerusalem Post*, November 26, at: www.jpost.com/printarticle.aspx?id=196877 (accessed November 14, 2016).
Shipler, David K. 2002. "Soothing Israel's Fears." *New York Times*, January 7, at: www.nytimes.com/2002/01/07/opinion/soothing-israel-s-fears.html (accessed May 29, 2015).
State of Israel vs. Yigal Amir. 1996. March 27, at: www.nevo.co.il/Psika_word/mechozi/M-PE-2-003-L.doc (accessed April 22, 2017) [Hebrew].
Sternhell, Zeev. 2015. "From a Curfew on Taibeh to a Military Government in Nablus." *Haaretz*, May 29, at: www.haaretz.co.il/opinions/.premium-1.2646942 (accessed May 29, 2015) [Hebrew].
Tal, Rami. 1997. "Moshe Dayan: Soul Searching," *Yedioth Ahronoth*, 27 April 1997 [Hebrew].

UN Archives. 1978. File S-0899–0008, Peacekeeping – Middle East 1945–1981, at: https://search.archives.un.org/uploads/r/united-nations-archives/4/6/5/465 c597ce8ea3f622ccfc21b666dcffd50c73181b310ff19071be08863dac70d/S-08 99-0008-07-00001.pdf (accessed April 22, 2017).
Weitz, Gidi. 2016. "Secret 1978 Talks Lay Bare the Hawk That Peacemaker Peres Once Was," *Haaretz*, October 11, at: www.haaretz.com/israel-news/.pre mium-1.747031 (accessed November 24, 2016).
Winograd Commission [The Commission of Inquiry into the Events of Military Engagement in Lebanon 2006]. 2007. *Interim Report*. At: www.vaadatwino.go v.il/pdf/%D7%93%D7%95%D7%97%20%D7%97%D7%9C%D7%A7%D 7%99.pdf (accessed February 13, 2015) [Hebrew].
Wong, Edward. 2006. "US Is Seeking Better Balance in Iraqi Police." *New York Times*, March 7.
Yaar, Ephraim, and Tamar Hermann. 2006. *Peace Index: December 2006*. Tel Aviv: Tel Aviv University, at: www.peaceindex.org/files/peacein dex2006_12_3.pdf (accessed April 22, 2017).

Articles and Books

Abu, Iyad [Salah Khalaf]. 1981. *My Home, My Land*. New York: Times.
Abul-Husn, Latif. 1998. *The Lebanese Conflict: Looking Inward*. Boulder: Lynne Rienner.
Ajami, Fouad. 1986. *The Vanished Imam: Musa Al Sadr and the Shia of Lebanon*. Ithaca: Cornell University Press.
Ajami, Fouad. 1992. *The Arab Predicament: Arab Political Thought and Practice since 1967*. 2nd edn. New York: Cambridge University Press.
Ajay, Nicholas Z., Jr. 1974. "Political Intrigue and Suppression in Lebanon during World War I." *International Journal of Middle East Studies* 5 (2): 140–160.
Akarli, Engin D. 1993. *The Long Peace: Ottoman Lebanon, 1861–1920*. Berkeley: University of California Press.
Alagappa, Muthia, ed. 2001. *Coercion and Governance: The Declining Political Role of the Military in Asia*. Stanford: Stanford University Press.
Alagha, Joseph E. 2011. *Hizbullah's Documents: From the 1985 Open Letter to the 2009 Manifesto*. Amsterdam: Amsterdam University Press.
Alimi, Eitan Y. 2007. *Israeli Politics and the First Palestinian Intifada: Political Opportunities, Framing Processes and Contentious Politics*. London: Routledge.
Alin, Erika G. 1994. *The United States and the 1958 Lebanon Crisis*. Lanham: University Press of America.
Almog, Shulamit. 2009. "From 'Paratroopers' to 'Waltz with Bashir': The Absence of Law from Israeli War Films." *Studies in Law, Politics, and Society* 50: 19–64.
Anderson, Benedict. 1991. *Imagined Communities: Reflections on the Origin and Spread of Nationalism*. 2nd edn. London: Verso.
Anderson, Lisa. 1987. "The State in the Middle East and North Africa." *Comparative Politics* 20 (1): 1–18.
Aoun, Fuad. 1988. *The Army Remains the Solution*. Lebanon: s.n. [Arabic].

Arendt, Hannah. 1963. *Eichmann in Jerusalem: A Report on the Banality of Evil*. New York: Viking Press.
Arendt, Hannah. 1973 [1951]. *The Origins of Totalitarianism*. 2nd edn. New York: Harcourt.
Aronson, Shlomo, and Dan Horowitz. 1971. "The Strategy of Controlled Reprisal: The Israeli Example." *State and Government* 1 (1): 77–99 [Hebrew].
Assi, Abbas, and James Worrall. 2015. "Stable Instability: The Syrian Conflict and the Postponement of the 2013 Lebanese Parliamentary Elections." *Third World Quarterly* 36 (10): 1944–1967.
Attié, Caroline. 2003. *Struggle in the Levant: Lebanon in the 1950s*. London: I.B. Tauris.
Atzili, Boaz. 2006. "When Good Fences Make Bad Neighbors: Fixed Borders, State Weakness, and International Conflict." *International Security* 31 (3): 139–173.
Atzili, Boaz. 2010. "State Weakness and 'Vacuum of Power' in Lebanon." *Studies in Conflict & Terrorism* 33 (8): 757–782.
Atzili, Boaz. 2011. *Good Fences, Bad Neighbors: Border Fixity and International Conflict*. Chicago: University of Chicago Press.
Avi-Ran [Erlich], Reuven. 1991. *The Syrian Involvement in Lebanon since 1975*. Boulder: Westview.
Ayoob, Mohammed. 1995. *The Third World Security Predicament: State Making, Regional Conflict, and the International System*. Boulder: Lynne Rienner.
Azar, Edward E., ed. 1984. *The Emergence of a New Lebanon: Fantasy or Reality?* New York: Praeger.
Azar, Edward E., and Robert F. Haddad. 1986. "Lebanon: An Anomalous Conflict?" *Third World Quarterly* 8 (4): 1337–1350.
Azoulay, Ariella, and Adi Ophir. 2012. *The One-State Condition: Occupation and Democracy in Israel/Palestine*. Stanford: Stanford University Press.
Baaklini, Abdo I. 1976. *Legislative and Political Development: Lebanon, 1842–1972*. Durham: Duke University Press.
Badran, Amneh. 2009. *Zionist Israel and Apartheid South Africa: Civil Society and Peace Building in Ethnic-National States*. London: Routledge.
Baer, Robert. 2002. *See No Evil: The True Story of a Ground Soldier in the CIA's War on Terrorism*. New York: Three Rivers.
Baqraduni [Pakradouni], Karim. 1984. *The Lost Peace*. Beirut: 'Abra al-Sharq lil-Manshurat [Arabic].
Barak, Oren. 2001. "Commemorating Malikiyya: Political Myth, Multiethnic Identity and the Making of the Lebanese Army." *History & Memory* 13 (1): 60–84.
Barak, Oren. 2002. "Intra-Communal and Inter-Communal Dimensions of Conflict and Peace in Lebanon." *International Journal of Middle East Studies* 34 (4): 619–644.
Barak, Oren. 2003. "Lebanon: Failure, Collapse, and Resuscitation." In *State Failure and State Weakness in a Time of Terror*, ed. Robert I. Rotberg, pp. 305–339. Washington, DC: The Brookings Institution Press.
Barak, Oren. 2005a. "The Failure of the Israeli–Palestinian Peace Process, 1993–2000." *Journal of Peace Research* 42 (6): 719–736.

Barak, Oren. 2005b. "National Visions and Multi-Communal Realities: Lebanon and Israel/Palestine in a Comparative Perspective." In *Arab–Jewish Relations: From Conflict to Resolution?*, eds. Elie Podeh and Asher Kaufman, pp. 169–189. Brighton: Sussex Academic Press.

Barak, Oren. 2006. "Towards a Representative Military? The Transformation of the Lebanese Officer Corps since 1945." *Middle East Journal* 60 (1): 75–93.

Barak, Oren. 2007a. "'Don't Mention the War?' The Politics of Remembrance and Forgetfulness in Postwar Lebanon." *Middle East Journal* 61 (1): 49–70.

Barak, Oren. 2007b. "Dilemmas of Security in Iraq." *Security Dialogue* 38 (4): 455–475.

Barak, Oren. 2009a. *The Lebanese Army: A National Institution in a Divided Society.* Albany: State University of New York Press.

Barak, Oren. 2009b. "National Visions and Multi-Communal Realities: Lebanon and Israel/Palestine in a Comparative Perspective." *Theory and Criticism* 35: 193–217 [Hebrew].

Barak, Oren. 2010. "Ambiguity and Conflict in Israeli–Lebanese Relations." *Israel Studies* 15 (3): 163–188.

Barak, Oren. 2012. "Representation and Stability in Postwar Lebanon." *Representation* 48 (3): 321–333.

Barak, Oren. 2014. "Civil-Security Relations in Israel: Looking through the Mirror." In *Civil–Military Relations in Israel: Essays in Honor of Stuart A. Cohen*, eds. Elisheva Rosman-Stollman and Aharon Kampinsky, pp. 29–45. Lanham: Lexington Books.

Barak, Oren. 2016. "Toward a Shared Vision of Israel and Israel/Palestine." In *Israel and Palestine: Alternative Perspectives on Statehood*, eds. John Ehrenberg and Yoav Peled, pp. 283–290. Lanham: Rowman & Littlefield.

Barak, Oren, and Chanan Cohen. 2014. "The Modern Sherwood Forest." In *Nonstate Actors in Intrastate Conflicts*, eds. Dan Miodownik and Oren Barak, pp. 12–33. Philadelphia: University of Pennsylvania Press.

Barak, Oren, and Gideon Rahat, eds. 2012. "Representation(s) in the Middle East." Special Issue of *Representation* 48 (3): 249–333.

Barak, Oren, and Eyal Tsur. 2012a. "The Military Careers and Second Careers of Israel's Military Elite, 1948–2010." *Middle East Journal* 66 (3): 473–492.

Barak, Oren, and Eyal Tsur. 2012b. "The Social Origins of Israel's Military Elite, 1948–2010." *Middle East Journal* 66 (2): 211–230.

Barakat, Cherbel R. 2011. *Madameek Courses: A Struggle for Peace in a Zone of War*. Trans. Maroun Sakr. Bloomington: AuthorHouse.

Barakat, Halim, ed. 1988. *Toward a Viable Lebanon*. London: Croom Helm.

Bareli, Avi. 2014. *Authority and Participation in a New Democracy: Political Struggles in Mapai, Israel's Ruling Party, 1948–1953*. Boston: Academic Studies Press.

Barnett, Michael N. 1992. *Confronting the Costs of War: Military Power, State, and Society in Egypt and Israel*. Princeton: Princeton University Press.

Barnett, Michael N. 1998. *Dialogues in Arab Politics*. New York: Columbia University Press.

Barnett, Michael N. 1999. "Culture, Strategy and Foreign Policy Change: Israel's Road to Oslo." *European Journal of International Relations* 5 (1): 5–36.
Barrington, Lowell. 1997. "'Nation' and 'Nationalism': The Misuse of Key Concepts in Political Science." *Political Science and Politics* 30 (4): 712–716.
Barry, Brian. 1975. "The Consociational Model and Its Dangers." *European Journal of Political Research* 3 (4): 393–412.
Bar-Siman-Tov, Yaacov. 2009. "Introduction." In *The Disengagement Plan – An Idea Shattered*, ed. Yaacov Bar-Siman-Tov, pp. 11–16. Jerusalem: The Jerusalem Institute for Israel Studies [Hebrew].
Bar-Tal, Daniel, Eran Halperin, and Tamir Magal. 2009. "The Paradox of Security Views in Israel: A Social-psychological Explanation." In *Existential Threats and Civil-Security Relations*, eds. Oren Barak and Gabriel Sheffer, pp. 219–248. Lanham: Lexington Books.
Bar-Tal, Daniel, and Izhak Schnell. 2013. *The Impacts of Lasting Occupation: Lessons from Israeli Society*. New York: Oxford University Press.
Bartov, Hanoch. 2002. *Daddo: 48 Years and 20 More Days*. 2nd edn. 2 Vols. Or Yehuda: Dvir [Hebrew].
Bar-Tuvia, Shani, and Oren Barak. 2014. "The Gatekeepers: A Critical Perspective." *Theory and Criticism* 43: 291–300 [Hebrew].
Bar-Yosef, Eitan. 2007. "A Villa in the Jungle: Herzl, Zionist Culture, and the Great African Adventure." In *Theodor Herzl between Europe and Zion*, eds. Mark Gelber and Vivian Liska, pp. 85–102. Tübingen: Niemeyer.
Bäuml, Yair. 2007. *A Blue and White Shadow: The Israeli Establishment's Policy and Actions among Its Arab Citizens: The Formative Years, 1958–1968*. Haifa: Pardes [Hebrew].
Becke, Johannes. 2014. "Towards a De-Occidentalist Perspective on Israel: The Case of the Occupation." *Journal of Israeli History* 33 (1): 1–23.
Beilin, Yossi. 2001. *Manual for a Wounded Dove*. Tel Aviv: Miskal [Hebrew].
Ben-Ami, Shlomo. 2004. *A Front without a Rearguard: A Voyage to the Boundaries of the Peace Process*. Tel Aviv: Miskal [Hebrew].
Ben-Ari, Eyal, Zeev Lerer, Uzi Ben-Shalom, and Ariel Vainer. 2010. *Rethinking Contemporary Warfare: A Sociological View of the Al-Aqsa Intifada*. Albany: State University of New York Press.
Ben-Eliezer, Uri. 1995. "A Nation-in-Arms: State, Nation, and Militarism in Israel's First Years." *Comparative Studies in Society and History* 37 (2): 264–285.
Ben-Eliezer, Uri. 1997. "Rethinking the Civil-Military Relations Paradigm: The Inverse Relation between Militarism and Praetorianism through the Example of Israel." *Comparative Political Studies* 30 (3): 356–374.
Ben-Eliezer, Uri. 1998a. "Is a Military Coup Possible in Israel? Israel and French-Algeria in Comparative Historical-Sociological Perspective." *Theory and Society* 27 (3): 311–349.
Ben-Eliezer, Uri. 1998b. *The Making of Israeli Militarism*. Bloomington: Indiana University Press.
Ben-Eliezer, Uri. 2012. *Old Conflict, New War: Israel's Politics toward the Palestinians*. New York: Palgrave Macmillan.
Ben-Porat, Guy. 2006. *Global Liberalism, Local Populism*. Syracuse: Syracuse University Press.

Benvenisti, Eyal. 2012. *The International Law of Occupation*. Oxford: Oxford University Press.
Benvenisti, Meron. 1984. *The West Bank Data Project: A Survey of Israel's Policies*. Washington, DC: American Enterprise Institute for Public Policy Research.
Benvenisti, Meron. 1986. *Conflicts and Contradictions*. New York: Villard Books.
Benvenisti, Meron. 1995. *Intimate Enemies: Jews and Arabs in a Shared Land*. Berkeley: University of California Press.
Benvenisti, Meron. 2007. *Son of the Cypresses: Memories, Reflections, and Regrets from a Political Life*. Berkeley: University of California Press.
Ben-Yehuda, Nachman. 1996. *The Masada Myth: Collective Memory and Mythmaking in Israel*. Madison: University of Wisconsin Press.
Benziman, Yuval. 2013. "'Mom, I'm Home': Israeli Lebanon–War Films as Inadvertent Preservers of the National Narrative." *Israel Studies* 18 (3): 112–132.
Bergman, Ronen. 2009. *By Any Means Necessary: Israel's Covert War for Its POWs and MIAs*. Or Yehuda: Kinneret, Zmora-Bitan, Dvir [Hebrew].
Bhavnani, Ravi, Dan Miodownik, and Hyun Jin Choi. 2011. "Three Two Tango: Territorial Control and Selective Violence in Israel, the West Bank, and Gaza." *Journal of Conflict Resolution* 55 (1): 133–158.
Bilgin, Pinar, and Adam D. Morton. 2004. "From 'Rogue' to 'Failed' States? The Fallacy of Short-termism." *Politics* 24 (3): 169–180.
Binder, Leonard, ed. 1966. *Politics in Lebanon*. New York: Wiley.
Birkenstein, Jeff, Anna Froula, and Karen Randell, eds. 2010. *Reframing 9/11: Film, Popular Culture and the "War on Terror."* New York: Continuum.
Bishara, Marwan. 2001. *Palestine/Israel: Peace or Apartheid: Prospects for Resolving the Conflict*. London: Zed Books.
Blanford, Nicholas. 2006. *Killing Mr. Lebanon: The Assassination of Rafik Hariri and Its Impact on the Middle East*. London: I.B. Tauris.
Blum, Gabriella. 2007. *Islands of Agreement: Managing Enduring Armed Rivalries*. Cambridge, MA: Harvard University Press.
Bou-Nacklie, N.E. 1993. "Les Troupes Spéciales: Religious and Ethnic Recruitment, 1916–46." *International Journal of Middle East Studies* 25 (4): 645–660.
Bou-Nacklie, N.E. 1994. "The 1941 Invasion of Syria and Lebanon: The Role of the Local Paramilitary." *Middle Eastern Studies* 30 (3): 355–373.
Bowen, Jeremy. 2013. *Six Days: How the 1967 War Shaped the Middle East*. New York: Macmillan.
Brecher, Michael. 1972. *The Foreign Policy System of Israel: Setting, Images, Process*. New Haven: Yale University Press.
Bregman, Ahron. 2014. *Cursed Victory: A History of Israel and the Occupied Territories*. London: Allen Lane.
Brynen, Rex. 1990. *Sanctuary and Survival: The PLO in Lebanon*. Boulder: Westview.
Buheiry, Marwan. 1987. "External Interventions and Internal Wars in Lebanon: 1770–1982." In *The Formation and Perception of the Modern Arab World: Studies by Marwan R. Buheiry*, ed. Laurence I. Conard, pp. 129–139. Princeton: Darwin Press.

Burk, James. 2002. "Theories of Democratic Civil-Military Relations." *Armed Forces & Society* 29 (1): 7–29.
Burns, E.L.M. 1962. *Between Arab and Israeli*. Toronto: Clarke, Irwin.
Buzan, Barry, Ole Wæver, and Japp De Wilde. 1998. *Security: A New Framework for Analysis*. Boulder: Lynne Rienner.
Byrne, Sean. 1999. "Israel, Northern Ireland, and South Africa at a Crossroads: Understanding Intergroup Conflict, Peace-Building, and Conflict Resolution." *International Journal of Group Tensions* 28 (3–4): 231–253.
Cammett, Melani. 2014. *Compassionate Communalism: Welfare and Sectarianism in Lebanon*. Ithaca: Cornell University Press.
Cawthra, Gavin, and Robin Luckham, eds. 2003. *Governing Insecurity: Democratic Control of Military and Security*. London: Zed.
Cederman, Lars-Erik, Andreas Wimmer, and Brian Min. 2010. "Why Do Ethnic Groups Rebel? New Data and Analysis." *World Politics* 62 (1): 87–119.
Chalouhi, Robert G. 1978. "The Crisis in Lebanon: A Test of Consociational Democracy." PhD Thesis, University of Florida.
Chamberlin, Paul T. 2012. *The Global Offensive: The United States, the Palestine Liberation Organization, and the Making of the Post-Cold War Order*. New York: Oxford University Press.
Chamoun, Camille. 1963. *Crise au Moyen-Orient*. Paris: Gallimard.
Chamoun, Camille. 1977. *Crisis in Lebanon*. Beirut: Al-Fikr al-Hurr [Arabic].
Chandra, Kanchan. 2009. "Making Causal Claims about the Effect of Ethnicity." In *Comparative Politics: Rationality, Culture, and Structure*, eds. Mark Lichbach and Alan Zuckerman, 2nd edn., pp. 376–381. Cambridge: Cambridge University Press.
Chatarjee, Partha, 1993. *The Nation and Its Fragments*. Princeton: Princeton University Press.
Chiha, Michel. 1966. *Lebanon: At Home and Abroad*. Beirut: Cénacle Libanais.
Childs, Steven G. 2012. "Points of the Star, Branches of the Cedar: Israeli and Lebanese Military Integration Policies." *Democracy and Security* 8 (3): 247–265.
Cizre, Ümit. 2001. "Turkey's Kurdish Problem: Borders, Identity and Hegemony." In *Right-Sizing the State: The Politics of Moving Borders*, eds. Brendan O'Leary, Ian Lustick, and Thomas Callaghy, pp. 222–252. New York: Oxford University Press.
Cohen, Avner. 1998. *Israel and the Bomb*. New York: Columbia University Press.
Cohen, Avner. 2013. *The Worst-Kept Secret: Israel's Bargain with the Bomb*. New York: Columbia University Press.
Cohen, Hillel. 2008. *Army of Shadows: Palestinian Collaboration with Zionism, 1917–1948*. Berkeley: University of California Press.
Cohen, Hillel. 2010. *Good Arabs: The Israeli Security Agencies and the Israeli Arabs, 1948–1967*. Berkeley: University of California Press.
Collings, Deirdre, ed. 1994. *Peace for Lebanon?* Boulder: Lynne Rienner.
Connor, Walker. 1994. *Ethnonationalism*. Princeton: Princeton University Press.
Cooke, Miriam. 1988. *War's Other Voices: Women Writers on the Lebanese Civil War*. Cambridge: Cambridge University Press.
Corm, Georges. 1988. "Myths and Realities of the Lebanese Conflict." In *Toward a Viable Lebanon*, ed. Halim Barakat, pp. 258–274. London: Croom Helm.

Dagher, Carole H. 2000. *Bring Down the Walls: Lebanon's Post-War Challenge.* New York: Palgrave.
Dahan, Momi. 2013. *The Israeli Economy: Has the Melting Pot Succeeded?* Jerusalem: The Israel Democracy Institute, at: http://en.idi.org.il/analysis/articles/the-israeli-economy-has-the-melting-pot-succeeded (accessed September 2, 2015) [Hebrew].
Danguri, Yehuda. 1998. *A Four-Leaves Clover.* Pardes Hana: Tempo [Hebrew].
Darwish, Mahmoud. 2013. *Memory for Forgetfulness: August, Beirut, 1982.* Trans. Ibrahim Muhawi. Berkeley: University of California Press.
Dayan, Moshe. 1976. *Milestones: An Autobiography.* Jerusalem: Idanim [Hebrew].
Deeb, Marius K. 1980. *The Lebanese Civil War.* New York: Praeger.
Deeb, Mary-Jane, and Marius K. Deeb. 1991. "Regional Conflict and Regional Solutions: Lebanon." *Annals of the American Academy of Political and Social Science* 518: 82–94.
Dekmejian, R. Hrair. 1975. *Patterns of Political Leadership: Egypt, Israel, Lebanon.* Albany: State University of New York Press.
Dor, Daniel. 2004. *Intifada Hits the Headlines: How the Israeli Press Misreported the Outbreak of the Second Palestinian Uprising.* Bloomington: Indiana University Press.
Dowty, Alan. 2012. *Israel/Palestine.* 3rd edn. Cambridge: Polity.
Dowty, Alan. 2013. "How It Began: Europe vs. the Middle East in the Orientation of the First Zionist Settlers." In *Israeli Identity: Between Orient and Occident*, ed. David Tal, pp. 15–25. London: Routledge.
Drezner, Daniel D. 2011. *Theories of International Politics and Zombies.* Princeton: Princeton University Press.
Dumper, Michael. 2014. *Jerusalem Unbound: Geography, History, and the Future of the Holy City.* New York: Columbia University Press.
Eban, Abba. 1978. *Memoirs.* Tel Aviv: Maariv, 2 Vols. [Hebrew].
Edelstein, David M. 2004. "Occupational Hazards: Why Military Occupations Succeed or Fail." *International Security* 29 (1): 49–91.
Edelstein, David M. 2008. *Occupational Hazards: Success and Failure in Military Occupation.* Ithaca: Cornell University Press.
Efrat, Elisha. 2006. *The West Bank and Gaza Strip: A Geography of Occupation and Disengagement.* London: Routledge.
Eilam, Uzi. 2009. *Eilam's Arc: Advanced Technology, the Secret of Israeli Strength.* Tel Aviv: Yedioth Ahronoth [Hebrew].
Eiran, Ehud. 2013. *Israel and Weak Neighboring States: Lessons from the Israeli Experience in Lebanon.* Ramat Gan: Mitvim – The Israeli Institute for Regional Foreign Policies, at: www.mitvim.org.il/images/Israel_and_Weak_Neighboring_States_-_Dr._Ehud_Eiran.pdf (accessed June 10, 2015).
Eisenberg, Laura Zittrain. 1994. *My Enemy's Enemy: Lebanon in the Early Zionist Imagination, 1900–1948.* Detroit: Wayne State University Press.
Eisenberg, Laurie Zittrain. 1997. "Israel's South Lebanon Imbroglio." *Middle East Quarterly* 4 (2): 60–69.
Eisenberg, Laurie Zittrain. 2000. "Do Good Fences Make Good Neighbors?: Israel and Lebanon after the Withdrawal." *Middle East Review of International Affairs* 4 (3): 17–31.

Eisenberg, Laurie Zittrain. 2009. "History Revisited or Revamped? The Maronite Factor in Israel's 1982 Invasion of Lebanon." *Israel Affairs* 15 (4): 372–396.

Eisenberg, Laurie Zittrain. 2010. "From Benign to Malign: Israeli–Lebanese Relations, 1948–1978." In *Israel and Hizbollah: An Asymmetric Conflict in Historical and Comparative Perspective*, eds. Clive Jones and Sergio Catignani, pp. 10–24. London: Routledge.

Eitan, Rafael. 2001. *The Fourth Parachute Got Open*. Tel Aviv: Miskal [Hebrew].

Elad, Moshe. 2015. *If You Wish It, It Is The West Bank*. Haifa: Pardes [Hebrew].

El-Husseini, Rola. 2012. *Pax Syriana: Elite Politics in Postwar Lebanon*. Syracuse: Syracuse University Press.

El-Khazen, Farid. 1991. *The Communal Pact of National Identities: The Making and Politics of the 1943 National Pact*. Papers on Lebanon, No. 12. Oxford: Centre for Lebanese Studies.

El-Khazen, Farid. 1994. *Lebanon's First Postwar Parliamentary Election, 1992: An Imposed Choice*. Prospects for Lebanon, No. 8. Oxford: Centre for Lebanese Studies.

El-Khazen, Farid. 2000. *The Breakdown of the State in Lebanon, 1967–1976*. London: I.B. Tauris.

Enloe, Cynthia. 1980. *Ethnic Soldiers: State Security in Divided Societies*. Athens: University of Georgia Press.

Entelis, John P. 1974. *Pluralism and Party Transformation in Lebanon: Al-Kata'ib, 1936–1970*. Leiden: Brill.

Entelis, John P. 1979. "Ethnic Conflict and the Reemergence of Radical Christian Nationalism in Lebanon." *Journal of South Asian and Middle Eastern Studies* 2 (3): 6–25.

Erlich, Reuven. 1997. "The Conception of the Security Zone and Its Ability to Pass the Test of Reality." In *The Security Zone in Lebanon*, ed. Yaacov Bar-Siman-Tov, pp. 9–28. Jerusalem: The Leonard Davis Institute for International Relations, The Hebrew University of Jerusalem [Hebrew].

Erlich, Reuven. 2000. *The Lebanon Tangle: The Policy of the Zionist Movement and the State of Israel towards Lebanon – 1918–1958*. Tel Aviv: Ministry of Defense [Hebrew].

Erlich, Reuven. 2011. "Israel's Unilateral Withdrawals from Lebanon and the Gaza Strip: A Comparative Overview," at: www.terrorism-info.org.il/data/pdf/PDF_11_174_2.pdf (accessed June 9, 2015).

Esman, Milton J. 1988. "How Unique Is the Middle East." In *Ethnicity, Pluralism and the State in the Middle East*, eds. Milton Esman and Itamar Rabinovich, pp. 271–287. Ithaca: Cornell University Press.

Esman, Milton J., and Itamar Rabinovich, eds. 1988. *Ethnicity, Pluralism and the State in the Middle East*. Ithaca: Cornell University Press.

Evans, Peter, Dietrich Rueschemeyer, and Theda Skocpol, eds. 1985. *Bringing the State Back In*. Cambridge: Cambridge University Press.

Even, Shmuel. 2015. "'The Decision That Changed History': Ten Years since the Disengagement from the Gaza Strip." *Strategic Assessment* 18 (2): 73–88.

Evron, Yair. 1987. *War and Intervention in Lebanon: The Israeli–Syrian Deterrence Dialogue*. London: Croom Helm.

Eyal, Gil. 2002. "Dangerous Liaisons between Military Intelligence and Middle Eastern Studies in Israel." *Theory and Society* 31 (5): 653–693.
Fahmy, Khaled. 1997. *All the Pasha's Men: Mehmed Ali, His Army and the Making of Modern Egypt*. Cambridge: Cambridge University Press.
Farah, Ceasar E. 2000. *The Politics of Interventionism in Ottoman Lebanon, 1830–1861*. London: I.B. Tauris.
Faris, Hani A. 1994. "The Failure of Peacemaking in Lebanon, 1975–89." In *Peace for Lebanon?*, ed. Deirdre Collings, pp. 17–30. Boulder: Lynne Rienner.
Faris, Hani A., ed. 2013. *The Failure of the Two-State Solution: The Prospects of One State in the Israel-Palestine Conflict*. London: I.B. Tauris.
Fawaz, Leila T. 1994. *An Occasion for War: Civil Conflict in Lebanon and Damascus in 1860*. Berkeley: University of California Press.
Fawaz, Leila T. 2014. *A Land of Aching Hearts: The Middle East in the Great War*. Cambridge, MA: Harvard University Press.
Fazal, Tanisha M. 2007. *State Death: The Politics and Geography of Conquest, Occupation, and Annexation*. Princeton: Princeton University Press.
Fieldhouse, David K. 2006. *Western Imperialism in the Middle East, 1914–1958*. Oxford: Oxford University Press.
Finer, Samuel. 1975. "State- and Nation-Building in Europe: The Role of the Military." In *The Formation of National States in Western Europe*, ed. Charles Tilly, pp. 84–163. Princeton: Princeton University Press.
Firro, Kais M. 2002. *Inventing Lebanon: Nationalism and the State under the Mandate*. London: I.B Tauris.
Fitzgerald, F. Scott. 1986 [1925]. *The Great Gatsby*. New York: Collier.
Foley, Sean. 2005. "It Would Surely Be the Second: Lebanon, Israel, and the Arab–Israeli War of 1967." *Middle East Review of International Affairs* 9 (2): 45–56.
Foucault, Michel. 1979. *Discipline and Punish*. Trans. Alan Sheridan. New York: Vintage Books.
Freilich, Charles D. 2012. *Zion's Dilemmas: How Israel Makes National Security Policy*. Ithaca: Cornell University Press.
Friedman, Robert I. 1994. *Zealots for Zion: Inside Israel's West Bank Settlement Movement*. New Brunswick: Rutgers University Press.
Friedman, Thomas L. 1989. *From Beirut to Jerusalem*. New York: Farrar Straus Giroux.
Frieha, Adel. 1980. *L'Armée et l'Etat au Liban*. Paris: Libraire Generale de Droit et Jurispridance.
Friling, Tuvia. 2016. "What Do Those Who Claim Zionism Is Colonialism Overlook?" In *Handbook of Israel: Major Debates*, eds. Eliezer Ben-Rafael, Julius H. Schoeps, Yitzhak Sternberg, and Olaf Glöckner, pp. 848–872. 2 Vols. Berlin: De Gruyter.
Gal, Irit, and Ilana Hammerman. 2002. *From Beirut to Jenin*. Tel Aviv: Am Oved [Hebrew].
Galnoor, Itzhak, and Dana Blander. 2013. *The Political System of Israel. Formative Years; Institutional Structure; Political Behavior; Unsolved Problems; Democracy in Israel*. Tel Aviv: Am Oved [Hebrew].
Gaub, Florence. 2010. *Military Integration after Civil Wars: Multiethnic Armies, Identity and Post-Conflict Reconstruction*. New York: Routledge.

Gaunsen, A.B. 1987. *The Anglo-French Clash in Lebanon and Syria, 1940–45.* New York: St. Martin's.
Gavison, Ruth. 1999. "Jewish and Democratic? A Rejoinder to the 'Ethnic Democracy Debate.'" *Israel Studies* 4 (1): 44–72.
Gazit, Orit. 2011. *Betrayal, Morality and Transnationalism: Identity Construction Processes of the "South Lebanese Army" in Israel since May 2000.* PhD Thesis, The Hebrew University of Jerusalem [Hebrew].
Gazit, Shlomo. 2003. *Trapped Fools: Thirty Years of Israeli Policy in the Territories.* London: Frank Cass.
Gazit, Shlomo. 2016. *At Key Points of Time.* Rishon LeZion: Miskal [Hebrew].
Geary, Patrick J. 2002. *The Myth of Nations: The Medieval Origins of Europe.* Princeton: Princeton University Press.
Gelber, Yoav. 1986. *The Emergence of a Jewish Army.* Jerusalem: Yad Ben-Zvi [Hebrew].
Gellner, Ernest. 1983. *Nations and Nationalism.* Oxford: Blackwell.
Gemayel, Amine. 1985. "The Price and the Promise." *Foreign Affairs* 63 (4): 759–777.
Gendzier, Irene L. 2006. *Notes from the Minefield: United State Intervention in Lebanon and the Middle East, 1945–1958.* New York: Columbia University Press.
Gerber, Haim. 2003. "Zionism, Orientalism, and the Palestinians." *Journal of Palestine Studies* 33 (1): 23–41.
Gerber, Haim. 2008. *Remembering and Imagining Palestine: Identity and Nationalism from the Crusades to the Present.* Houndmills, Basingstoke: Palgrave Macmillan.
Gerges, Fawaz A. 2001. "Israel's Retreat from South Lebanon: Internal and External Implications." *Middle East Policy* 8 (1): 106–116.
Giddens, Anthony. 1991. *Modernity and Self-Identity: Self and Society in the Late Modern Age.* Stanford: Stanford University Press.
Gilboa, Amos. 2015. *The True Story How Israel Left Lebanon (May 2000) Code Name "Dawn."* Jerusalem: Efi Meltzer [Hebrew].
Gluska, Ami. 2007. *The Israeli Military and the Origins of the 1967 War: Government, Armed Forces and Defense Policy, 1963–1967.* New York: Routledge.
Goddard, Stacie E. 2010. *Indivisible Territory and the Politics of Legitimacy: Jerusalem and Northern Ireland.* New York: Cambridge University Press.
Goertz, Gary, and Paul F. Diehl. 1992. "Toward a Theory of International Norms: Some Conceptual and Measurement Issues." *Journal of Conflict Resolution* 36 (4): 634–664.
Golani, Motti. 2001. "Chief of Staff in Quest of a War: Moshe Dayan Leads Israel into War." *Journal of Strategic Studies* 24 (1): 49–70.
Goldstein, Yossi. 2003. *Eshkol – Biography.* Jerusalem: Keter [Hebrew].
Gordon, David C. 1983. *The Republic of Lebanon: Nation in Jeopardy.* Boulder: Westview.
Gordon, Neve. 2008. *Israel's Occupation.* Berkeley: University of California Press.
Gorenberg, Gershom. 2006. *The Accidental Empire: Israel and the Birth of the Settlements, 1967–1977.* New York: Times Books.

Bibliography

Goria, Wade. 1985. *Sovereignty and Leadership in Lebanon, 1943–1976.* London: Ithaca Press.
Goulding, Marrack. 2003. *Peacemonger.* Baltimore: Johns Hopkins University Press.
Greenstein, Ran. 1995. *Genealogies of Conflict: Class, Identity, and State in Palestine/Israel and South Africa.* Hanover: Wesleyan University Press.
Greenstein, Ran. 2014. *Zionism and Its Discontents: A Century of Radical Dissent in Israel/Palestine.* London: Pluto Press.
Grinberg, Lev Luis. 2010. *Politics and Violence in Israel/Palestine: Democracy versus Military Rule.* London: Routledge.
Guelke, Adrian. 2012. *Politics in Deeply Divided Societies.* Cambridge: Polity.
Gur, Mordechai. 1981. "The War of the Israeli Army against Terrorist Activity." In *Elazar Papers: The Annual Symposium in Memory of General David Elazar,* pp. 41–50. Tel Aviv: Amikam [Hebrew].
Gur, Mordechai. 1998. *Chief of Staff.* Tel Aviv: Maarachot [Hebrew].
Gurr, Ted R., and Barbara Harff. 1994. *Ethnic Conflicts in World Politics.* Boulder: Westview.
Habibi, Emile. 1974. *The Secret Life of Saeed the Pessoptimist.* Haifa: Dar al-Ittihad [Arabic].
Haidar, Aziz, ed. 2005. *Arab Society in Israel: Populations, Society, Economy.* Jerusalem: The Van Leer Jerusalem Institute and Hakibbutz Hameuchad [Hebrew].
Hakim, Carole. 2013. *The Origins of the Lebanese National Idea, 1840–1920.* Berkeley: University of California Press.
Haklai, Oded, and Neophytos Loizides, eds. 2015. *Settlers in Contested Lands: Territorial Disputes and Ethnic Conflicts.* Stanford: Stanford University Press.
Haley, Edward P., and Lewis W. Snider, eds. 1979. *Lebanon in Crisis: Participants and Issues.* Syracuse: Syracuse University Press.
Hamizrachi, Beate. 1988. *The Emergence of the South Lebanon Security Belt.* New York: Praeger.
Hamzeh, Nizar. 2004. *In the Path of Hizbullah.* Syracuse: Syracuse University Press.
Handel, Michael I. 1994. "The Evolution of Israeli Strategy: The Psychology of Insecurity and the Quest for Absolute Security." In *The Making of Strategy: Rulers, States, and War,* eds. Williamson Murray, MacGregor Knox, and Alvin H. Bernstein, pp. 534–578. Cambridge: Cambridge University Press.
Hanf, Theodor. 1993. *Coexistence in Wartime Lebanon: Decline of a State and Rise of a Nation.* London: I.B. Tauris.
Harel, Amos, and Avi Issacharoff. 2004. *The Seventh War.* Tel Aviv: Miskal [Hebrew].
Harel, Amos, and Avi Issacharoff. 2008. *34 Days: Israel, Hezbollah, and the War in Lebanon.* New York: Palgrave Macmillan.
Harik, Iliya F. 1968. *Politics and Change in a Traditional Society; Lebanon, 1711–1845.* Princeton: Princeton University Press.
Harik, Iliya F. 1990. "The Origins of the Arab State System." In *The Arab State,* ed. Giacomo Luciani, pp. 1–28. Berkeley: University of California Press.

Harik, Iliya F. 2006. "Democracy, 'Arab Exceptionalism,' and Social Science." *Middle East Journal* 60 (4): 664–684.
Harik, Judith P. 1993. "Change and Continuity among the Lebanese Druze Community: The Civil Administration of the Mountains, 1983–1990." *Middle Eastern Studies* 29 (3): 377–398.
Harik, Judith P. 1994. *The Public and Social Services of the Lebanese Militias*. Papers on Lebanon, No. 14. Oxford: Centre for Lebanese Studies.
Harik, Judith P. 2004. *Hezbollah: The Changing Face of Terrorism*. London: I.B. Tauris.
Harris, William W. 1997. *Faces of Lebanon: Sects, Wars and Global Extensions*. Princeton: Markus Wiener Publishers.
Hartzell, Caroline A., and Matthew Hoddie. 2003. "Institutionalizing Peace: Power Sharing and Post-Civil War Conflict Management." *American Journal of Political Science* 47 (2): 318–332.
Hartzell, Caroline A., and Matthew Hoddie. 2015. "The Art of the Possible: Power Sharing and Post-Civil War Democracy." *World Politics* 67 (1): 37–71.
Heller, Joseph. 2003. *From Brit Shalom to the Ihud: Judah Leib Magnes and the Struggle for a Bi-national State*. Jerusalem: The Hebrew University Magnes Press [Hebrew].
Heller, Patrick. 2000. "Degrees of Democracy: Some Comparative Lessons from India." *World Politics* 52 (4): 484–519.
Herbst, Jeffrey. 2014. *States and Power in Africa: Comparative Lessons in Authority and Control*. 2nd edn. Princeton: Princeton University Press.
Hermann, Tamar S. 2009. *The Israeli Peace Movement: A Shattered Dream*. New York: Cambridge University Press.
Hermann, Tamar. 2010. "Pacifism and Anti-Militarism in the Period Surrounding the Birth of the State of Israel." *Israel Studies* 15 (2): 127–148.
Hilterman, Joost R. 1991. *Behind the Intifada: Labor and Women's Movements in the Occupied Territories*. Princeton: Princeton University Press.
Hobsbawm, Eric. 1990. *Nations and Nationalism since 1780*. Cambridge: Cambridge University Press.
Hof, Fredrick. 1985. *Galilee Divided: The Israel-Lebanon Frontier, 1916–1984*. Boulder: Westview.
Horowitz, Dan. 1982. "Dual Authority Polities." *Comparative Politics* 14 (3): 329–349.
Horowitz, Dan. 1993. *The Heavens and the Earth: A Self-Portrait of the 1948 Generation*. Jerusalem: Keter [Hebrew].
Horowitz, Dan, and Moshe Lissak. 1978. *Origins of the Israeli Polity*. Chicago: University of Chicago Press.
Horowitz, Dan, and Moshe Lissak. 1989. *Trouble in Utopia: The Overburdened Polity of Israel*. Albany: State University of New York Press.
Horowitz, Donald. 1985. *Ethnic Groups in Conflict*. Berkeley: University of California Press.
Horowitz, Michael C. 2010. "Nonstate Actors and the Diffusion of Innovations: The Case of Suicide Terrorism." *International Organization* 64 (1): 33–64.
Hoss, Salim el-. 1991. *The Era of Decision and Caprice*. Beirut: Dar al-'Ilm lil-Malayin [Arabic].

Hourani, Albert. 1976. "Ideologies of the Mountain and the City." In *Essays on the Crisis in Lebanon*, ed. Roger Owen, pp. 33–41. London: Ithaca Press.

Hourani, Albert. 1988. "Visions of Lebanon." In *Toward a Viable Lebanon*, ed. Halim Barakat, pp. 3–11. London: Croom Helm.

Howard, Michael. 1979. "War and the Nation-State." *Daedalus* 108 (4): 101–110.

Hudson, Michael C. 1968. *The Precarious Republic: Political Modernization in Lebanon*. New York: Random House.

Hudson, Michael C. 1988, "The Problem of Authoritative Power in Lebanese Politics: Why Consociationalism Failed." In *Lebanon: A History of Conflict and Consensus*, eds. Nadim Shehadi and Dana Haffar Mills, pp. 224–239. London: Centre for Lebanese Studies and I.B. Tauris.

Hughes, Matthew. 2005. "Lebanon's Armed Forces and the Arab-Israeli War, 1948–49." *Journal of Palestine Studies* 34 (2): 24–41.

Hughes, Matthew. 2009. "The Banality of Brutality: British Armed Forces and the Repression of the Arab Revolt in Palestine, 1936–39." *The English Historical Review* 124 (507): 313–354.

Hunter, F. Robert. 1993. *The Palestinian Uprising: A War by Other Means*. Berkeley: University of California Press.

Huntington, Samuel. 1968. *Political Order in Changing Societies*. New Haven: Yale University Press.

Hurewitz, J.C. 1969. *Middle East Politics: The Military Dimension*. New York: Praeger.

Ibrahim, Saad Eddin. 1998. "Ethnic Conflict and State-Building in the Arab World." *International Social Science Journal* 50 (156): 230–242.

Jabra, Nancy W., and Jabra, Joseph G. 1984. "Education and Political Development in the Middle East." *Journal of Asian and African Studies* 19 (3–4): 202–218.

Jackson, Richard. 2005. *Writing the War on Terrorism: Language, Politics and Counter-Terrorism*. Manchester: Manchester University Press.

Jackson, Robert H. 1990. *Quasi-States: Sovereignty, International Relations and the Third World*. Cambridge: Cambridge University Press.

Jackson, Robert H., and Carl G. Rosberg. 1982. "Why Africa's Weak States Persist: The Empirical and the Juridical in Statehood." *World Politics* 35 (1): 1–24.

Job, Steven. 1992. "The Insecurity Dilemma: National, Regime, and State Securities in the Third World." In *The Insecurity Dilemma*, ed. Steven Job, pp. 11–36. Boulder: Lynne Rienner.

Johnson, Michael. 1977. "Political Bosses and Their Gangs: Zu'ama and Qabadayat in the Sunni Muslim Quarters of Beirut." In *Patrons and Clients in Mediterranean Societies*, eds. Ernest Gellner and John Waterbury, pp. 207–224. London: Duckworth.

Johnson, Michael. 1986. *Class and Client in Beirut: The Sunni Muslim Community and the Lebanese State, 1840–1985*. London: Ithaca Press.

Johnson, Michael. 2001. *All Honourable Men: The Social Origins of War in Lebanon*. London: I.B. Tauris.

Judt, Tony, 2003. "Israel: The Alternative." *New York Review of Books* 50 (16): 8–11.

Junblat, Kamal. 1959. *The Truth about the Lebanese Revolution*. Beirut: Dar al-Nashr al-'Arabiyah [Arabic].
Junblat, Kamal. 1987. *This Is My Testament*. 2nd edn. Mukhtara: al-Dar al-Taqaddumiyya [Arabic].
Kalawoun, Nasser. 2000. *The Struggle for Lebanon: A Modern History of Lebanese-Egyptian Relations*. London: I.B. Tauris.
Kanaaneh, Rhoda. 2008. *Surrounded: Palestinian Soldiers in the Israeli Military*. Stanford: Stanford University Press.
Kaufman, Asher. 2004. *Reviving Phoenicia: In Search of Identity in Lebanon*. London: I.B. Tauris.
Kaufman, Asher. 2010a. "Forgetting the Lebanon War? On Silence, Denial, and the Selective Remembrance of the 'First' Lebanon War." In *Shadows of War: A Social History of Silence in the Twentieth Century*, eds. Efrat Ben-Ze'ev, Ruth Ginio, and Jay Winter, pp. 197–216. Cambridge: Cambridge University Press.
Kaufman, Asher. 2010b. "From the Litani to Beirut: Israel's Invasions of Lebanon, 1978–85." In *Israel and Hizbollah: An Asymmetric Conflict in Historical and Comparative Perspective*, eds. Clive Jones and Sergio Catignani, pp. 25–38. London: Routledge.
Kaufman, Asher. 2013. *Contested Frontiers in the Syria-Lebanon-Israel Region: Cartography, Sovereignty, and Conflict*. Washington, DC: Woodrow Wilson Center and Johns Hopkins University Press.
Kaufmann, Chaim. 1996. "Possible and Impossible Solutions to Ethnic Civil Wars." *International Security* 20 (4): 136–175.
Kechichian, Joseph A. 1985. "The Lebanese Army: Capabilities and Challenges in the 1980s." *Conflict Quarterly* 5 (1): 15–39.
Kedar, Nir. 2003. "Ben-Gurion's Mamlakhtiyut: Etymological and Theoretical Roots." *Israel Studies* 7 (3): 117–133.
Kedar, Nir. 2008. "A Civilian Commander in Chief: Ben-Gurion's Mamlakhtiyut, the Army and the Law." *Israel Affairs* 14 (2): 202–217.
Kedar, Nir. 2013. "Ben-Gurion's View of the Place of Judaism in Israel." *Journal of Israeli History* 32 (2): 157–174.
Kedourie, Elie. 1992. *Politics in the Middle East*. Oxford: Oxford University Press.
Kemp, Adriana. 2004. "Dangerous Populations: State Territoriality and the Constitution of National Minorities." In *Boundaries and Belonging: States and Societies in the Struggle to Shape Identities and Local Practices*, ed. Joel Migdal, pp. 73–97. New York: Cambridge University Press.
Kenan, Amos. 1984. *The Road to Ein Harod*. Tel Aviv: Am Oved [Hebrew].
Kenig, Ofer. 2014. "The Social Representativeness of Cabinet Ministers in Israel: Are the Gaps Closing?" *Representation* 50 (2): 177–191.
Kerr, Malcolm H. 1978. *The Arab Cold War: Gamal 'Abd al-Nasir and His Rivals, 1958–1970*. New York: Oxford University Press.
Kerr, Michael. 2009. "'A Positive Aspect to the Tragedy of Lebanon': The Convergence of US, Syrian and Israeli Interests at the Outset of Lebanon's Civil War." *Israel Affairs* 15 (4): 355–371.
Khalaf, Samir. 1977. "Changing Patterns of Political Patronage in Lebanon." In *Patrons and Clients in Mediterranean Societies*, eds. Ernest Gellner and John Waterbury, pp. 185–205. London: Duckworth.

Khalaf, Samir, 1987. *Lebanon's Predicament*. New York: Columbia University Press.
Khalaf, Samir, 2002. *Civil and Uncivil Violence in Lebanon*. New York: Columbia University Press.
Khalaf, Twefik. 1976. "The Phalange and the Maronite Community: From Lebanonism to Maronitism." In *Essays on the Crisis in Lebanon*, ed. Roger Owen, pp. 43–57. London: Ithaca Press.
Khalidi, Rashid. 1986. *Under Siege: PLO Decision-Making during the 1982 War*. New York: Columbia University Press.
Khalidi, Rashid. 1997. *Palestinian Identity: The Construction of Modern National Consciousness*. New York: Columbia University Press.
Khalidi, Rashid. 2006. *The Iron Cage: The Story of the Palestinian Struggle for Statehood*. Boston: Beacon Press.
Khalidi, Walid. 1979. *Conflict and Violence in Lebanon: Confrontation in the Middle East*. Cambridge, MA: Center for International Affairs, Harvard University.
Khashan, Hilal. 1992. *Inside the Lebanese Confessional Mind*. Lanham: University Press of America.
Khashan, Hilal. 2009. "The Evolution of Israeli–Lebanese Relations: From Implicit Peace to Explicit Conflict." *Israel Affairs* 15 (4): 319–334.
Khatib, Lina. 2008. *Lebanese Cinema: Imagining the Civil War and Beyond*. London: I.B. Tauris.
Khuri, Bishara Khalil. 1960. *Lebanese Truths*. 3 Vols. Daroun-Harisa: Awrak Lubnaniyya [Arabic].
Kimche, David. 1991. *The Last Option: After Nasser, Arafat, and Saddam Hussein: The Quest for Peace in the Middle East*. New York: Charles Scribner's Sons.
Kimmerling, Baruch, 1989. "Boundaries and Frontiers of the Israeli Control System: Analytical Conclusions." In *The Israeli State and Society: Boundaries and Frontiers*, ed. Baruch Kimmerling, pp. 265–284. Albany: State University of New York Press.
Kimmerling, Baruch. 1993. "Patterns of Militarism in Israel." *European Journal of Sociology* 34 (2): 196–223.
Kimmerling, Baruch. 2001. *The Invention and Decline of Israeliness: State, Society, and the Military*. Berkeley: University of California Press.
Kimmerling, Baruch. 2012. *Clash of Identities: Explorations in Israeli and Palestinian Societies*. New York: Columbia University Press.
Kingston, Paul. 2013. *Reproducing Sectarianism: Advocacy Networks and the Politics of Civil Society in Postwar Lebanon*. Albany: State University of New York Press.
Klein, Menachem. 2010. *The Shift: Israel-Palestine from Border Struggle to Ethnic Conflict*. New York: Columbia University Press.
Klein, Menachem. 2014. *Lives in Common: Arabs and Jews in Jerusalem, Jaffa, and Hebron*. London: Hurst.
Kliot, Nurit 1986. *The Territorial Disintegration of a State: The Case of Lebanon*. Durham: University of Durham, Centre for Middle Eastern and Islamic Studies.
Knudsen, Are, and Michael Kerr, eds. 2013. *Lebanon: After the Cedar Revolution*. New York: Oxford University Press.
Kohn, Richard. 2009. "The Danger of Militarization in an Endless 'War' on Terrorism." *Journal of Military History* 73 (1): 177–208.

Kolinsky, Martin. 1993. *Law, Order, and Riots in Mandatory Palestine, 1928–35*. London: Macmillan.
Koya, Abdar Rahman, ed. 2006. *Hizbullah, Party of God: An Islamic Movement Perspective*. Petaling Jaya, Malaysia: The Other Press.
Krebs, Ronald. 2006. *Fighting for Rights: Military Service and the Politics of Citizenship*. Ithaca: Cornell University Press.
Kretzmer, David. 2002. *The Occupation of Justice: The Supreme Court of Israel and the Occupied Territories*. Albany: State University of New York Press.
Kretzmer, David. 2012. "The Law of Belligerent Occupation in the Supreme Court of Israel." *International Review of the Red Cross* 94 (885): 207–236.
Kriesberg, Louis. 2002. "The Relevance of Reconciliation Actions in the Breakdown of Israeli–Palestinian Negotiations, 2000." *Peace & Change* 27 (4): 546–571.
Labaki, Boutrus. 1992. "Lebanese Emigration during the War (1975–1989)." In *The Lebanese in the World*, eds. Albert Hourani and Nadim Shehadi, pp. 605–626. London: Centre for Lebanese Studies and I.B. Tauris.
Lahad, Antoine. 2003. *In the Eye of the Storm*. Haifa: Maktabat Kul Shay' [Arabic].
Lahoud, Fuad. 1976. *The Tragedy of the Lebanese Army*. Baabdaat: s.n. [Arabic].
Larkin, Craig. 2012. *Memory and Conflict in Lebanon: Remembering and Forgetting the Past*. London: Routledge.
Laron, Guy. 2010. "Playing with Fire: The Soviet-Israeli-Syrian Triangle, 1965–1967." *Cold War History* 10 (2): 163–184.
Laron, Guy. 2013. *Origins of the Suez Crisis: Postwar Development Diplomacy and the Struggle over Third World Industrialization, 1945–1956*. Washington, DC: Woodrow Wilson Center Press and Johns Hopkins University Press.
Laron, Guy. 2015. "The Domestic Sources of Israel's Decision to Launch the 1956 Sinai Campaign." *British Journal of Middle Eastern Studies* 42 (2): 200–218.
Leenders, Reinoud. 2012. *Spoils of Truce: Corruption and State-Building in Postwar Lebanon*. Ithaca: Cornell University Press.
Lehmbruch, Gerhard, 1974. "A Non-Competitive Pattern of Management in Liberal Democracies: The Case of Switzerland, Austria and Lebanon." In *Consociational Democracy: Political Accommodation in Segmented Societies*, ed. Kenneth D. Mcrae, pp. 90–97. Toronto: McClelland & Stewart.
Leibovich, Yeshayahu. 1992. *Judaism, Human Values, and the Jewish State*. Cambridge, MA: Harvard University Press.
Levenberg, Haim. 1993. *Military Preparations of the Arab Community in Palestine, 1945–1948*. London: Frank Cass.
Levy, Yagil. 2007. *Israel's Materialist Militarism*. Lanham: Lexington Books.
Levy, Yagil. 2012. *Israel's Death Hierarchy: Casualty Aversion in a Militarized Democracy*. New York: New York University Press.
Lia, Brynjar. 2006. *A Police Force without a State: A History of the Palestinian Security Forces in the West Bank and Gaza*. Reading: Ithaca Press
Libel, Tamir. 2013. "From the People's Army to the Jewish People's Army: The IDF's Force Structure between Professionalization and Militarization." *Defense & Security Analysis* 29 (4): 280–292.

Lichbach, Mark I. 1997. "Social Theory and Comparative Politics." In *Comparative Politics: Rationality, Culture, and Structure*, eds. Mark I. Lichbach and Alan S. Zuckerman, pp. 239–276. Cambridge: Cambridge University Press.
Liel, Alon. 1999. *Black Justice: The South African Upheaval*. Tel Aviv: Hakibutz Hameuchad [Hebrew].
Lijphart, Arend. 1968. *The Politics of Accommodation: Pluralism and Democracy in the Netherlands*. Berkeley: University of California Press.
Lijphart, Arend. 1977. *Democracy in Plural Societies*. New Haven: Yale University Press.
Lijphart, Arend. 1984. *Democracies: Patterns of Majoritarian and Consensus Government in Twenty-One Countries*. New Haven: Yale University Press.
Lijphart, Arend. 1998. "Consensus and Consensus Democracy: Cultural, Structural, Functional and Rational Choice Explanations." *Scandinavian Political Studies* 21 (2): 99–108.
Lijphart, Arend. 2004. "Constitutional Design for Divided Societies." *Journal of Democracy* 15 (2): 96–109.
Little, Douglas. 1996. "His Finest Hour? Eisenhower, Lebanon and the 1958 Middle East Crisis." *Diplomatic History* 20 (1): 27–54.
Lockman, Zachary, and Joel Beinin, eds. 1989. *Intifada: The Palestinian Uprising against Israeli Occupation*. Cambridge, MA: South End Press.
Longrigg, Stephen. 1958. *Syria and Lebanon under French Mandate*. London: Oxford University Press.
Louis, Wm Roger, and Avi Shlaim, eds. 2012. *The 1967 Arab–Israeli War: Origins and Consequences*. New York: Cambridge University Press.
Löwenheim, Oded, and Gadi Heimann. 2008. "Revenge in International Politics." *Security Studies* 17 (4): 685–724.
Luft, Gal. 2000. "Israel's Security Zone in Lebanon: A Tragedy?" *Middle East Quarterly* 7 (3): 13–20.
Lupovici, Amir. 2009. "Constructivist Methods: A Plea and Manifesto for Pluralism." *Review of International Studies* 35 (1): 195–218.
Lupovici, Amir. 2012. "Ontological Dissonance, Clashing Identities, and Israel's Unilateral Steps towards the Palestinians." *Review of International Studies* 38 (4): 809–833.
Lupovici, Amir. 2013. "Me and the Other in International Relations: An Alternative Pluralist International Relations 101." *International Studies Perspectives* 14 (3): 235–254.
Lustick, Ian S. 1979. "Stability in Deeply Divided Societies: Consociationalism versus Control." *World Politics* 31 (3): 325–344.
Lustick, Ian S. 1980. *Arabs in the Jewish State: Israel's Control of a National Minority*. Austin: University of Texas Press.
Lustick, Ian S. 1993. *Unsettled States, Disputed Lands: Britain and Ireland, France and Algeria, Israel and the West Bank-Gaza*. Ithaca: Cornell University Press.
Lustick, Ian S. 1997a. "Has Israel Annexed East Jerusalem?" *Middle East Policy* 5 (1): 34–45.
Lustick, Ian S. 1997b. "Lijphart, Lakatos, and Consociationalism." *World Politics* 50 (1): 88–117.

Lustick, Ian S. 1997c. "The Oslo Agreement as an Obstacle to Peace." *Journal of Palestine Studies* 27 (1): 61–66.

Lustick, Ian S. 1999. "Hegemony and the Riddle of Nationalism." In *Ethnic Conflict and International Politics in the Middle East*, ed. Leonard Binder, pp. 332–359. Gainesville: University Press of Florida.

Lustick, Ian S. 2001. "Thresholds of Opportunity and Barriers to Change in the Right-Sizing of States." In *Right-Sizing the State: The Politics of Moving Borders*, eds. Brendan O'Leary, Ian Lustick, and Thomas Callaghy, pp. 74–101. New York: Oxford University Press.

Lustick, Ian S. 2013. "What Counts Is the Counting: Statistical Manipulation as a Solution to Israel's 'Demographic Problem.'" *Middle East Journal* 67 (2): 185–205.

Maila, Joseph. 1992. *The Document of National Understanding: A Commentary*. Prospects for Lebanon No. 4. Oxford: Centre for Lebanese Studies.

Makdisi, Ussama. 2000. *The Culture of Sectarianism: Community, History, and Violence in Nineteenth-Century Ottoman Lebanon*. Berkeley: University of California Press.

Maktani, Rania. 1999. "The Lebanese Census of 1932 Revisited. Who Are the Lebanese?" *British Journal of Middle Eastern Studies* 26 (2): 219–241.

Mann, Michael. 1986. "The Autonomous Power of the State: Its Origins, Mechanisms and Results." In *States in History*, ed. John A. Hall, pp. 109–136. Oxford: Blackwell.

Mansfield, Edward D., and Jack L. Snyder. 2005. *Electing to Fight: Why Emerging Democracies Go to War*. Cambridge, MA: MIT Press.

Maoz, Zeev. 2009. *Defending the Holy Land: A Critical Analysis of Israel's Security and Foreign Policy*. Ann Arbor: University of Michigan Press.

Marayati, Abid A. 1968. *Middle Eastern Constitutions and Electoral Laws*. New York, Washington and London: Praeger.

Massad, Joseph. 2001. *Colonial Effects: The Making of National Identity in Jordan*. New York: Columbia University Press.

McCulloch, Allison. 2014. *Power-Sharing and Political Stability in Deeply Divided Societies*. London: Routledge.

McDermott, Anthony. 1996. "The Arab–Israeli Mixed Armistice Commissions of Yore: Relevant Today?" *Geopolitics and International Boundaries* 1 (1): 93–114.

McEvoy, Joanne, and Brendan O'Leary, eds. 2013. *Power Sharing in Deeply Divided Places*. Philadelphia: University of Pennsylvania Press.

McGarry, John, and Brendan O'Leary. 1993. *The Politics of Ethnic Conflict Regulation: Case Studies of Protracted Ethnic Conflicts*. London: Routledge.

McGarry, John, and Brendan O'Leary. 1999. *Policing Northern Ireland*. Belfast: Blackstaff.

McLaurin, Ronald. 1984. "Lebanon and Its Army: Past, Present and Future." In *The Emergence of a New Lebanon*, ed. Edward Azar, pp. 79–114. New York: Praeger.

McLaurin, Ronald. 1991. "From Professional to Political: The Redecline of the Lebanese Army." *Armed Forces and Society* 17 (4): 545–568.

Medding, Peter Y. 1990. *The Founding of Israeli Democracy, 1948–1967*. New York: Oxford University Press.

Meier, Daniel. 2014. "The Palestinian Fidâ'i as an Icon of Transnational Struggle: The South Lebanese Experience." *British Journal of Middle Eastern Studies* 41 (3): 322–334.

Mendelsohn, Barak. 2016. "Israel and Its Messianic Right: Path Dependency and State Authority in International Conflict." *International Studies Quarterly* 60 (1): 47–58.

Meo, Leila T. 1965. *Lebanon Improbable Nation: A Study in Political Development.* Bloomington: Indiana University Press.

Merom, Gil. 2003. *How Democracies Lose Small Wars: State, Society, and the Failures of France in Algeria, Israel in Lebanon, and the United States in Vietnam.* New York: Cambridge University Press.

Migdal, Joel S. 1988. *Strong Societies and Weak States: State-Society Relations and State Capabilities in the Third World.* Princeton: Princeton University Press.

Migdal, Joel S. 1996. "Society-Formation and the Case of Israel." In *Israel in Comparative Perspective: Challenging the Conventional Wisdom*, ed. Michael N. Barnett, pp. 173–198. Albany: State University of New York Press.

Migdal, Joel S. 1997. "Studying the State." In *Comparative Politics: Rationality, Culture, and Structure*, eds. Mark I. Lichbach and Alan S. Zuckerman, pp. 208–235. Cambridge: Cambridge University Press.

Migdal, Joel S. 2001. *Through the Lens of Israel: Explorations in State and Society.* Albany: State University of New York Press.

Migdal, Joel S. 2004. *State in Society: Studying How States and Societies Transform and Constitute One Another.* Cambridge: Cambridge University Press.

Mikdashi, Maya. 2011. "The Making of a Secular Democracy: Law, Marriage, and Empirical Irrelevance in Israel and Lebanon." *Jadaliyya*, October 29, at: www.jadaliyya.com/pages/index/3007/the-making-of-a-secular-democracy_law-marriage-and (accessed April 6, 2015).

Miller, Benjamin. 2007. *States, Nations, and the Great Powers: The Sources of Regional War and Peace.* Cambridge: Cambridge University Press.

Milson, Menachem. 1984. *Jordan and the West Bank.* Jerusalem: The Leonard Davis Institute for International Relations, The Hebrew University of Jerusalem [Hebrew].

Mishal, Shaul, and Avraham Sela. 2000. *The Palestinian Hamas: Vision, Violence, and Coexistence.* New York: Columbia University Press.

Mitchell, Timothy. 1991. "The Limits of the State: Beyond Statist Approaches and Their Critics." *American Political Science Review* 85 (1): 77–96.

Mitzen, Jennifer. 2006. "Ontological Security in World Politics: State Identity and the Security Dilemma." *European Journal of International Relations* 12 (3): 341–370.

Morag, Raya. 2012. "Perpetrator Trauma and Current Israeli Documentary Cinema." *Camera Obscura* 27 (2): 93–132.

Morag, Raya. 2013. *Waltzing with Bashir: Perpetrator Trauma and Cinema.* London: I.B. Tauris.

Morris, Benny. 1984. "Israel and the Lebanese Phalange: The Birth of a Relationship, 1948–1951." *Studies in Zionism* 5 (1): 125–144.

Morris, Benny. 1993. *Israel's Border Wars, 1949–1956.* Oxford: Oxford University Press.

Morris, Benny. 2008. *1948: A History of the First Arab–Israeli War*. New Haven: Yale University Press.
Morris, Benny. 2009. *One State, Two States: Resolving the Israel/Palestine Conflict*. New Haven: Yale University Press.
Morselli, Valentina. 2015. *"We Are the Last Frontier Against . . . ": National Role Conception and Primacy of Security in Israel's Road to the First and Second Lebanon Wars (1982, 2006)*. PhD Thesis, Université Libre de Bruxelles.
Mosse, George L. 1990. *Fallen Soldiers: Reshaping the Memory of the World Wars*. Oxford: Oxford University Press.
Muslih, Muhammad Y. 1988. *The Origins of Palestinian Nationalism*. New York: Columbia University Press.
Na'um, Sarkis. 1992. *Michel Aoun: Dream or Delusion?* Beirut: al-Mutawassit [Arabic].
Naor, Arye. 2015. "'A Simple Historical Truth': Judea, Samaria and the Gaza Strip in Menachem Begin's Ideology." *Israel Affairs* 21 (3): 462–481.
Naor, Dan. 2013. "The Quest for a Balance of Power in Lebanon during Suleiman Frangieh's Presidency, 1970–76." *Middle Eastern Studies* 49 (6): 990–1008.
Naor, Dan. 2014a. "In the Arena of the Zu'ama: Reviewing Hizbullah's Role in Lebanon." *Middle East Review of International Affairs* 1 (2): 8–17.
Naor, Dan. 2014b. "The Path to Syrian Intervention in Lebanon on the Eve of Civil War, 1970–1975." *British Journal of Middle Eastern Studies* 41 (2): 183–199.
Nasasra, Mansour, Sophie Richter-Devroe, Sarab Abu-Rabia-Queder, and Richard Ratcliffe, eds. 2015. *The Naqab Bedouin and Colonialism: New Perspectives*. London: Routledge.
Natali, Denise. 2001. "Manufacturing Identity and Managing Kurds in Iraq." In *Right-Sizing the State: The Politics of Moving Borders*, eds. Brendan O'Leary, Ian Lustick, and Thomas Callaghy, pp. 253–288. New York: Oxford University Press.
Navot, Nachik. 2015. *One Man's Mossad*. Or Yehuda: Kinneret, Zmora-Bitan, Dvir [Hebrew].
Ne'eman, Yuval. 1981. "Panel Discussion: Israel and Lebanon: Interests and Policy at Present and in the Future." In *Elazar Papers: The Annual Symposium in Memory of General David Elazar*, pp. 69–74. Tel Aviv: Amikam [Hebrew].
Neep, Daniel. 2012. *Occupying Syria Under the French Mandate: Insurgency, Space and State Formation*. New York: Cambridge University Press.
Nerguizian, Aram. 2009. *The Lebanese Armed Forces: Challenges and Opportunities in Post-Syria Lebanon*. Washington, DC: Center for Strategic and International Studies, at: http://csis.org/files/media/csis/pubs/090210_lafsecurity.pdf (accessed April 26, 2015).
Nevo, Joseph. 2008. "September 1970 in Jordan: A Civil War?" *Civil Wars* 10 (3): 217–230.
Newman, David. 1995. *Boundaries in Flux: The "Green Line" Boundary between Israel and the West Bank-Past, Present and Future*. Durham: International Boundaries Research Unit.

Nikolenyi, Csaba. 2013. "The Israeli Party System in Comparative Perspective: A 'Unique Case' or Part of the Western European Tradition." In *Israeli Identity: Between Orient and Occident*, ed. David Tal, pp. 65–82. London: Routledge.
Nir, Omri. 2011. *Nabih Berri and Lebanese Politics*. New York: Palgrave Macmillan.
Nisan, Mordechai. 2004. *The Conscience of Lebanon: A Political Biography of Etienne Sakr (Abu-Arz)*. London: Routledge.
Niv, Kobi. 2014. *Look Back into the Future: The Israeli Cinema and the Lebanon War of 1982*. Tel Aviv: Olam Hadash [Hebrew].
Nordlinger, Eric A. 1972. *Conflict Regulation in Divided Societies*. Cambridge, MA: Center for International Affairs, Harvard University.
Norris, Jacob. 2013. *Land of Progress: Palestine in the Age of Colonial Development, 1905–1948*. Oxford: Oxford University Press.
Norton, Augustus Richard. 1987. *Amal and the Shi'a: Struggle for the Soul of Lebanon*. Austin: University of Texas Press.
Norton, Augustus Richard. 2007. *Hizballah: A Short History*. Princeton: Princeton University Press.
O'Leary, Brendan. 2001a. "Introduction." In *Right-Sizing the State: The Politics of Moving Borders*, eds. Brendan O'Leary, Ian Lustick, and Thomas Callaghy, pp. 1–14. New York: Oxford University Press.
O'Leary, Brendan. 2001b. "The Elements of Right-Sizing and Right-Peopling the State." In *Right-Sizing the State: The Politics of Moving Borders*, eds. Brendan O'Leary, Ian Lustick, and Thomas Callaghy, pp. 15–73. New York: Oxford University Press.
O'Leary, Brendan, Ian Lustick, and Thomas Callaghy, eds. 2001. *Right-Sizing the State: The Politics of Moving Borders*. New York: Oxford University Press.
Oren, Amiram. 2009. *"Drafted Territories": The Creation of Israeli Army Hegemony over the State's Land and Its Expanses during Its Early Years, 1948–1956*. Tel Aviv: Madaf [Hebrew].
Oren, Amiram, Oren Barak, and Assaf Shapira. 2013. "'How the Mouse Got His Roar': The Shift to an 'Offensive-Defensive' Military Strategy in Israel in 1953 and its Implications." *International History Review* 35 (2): 356–376.
Oren, Michael B. 2003. *Six Days of War: June 1967 and the Making of the Modern Middle East*. New York: Presidio Press.
Oren, Nissan. 1982. "Prudence in Victory." In *Termination of Wars: Processes, Procedures and Aftermaths*, ed. Nissan Oren, pp. 147–163. Jerusalem: The Hebrew University Magnes Press.
O'Shea, Brendan. 2004. "Lebanon's 'Blue Line': A New International Border or Just Another Cease-fire Zone?" *Studies in Conflict & Terrorism*, 27 (1): 19–30
Ostfeld, Zehava. 1994. *An Army Is Born*. Tel Aviv: Ministry of Defense [Hebrew].
Owen, Roger, ed. 1976. *Essays on the Crisis in Lebanon*. London: Ithaca Press.
Owen, Roger. 2000. *State, Power and Politics in the Making of the Modern Middle East*. London: Routledge.
Oz, Amos. 2012 [1989]. *The Slopes of Lebanon*. Trans. Maurie Goldberg-Bartura. New York: Houghton Mifflin Harcourt.
Pa'il, Meir. 1979. *From the Hagana to the Defense Forces*. Tel Aviv: Zmora-Bitan Modan [Hebrew].

Pappe, Ilan. 2006. *A History of Modern Palestine: One Land, Two Peoples*. 2nd edn. New York: Cambridge University Press.
Parker, Richard C. 1996. "Kawkaba and the South Lebanon Imbroglio: A Personal Recollection, 1977–1978." *Middle East Journal* 50 (4): 547–558.
Parker, Richard C. 1993. *The Politics of Miscalculation in the Middle East*. Bloomington: Indiana University Press.
Pedahzur, Ami. 2012. *The Triumph of Israel's Radical Right*. New York: Oxford University Press.
Pedahzur, Ami, and Holly McCarthy. 2015. "Against All Odds: The Paradoxical Victory of the West Bank Settlers: Interest Groups and Policy Enforcement." *Israel Affairs* 21 (3): 443–461.
Pedatzur, Reuven. 1996. *The Triumph of Embarrassment: Israel and the Territories after the Six-Day War*. Tel Aviv: Yad Tabenkin–Galili Research Institute and Bitan [Hebrew].
Pelcovits, Nathan A. 1993. *The Long Armistice: UN Peacekeeping and the Arab–Israeli Conflict, 1948–1960*. Boulder: Westview Press.
Peled, Alon. 1998. *A Question of Loyalty: Military Manpower Policy in Multiethnic States*. Ithaca: Cornell University Press.
Peled, Yoav. 2014. *The Challenge of Ethnic Democracy: The State and Minority Groups in Israel, Poland and Northern Ireland*. London: Routledge.
Peled, Yossi. 1997. "The Background for the IDF's Presence in the Security Zone." In *The Security Zone in Lebanon: A Reconsideration*, ed. Yaacov Bar-Siman-Tov, pp. 29–34. Jerusalem: The Leonard Davis Institute for International Relations, The Hebrew University of Jerusalem [Hebrew].
Peres, Shimon. 1978. *Tomorrow Is Now*. Jerusalem: Mabat [Hebrew].
Peretz, Don. 1990. *Intifada: The Palestinian Uprising*. Boulder: Westview.
Peri, Yoram. 1983. *Between Battles and Ballots: The Israeli Military in Politics*. Cambridge: Cambridge University Press.
Peri, Yoram. 2006. *Generals in the Cabinet Room: How the Military Shapes Israeli Policy*. Washington, DC: United States Institute of Peace.
Picard, Elizabeth. 1996. *Lebanon, a Shattered Country: Myths and Realities of the Wars in Lebanon*. New York: Holmes and Meier.
Picard, Elizabeth. 2000. "Lebanon's War Economy." In *War, Institutions, and Social Change in the Middle East*, ed. Steven Heydemann, pp. 292–322. Berkeley: University of California Press.
Podeh, Elie. 2011. *The Politics of National Celebrations in the Arab Middle East*. New York: Cambridge University Press.
Podeh, Elie. 2015. *Chances for Peace: Missed Opportunities in the Arab-Israeli Conflict*. Austin: University of Texas Press.
Polakow-Suransky, Sasha. 2010. *The Unspoken Alliance: Israel's Secret Relationship with Apartheid South Africa*. New York: Pantheon Books.
Porath, Yehoshua. 1974. *The Emergence of the Palestinian-Arab National Movement, 1918–1929*. London: Frank Cass.
Porath, Yehoshua. 1977. *The Palestinian Arab National Movement, 1929–1939: From Riots to Rebellion*. London: Frank Cass.
Porath, Yehoshua. 1986. *In Search of Arab Unity, 1930–1945*. London: Frank Cass.

Porter, Patrick. 2009. *Military Orientalism: Eastern War through Western Eyes*. London: Hurst.
Posen, Barry, 1993. "The Security Dilemma and Ethnic Conflict." In *Ethnic Conflict and International Security*, ed. Michael Brown, pp. 103–124. Princeton: Princeton University Press.
Putnam, Robert D. 1988. "Diplomacy and Domestic Politics: The Logic of Two-Level Games." *International Organization* 42 (3): 427–460.
Qubain, Fahim I. 1961. *Crisis in Lebanon*. Washington, DC: The Middle East Institute.
Quinlivan, James. 1999. "Coup-Proofing: Its Practice and Consequences in the Middle East." *International Security* 24 (2): 131–165.
Ra'anan, Uri. 1990. "The Nation-State Fallacy." In *Conflict and Peacemaking in Multiethnic Societies*, ed. Joseph Montville, pp. 5–20. Lexington: Lexington Books.
Rabin, Yitzhak. 1996. *The Rabin Memoirs*. 2nd edn. Berkeley: University of California Press.
Rabinovich, Itamar. 1972. *Syria under the Ba'th 1963–1966: The Army-Party Symbiosis*. Jerusalem: Israel Universities Press.
Rabinovich, Itamar. 1981. "Lebanon during and after Its Civil War." In *Elazar Papers: The Annual Symposium in Memory of General David Elazar*, pp. 32–40. Tel Aviv: Amikam [Hebrew].
Rabinovich, Itamar. 1985. *The War for Lebanon, 1970–1985*. Ithaca: Cornell University Press.
Rahat, Gideon, and Reut Itzkovitch Malka. 2012. "Political Representation in Israel: Minority Sectors vs. Women." *Representation* 48 (3): 307–319.
Ram, Haggai. 2009. *Iranophobia: The Logic of an Israeli Obsession*. Stanford: Stanford University Press.
Randal, Jonathan C. 1983. *Going All the Way: Christian Warlords, Israeli Adventurers, and the War in Lebanon*. New York: Viking Press.
Ranta, Ronald. 2015. *Political Decision Making and Non-Decisions: The Case of Israel and the Occupied Territories*. Houndmills, Basingstoke: Palgrave Macmillan.
Rice, Condoleezza. 2011. *No Higher Honor: A Memoir of My Years in Washington*. New York: Crown.
Rihana, Sami. 1984–1988. *Histoire de l'Armée Libanaise Contemporaine*. 2 Vols. Beirut: Impermerie Rahbani.
Rihana, Sami. 1996. *History of the Modern Lebanese Army*. Beirut: Noblesse [Arabic].
Robinson, Shira. 2013. *Citizen Strangers: Palestinians and the Birth of Israel's Liberal Settler State*. Stanford: Stanford University Press.
Roeder, Philip G., and Donald S. Rothchild, eds. 2005. *Sustainable Peace: Power and Democracy after Civil Wars*. Ithaca: Cornell University Press.
Rogan, Eugene L., and Avi Shlaim, eds. 2007. *The War for Palestine: Rewriting the History of 1948*. 2nd edn. Cambridge: Cambridge University Press.
Rokach, Livia. 1986. *Israel's Sacred Terrorism*. 3rd edn. Belmont: Association of Arab-American University Graduates.
Ron, James. 2003. *Frontiers and Ghettos: State Violence in Serbia and Israel*. Berkeley: University of California Press.

Ronen, David. 1989. *The Year of the Shabak: Deployment in Judea and Samaria, First Year*. Tel Aviv: Ministry of Defense [Hebrew].
Rotberg, Robert I. 2002. "The New Nature of Nation-State Failure." *The Washington Quarterly* 25 (3): 85–96.
Rotberg, Robert I., ed. 2003. *State Failure and State Weakness in a Time of Terror*. Washington, DC: Brookings Institution Press.
Rotberg, Robert I., ed. 2004. *When States Fail: Causes and Consequences*. Princeton: Princeton University Press.
Rouhana, Nadim N. 1997. *Palestinian Citizens in an Ethnic Jewish State: Identities in Conflict*. New Haven: Yale University Press.
Rouhana, Nadim N., and Areej Sabbagh-Khoury. 2006. "Force, Privilege, and the Range of Tolerance." In *Knowledge and Silence: On Mechanisms of Denial and Repression in Israeli Society*, eds. Hanna Herzog and Kinneret Lahad, pp. 62–74. Jerusalem: The Van Leer Jerusalem Institute [Hebrew].
Rouhana, Nadim N., and Areej Sabbagh-Khoury. 2015. "Settler-Colonial Citizenship: Conceptualizing the Relationship between Israel and Its Palestinian Citizens." *Settler Colonial Studies* 5 (3): 205–225.
Rubinovitz, Ziv. 2010. "Blue and White 'Black September': Israel's Role in the Jordan Crisis of 1970." *The International History Review* 32 (4): 687–706.
Rubinovich, Ziv, and Gerald Steinberg. 2012. "Menachem Begin's Autonomy Plan: Between Political Realism and Ideology." *The Public Sphere* 6: 75–94 [Hebrew].
Saad-Ghorayeb, Amal. 2002. *Hezbollah: Politics and Religion*. London: Pluto Press.
Said, Edward W. 1979. *Orientalism*. New York: Vintage Books.
Said, Edward W. 1989. "The Orientalist Express: Thomas Friedman Wraps up the Middle East." *Village Voice* 36 (42), October 17.
Said, Edward W. 2001. *The End of the Peace Process: Oslo and After*. New York: Vintage Books.
Salem, Elie A. 1973. *Modernization without Revolution: Lebanon's Experience*. Bloomington: Indiana University Press.
Salem, Elie A. 1993. *Violence and Diplomacy in Lebanon: The Troubled Years, 1982–1988*. London: I.B. Tauris.
Salibi, Kamal S. 1965. *The Modern History of Lebanon*, London: Weidenfeld & Nicholson.
Salibi, Kamal S. 1976. *Crossroads to Civil War*. New York: Caravan.
Salibi, Kamal S. 1988. *A House of Many Mansions: The History of Lebanon Reconsidered*. London: I.B. Tauris.
Sayigh, Rosemary. 1992. *Too Many Enemies: The Palestinian Experience in Lebanon*. London: Zed.
Sayigh, Yezid. 1991. "The Gulf Crisis: Why the Arab Regional Order Failed." *International Affairs* 67 (3): 487–507.
Sayigh, Yezid. 1997. *Armed Struggle and the Search for State: The Palestinian National Movement*. New York: Oxford University Press.
Schiff, Ze'ev, and Ehud Ya'ari. 1984. *Israel's Lebanon War*. New York: Simon & Schuster.
Schiff, Ze'ev, and Ehud Ya'ari. 1989. *Intifada: The Palestinian Uprising – Israel's Third Front*. New York: Simon & Schuster.

Bibliography 255

Schmitt, Carl. 2004 [1963]. "Theory of the Partisan: Intermediate Commentary on the Concept of the Political." *Telos* 127: 11–78.

Schulze, Kirsten E. 1998. *Israel's Covert Diplomacy in Lebanon*. Houndmilles, Basingstoke: Macmillan.

Seale, Patrick. 1965. *The Struggle for Syria*. Oxford: Oxford University Press.

Seale, Patrick. 1988. *Asad of Syria: The Struggle for the Middle East*. London: I.B. Tauris

Seaver, Brenda M. 2000. "The Regional Sources of Power-Sharing Failure: The Case of Lebanon." *Political Science Quarterly* 115 (2): 247–271.

Segev, Tom. 2000. *One Palestine, Complete: Jews and Arabs under the Mandate*. New York: Henry Holt & Co.

Segev, Tom. 2007. *1967: Israel, the War, and the Year that Transformed the Middle East*. New York: Metropolitan Books.

Sela, Avraham. 1998. *The Decline of the Arab-Israeli Conflict*. Albany: State University of New York Press.

Sela, Avraham. 2007. "Civil Society, the Military, and National Security: The Case of Israel's Security Zone in South Lebanon." *Israel Studies* 13 (1): 53–78.

Sela, Avraham. 2009. "Difficult Dialogue: The Oslo Process in Israeli Perspective." *Macalester International* 23 (11), at: http://digitalcommons.macalester.edu/cgi/viewcontent.cgi?article=1214&context=macintl (accessed March 24, 2013).

Sela, Avraham. 2014. "The PLO at Fifty: A Historical Perspective." *Contemporary Review of the Middle East* 1 (3): 269–333.

Sela, Avraham, and Oren Barak. 2014. "Domestic-Regional Interactions and Outside Intervention in Intrastate Conflicts: Insights from Lebanon." In *Nonstate Actors in Intrastate Conflicts*, eds. Dan Miodownik and Oren Barak, pp. 166–186. Philadelphia: University of Pennsylvania Press.

Sela, Avraham, and Moshe Ma'oz, eds. 1997a. *The PLO and Israel: From Armed Conflict to Political Solution, 1964–1994*. New York: St. Martin's Press.

Sela, Avraham and Moshe Ma'oz. 1997b. "The PLO in Regional Arab Politics: Taming a Non-state Actor." In *The PLO and Israel: From Armed Conflict to Political Solution, 1964–1994*, eds. Avraham Sela and Moshe Ma'oz, pp. 97–119. New York: St. Martin's Press.

Selby, Jan. 2003. "Dressing Up Domination as 'Cooperation': The Case of Israeli–Palestinian Water Relations." *Review of International Studies* 29 (1): 121–138.

Seliktar, Ofira. 2009. *Doomed to Failure? The Politics and Intelligence of the Oslo Peace Process*. Santa Barbara: ABC-CLIO.

Shafir, Gershon. 2016. "Is Israel a Colonialist State?" In *Handbook of Israel: Major Debates*, eds. Eliezer Ben-Rafael, Julius H. Schoeps, Yitzhak Sternberg, and Olaf Glöckner, pp. 794–808. 2 Vols. Berlin: De Gruyter.

Shafir, Gershon, and Yoav Peled. 2002. *Being Israeli: The Dynamics of Multiple Citizenship*. Cambridge: Cambridge University Press.

Shamir, Yitzhak. 1994. *Summing Up: An Autobiography*. Boston: Little, Brown & Company.

Shapiro, Michael. 2009. *Cinematic Geopolitics*. New York: Routledge.

Sharett, Moshe. 1978. *Personal Diary*. 8 Vols. Tel Aviv: Maariv [Hebrew].

Sharfman, Daphna. 2014. *Palestine in the Second World War: Strategic Plans and Political Dilemmas*. Brighton: Sussex Academic Press.
Sharkansky, Ira. 1999. *Ambiguity, Coping, and Governance: Israeli Experiences in Politics, Religion, and Policymaking*. Westport: Praeger.
Sheffer, Gabriel. 1996. *Moshe Sharett: Biography of a Political Moderate*. Oxford: Oxford University Press.
Sheffer, Gabriel, and Oren Barak, eds. 2010. *Militarism and Israeli Society*. Bloomington: Indiana University Press.
Sheffer, Gabriel, and Oren Barak. 2013. *Israel's Security Networks: A Theoretical and Comparative Perspective*. New York: Cambridge University Press.
Shehadi, Nadim. 1987. *The Idea of Lebanon: Economy and State in the Cénacle Libanais*. Papers on Lebanon, No. 5. Oxford: Centre for Lebanese Studies.
Shehadi, Nadim, and Dana Haffar Mills, eds. 1988. *Lebanon: A History of Conflict and Consensus*. London: Centre for Lebanese Studies and I.B. Tauris.
Shelef, Nadav G. 2010. *Evolving Nationalism: Homeland, Identity, and Religion in Israel, 1925–2005*. Ithaca: Cornell University Press.
Shenhav, Yehouda. 2012. *Beyond the Two-State Solution: A Jewish Political Essay*. Cambridge: Polity.
Shenhav, Yehouda, and Hannan Hever. 2004. "Trends in Post-colonial Research." In *Colonialism and the Postcolonial Dituation*, eds. Yehouda Shenhav and Hannan Hever, pp. 189–201. Jerusalem and Tel Aviv: The Van Leer Jerusalem Institute and Hakibbutz Hameuchad [Hebrew].
Sher, Gilad. 2001. *Just Beyond Reach: The Israeli–Palestinian Peace Negotiations 1999–2001*. Tel Aviv: Miskal [Hebrew].
Shilon, Avi. 2012. *Menachem Begin: A Life*. Trans. Danielle Zilberberg and Yoram Sharett. New Haven: Yale University Press.
Shlaim, Avi. 1988a. *Collusion across the Jordan: King Abdullah, the Zionist Movement and the Partition of Palestine*. New York: Columbia University Press.
Shlaim, Avi. 1988b. "Israeli Interference in Internal Arab Politics: The Case of Lebanon." In *The Politics of Arab Integration*, eds. Giacomo Luciani and Ghassan Salamé, pp. 232–255. New York: Croom Helm.
Shlaim, Avi. 1997. "The Protocol of Sèvres, 1956: An Anatomy of a War Plot." *International Affairs* 73 (3): 509–530.
Shlaim, Avi. 2012. "Israel: Poor Little Samson." In *The 1967 Arab-Israeli War: Origins and Consequences*, eds. Wim Roger Louis and Avi Shlaim, pp. 22–55. New York: Cambridge University Press.
Shohat, Ella. 2010. *Israeli Cinema: East/West and the Politics of Representation*. London: I.B. Tauris.
Shultz, George P. 1993. *Turmoil and Triumph: My Years as Secretary of State*. New York: Charles Scribner's Sons.
Sirriyeh, Hussein. 1976. "The Palestinian Armed Presence in Lebanon since 1967." In *Essays on the Crisis in Lebanon*, ed. Roger Owen, pp. 73–89. London: Ithaca Press.
Sisk, Timothy. 1996. *Power-Sharing and International Mediation in Ethnic Conflicts*. Washington, DC: United States Institute of Peace.
Slyomovics, Susan. 2013. "Memory Studies: Lebanon and Israel/Palestine." *International Journal of Middle East Studies* 45 (3): 589–601.

Smith, Anthony D. 1986. *The Ethnic Origins of Nations*. Oxford: Blackwell.
Smith, Barbara J. 1993. *The Roots of Separatism in Palestine: British Economic Policy, 1920–1929*. Syracuse: Syracuse University Press.
Smooha, Sammy. 1997. "Ethnic Democracy: Israel as an Archetype." *Israel Studies* 2 (2): 198–241.
Smooha, Sammy. 2002. "The Model of Ethnic Democracy: Israel as a Jewish and Democratic State." *Nations and Nationalism* 8 (4): 475–503.
Smooha, Sammy, and Theodor Hanf. 1992. "The Diverse Modes of Conflict Regulation in Deeply Divided Societies." *International Journal of Comparative Sociology* 33 (1–2): 26–47.
Snider, Lewis W. 1984. "The Lebanese Forces: Their Origins and Role in Lebanon's Politics." *Middle East Journal* 38 (1): 1–33.
Snyder, Jack. 1991. *Myths of Empire: Domestic Politics and International Ambition*. Ithaca: Cornell University Press.
Sobelman, Daniel. 2004. *New Rules of the Game*. Tel Aviv: Jaffee Center for Strategic Studies.
Sobelman, Daniel. 2010. "Hizbollah: From Terror to Resistance." In *Israel and Hizbollah: An Asymmetric Conflict in Historical and Comparative Perspective*, eds. Clive Jones and Sergio Catignani, pp. 49–66. London: Routledge.
Söyler, Mehtap. 2013. "Informal Institutions, Forms of State and Democracy: The Turkish Deep State." *Democratization* 20 (2): 310–334.
Spagnolo, John P. 1977. *France and Ottoman Lebanon: 1861–1914*. London: Ithaca Press.
Sprinzak, Ehud. 1991. *The Ascendance of Israel's Radical Right*. New York: Oxford University Press.
Spruyt, Hendrik. 1996. *The Sovereign State and Its Competitors: An Analysis of Systems Change*. Princeton: Princeton University Press.
Spruyt, Hendrik. 2005. *Ending Empire: Contested Sovereignty and Territorial Partition*. Ithaca: Cornell University Press.
Spruyt, Hendrik. 2014. "Territorial Concessions, Domestic Politics, and the Israeli–Palestinian Conflict." In *Democracy and Conflict Resolution: The Dilemmas of Israel's Peacemaking*, eds. Miriam Elman, Oded Haklai, and Hendrik Spruyt, pp. 29–66. Syracuse: Syracuse University Press.
Steele, Brent. 2005. "Ontological Security and the Power of Self-Identity: British Neutrality and the American Civil War." *Review of International Studies* 31 (3): 519–540.
Stein, Kenneth W. 1999. *Heroic Diplomacy: Sadat, Kissinger, Carter, Begin, and the Quest for Arab-Israeli Peace*. London: Routledge.
Steinmetz, George, ed. 1999. *State/Culture: State-Formation after the Cultural Turn*. Ithaca: Cornell University Press.
Sternberg, Yitzhak. 2016. "The Colonialism/Colonization Perspective on Zionism/Israel." In *Handbook of Israel: Major Debates*, eds. Eliezer Ben-Rafael, Julius H. Schoeps, Yitzhak Sternberg, and Olaf Glöckner, pp. 823–847. 2 Vols. Berlin: De Gruyter.
Sternhell, Zeev. 2009. *The Founding Myths of Israel: Nationalism, Socialism, and the Making of the Jewish State*. Princeton: Princeton University Press.

Stirk, Peter M.R. 2009. *The Politics of Military Occupation*. Edinburgh: Edinburgh University Press.

Stoakes, Frank. 1975. "The Supervigilantes: The Lebanese Kataeb Party as a Builder, Surrogate and Defender of the State." *Middle Eastern Studies* 11 (3): 215–236.

Suleiman, Michael. 1967. *Political Parties in Lebanon: The Challenge of a Fragmented Political Culture*. Ithaca: Cornell University Press.

Susser, Asher. 1986. *Western Power Rivalry and Its Interaction with Local Politics in the Levant, 1941–1946*. PhD Thesis, Tel Aviv University.

Tabory, Mala. 1986. *The Multinational Force and Observers in the Sinai: Organization, Structure, and Function*. Boulder: Westview.

Tamir, Moshe. 2005. *Undeclared War*. Tel Aviv: Ministry of Defense [Hebrew].

Taqi al-Din, Riad H. 1987. *The Druze Military Experience*. Kafarnabrakh: Sharikat Matabi' al-Jabal al-Akhdar [Arabic].

Taqi al-Din, Riad. 1998. *An Army Revived, 1988–1994*. Lebanon: s.n. [Arabic].

Tarrow, Sidney. 2012. *Strangers at the Gates: Movements and States in Contentious Politics*. New York: Cambridge University Press.

Telhami, Shibley, and Michael N. Barnett. 2002. "Introduction: Identity and Foreign Policy in the Middle East." In *Identity and Foreign Policy in the Middle East*, eds. Shibley Telhami and Michael N. Barnett, pp. 1–25. Ithaca: Cornell University Press.

Tessler, Mark A. 1994. *A History of the Israeli–Palestinian Conflict*. Bloomington: Indiana University Press.

Thomas, Martin. 2008. *Empires of Intelligence: Security Services and Colonial Disorder after 1914*. Berkeley: University of California Press.

Thomas, Martin. 2014. *Fight or Flight: Britain, France, and Their Roads from Empire*. Oxford: Oxford University Press.

Thomson, Janice. 1994. *Mercenaries, Pirates, and Sovereigns*. Princeton: Princeton University Press.

Thompson, Elizabeth F. 1999. *Colonial Citizens: Republican Rights, Paternal Privilege, and Gender in French Syria and Lebanon*. New York: Columbia University Press.

Thompson, Elizabeth F. 2013. *Justice Interrupted: The Struggle for Constitutional Government in the Middle East*. Cambridge, MA: Harvard University Press.

Tidy, Joanna. 2012. "The Social Construction of Identity: Israeli Foreign Policy and the 2006 War in Lebanon." *Global Society* 26 (4): 535–556.

Tilley, Virginia. 2005. *The One-State Solution: A Breakthrough for Peace in the Israeli–Palestinian Deadlock*. Ann Arbor: University of Michigan Press.

Tilly, Charles. 1975. "Reflections on the History of European State-Making." In *The Formation of National States in Western Europe*, ed. Charles Tilly, pp. 3–84. Princeton: Princeton University Press.

Tilly, Charles. 1992. *Coercion, Capital, and European States, AD 990–1992*. Oxford: Blackwell.

Tlass, Mustafa. ed. 1985. *The Israeli Invasion of Lebanon*. Damascus: Dar Tlass Lil-Dirasat wa-al-Tarjameh wa-al-Nashr [Arabic].

Tolstoy, Leo. 2002 [1878]. *Anna Karenina*. Trans. Richard Pevear and Larissa Volkhonsky. New York: Penguin Books.

Tonge, Jonathan. 2014. *Comparative Peace Processes*. Cambridge: Polity.
Tsafrir, Eliezer. 2006. *Labyrinth in Lebanon: A Traffic Cop in the Lebanese Tangle*. Tel Aviv: Yedioth Ahronoth [Hebrew].
Tsur, Nadir. 2013. "Vocabulary and the Discourse on the 1967 Territories." In *The Impacts of Lasting Occupation: Lessons from Israeli Society*, eds. Daniel Bar-Tal and Izhak Schnell, pp. 471–506. New York: Oxford University Press.
Van Benthuysen, John. 2015. "In-between Anarchy and Interdependence: From State Death to Fragile and Failing States." *Third World Quarterly* 36 (1): 22–39.
Van Creveld, Martin. 1998. *The Sword and the Olive: A Critical History of the Israeli Defense Force*. New York: Public Affairs.
Van Dam, Nikolaos. 1979. *The Struggle for Power in Syria: Sectarianism, Regionalism and Tribalism in Politics, 1961–1980*. New York: St. Martin's Press.
Vocke, Herald. 1978. *The Lebanese War: Its Origins and Political Dimensions*. New York: St. Martin's Press.
Volk, Lucia. 2010. *Memorials and Martyrs in Modern Lebanon*. Bloomington: Indiana University Press.
Wæver, Ole. 2009. "What Exactly Makes a Continuous Existential Threat Existential – and How Is It Discontinued?" In *Existential Threats and Civil-Security Relations*, eds. Oren Barak and Gabriel Sheffer, pp. 19–36. Lanham: Lexington Books.
Waldman, Adir. 2003. *Arbitrating Armed Conflict: Decisions of the Israel–Lebanon Monitoring Group*. New York: Juris Publishing.
Wallach, Yair. 2011a. "Creating a Country through Currency and Stamps: State Symbols and Nation-Building in British-ruled Palestine." *Nations and Nationalism* 17 (1): 129–147.
Wallach, Yair. 2011b. "Trapped in Mirror-Images: The Rhetoric of Maps in Israel/Palestine." *Political Geography* 30 (7): 358–369.
Weber, Max. 1949. *The Methodology of the Social Sciences*. Trans. Edward A. Shils and Henry A. Finch. Glencoe: The Free Press.
Weber, Max. 2003. *The Essential Weber: A Reader*. London: Routledge.
Wedeen, Lisa. 1999. *Ambiguities of Domination: Politics, Rhetoric, and Symbols in Contemporary Syria*. Chicago: Chicago University Press.
Weisburd, David. 1989. *Jewish Settler Violence: Deviance as Social Reaction*. University Park: Penn State University Press.
Weiss, Max. 2010. *In the Shadow of Sectarianism: Law, Shi'ism, and the Making of Modern Lebanon*. Cambridge, MA: Harvard University Press.
Weitz, Yechiam. 2014. "From Peace in the South to War in the North: Menachem Begin as Prime Minister, 1977–1983." *Israel Studies* 19 (1): 145–165.
Weizman, Eyal. 2012. *Hollow Land: Israel's Architecture of Occupation*. London: Verso.
Wendt, Alexander. 1999. *Social Theory of International Politics*. Cambridge: Cambridge University Press.
Wimmer, Andreas, Lars-Erik Cederman, and Brian Min. 2009. "Ethnic Politics and Armed Conflict: A Configurational Analysis of a New Global Data Set." *American Sociological Review* 74 (2): 316–337.
Yamak, Labib Z. 1966. *The Syrian Social Nationalist Party: An Ideological Analysis*. Cambridge, MA: Harvard University Press.

Yaniv, Avner. 1987. *Dilemmas of Security: Politics, Strategy, and the Israeli Experience in Lebanon*. New York: Oxford University Press.

Yiftachel, Oren. 1992. "The State, Ethnic Relations and Democratic Stability: Lebanon, Cyprus and Israel." *GeoJournal* 28 (3): 319–332.

Yiftachel, Oren. 2001. "'Right-Sizing' or 'Right-Shaping?' Politics, Ethnicity and Territory in Plural States." In *Right-Sizing the State: The Politics of Moving Borders*, eds. Brendan O'Leary, Ian Lustick, and Thomas Callaghy, pp. 358–387. New York: Oxford University Press.

Yiftachel, Oren. 2006. *Ethnocracy: Land and Identity Politics in Israel/Palestine*. Philadelphia: University of Pennsylvania Press.

Yishai, Yael. 1985. "Israeli Annexation of East Jerusalem and the Golan Heights: Factors and Processes." *Middle Eastern Studies* 21 (1): 45–60.

Yosef, Raz. 2011. *The Politics of Loss and Trauma in Contemporary Israeli Cinema*. London: Routledge.

Young, Iris M. 2005. "Self-determination as Non-domination: Ideals Applied to Palestine/Israel." *Ethnicities* 5 (2): 139–159.

Young, Michael. 2010. *The Ghosts of Martyrs Square: An Eyewitness Account of Lebanon's Life Struggle*. New York: Simon & Schuster.

Zacher, Mark. 2001. "The Territorial Integrity Norm: International Boundaries and the Use of Force." *International Organization* 55 (2): 215–250.

Zamir, Meir. 1982. "Smaller and Greater Lebanon: The Squaring of a Circle?" *The Jerusalem Quarterly* 23: 34–53.

Zamir, Meir. 1985. *The Formation of Modern Lebanon*. London: Croom Helm.

Zamir, Meir. 1993. *The Formation of Modern Lebanon*. Tel Aviv: Maarachot and Ministry of Defense [Hebrew].

Zamir, Meir. 1997. *Lebanon's Quest: The Road to Statehood, 1926–1939*. London: I.B. Tauris.

Zamir, Meir. 2002. *The Fractured Cedar: Lebanon's Road to Statehood, 1926–1939*. Tel Aviv: Ministry of Defense.

Zeedan, Rami. 2015. *Battalion of Arab: The History of the Minorities Unit in the IDF from 1948 to 1956*. Ben Shemen: Modan [Hebrew].

Zertal, Idith. 2005. *Israel's Holocaust and the Politics of Nationhood*. Trans. Chaya Galai. Cambridge: Cambridge University Press.

Zertal, Idith, and Akiva Eldar. 2007. *Lords of the Land: The War over Israel's Settlements in the Occupied Territories, 1967-2007*. New York: Nation Books.

Zerubavel, Yael. 1995. *Recovered Roots: Collective Memory and the Making of Israeli National Tradition*. Chicago: University of Chicago Press.

Zipori, Mordechai. 1997. *In a Straight Line*. Tel Aviv: Miskal – Yedioth Ahronoth and Chemed Books [Hebrew].

Zisser, Eyal. 1995. "The Maronites, Lebanon and the State of Israel: Early Contacts." *Middle Eastern Studies* 31 (4): 889–918.

Zisser, Eyal. 2000. *Lebanon: The Challenge of Independence*. London: I.B. Tauris.

Zisser, Eyal. 2009. *Lebanon: Blood in the Cedars: From the Civil War to the Second Lebanon War*. Tel Aviv: Hakibbutz Hameuchad [Hebrew].

Zisser, Eyal. 2009. "The Israeli-Syrian-Lebanese Triangle: The Renewed Struggle over Lebanon." *Israel Affairs* 15 (4): 397–412.

Index

Abdullah, Emir/King, 99, 107
Africa, 27, 155
　North Africa, 51, 101
Ahdab, Khayr al-Din al-, 66
Akarli, Engin, 63
Algeria, 19, 20, 29, 31, 38, 222
　Algerian model, 97, 131
　Algerian War (1954–1962), 97
　FLN (Front Libération Nationale), 97
Algiers, 178
Allied Powers (First World War), 9, 46, 47, 51, 98
Allon, Yigal, 116, 169, 183, 184, 185, 186, 200
Almog, Shulamit, 207
Al-Najaddah, 67
Amal Movement, 80, 81, 87, 90, 91, 205
Amir, Yigal, xxii, 130
Andrews, Lewis, 103
Annexation, 18, 37, 54, 115, 117, 137, 141
Aoun, Michel, xxiii, 8, 80, 84, 87, 88, 250
Apartheid, 29, 97, 222
Arab League (League of Arab States), xix, 7, 21, 50, 68, 84
Arab Liberation Army (ALA), 160, 161
Arab Spring, xv, 29, 86, 89
Arab states, xx, 7, 8, 9, 10, 12, 53, 55, 68, 73, 75, 86, 110, 112, 114, 116, 127, 129, 130, 149, 152, 156, 160, 161, 162, 166, 167, 168, 171, 175, 176, 195, 197
Arab summits, xxi
Arab-Israeli conflict, 73, 149, 172
Arab-Israeli War of 1973, 38, 127, 128, 135, 148, 149, 180, 181, 184, 199
Arafat, Yasser, xxii, 128, 129, 131, 147, 168, 171, 197, 198, 210, 212
Arens, Moshe, 201, 214
Argentina, 214
Armenians, 58
Armistice agreements, xx, 9, 52, 104, 167, 174, 177

Armistice regime, 177, 187
Ashkenazi Jews, 135
Asia, 27
Assad, Bashar al-, 35, 84, 89, 222
Assad, Hafez al-, 13, 71, 127, 157, 181, 182, 184, 199, 201
Athens, 178, 179
Auschwitz, 169
Awali River, 196
Axis Powers, 101

B'Tselem, 119, 124, 129
Baath Party, 13, 35, 181
Baghdad, 222
Balfour Declaration (1917), 51, 98, 100
Barak, Ehud, xxii, 57, 131, 132, 147, 204
Begin, Menachem, 1, 54, 134, 147, 158, 180, 189, 190, 191, 192, 193, 195, 197, 198, 199, 200, 201, 202, 203, 205, 208
Beirut, xix, xxii, 2, 6, 7, 8, 13, 48, 63, 66, 75, 84, 86, 89, 159, 160, 161, 162, 163, 173, 178, 180, 192, 193, 196, 197, 204, 210, 216, 244
　International airport, xx, 92, 178, 179
　Southern Suburb of, 87
　West Beirut, 89
Beirut Declaration (2004), 146
Ben-Ami, Shlomo, 215
Ben-Eliezer, Uri, 132
Ben-Gal, Avigdor, 198, 199, 200
Ben-Gurion, David, 21, 52, 106, 107, 108, 110, 133, 134, 165, 166, 167, 200
Bethlehem, 117
Boustani, Emile, 171
Brit Shalom, 103
Britain, xix, 9, 19, 28, 29, 38, 50, 53, 58, 98, 99, 100, 101, 102, 104, 105, 110, 121, 136, 149, 199, 222, 223
　British army, 101, 103
　White Paper (1939), 98
Byron, Lord, 26

261

Index

Cairo Accord, xxii
Cairo Agreement (1969), xx, 159, 171, 172, 174, 180, 184
Camp David Accords (1978), xxi, 128, 195, 197, 203
Camp David summit (1978), 147
Camp David summit (2000), xxii, 131, 147
Carter, Jimmy, 54, 190, 191
Chamoun, Camille, 1, 2, 71, 161, 167, 194, 195
Chamoun, Dani, 195
Chehab, Fouad, xx, 75, 138, 150, 161
Chiha, Michel, 72
China, 21, 149, 221
Chouf, 203
Clinton, Bill, xxii, 131
Cold War, 21, 61, 128, 140
Colonialism, 27, 51, 99
 Colonial power, 20
 Colonies, 20
Communism, 67
Communities, 3, 28, 31, 32, 33, 34, 35, 36, 37, 41, 42, 43, *See* Ethnic groups
Comparative politics, 6, 16, 223
Conflict management, xii, xiii
Conflict regulation, xii, xiii, 32, 33, 34, 42, 43, 76, 104, 133, 174
Conflict resolution, xii, xiii
Corm, Georges, 157
Crimean Peninsula, 22, 221
Cyprus, 223
Czechoslovakia, 43

Damascus, 13, 181
Dayan, Moshe, 53, 116, 119, 165, 166, 167, 174, 178, 179, 190, 198
de Gaulle, Charles, 19, 20, 31, 129
De-militarization, 4, 39, 76, 149, *See also* Militarization
De-securitization, 43, 152, *See also* Securitization
DFLP (Democratic Front for the Liberation of Palestine), 168
Diskin, Yuval, 120
Divided societies, xii, xv, 2, 3, 5, 6, 12, 14, 15, 16, 27, 31, 32, 33, 34, 35, 36, 37, 39, 40, 41, 42, 43, 44, 45, 49, 54, 57, 58, 60, 64, 77, 86, 95, 97, 99, 115, 121, 123, 127, 129, 130, 137, 138, 140, 144, 146, 147, 148, 149, 151, 154, 155, 202, 210, 219, 222, 224

East Jerusalem, xx, xxiii, 2, 10, 17, 52, 54, 105, 106, 107, 117, 119, 122, 123, 124, 126, 129, 145, 191
 Western Wall, 117
East Timor, 221
Eban, Abba, 2, 54, 169, 170
Egypt, xx, xxi, 4, 9, 10, 11, 12, 38, 50, 52, 53, 54, 86, 99, 104, 105, 114, 122, 127, 130, 159, 168, 170, 172, 175, 179, 180, 182, 189, 199, 201, 220
Egyptian-Israeli peace process, 128, 190, 195
Egyptian-Israeli peace treaty (1979), xxi, 11, 54, 122, 128, 130, 176, 195, 201
Egyptian-Israeli relations, 156
Eichmann, Adolf, 108, 198
Eitan, Rafael, 158, 178, 197, 199, 201, 212
Elazar, David, 169
Eritrea, 222
Erlich, Simcha, 203
Eshkol, Levi, 53, 55, 116, 198
Ethiopia, 222
Ethnic groups, 3, *See* Communities
Ethno-securitism, 146, 151
Etzel, 102, 110, 200
Europe, 58, 64, 67, 102, 221
 Colonial powers, 1
 European powers, xix, 27, 46, 47, 62, 64
 European Union, 131
 Jews in, 191
 Western Europe, 24
Expanded states, 4, 5, 18, 19, 22, 36, 37, 38, 39, 40, 41, 42, 57, 122, 123, 154, 203, 219

Failed states, 27, 30, 209
Fascism, 67
Fatah, 90, 119, 131, 168, 169, 171, 178, 179, 192, 210, 212
Fatah al-Islam, 89
Faysal, Emir/King, 47, 99
Fedayeen, 163, *See* Fidayin
Fidayin, 114, 162, 175, *See* Fedayeen
Films, 205
 In Israel, 159
 In Lebanon, 159
First Arab-Israeli War, xix, xx, 9, 12, 52, 73, 95, 96, 101, 103, 104, 109, 111, 116, 130, 137, 140, 143, 157, 160, 161, 192, 200
 Arab armies in, 106
 Jewish militias in, 106
 Palestinian militias in, 106
 Volunteers in, 106

Index

First World War, xix, 6, 9, 46, 47, 48, 49, 51, 58, 63, 64, 98
Fitzgerald, F. Scott, 24
Ford, Gerald, 184
France, xix, 1, 6, 7, 8, 12, 19, 20, 21, 23, 29, 31, 38, 46, 47, 48, 49, 50, 53, 58, 60, 63, 64, 65, 66, 68, 75, 86, 97, 98, 99, 158, 160, 167, 222
   Revolution, 23
Franco-Lebanese treaty (1936), 65
Frangieh, Suleiman, 180, 182
Free Patriotic Movement, 87, 91
Freedom House, 22, 78
Frontiers, 34, 35, 36, 57, 110, 111, 122, 125, 140, 214
   Frontierization, 125
Future Movement, 87, 89, 91

Galilee, 95, 114, 171
Gaza District, 118, *See* Gaza Strip
Gaza Strip, xx, xxi, xxii, xxiii, 2, 10, 11, 12, 17, 19, 20, 22, 35, 52, 54, 56, 57, 95, 105, 107, 115, 117, 119, 120, 123, 124, 126, 129, 130, 132, 137, 140, 142, 145, 168, 190, 203, 214, 215, 216, 217
   Refugee camps in, 105
Gaza War (2008–2009), xxiii, *See* Israel: Operation Cast Lead
Gazit, Shlomo, 116, 193, 194
Gemayel family, 190, 200
Gemayel, Amine, 195
Gemayel, Bashir, xxi, 13, 81, 189, 195, 202, 204, 216, 221
Gemayel, Pierre, 67, 81, 92, 157, 194, 195
Germany, 149
Ghettos, 34, 35, 36, 57, 125, 214
Golan, xx, 10, 11, 17, 18, 38, 53, 127, 199, 217
   Israeli occupation of, 203
Goldstein, Baruch, xxii, 130
Gouraud, Henri, 48
Great Britain, 51, *See* Britain
Great powers, 21, 37, 39, 58, 59, 138, 148, 167
Greater Israel, 2, 10, 45, 50, 54, 56, 57, 115, 138, 141, 219
Greater Lebanon (*grand liban*), xix, 1, 2, 6, 9, 45, 48, 50, 57, 58, 60, 61, 62, 65, 68, 138, 141, 142, 219
Greater Syria, 67, 182, 204
Greek War of Independence, 26
Green Line, 10, 118, 125, 131, 140
Gulf War (1991), xxi, 11, 21, 50, 128, 140
Gur, Mordechai, 175, 176, 179

Gush Emunim, 135, 202
Gush Etzion, 106

Haddad, Saad, xxi, 78, 186, 190, 193, 194, 196, 203
Hagana, 100, 102, 199, 200
Haig, Alexander, 191, 201
Hamas, xxii, xxiii, 12, 17, 57, 119, 126, 131, 132, 145, 209, 210, 213, 214, 215
Hariri, Rafiq al-, xxii, 8, 84, 85, 87, 89, 91, 92
Hasbaiya, 196
Hashemite family, 47, 99
Hazak, Reuven, 211, 212
Hebron, 95, 117, 123, 130
Helou, Charles, 75, 172
Herut, 110, 117, 133
Hitchcock, Alfred, 147
Hizbullah, xv, xxii, 8, 13, 14, 81, 82, 85, 86, 87, 89, 90, 91, 92, 93, 94, 142, 146, 149, 150, 158, 187, 204, 205, 209, 210, 211, 212, 213, 214, 215, 216, 217, 218, 221, 224
   Resistance, 8, 85, 90, 92, 213, 218, 221
Holocaust, 52, 54, 108
Holy Places, 109
Holy sites, 102, 117
Hoyek, Elias, 47
Hussein, King, 169, 184
Husseini, Mufti Haj Amin al-, 102, 106

India, 22, 149
Indonesia, 221
Inter-communal relations, 31, 33, 37, 43, 221, 222
   Control, 32, 33, 34, 35, 36, 37, 42, 43, 63, 65, 71, 79, 109, 111, 112, 113, 114, 121, 128, 133, 137, 142, 143, 154, 198, 200, 201, 203, 205, 219, 222
   Power sharing, 7, 8, 33, 34, 35, 36, 42, 43, 63, 65, 69, 71, 72, 73, 76, 77, 78, 79, 80, 81, 82, 88, 93, 110, 133, 139, 140, 142, 143, 144, 145, 146, 150, 154, 219, 222
   Repression, 33, 34, 35, 43, 79, 133, 137, 142, 143, 151, 154, 196, 222
   Stalemate, 33, 35, 36, 79, 142, 143, 150, 154, 222
International Relations, xii, 6, 16, 155, 159, 223, 243
Intifada, 134, 145
   First Palestinian Intifada, xxi, 2, 11, 56, 96, 115, 121, 122, 123, 126, 127, 128, 137, 140, 143, 213, 216

Intifada (cont.)
  Second Palestinian Intifada, xxii, 11, 56, 92, 123, 125, 127, 128, 131, 206, 214, 215
Iran, 13, 58, 86, 91, 94, 149, 155, 156, 214
Iraq, xxi, 9, 13, 21, 27, 29, 32, 50, 57, 58, 86, 99, 101, 105, 144, 149, 166, 192, 222, 223, 228
  British rule in, 99
  Iraqi army, 27
  Kurdish community in, 32, 223
  Palestinian refugees in, 105
  Shi'i community in, 32, 223
  Sunni community in, 32, 222
Ireland, 19, 222
Islamic Jihad, xxii, 145, 214
Islamic State, 222
Israel, xv, xx, xxi, xxii, xxiii, 1, 2, 3, 4, 5, 7, 8, 9, 10, 11, 12, 13, 16, 17, 18, 19, 20, 21, 22, 23, 28, 29, 30, 31, 34, 38, 50, 51, 52, 53, 54, 55, 56, 57, 61, 75, 77, 78, 80, 83, 84, 85, 86, 90, 91, 92, 94, 96, 97, 98, 101, 105, 106, 107, 108, 109, 110, 111, 112, 113, 114, 115, 116, 117, 118, 119, 120, 121, 122, 123, 124, 125, 126, 127, 128, 129, 130, 131, 132, 133, 135, 136, 137, 139, 140, 142, 145, 146, 147, 149, 155, 156, 158, 159, 160, 161, 162, 163, 164, 165, 166, 167, 168, 169, 170, 171, 172, 173, 174, 175, 176, 177, 178, 179, 180, 182, 183, 184, 185, 186, 188, 189, 190, 191, 192, 193, 194, 195, 196, 197, 198, 199, 200, 201, 202, 203, 204, 205, 206, 207, 208, 209, 210, 211, 212, 213, 214, 215, 216, 217, 218, 220, 221, 222, 234, 260
  Autonomy Plan, 195, 197, 198, 203
  Bedouin community in, xx, 111, 112
  Begin Doctrine, 192
  Bus 300 Affair, 212
  Cabinet, 109, 117, 135, 190
  Christian community in, xx
  Circassian community in, xx, 111, 112, 136
  Civil Support Administration in Lebanon, 211
  Communal approach in, 111, 122, 157, 163, 164, 165, 166, 167, 168, 189, 190, 191, 193, 202, 217, 220
  Confiscation of Palestinian land in, xx, 10, 111, 113
  Coordinator of Israel's Operations in Lebanon, 170, 204, 207, 211
  Court system, 117
  Culture, 155
  Declaration of the Establishment of the State of Israel, 108
  Disengagement Plan (2005), xxiii, 11, 57, 123, 124, 126, 132, 137, 140, 215
  Druze community in, xx, 111, 112, 136
  Economy, 135, 141, 155
  Emergency laws, 103
  Ethnic democracy in, 96
  Foreign relations, 155
  Foreign workers in, 56
  Four Mothers movement, 212
  General Security Service (*Shin Bet, Shabak*), 113, 120, 121, 125, 128, 148, 196, 203, 211, 212
  Good Fence policy, xx, 183, 209
  High Court of Justice, 129
  Inter-communal relations in, 111, 112, 114, 120
  Interior Ministry, 56
  Israel Defense Forces (IDF), xii, xx, xxi, 1, 9, 10, 14, 52, 53, 57, 101, 106, 107, 111, 112, 113, 114, 116, 120, 125, 126, 128, 131, 135, 136, 137, 140, 148, 158, 161, 163, 165, 166, 168, 169, 170, 171, 172, 173, 175, 177, 178, 180, 184, 185, 189, 194, 196, 197, 200, 202, 203, 204, 206, 207, 208, 209, 211, 212, 214, 215, 217
  Jewish community in, 10, 14, 15, 45, 53, 107, 108, 109, 110, 111, 112, 113, 114, 118, 133, 137, 139, 148, 153
  Jewish immigration (*aliya*), 107
  Kahan Commission of Inquiry, xxi, 191
  Knesset (parliament), xi, 10, 109, 117, 119, 130, 131, 135, 170, 180, 185, 192, 200, 202, 212
  Law of Return, 56
  Litani Operation (1978), xxi, 7, 13, 174, 186, 188, 192, 193
  Maps of, 17, 118
  Military elite, 135
  Military Government over Palestinian citizens, xx, 10, 109, 112, 114, 137
  Military strategy, 148, 156
  Ministry of Defense, xv, 1, 165
  Ministry of Education, 113
  Ministry of Foreign Affairs, 2, 164, 166, 174, 176, 183, 195, 200
  Muslim community in, xx
  National religious Jews, 135
  National Unity Government, 117, 127, 133, 198
  Operation Accountability (1993), xxii

Index

Operation Cast Lead (2008–2009), xxiii
Operation Grapes of Wrath (1996), xxii, 134, 158, 209, 213
Operation Pillar of Defense (2012), xxiii
Operation Protective Edge (2014), xxiii
Operation Uproar 2 (1970), 175
Oranim plan (1982), 196
Palestinian community in, xx, xxii, 10, 12, 54, 108, 109, 110, 111, 112, 113, 114, 118, 119, 120, 121, 122, 133, 136, 137, 139, 145, 148, 153, 190
Politics, 155
Preventive strategy, 192
Refugees in, 56
Religious parties in, 108
Representation in, 109, 135
Security in, 109, 111, 112, 120, 128, 168
Security networks in, 54, 55, 113, 117, 122, 135, 137, 149, 156, 158, 193, 220
Security sector in, xx, xxii, 57, 109, 112, 113, 118, 121, 125, 127, 128, 131, 137, 139, 140, 148, 150, 196
Security Zone in Lebanon, xxi, xxii, 8, 13, 14, 85, 158, 171, 186, 193, 208, 209, 211, 213, 218, 221
Separation barrier in West Bank, 56, 125
Separation of religion and state, 108
Settler movement, 55, 137
Society, 155
South Lebanon Area (ADAL), 186, 193
State Attorney's Office, 125
State formation in, 107, 108, 111, 112, 114, 116, 120, 136, 137, 148
Statism (*mamlachtiyut*), 107, 111, 166
Statist approach in, 111, 122, 133, 139, 163, 164, 166, 167, 168, 176, 178, 185, 187, 189, 190, 191, 193, 217, 220
Triangle area, 114
Ultra-religious groups in, 111
War of Independence, xix, 200. *See* First Arab-Israeli War
Winograd Commission of inquiry, 209
Withdrawal from Lebanon (1985), xxi, 13, 211, 218, 221
Withdrawal from Lebanon (2000), xxii, 8, 85, 158, 204, 211, 214, 218, 221
Israel/Palestine, xi, xiii, xix, 3, 4, 5, 6, 10, 11, 12, 13, 14, 15, 16, 18, 20, 29, 31, 34, 35, 39, 44, 45, 50, 51, 54, 55, 56, 57, 58, 95, 96, 97, 98, 104, 115, 122, 123, 125, 126, 127, 130, 132, 135, 136, 137, 138, 139, 140, 141, 142, 143, 144, 145, 146, 147, 148, 150, 151, 153, 154, 155, 156, 160, 168, 169, 171, 176, 181, 182, 187, 188, 189, 190, 202, 204, 210, 211, 212, 213, 214, 215, 216, 217, 218, 219, 220, 221, 222, 223, 224
Confiscation of Palestinian land in, 118, 119, 122
Ethnocracy in, 97
Geographical regions in, 95
Inter-communal relations in, 11, 122, 142, 143, 144, 146, 153
Jewish community in, 3, 4, 5, 9, 11, 16, 45, 46, 54, 55, 56, 58, 95, 96, 116, 117, 120, 121, 127, 128, 131, 133, 134, 135, 136, 137, 138, 141, 144, 145, 146, 148, 150, 153, 203, 216, 219, 224
Palestinian community in, 3, 4, 9, 11, 30, 45, 54, 55, 56, 95, 96, 116, 119, 120, 121, 122, 124, 126, 127, 128, 129, 131, 132, 136, 140, 143, 145, 148, 150, 153, 195, 196, 197, 198, 214, 215, 219, 224
Palestinian refugees in, 130
State formation in, 141
Israeli Communist Party (*Maki*), 109, 110
Israeli-Arab War of 1967, xx, 3, 7, 11, 12, 13, 16, 17, 21, 23, 50, 51, 53, 55, 75, 95, 96, 107, 111, 115, 116, 133, 135, 137, 148, 149, 155, 156, 157, 161, 168, 169, 171, 174, 176, 186, 189, 197, 198, 213, 220
Israeli-Jordanian peace treaty (1994), xxii, 130, 156
Israeli-Jordanian relations, 156
Israeli-Lebanese border, xx, 9, 89, 159, 161, 162, 164, 171, 174, 176, 177, 185, 187, 192, 216
Blue Line, xxii, 204
Israeli-Lebanese border area, 7, 13, 75, 85, 158, 161, 169, 172, 173, 174, 180, 182, 183, 185, 186, 193, 194, 211, 220, 221
Israeli-Lebanese relations, 5, 12, 13, 155, 156, 157, 158, 159, 160, 161, 163, 164, 168, 177, 187, 189, 192, 205, 207, 220, 224
Armistice Agreement (1949), 12, 155, 157, 161, 162, 164, 174, 175, 177, 178, 198, 224
Israeli-Lebanese agreement (1983), xxi, 79
Israel-Lebanon Mixed Armistice Commission (ILMAC), xx, 157, 162, 163, 166, 174, 175, 176, 177, 178, 220, 224
Israeli-Palestinian conflict, xiii, 96, 118, 127, 129, 130, 137, 140, 141, 143, 146, 147

266   Index

Israeli-Palestinian peace process, xxii, 11, 29, 56, 97, 115, 123, 124, 126, 127, 128, 131, 132, 137, 140, 143, 220
   Cairo Accord (1994). *See* Gaza-Jericho Agreement
   Gaza-Jericho Agreement (1994), xxii
   Interim Agreement on the West Bank and Gaza Strip (1995), xxii
   Wye River Memorandum (1998), 134
Israeli-Syrian relations, 156

Jabal Wastani, 196
Jericho, 130
Jerusalem, 1, 17, 95, 99, 102, 117, 119, 123, 130, 132, 147, 195
   Old City, 106
   Special International Regime for, 104
Jewish Agency, 111, 165
Jewish National Fund, 111
Jews, xxii, xxiii, 29, 129, 201
Jezzine, 87
Jibril, Ahmad, 213
Johnson, Lyndon B., 21
Jordan, xv, xx, xxi, xxii, 7, 10, 12, 13, 34, 50, 52, 53, 54, 57, 98, 105, 115, 121, 126, 127, 130, 156, 168, 169, 171, 175, 179, 180, 182, 184, 185, 186, 187, 196, 197, 203, 220, 221, 222
   Black September, 13, 169, 179, 184
   Hashemite family, 179
   Jordanian army, xx, 168, 175
   Palestinian refugees in, 105
Jordan River, xi, 9, 52, 58, 98, 105, 168, 169
Judea and Samaria, 2, *See* West Bank
Junblat, Kamal, 182

Kafar Qassem Massacre (1956), 114, 190
Karameh, Battle of (1968), 156, 168, 175
Kawkaba, 196
Kerry, John, xiii, 144
Khoury, Bechara al-, 70, 161
Kimche, David, 1, 176, 195, 200, 207
Kiryat Shmonah, 169
Kissinger, Henry, 179, 183, 184, 185
Kurds, 58
Kuwait, 21

Labor Party, xxii, 2, 109, 118, 127, 128, 133, 169, 190, 202, 209
Lahad, Antoine, 211
Lahoud, Emile, 88
Land Day (1976), xx, 190
Land of Israel (*Eretz Israel*), xi, 3, 54, 100, 108

League of Nations, xix
Lebanese civil war (1958), xx, 51, 61, 70, 71, 73, 75, 81, 92, 149, 157, 167, 189
Lebanese civil war (1975–1990), xiii, xx, xxi, 7, 12, 13, 30, 46, 51, 58, 60, 61, 62, 67, 71, 76, 78, 79, 80, 82, 83, 84, 85, 86, 88, 91, 92, 93, 99, 139, 142, 143, 145, 146, 149, 150, 152, 159, 182, 189, 207, 209, 210, 220, 221
Lebanese Communist Party, 67
Lebanese Forces (militia), xxi, 13, 81, 86, 90, 91, 189, 202, 203, 204, 221
Lebanon, vii, xii, xv, xix, xx, xxi, xxii, xxiii, 1, 2, 3, 4, 5, 6, 7, 8, 9, 10, 11, 12, 13, 14, 15, 16, 18, 21, 27, 30, 31, 34, 35, 38, 39, 41, 44, 45, 47, 48, 49, 50, 51, 52, 57, 58, 60, 61, 62, 63, 64, 65, 66, 67, 68, 69, 70, 71, 72, 73, 74, 75, 76, 77, 78, 80, 81, 82, 83, 84, 85, 86, 87, 89, 90, 91, 92, 93, 95, 96, 98, 99, 101, 104, 107, 120, 126, 138, 140, 141, 143, 144, 145, 146, 147, 148, 149, 150, 151, 153, 154, 155, 156, 157, 158, 159, 160, 161, 162, 163, 164, 165, 166, 167, 168, 169, 170, 171, 172, 173, 174, 175, 176, 177, 178, 179, 180, 181, 182, 183, 184, 185, 186, 187, 188, 189, 190, 191, 192, 193, 194, 195, 196, 197, 198, 199, 200, 201, 202, 204, 205, 206, 207, 208, 209, 210, 211, 212, 213, 214, 215, 216, 217, 218, 219, 220, 221, 222, 223, 224
   Alawite community in, 8, 35, 85, 89
   Armenian community in, 49, 85
   Biqaʻ, xix, 6, 48, 60, 75, 88, 165, 196, 199
   Cabinet, 63, 79, 82, 83, 85, 86, 87, 91, 139, 142, 213
   Cantons in, 7, 79, 83, 93, 143
   Christian communities in, 1, 6, 7, 9, 45, 47, 48, 49, 53, 56, 58, 63, 65, 66, 69, 71, 74, 75, 76, 77, 79, 80, 81, 83, 85, 87, 88, 96, 139, 142, 143, 149, 150, 157, 160, 167, 182, 183, 191, 192, 193, 195, 196, 197, 200, 202, 203, 206
   Civil society in, 146
   Communities in, xiii, 4, 7, 27, 50, 60, 61, 64, 65, 68, 70, 71, 72, 73, 74, 81, 82, 83, 85, 86, 87, 88, 96, 100, 138, 141, 142, 147, 149, 151, 198, 205
   Constitutional Crisis (1952), 70, 75
   Deep state in, 89, 94, 150
   Druze community in, xxi, 6, 7, 8, 45, 46, 49, 63, 66, 71, 74, 75, 80, 85, 91, 96, 142, 160, 182, 203, 205, 206, 217
   Economy, 141

Electoral laws, 65
Free Lebanon State (1979), 78, 193
French High Commissioner (in Mandate period), 65
French Mandate in, xix, 64, 66, 140, 143
General Directorate of General Security (*Surete Générale*), 61, 87
General Directorate of State Security, 61, 87
Geographical regions in, 27, 50, 60, 64, 65, 73, 83, 88, 138
Government of National Reconciliation, 83
Higher Defense Council, 83
Immobilism in, 71
Inter-communal relations in, 62, 64, 67, 68, 69, 70, 71, 73, 78, 79, 80, 81, 87, 94, 142, 144, 146, 152, 161
Internal Security Forces (ISF), 61, 83, 87
Israeli occupation of, 203, 204, 206, 208, 209, 212, 218
Large families (or clans) in, 27, 50, 60, 64, 65, 73, 88, 138
Lebanese Armed Forces (LAF), xi, xx, xxiii, 8, 9, 14, 61, 66, 74, 75, 76, 78, 79, 80, 81, 83, 84, 85, 88, 89, 139, 149, 150, 158, 160, 161, 162, 171, 172, 173, 175, 177, 179, 180, 181, 185, 186, 193, 194, 209, 214
Lebanese Constitution, 64, 65, 99
Maronite community in, 1, 2, 5, 6, 9, 12, 13, 14, 15, 16, 38, 45, 46, 47, 48, 49, 50, 51, 58, 62, 63, 64, 65, 66, 67, 68, 69, 71, 74, 75, 76, 79, 80, 82, 83, 85, 86, 87, 90, 91, 92, 93, 96, 98, 99, 138, 139, 142, 148, 150, 157, 158, 160, 161, 164, 165, 166, 171, 172, 173, 182, 183, 189, 190, 191, 194, 195, 198, 199, 200, 201, 202, 203, 204, 205, 207, 211, 217, 220
Mount Lebanon, xix, 2, 4, 6, 45, 46, 47, 48, 49, 50, 51, 58, 60, 61, 62, 64, 75, 87, 88, 93, 98, 143. *See also Mutasarrifiyya*, Autonomous district of Mount Lebanon
Muslim communities in, 1, 6, 12, 65, 66, 69, 71, 74, 75, 77, 80, 81, 83, 88, 93, 139, 142, 143, 150, 157, 160, 166, 171, 174, 184
National Unity Government, 92
Neutrality of, 93, 149
North Lebanon, xix, 6, 48, 88
Orthodox community in, 49, 63, 85
Palestinian refugee camps in, xix, 161, 163, 180, 204, 210, 216
Palestinian refugees in, xix, 105, 161, 162
Palestinians in, 206
Parliament, xxi, xxiii, 8, 63, 65, 79, 82, 85, 86, 87, 91, 99, 139, 161, 213
Parties-militias in, xii, 67, 73, 77, 78, 79, 80, 81, 83, 84, 85, 86, 91, 93, 143, 146, 149, 152, 182, 183, 189, 190, 191, 194, 198, 199, 200, 205, 221
Peace process, 147, 152, 154, 220
Political bosses (*zu'ama'*) in, 7, 71, 91
Political sectarianism in, 82
Population census (1932), xix, 9, 11, 48
President, xv, xxiii, 62, 69, 74, 79, 82, 83, 87, 88, 139, 195
Prime Minister, 62, 66, 69, 82, 83, 84, 87
Representation in, 65, 69, 73, 87, 88, 99, 139, 152
Security in, 64, 66, 67, 70, 71, 73, 76, 79, 80, 81, 82, 83, 87, 89, 94, 146, 149, 152, 153
Security network in, 75, 150
Security sector in, 61, 62, 63, 67, 69, 73, 74, 76, 79, 80, 81, 83, 89, 93, 138, 139, 146, 149, 150, 151, 171
Shi'i community in, xxi, 6, 7, 8, 45, 48, 49, 63, 66, 69, 71, 80, 81, 82, 85, 86, 87, 90, 92, 94, 96, 142, 149, 150, 158, 160, 202, 203, 204, 205, 206, 210, 211, 215, 217, 218
South Lebanon, xix, xx, xxi, xxii, 6, 7, 8, 13, 48, 80, 87, 88, 94, 158, 162, 169, 175, 184, 185, 186, 192, 193, 194, 196, 197, 199, 203, 208, 210, 211, 212, 216
South Lebanon, Christian militia in, xx, xxi, 78, 186, 190, 194, 196, 203
Speaker of Parliament, xv, 66, 69, 82, 87
State failure, 4, 5, 27, 73, 76, 93, 158, 159, 187
State formation in, 62, 64, 67, 70, 71, 72, 73, 82, 83, 141
Sunni community in, 6, 7, 8, 45, 48, 49, 63, 65, 66, 67, 68, 69, 71, 75, 79, 82, 83, 84, 85, 87, 89, 93, 159, 161, 172, 174, 206
Syrian refugees in, 8, 84
Tribes in, 60, 64
Troika, 62, 82, 87
Lebanon War of 1982, xxi, 2, 7, 8, 11, 16, 38, 80, 90, 91, 112, 120, 127, 133, 148, 156, 157, 158, 159, 178, 188, 189, 191, 197, 200, 202, 203, 204, 205, 206, 209, 210, 211, 212, 213, 215, 216, 217, *See* Operation Peace for Galilee

Index

Lehi, 102, 146
Leibowitz, Yeshayahu, 108, 120
Levant, 6, 21, 46, 47, 48, 49, 64, 66
   Christian communities in, 66
   Muslim communities in, 66
Lewis, Samuel, 191, 194
Libya, 13, 29, 86, 149
Likud Party, 54, 127, 130, 131, 133, 134, 158, 189, 190, 220
Litani River, 89, 165, 167, 192
Lubrani, Uri, 170, 175, 204, 207

Magnes, Judah, 103
Malikiyya, Battle of (1948), 9, 161
Mapai, 107, 108, 109, 110, 133, 164
March 14 Camp, 85
March 8 Camp, 85
Meir, Golda, 164, 169, 172
Meretz, 2
Middle East, 1, 2, 5, 14, 47, 50, 51, 58, 73, 86, 90, 97, 101, 157, 158, 164, 165, 168, 178, 192, 197, 221
   Mandate system in, 99
Middle East peace process, 184, 190
   Madrid Conference (1991), xxi, 56, 128, 175
   Reagan Plan (1982), 203, 217
Militarism, 146
   Ethno-militarism, 43, 104, 146, 151
Militarization, 4, 36, 38, 39, 73, 76, 102, 104, 148, 152
   Ethno-militarization, 153
Mizrahi Jews, 135
Modernization school, 32, 33
Morocco, 21, 50, 221
Mossad, 2, 108, 164, 191, 195, 197, 200, 208
Mubarak, Hosni, 189
Mughniya, 'Imad, 90, 92
Musawi, Abbas, 209, 212, 214
Mustaqbal Movement, 89
Mutasarrifiyya, Autonomous district of Mount Lebanon, xix, 6, 46, 47, 48, 53, 60, 62, 63, 64, 65, 93, 140, 219
   Administrative council, 63
   Governor, 62, 63

Nahariya, 202
Nahr al-Bared refugee camp, 89
Nakba, xix, 104, *See* First Arab-Israeli War
Naqoura, 162, 175
Nasrallah, Hassan, 87, 215
Nasser, Gamal Abdul, 10, 38, 53, 61, 159, 172
Nation in arms, 151

National Liberal Party, 194
National Pact (1943), xix, 6, 7, 46, 62, 65, 68, 69, 71, 72, 75, 82, 83, 93, 139, 143, 156, 160
Nation-state, 2, 3, 5, 6, 10, 14, 15, 28, 45, 46, 48, 49, 57, 58, 59, 64, 96, 105, 138, 139, 140, 148, 219
Navot, Nachum, 191, 197
Nazis, 108
Netanyahu, Benjamin, 2, 126, 130, 134, 145
New states, 27, 33
North America, 24
North Cyprus, 221
Northern Ireland, 21, 22, 50, 57, 97, 121, 122, 144, 223, 224

Olmert, Ehud, 57, 132
Ontological security, 3
Operation Peace for Galilee, xxi, 197, 202, 205, *See* Lebanon War of 1982
Orientalism, 207, 212
Orwell, George, 205
Oslo Agreement (1993), xxii, 2, 20, 56, 128, 130, 137, 146, 147, 224
Oslo Process, 11, 140, 145, *See* Israeli-Palestinian peace process
Ottoman Empire, xix, 6, 9, 46, 47, 49, 50, 58, 62, 64, 98
Ottoman army, 47
Oz, Amos, 205

Pakradouni, Karim, 67
Palestine, xi, 10, 98, 99, 100, 101, 102, 103, 104, 105, 160, 161, 163
   Arab Higher Council, 106
   Arab state in, 52, 104
   Bi-national state in, 103
   British Mandate in, xix, xx, 3, 5, 9, 10, 12, 52, 54, 98, 99, 100, 101, 102, 103, 104, 106, 107, 110, 113, 133, 136, 140, 160, 161, 199, 200
   Christian communities in, 102
   Druze community in, 102
   Inter-communal relations in, 100, 102, 103, 104, 105, 140
   Jewish community in, xix, 9, 51, 52, 58, 98, 99, 100, 101, 102, 103, 104, 105, 106, 107, 110, 133, 136, 148, 160, 199
   Jewish militias in, 107
   Jewish national home in, 9, 100
   Muslim community in, 102
   Palestinian community in, 9, 51, 100, 101, 102, 103, 104, 105, 106, 110, 133, 136, 148, 160

Index

Palestinian refugees in, 105
Parties-militias in, 102, 199
Representation in, 106
Security in, 100, 106, 136
State formation in, 100, 104, 105
Zionist settlers in, 51
Palestine (*Filastin*), 3
Palestine War, xix, *See* First Arab-Israeli War
Palestinian armed factions in, 197, 199
Palestinian National Authority (PNA or PA), xxii, 41, 56, 125, 126, 130, 131, 132, 137
Palestinian Police, 147
Palestinian revolt (1936–1939), xix, 9, 102, 103, 104, 106, 199
Palestinian state, 11, 121, 130, 132, 145, 197, 198, 203
Palestinians, xxi, xxiii, 10, 12, 51, 52, 98, 105, 107, 127, 159, 168, 169, 176, 180, 182, 203, 215, 216, 221
   Economy, 126
   Fedayin, 175, 179
   Palestinian Armed factions, xx, 7, 13, 70, 75, 77, 79, 85, 91, 92, 120, 126, 127, 145, 149, 168, 169, 170, 171, 172, 173, 179, 180, 181, 182, 184, 185, 186, 187, 192, 193, 194, 196, 200, 201, 203, 210, 211, 212, 213, 215, 217, 218, 220
   Palestinian armed struggle, 168, 210
   Palestinian national movement, 168
   Palestinian refugees, 10, 52, 95, 107, 130, 132, 137, 147
Palmach, 102, 200
Paris Peace Conference (1919), 47
Parker, Richard, 194
Partition, 35, 143, 144, 222
Peled, Yossi, 208, 209
Peres, Shimon, xxii, 57, 131, 170, 180, 183, 185, 202, 209
PFLP (Popular Front for the Liberation of Palestine), 168
Phalanges Party, 13, 67, 81, 90, 92, 149, 157, 158, 171, 189, 190, 191, 194, 200, 202, 220
Phoenicians, 72
PLO (Palestine Liberation Organization), xxi, xxii, 2, 56, 91, 120, 127, 128, 129, 131, 140, 147, 168, 169, 174, 180, 184, 186, 196, 197, 198, 199, 203, 210, 212, 216, 217, 220
Poland, 43
Popular Front for the Liberation of Palestine-General Command, 213

Posen, Barry, 152
Progressive Socialist Party (PSP), 80, 91, 205

Qana, xxii, 209
Qassem, Na'im, 90
Qatar, 86
Quasi states, 30

Rabin, Yitzhak, xiii, xxii, 20, 29, 31, 57, 128, 129, 130, 131, 134, 135, 147, 170, 176, 179, 182, 183, 184, 185, 186, 190, 191, 199, 214
Reagan, Ronald, 191, 198, 201
Realism, 5, 158
Role expansion, 36
Rosen, Meir, 174
Russia, 22, 29, 149, 221

Saad, Antoun, 175, 177, 179
Sabra and Shatila Massacre (1982), xxi, 13, 191, 204, 216, 221
*Sabra*s, 107
Sadat, Anwar al-, xxi, 127, 147, 195
Saniora, Fouad, 89
Sarid, Yossi, 202, 212
Sasson, Talia, 125
Saudi Arabia, xxi, 8, 84, 86
Savoy Hotel
   Attack on (1975), 170, 192
Schiff, Ze'ev, 175
Secession, 144
Second Lebanon War. *See* War between Israel and Hizbullah (2006)
Second World War, 21, 52, 101
Sectarianization, 43, 76
Securitism
   Ethno-securitism, 43
Securitization, 37, 42, 43, 118, 136, 152, 153, 154
Security, 36, 37, 39, 42, 43, 221, 222
   Security policy, 37, 39
Security dilemma, 5, 152, 158
Security sector, 30, 32, 36, 37, 38, 39
   Command and control of, 41, 222
   Composition of, 40, 222
   Identity of, 41, 222
   Objective control of, 151
   Operation of, 42, 222
Serbia, 34, 57, 97, 223
Shalit, Gilad, 215
Shalom, Avraham, 120, 121, 169
Shamir, Yitzhak, 134, 208, 209
Sharett, Moshe, 164, 165, 166
Sharon, Ariel, xxi, 11, 131, 132, 158, 189, 190, 197, 201

270   Index

Shebaa Farms, xxii, 213, 215, 224
Shiloah, Reuven, 164
Sidon, 84, 87, 161, 206
Sierra Leone, 87
Sinai Peninsula, xx, 10, 11, 21, 38, 53, 54, 55, 127, 129, 176, 195
   Jewish settlements in, xxi, 195
Singapore, 149, 222
Small states, 222
Socialism, 103
South Africa, 29, 57, 97, 144, 149, 222, 223, 224
South Lebanese Army (SLA), xxi, xxii, 8, 85, 86, 158, 171, 209, 211, 217, 221
South Sudan, 29, 49, 222
Soviet Union, xxi, 21, 27, 53, 55, 58, 135, 167, 198, 201, 222
State expansion, 14, 15, 18, 23, 28, 30, 31, 33, 34, 35, 36, 39, 42, 43, 50, 59, 69, 97, 126, 155, 159, 166, 222
State failure, 27
State formation, process of, 15, 23, 24, 27, 30, 31, 33, 34, 35, 36, 42, 43, 138, 221, 222
   National integration, xi, 24, 26, 28, 29, 30, 41, 138, 146, 153
   State building, 24, 26, 27, 28, 29, 30, 32, 35, 138
   State construction, 24, 26, 28, 29, 30, 138
Straits of Tiran, 10, 53
Sudan, 29, 49, 222
Suez War (1956), 21, 38, 53, 55, 114, 116, 148, 166
Suleiman, Michel, 88
Sulh, Riad al-, 159, 161
Sykes-Picot Agreement (1916), 47
Syria, xix, xx, xxi, xxiii, 6, 7, 8, 9, 10, 12, 13, 21, 29, 35, 38, 47, 50, 52, 53, 57, 58, 61, 66, 67, 68, 69, 71, 77, 80, 83, 84, 85, 86, 89, 90, 92, 94, 100, 101, 105, 127, 130, 142, 144, 149, 150, 156, 157, 158, 159, 163, 165, 166, 168, 170, 175, 179, 180, 181, 182, 183, 184, 185, 186, 187, 190, 191, 194, 197, 199, 200, 201, 203, 204, 206, 209, 210, 213, 217, 220, 221, 222, 223
   Alawite community in, 66, 222, 223
   Civil war in, 8, 84, 142, 146
   Palestinian refugees in, 105
   Parliament, 100
   Special relations with Lebanon, 8, 146
   Sunni community in, 223
   Syrian army, xxi, 38, 89, 150, 160, 183, 185, 193, 194, 196, 210
   Withdrawal from Lebanon (2005), xxiii, 8, 21, 50, 84, 85, 89, 142, 146
Syrian Social Nationalist Party (SSNP), 67, 68, 204
Syrian-Lebanese border, 84

Ta'if (Saudi Arabia), xxi
Ta'if Agreement (1989), xxi, 7, 8, 50, 62, 65, 77, 79, 81, 82, 83, 84, 87, 91, 94, 139, 142, 146, 147, 220
Tamir Moshe, 211
Tamir, Yael, 118
Tel Aviv, xxii, 170
Territories, 2, 3, 7, 11, 17, 18, 20, 21, 29, 34, 54, 55, 56, 57, 58, 96, 97, 103, 111, 115, 116, 117, 118, 119, 120, 121, 122, 123, 124, 125, 126, 127, 128, 129, 131, 134, 135, 136, 137, 140, 143, 145, 147, 148, 149, 150, 153, 178, 186, 187, 190, 195, 197, 198, 200, 202, 203, 206, 211, 212, 213, 214, 215, 220
   Coordinator of Israel's Operations in, 116, 211
   Irreversibility of Israel's occupation of, 191
   Israeli Civil Administration in, 196, 211
   Israeli Military Government in, 116, 118, 196
   Israeli occupation of, 10, 11, 50, 97, 118, 119, 121, 122, 126, 127, 133, 191, 196
   Jewish militias in, 125
   Jewish settlements in, xiii, xxiii, 10, 11, 20, 51, 57, 119, 123, 124, 125, 126, 130, 132, 135, 136, 137, 140, 147, 190, 200, 203
   Jewish settlers in, 11, 29, 51, 56, 57, 119, 123, 124, 125, 126, 132, 134, 137, 150, 190, 196
   Jewish unauthorized outposts in, 123, 125, 133
   Palestinian community in, 145
   Village Committees in, 196
   Water resources in, 119, 126
Terrorism, 42, 120, 121, 128, 169, 172, 173, 176, 179, 180, 181, 198, 212
The Hebrew University of Jerusalem, 103, 108, 199
Tibet, 21, 221
Transjordan, 9, 10, 52, 98, 99, 104, *See* Jordan
Tripoli, 8, 66, 84, 89, 161, 165, 210
Troupes Spéciales, 66
Tunisia, 210

Index

Turkey, 21, 22, 43, 50, 57, 58, 156, 214, 221, 222
  Kurdish community in, 222
Tyre, 165, 192, 202

Ukraine, 22, 29
United Nations, xx, xxi, xxii, 8, 9, 10, 14, 21, 53, 86, 104, 109, 161, 162, 167, 172, 174, 176, 177, 186, 192, 220
  Charter of, 109
  Partition Plan for Palestine (1947), 9, 52, 104
  United Nations Interim Forces in Lebanon (UNIFIL), xxi, 14, 89, 193
  United Nations Truce Supervision Organization (UNTSO), 163
United States, xiii, xx, xxi, 7, 8, 17, 21, 32, 53, 54, 55, 58, 61, 80, 84, 86, 103, 131, 132, 144, 149, 157, 158, 164, 167, 169, 176, 177, 178, 183, 184, 185, 186, 190, 191, 192, 193, 194, 197, 198, 201, 209, 217
  Invasion of Iraq, 27, 29, 32, 222, 223

Violent non-state actors, 8, 67, 73, 74, 83, 85, 90, 91, 93, 94, 114, 143, 149, 182, 186, 211
Violent transnational non-state actors, 24, 78, 143, 149, 222

Waldheim, Kurt, 174, 192

War between Israel and Hizbullah (2006), xxiii, 8, 86, 89, 93, 157, 188, 206, 209, 210, 211, 215, 221, *See* Second Lebanon War
War of Attrition (1969–1970), 148
Weisglass, Dov, 132
Weizman, Ezer, 190, 193
West Bank, xx, xxi, xxii, xxiii, 2, 10, 11, 17, 19, 20, 22, 34, 35, 50, 52, 54, 56, 95, 105, 106, 107, 115, 117, 119, 120, 122, 123, 124, 126, 129, 132, 137, 142, 145, 168, 169, 190, 195, 197, 203, 214, 216, 217, 221
  Refugee camps in, 105
West Beirut, 92
Western Sahara, 21, 50, 221
Wilson, Woodrow, 48
Wimmer, Andreas, 32
World powers, 19

Yafi, Abdullah, 172
Yemen, 49, 86
Yugoslavia, 27, 222, 223

Zeira, Eli, 180
Zionist movement, xiii, 9, 50, 51, 52, 55, 98, 99, 100, 103, 104, 112, 113, 157, 199
  Jewish Agency, 55
  Jewish National Fund, 55
Zipori, Mordechai, 200, 205